JACQUELINE COGDELL DJEDJE

Fiddling in West Africa

Touching the Spirit in Fulbe, Hausa, and Dagbamba Cultures

INDIANA UNIVERSITY PRESS
Bloomington and Indianapolis

This book is a publication of

Indiana University Press
601 North Morton Street
Bloomington, IN 47404-3797 USA

http://iupress.indiana.edu

Telephone orders   800-842-6796
Fax orders   812-855-7931
Orders by e-mail   iuporder@indiana.edu

Library of Congress Cataloging-in-Publication Data

DjeDje, Jacqueline Cogdell.
  Fiddling in West Africa : touching the spirit in Fulbe, Hausa, and Dagbamba cultures / Jacqueline Cogdell DjeDje.
      p.   cm.
  Includes bibliographical references (p.), discography (p.), videography (p.), and index.
  ISBN-13: 978-0-253-34924-8 (cloth : alk. paper)
  ISBN-13: 978-0-253-21929-9 (pbk. : alk. paper) 1. Music—Africa, West—History and criticism. 2. Fiddling—Africa, West. I. Title.
  ML3760.D55 2007
  787.20966—dc22

                                                                                          2007020501

1 2 3 4 5   13 12 11 10 09 08

A two CD compilation of music from West Africa, which includes music examples discussed in this book, has been published by UCLA Ethnomusicology Publications. At the time of this book's publication, it is available for purchase at http://www.ethnomusic.ucla.edu/publications/index.htm.

Dedicated to

Dominique, my daughter,

And in memory of my teacher, Salisu Mahama,

and other fiddlers who have passed on.

Contents

Acknowledgments   ix

Introduction:
A Master Fiddler and a Significant but Little-Known Tradition   1

1. Fiddling in West Africa: Understanding the Culture Area   11

2. An Affirmation of Identity: Fulbe Fiddling in Senegambia   43

3. Calling the Bori Spirits: Hausa Fiddling in Nigeria   103

4. In Service to the King: Dagbamba Fiddling in Ghana   169

Conclusion   242

Appendix:
Distribution of the One-Stringed Fiddle (Listed by Country)   251

Notes   257
List of References   299
Discography and Videography: Selected Recordings of One-Stringed
Fiddle Music from West Africa   319
Index   325

Acknowledgments

Many foundations, organizations, institutions, and people are responsible for helping me write this book and bring it to closure.

Several foundations and institutions financially supported my research in West Africa. Among these are the Ford Foundation, the United States Department of Education, and many units at the University of California, Los Angeles (UCLA), my home institution: the Academic Senate, the Institute of American Culture/Ralph Bunche Center for Afro-American Studies, and the International Studies Overseas Program (now known as the International Institute)/the James C. Coleman African Studies Center.

Without the assistance of staff at libraries and research centers in West Africa and the United States, this project would not have been completed. In Ghana, these include the Institute of African Studies, the International Centre for African Music and Dance, libraries at the University of Ghana, Legon, and the Ghanaian Broadcasting Center. In Nigeria, these include the Centre for Nigerian Cultural Studies of Ahmadu Bello University, Linguistic Studies at Abudullai Bayero College, the School of Music of Kano State, and the Ministry of Information and Cultural Affairs in Kano. In the United States, these include several units at UCLA (the Ethnomusicology Archive, the Music Library, the Office of Instructional Development and Photographic Services, the College Library, and the Charles E. Young Research Library) and Indiana University's Archive of Traditional Music in Bloomington.

My deepest gratitude goes to the many musicians who shared information about their culture, lives, and work experiences. In Ghana, these include Aruatu Gondze, Sulemana Iddrisu, Salifu Issah, and Alhassan Iddi Sulemana of Yendi; Abu Gondze of Tamale; Alhassan Gondze and members of his family in Savelugu; Iddrisu Gondze of Tampion; Salisu Lali of Bimbilla; Salisu Mahama of Legon/Accra; and Abubakari Salifu Meiregah of Bimbilla/Accra. In Nigeria, I interviewed Haruna Bande, Balan Na Bassa, Usman Garba, Mamman Landi, Garba Liyo, Umarun Mayani, Ibrahim Mohammadan, Momman Nabarau, Musa Dan Gado Saminaka, and Ahmadu Samunaka. In Senegambia, I interviewed Salif Badjie, Samba Juma Bah, Majaw Bai, Mamadou Baldeh, Maulday Baldeh, Seiniwa Baldeh, Ebrima Barry, Juldeh Camara, Ousainou Chaw, Jansewo Jallow, Ngansumana Jobateh, Nyega Kandeh, and Tamba Kandeh.

Throughout my research in West Africa, numerous individuals assisted by identifying people to interview, translating song texts, providing me with information about their culture, or welcoming me as a guest in their homes. In Ghana, I am indebted to Fuseini Abdullahi, Chester Amevuvor, Esther Appiah, Shine Attitsogbui and family, Patsy Dowuna-Hammond, M. Iddi, J. H. Kwabena

Nketia and family, Sulemana Salisua, Abdullahi Yakubu, and staff in Mensah Sarbah Hall at the University of Ghana, Legon, and at Alhassan Hotel in Tamale. In Nigeria, there were Ibrahim Abdullahi, Sheyu U. Aliyu, Peter Badejo, Fremont E. Besmer, Michael Crowder, Akin Euba, Ibraheem A. Garba, Gershon and Ruth Guyit and family, Benji Ishaku, Mohammad Kassim Hassan, Mallam Awwal Ibrahim, Salihu Y. Ingawa, Yusuf Isa, Benji Ishaku, Maikudi Karaye, Toro Karunwi, Auwalu Landi, Shehu Garba Liyo, J. O. Olayiwola, Mosun Omibiyi-Obidike, Duro Oni and family, Joke A. Sanni, Tunji Vidal, Jim and Sue Vilée, Mohammed Zubairu, and staff at the Royal Tropicana Hotel in Kano. In Senegambia, I am indebted to Matarr Baldeh, Buba Kandeh and family, Mamma Kandeh and family, Sidia Jatta, Bakari Sidibe, Mohammed Sissoho, and the family of Papa Susso. In the United States, several individuals assisted by reading portions of the manuscript, making suggestions about sources and people to contact, or helping with the translations of song texts. Among these include Kwashi Amevuvor and family, Lois Anderson, Donna Armstrong, Akayaa Atule, Francis Awe, Eric Charry, Michael Coolen, Christopher Ehret, Brian Eisenberg, Veit Erlmann, David Fuller, Dieynaba Gaye, Gloria J. Gibson, Maina Gimba, Roderic Knight, Lynn Kostman, David Martinelli, Eddie Meadows, Abdoulaye Oumar, Karin Patterson, Jihad Racy, Daniel B. Reed, Russell Schuh, Aliyu Moddibbo Umar, Carol Card Wendt, and Lawan Danladi Yalwa.

Several students and staff members in the UCLA Department of Ethnomusicology assisted by conducting library research, reading portions of the manuscript, and helping with the musical transcriptions, translations, and permissions: Ric Alviso, Paul Humphreys, Jean Kidula, Brian Schrag and family, Alissa Simon, and Kathleen Noss Van Buren.

I am deeply grateful to the editors at Indiana University Press (Miki Bird, Linda Oblack, Jane Behnken, Suzanne Ryan, Gayle Sherwood, and especially Donna Wilson) who encouraged and supported me. To the anonymous referees who critically assessed early drafts of the manuscript and offered helpful insights and comments, I thank you.

Finally, my immense gratitude goes to my mentor, J. H. Kwabena Nketia, who initially proposed my research on West African fiddling. I also thank Salisu Mahama and M. D. Sulley who guided me through the initial stages of the research.

To my family, Eddie, Dominique, Longben, and Kaya, I thank you for your support and patience.

Fiddling in West Africa

Introduction: A Master Fiddler and a Significant but Little-Known Tradition

On Saturday, August 11, 1990, I left Accra, Ghana's capital city, accompanied by my research associate M. D. Sulley—a native speaker and teacher of Dagbani language at the University of Ghana, Legon—and traveled approximately four hundred miles north to Dagbon, home of the Dagbamba people. The purpose of the journey was to work with Salisu Mahama, my *gondze* (fiddle) teacher.[1] An exceptional performer and an authority on Dagbamba fiddling culture, Salisu had taught at the University of Ghana, Legon, from the late 1960s to the early 1980s. I had worked with this acknowledged master since 1972 and had recorded him many times, both alone and with other musicians. This time, however, would be different. Having retired from teaching, Salisu had returned to his hometown of Savelugu. This time I would document the history of Dagbamba fiddling and record Salisu playing the gondze with members of his own family. It was he who had desired and arranged for this. At this point in his life, Salisu wanted to make sure that people throughout the world knew about fiddling in West Africa and, especially, in Dagbon. He felt that this opportunity would never come again, and it held special significance for him.

After a twelve-hour bus ride, we arrived in Tamale, the commercial capital of the Dagbamba. Although the third- or fourth-largest city in the country, Tamale was less Westernized than Accra. As the economic and transport hub for northern Ghana, however, it bustled with activity. The developing urban center was dotted with single- and multi-story Western-style buildings—banks, chain stores, restaurants, markets, hotels, etc.—as well as small parks and flower gardens. The many automobiles and *tros-tros* (vans and lorries used as multi-passenger vehicles) traveling the red dirt roads frequently filled the air with a fine dust. Salisu had thought it best that Sulley and I spend the first leg of our journey in Tamale before continuing on to Savelugu. The city offered amenities that wouldn't be available in his hometown, and Salisu had said that he would commute the approximately fifteen-mile distance to work with us.

When Salisu arrived at Tamale's Alhassan Hotel on the morning of August 12, I saw a man who had aged gracefully and was much thinner than he had been eighteen years before. Typical of northern Ghanaians, most of whom are Muslims, Salisu wore a white Muslim cap and a flowing, long-sleeved white gown that reached his ankles and covered a matching shirt and pants. I remembered him frequently dressing in this manner when he taught at Legon.

Probably due to his illness, his demeanor was not as jovial or lively as it used to be. Although I could tell by his smile that he was pleased to see me, there was also a certain formality about his behavior. He knew that we had come on an important mission, and there was no time to waste. As a result, Sulley and I immediately began interviewing him about the early history and development of gondze in Dagbon. After two days of Salisu recounting the oral traditions of Dagbamba kings and explaining how the lives of rulers were linked and interwoven with those of fiddlers, we decided that it was time to visit Savelugu.

Arriving at Savelugu's transport station in the early morning of August 14, Sulley and I were met by Iddrisu, Salisu's oldest son, who served as our guide through town en route to the gondze quarters where the fiddlers lived. Savelugu was a small town. Some people rode bicycles, but cars and motor bikes were scarce. The young and middle-aged men and women who walked along the roads and paths (sometimes carrying loads of wood, vegetables, or fruit on their heads) gave the place a relaxed feel. While most commercial buildings were square or rectangular with tin roofs, the homes were arranged in clusters (known as compounds) of round and square structures made from wattle and daub with grass-thatched roofs; the houses making up the compound were encircled or connected by six-foot-high walls also made of wattle and daub. Trees and ample gardens were scattered throughout the town. At different points along the road, vendors sold bananas, ground nuts, cigarettes, and other products at stalls. Sulley, who had been raised in the north and had traveled widely through the region as a child, remarked how much the town had grown. According to Iddrisu, the population of Savelugu was now about five thousand. Although there was no electricity or running water, it had a school and several entertainment spots: Bukateen Disco (a nightclub), a dance hall, a video hall where *Rambo* was scheduled to play that evening, a chop (or beer) bar, and lotto.

Upon arrival at the gondze quarters, I discovered that fiddlers in Savelugu lived in a manner similar to those in other Dagbamba towns. The gondze compound, which was located next to the king's palace because the musicians were part of the royal entourage, was architecturally no different from other Dagbamba residences. After passing through the entrance or first building of the compound, I saw small children playing and women cooking in a large open area that functioned as a location for family interactions as well as a place for the fiddlers to perform. Around the space were several structures where family members slept. Like other Dagbamba families, that of the gondze was composed of two or more men with their wives and dependents. Children born into the family resided in the compound until they married or left to live with gondze families in other parts of Dagbon or Ghana. The eldest male in the family, one of Salisu's uncles, was the head of the household and made major decisions affecting the fiddlers.

When we met Salisu inside the gondze quarters, he appeared extremely happy and animated, with a mood and demeanor quite different from those we had encountered during our meetings in Tamale. He had always spoken of his family and the elders of Savelugu, and I could see how satisfied he was to have me finally meet them. What happened next was a ritual I had experienced in my research with Salisu and Sulley in other parts of Dagbon. Before pursuing any work in a Dagbamba village or town, formal greetings had to be made to the traditional ruler who would grant us permission and his blessings before we could begin. Thus, Salisu had arranged for us to visit the palace to meet Naa Abudulai Mahama III, the Yo Naa, or ruler, of Savelugu, the capital of one of the three provinces in Dagbon.[2]

Constructed in the nineteenth century, the Yo Naa's palace was architecturally similar to other dwellings in Savelugu, but it was larger and held more and larger buildings within the compound walls. The sitting room where I met the Yo Naa, who appeared to be in his fifties or sixties, was round. While no decorations or ornamentation appeared on the walls, a wooden post in the middle of the room extended from the floor through the roof and seemed to ground the structure. The Yo Naa's "throne," a low, square wooden dais covered with animal skins (emblems of royalty), was situated behind the tall post and faced the entrance to the room. Dressed in a blue smock made from locally woven strips of cotton cloth and a navy blue traditional cap tilted to the side of his head (the typical attire of a Dagbamba male), the Yo Naa was sitting on the skins when we entered. I was struck when he addressed me in flawless English. Not only does he rarely speak directly to commoners, custom should have demanded that he speak in Dagbani, the local language, through the intermediary of his linguists. Salisu would later reveal that he had encouraged the Yo Naa to address me in English even though the leader was reluctant to do so, especially when his four elders entered the room and sat around the edge of the throne in front of him. I increasingly realized how important this visit was to Salisu, the trouble he had taken to ensure that I understand fully his background and hear him perform in his hometown among his family and friends.

It was about mid-morning when Sulley and I were escorted by Salisu and members of his family to the grounds of the local school where the four male gondze musicians and two *zaabia* (one female and one male rattle player) sat on a bench underneath a tree for the upcoming performance. Although there were slight variations, all gondze wore the same attire: a pair of Western trousers, a locally made Muslim-style or traditional Dagbamba cap, and a wide, flowing, locally made smock in stripes of white and blue. The woman zaabia wore a colorful Western-style striped blouse; an ankle-length, floral-patterned wraparound skirt; and a royal blue floral scarf covering her head. All of the performers assembled were related to Salisu. In addition to his son, there was a nephew (Babu) and brothers and children of his uncle. Curious about the assembly, ten young boys and girls between the ages of eight and twelve accompanied us to the school yard and stood near the tree in anticipation.

Although Salisu was relaxed among family and friends, he remained a perfectionist about his performances. He also knew much about sound recording because faculty and researchers at the University of Ghana had often recorded him. Therefore, when I indicated that the winds were high and, given our position underneath the tree, there would be a lot of background noise on the recording, he did not question my request when I asked the zaabia to sit to the left of the gondze, as opposed to their usual position on both sides of the musicians, so their sound would not dramatically affect that of the fiddle.

The entire recording session took about three hours with approximately seventy songs played and the performance divided into six parts.[3] I asked Salisu to start by performing praise songs in honor of the Ya Naas and other rulers of Dagbon because the songs constituted an important repertory of songs for fiddlers. Not only are they used to preserve Dagbamba history, proverbs in praises help advise and educate people about life's problems. Salisu was unique among fiddlers in Dagbon. He had a strong voice and a florid and improvisatory style of playing the fiddle. In addition, he was able to organize and insert catchy phrases and proverbial sayings that made the song text interesting. I admired his playing for its complexity and was amazed by his ability to produce so many intricate nuances and melodic ornaments on an instrument with only one string. Sulley often stated that whenever Salisu entered a Dagbamba town and started performing, everyone there knew he had arrived without seeing him because they recognized his distinctive playing and singing.

The group began with "Albanda," a praise song for Ya Naa Yakuba I, who lived during the nineteenth century. Salisu performed as the lead gondze and vocalist. In addition to playing repetitive patterns on the rattle and gondze, the zaabia and other gondze sang the chorus. Although all the gondze played the same ostinato pattern, each ornamented it differently, creating a dense, multilayered flowing melodic sound. After performing the twelfth song, which ended part 1, the group did not take a break. Instead, Babu immediately took over as leader by singing the vocal lead. Later, after the recording was over, Salisu told me that he had given Babu and others an opportunity to lead because this was a way of encouraging younger musicians. He also knew that young fiddlers would not play or sing their best if he performed the lead, for they would be trying to listen to him.

With Babu as leader, the group started part 2 with "Nantoh," "Bawuna," and "Naanigoo," praise songs in honor of several Dagbamba kings who lived during the nineteenth century (Ya Naa Yakuba I, Ya Naa Abudulai I, and Ya Naa Andani II, respectively). After continuing with songs for other rulers, the group took a short break before starting the next series of songs. The third part of the recording was led by Iddrisu. Under his lead, however, the members of the vocal chorus seemed to lack the enthusiasm they had evidenced earlier. Noting this, Salisu stopped the group after part 3 and began speaking to them. I am not sure what he said, but during the break they tuned their fiddles by playing the tuning-up melody (*zugubu*). By this time, twenty more people from town had come to the school yard, probably because they heard the sound of the fiddling.

When the group started part 4, Babu again took over as leader. Still there were few people singing the chorus. After the fourth song, "Yenchebli," Salisu stopped the group again for another break. It was becoming apparent that he was not satisfied with the performance. It seemed to me that he was frustrated

Salisu Mahama (on right), playing the fiddle and listening to his nephew, Babu, sing during a performance. Photograph by Jacqueline Cogdell DjeDje. August 1990.

because many of the young performers did not know the texts of some of the rarely performed songs they were being asked to play. Among these was "Yenchebli," a praise song in honor of the legendary figure from Grumaland (in present-day Burkina Faso) whom some Dagbamba fiddlers credit with the beginnings of fiddling in West Africa. At this point, Salisu turned the performance into a teaching session. When part 5 began, he had once again assumed the role of leader, singing two praise songs in honor of Yenchebli with no response from the vocal chorus. As the fiddlers and rattlers played repetitive patterns on their instruments, Salisu's florid playing on the fiddle was sharply foregrounded.

After Salisu finished the praises for Yenchebli, Babu continued as leader on the remaining songs in part 5. With little response from the chorus, Babu sang the vocal lead with only fiddle and rattle accompaniment. By the time the performers reached the seventh song, however, the chorus began to sing with greater enthusiasm. When they started performing some of the praise songs for the different Yamba Naas (chiefs of gondze)—for example, "Karinbandana" for Sulemana Ntoli and "Yeda Nai Ya" for Sulemana Bla—there was even greater participation from the chorus. By this point, the school grounds were filled with at least seventy-five local residents who formed a semicircle in front of the musicians with several listeners lingering on its fringes. Some older people were present, but the majority of the audience was between the ages of six and thirty-five. While the males were dressed in Western-style pants and shirts, the females were attired in a manner similar to that of the female zaabia. Although many people arrived almost two hours after the performance had begun, the performers did not seem to mind. Most members of the community had finished with their chores for the day and perhaps had been informed by others in the audience who had gone to tell them what was taking place. I also believe they came because they heard the sound of fiddling, especially after the playing became more intense. It was not an everyday occurrence for foreigners to visit Savelugu for the sole purpose of recording fiddle music. On that day, Salisu and his relatives were "stars" in the eyes of their neighbors, and people wanted to see them.

As the performers continued, women and men in the audience began entering the circle to dance. At one point, a man and a woman danced alone in the circle, each performing a separate dance. While the woman's movements were reserved as she gracefully moved her body from side to side, the man made large turns to the right and left so that his smock swirled about him. As people danced, the female zaabia got up, entered the circle, and stood close to the dancers, so she could better coordinate her rhythms with their movements. When this happened, sound and movement became more intense: the zaabia moved with the dancers as she played the rattle more quickly women in the audience began to ululate, and the fiddlers began to repeat the main melody of songs more rapidly without any singing.

When the performance reached a climax toward the end of part 5, Salisu took over as leader of the group without stopping for a break. Once he started playing part 6, not only did more people participate by moving and dancing, but the singing and playing of the musicians became more vibrant. The music achieved a lilting, dance-like feel as Salisu played the fiddle and danced in response to the excitement from the audience. At one point a boy of about four from the gondze family joined the group with his small fiddle. About two or three songs before ending the performance, Salisu led the group in playing Sulley's praise song so Sulley could dance. Then Salisu played "Sakpalenga," the first song I learned when I began my fiddle lessons with him in 1972. He ended the recording session with "Bawuna" and one final zugubu, which he played solo for about twenty-five seconds as a cadence. When the last note was played, Salisu had a smile on his face and glimmer in his eye. He was clearly pleased with the participation of everyone who helped to make the performance a success.

I know Salisu had hoped that, in addition to our documenting him playing gondze with his family, our presence would demonstrate to the youth of Savelugu that the Dagbamba had a unique and important musical tradition that should not be discarded. Salisu was becoming increasingly concerned with the maintenance of the fiddle tradition as he grew older. He hoped that instead of looking to Western culture for a sense of identity, the young people of Dagbon would express pride in and support of their own traditions. Otherwise, the art of fiddling would gradually be lost.

* * *

Salisu's wish that I hear him play with family members in his hometown and that I communicate the importance of the fiddle to a Western audience is easily understood.[4] Although the fiddle has been prominent in several regions of Africa since the precolonial era and may in fact date to the eleventh or twelfth century, researchers have largely ignored it. Articles have been written on melodic instruments (see Gray 1991), but few books on African music have treated the subject, with the exception of studies on the xylophone (Tracey 1948), the *mbira* (Berliner 1978), and a general discussion of string instruments (Wegner 1984). Rather, most published monographs deal with drums and drumming (Nketia 1963, Euba 1990, Locke and Lunna 1990, Wilson 1992), thus creating a skewed and inaccurate view of African music.[5] Interestingly, while the number of print sources on West African fiddling is small, the amount of sound material is relatively substantial (see discography). In addition to three audio recordings that focus entirely on fiddling, a large number of audio and a few video recordings include selections by West African artists performing the fiddle.[6]

Because scholars have given little attention to African fiddling, we do not understand the processes by which performance practices are transmitted and adapted, nor do we know what may have contributed to different practices. Furthermore, we cannot explain why the tradition continued to be important in West Africa through the first two decades of the postcolonial era but began to decline in the late twentieth century. Therefore, several questions are central to this study. Who performs the fiddle and what is the history of fiddling among West Africans? In what context is the fiddle used and why is it performed in these contexts? What are the aesthetics, beliefs, and attitudes related to fiddling that make it popular or unpopular? Stylistically, how is fiddling similar to or different from other West African performance traditions?

Absent a substantial body of published research, this study relies principally on data that I collected during fieldwork in West Africa over a thirty-year period: 1972–1974, 1990, 1994, 1995, and 2003.[7] I have also consulted commercial recordings; writings by Arabs and Africans; the journals and reports of European colonial officers, explorers, and early travelers in Africa; photographs, newspaper advertisements, and linguistic sources; and material gathered by researchers in ethnomusicology, music, folklore, anthropology, history, and other disciplines.

As I hope will be apparent from the above description of Salisu's recording session in Savelugu, fiddling in this study does not refer solely to playing the instrument. The person who plays the instrument, the performance context, the meanings surrounding the instrument and music event, as well as the music performed are all important. Fiddling is most often identified with people who live in Sudanic West Africa,[8] an area that has not received much scholarly attention but that has been substantially influenced by North Africa and the Arab world. The fiddle can also be found among selected societies in the West African forest regions, although this is the result of contacts with peoples in the grasslands (or savannah).

The fiddle in West Africa has multiple identities that shift due to differences in geography and ideology. For some individuals included in this study, the sound of the fiddle touches the spirit. Not only does fiddle music stir up "a state of ecstasy and joy," it causes many to feel healed and proud. Others indicate that it awakens their soul and gives them inner peace (Sulemana 1995b). As Jihad Racy explains, "like living organisms, instruments adapt to different cultural settings, thus dropping or maintaining some of their older connotations and acquiring new functions and meanings. Consequently, the study of musical instruments may necessitate applying a combination of historical, anthropological, musicological, and organological approaches" (Racy 1999). Therefore, instead of using the findings from one ethnic group or society to generalize about the whole, I have prepared a multi-sited ethnography that moves from a conventional single-site location to multiple sites of observation and participation (Marcus 1995). This allows for examination of the circulation of cultural meanings, objects, and identities in diffuse time-space.[9] Using this methodology, we learn that the role of the fiddle in societies is not fixed; variations in location, history, cultural systems, and individual preferences affect meaning. The sites selected for this study—Senegambia (home to the Fulbe people), Nigeria (home to the Hausa), and Ghana (the Dagbamba)—are significant because the role of fiddling among people in each location is distinct, providing an excellent cross section of the tradition. Also, the sites represent three of the major culture clusters or subregions (Western Sudan, Central Sudan, and Voltaic) in Sudanic West Africa (DjeDje 1998, Monts 1982; see chapter 1).[10]

Multi-sited ethnography is not merely a different kind of controlled comparison, although comparative analysis may be used to demonstrate diversity and define aspects of shared behavior.[11] Marcus states, "in multi-sited ethnography, comparison emerges from putting questions to an emergent object of study whose . . . relationships are not known beforehand, but are themselves a contribution of making an account that has different, complexly connected real-world sites of investigation" (Marcus 1995:102). It is of note that my own approach to the subject of fiddling changed when I integrated the Fulbe data into the previously collected material on the Hausa and Dagbamba. After examining the three groups collectively, I came to view fiddling not as a discrete unit in several West African locations, but as a *whole* with interconnected parts. In addition, four issues emerged as important to the tradition: place (the geographical and sociocultural environment); ethnicity (the ethnic identity of the people and their relationship with those around them); religion (the belief system and its role in society); and status (the social standing of performers in relation to others in the society).

One of these forces invariably tends to be more important in a particular culture than it is in others. In Senegambia, ethnicity is central to fiddling because the fiddle distinguishes the Fulbe from other ethnic groups, thus transforming them from being Senegambians to being Fulbe in Senegambia. In Hausaland, many Muslims regard fiddling with disdain, but it empowers practitioners of Bori (the indigenous religion) and others (e.g., women) who are marginalized in Hausa society. The tensions between these religious groups have greatly affected the meaning of fiddling among the Hausa. Among the Dagbamba, fiddlers—as in the case of Salisu Mahama—have a high social status and are considered to be the most beloved performers attached to the king. Because most musicians in Sudanic societies have a low status (DjeDje 1998), the Dagbamba situation is unique and has caused interesting developments in musicking[12] in this culture. Studying the fiddle tradition, then, provides a window for understanding the significance and complexity of ethnicity, religion, and social status in Sudanic West Africa.

Scholars who use a multi-sited ethnography focus their studies through several techniques. They may research a people, an object, a metaphor, a plot (story or allegory), a life (or biography), or a conflict (Marcus 1995:105–110). In this book, I follow an object (the fiddle), realizing all the time that the object could not have moved without people. I agree with scholars who believe that fiddling in West Africa is the result of Arab influence. However, the manner in which the fiddling tradition was dispersed to become "African" fiddling is a topic that has not been discussed. I argue that the dispersion of the fiddle in West Africa is related to the Fulbe, a nomadic people who originated in the Senegal valley and migrated across West Africa from Senegal to Lake Chad. Wherever the Fulbe are located, you will quite probably find the fiddle. When the fiddle was absorbed by groups with whom the Fulbe came in contact, the instrument's identity was reshaped to fit the history and ideology of the people who adopted it. In his essay "Intra-African Streams of Influence," Gerhard Kubik indicates that a trait, or a cluster of traits, can spread geographically to take root elsewhere by four avenues: (1) human migration, (2) contacts between neighboring groups, (3) long-distance travel, (4) and media (Kubik 1998:296–298). I believe that all of these processes affected fiddling in West Africa, but each has been significant at different points in history.

Duplication of information cannot be avoided in a multi-sited ethnography. Occasionally, the same statements are made about use, learning, and performance style. But as Nketia has noted, "this duplication should ultimately enable us to get a better picture of the continental or regional characteristics of the music of Africa and their distribution than we have at present" (Nketia 1972:273). Nketia believes that we must examine the variety of musical expressions found in Africa to enlarge our knowledge and to appreciate each type of expression in its own right. In this way we can avoid getting into a state of mind that prejudges a musical tradition on the basis of familiarity with a limited geographical area. In addition, we must systematically examine the music of African cultures to delimit the identical or common elements and the differences. The examination of the latter must be concerned with the extent, distribution, and function of differences. We need to discover which are mutually exclusive or totally unrelated elements and which are similar elements or possible variants. In other words, our study of African music should lead to the identification of style types within which similarities and divergent forms operate (Nketia 1972:279).

Music analysis is prominent in this book because of my interest in understanding how identity and culture relate to sound and in learning whether the enduring and generic characteristics often identified with African music are apparent in West African fiddling (Nketia 1978). The music examples come from commercial recordings and from field recordings I collected in West Africa. All music transcriptions are presented in Western staff notation and transposed to pitch G^3 (the open string) because this is the general area where West African fiddles are tuned; G below middle C on the Western piano constitutes pitch one for all songs. Although Western notation is used as a tool to represent sound, practices that would be unorthodox in the Western system are employed. First, no time signature is used, but the quarter note constitutes the basic unit of measurement for all songs. Second, a single rest to accommodate beats within a measure is not always used. Instead, rests are sometimes presented in accordance with the number of beats performed in the measure. Third, the signature signs placed at the beginning of measures do not signify that the music is in a particular key such as G major or g minor. Rather, the signs have been employed to avoid having to insert them repeatedly in the transcription, thus making the music easier to read. Fourth, instead of bar lines at the end of each measure serving as an indication of a regular recurrent main beat, they are used to divide the repetitive main melody, melodic cycle, or ostinato performed by fiddlers. This recurring melody, whether it consists of nine, twelve, or twenty-four beats, constitutes the formal structure upon which further variation is created. Fifth, the repetitive rhythmic pattern performed by percussionists, which does not always correspond with the melodic cycle, is referred to as either rhythmic timeline, rhythmic pattern, or rhythmic cycle. The amount of time it takes for the timeline to be performed is called the time span. Finally, additive rhythms refer to durational values of notes extending beyond the regular division of the cycle, while divisive rhythms are accented pulses articulated during regular divisions of the cycle.[13]

In many ways, this book satisfies a gap in African music studies because it embraces the history of both traditional[14] and contemporary Africa but with emphasis on a region that has been influenced by Arab culture (Nketia 1998: 48). Although much research on contemporary Africa focuses on societies that have been so greatly influenced by the West that forces unique to the locale are ignored or omitted, recent studies demonstrate that researchers are broadening their approach (see, for example, the Society for Ethnomusicology's "Current Bibliography" section on African music in their journal and on their website). Thus, this book contributes to the body of literature that examines local culture change.

1   Fiddling in West Africa: Understanding the Culture Area

Soon after [they] appeared in another Squadron, all the young Men, divided, like the Women, into Companies with Drums and Fiddles. They made their Procession round the Fire, and quitting this Dress and Weapons, began to wrestle singly with great Agility. . . . This Exercise was followed by a Sort of Ball to their Violins, both Sexes showing their Skill in Dancing, which is their favourite Diversion, and of which they never tire.

—Jean Baptiste Labat, 1728. Quoted in Astley (1968:298)

Musically, West Africa is perhaps the best-known and least-understood culture area on the African continent. Although as the quotation above clearly demonstrates, West African musicians have used the fiddle for at least three hundred years, the region is usually identified with drumming. In spite of recent scholarly publications on various ethnic groups, much of the general public continues to regard West African music as homogenous, as opposed to a locus of diverse cultural and performance traditions (DjeDje 1998).

The one-stringed fiddle (or bowed lute) is found primarily in an area called the Sudan that extends across the African continent from Senegal to Ethiopia. Historians usually divide the Sudan into three sections: the Western Sudan (Mauritania, Senegal, The Gambia, Guinea-Bissau, Guinea, Mali, and parts of Burkina Faso), the Central Sudan (parts of Burkina Faso, Ghana, Togo, Benin, Nigeria, Niger, Cameroon, and Chad), and the Eastern Sudan (parts of Chad, Sudan, Ethiopia, and Eritrea). My discussion here concerns primarily Sudanic West Africa, which includes the Western and Central Sudan (see Map 1.1).

A History of Sudanic West Africa

The peoples of Sudanic West Africa belong to several language families (Niger-Congo, Songhai (or Songhay), Saharan, Chari-Nile, Berber, and Chad) and have resided in this region for thousands of years.[1] While some commonalities existed among them historically, their religious and political systems were not identical. The indigenous religions of most groups were monotheistic with a single divine force identified metaphorically with the sky and symbolized by lightning. In some ancient states, the political structure was based on a sacral kingship with people believing in an afterlife for their leaders. This idea probably originated in the east and was introduced by the Songhai peoples to the states immediately east and west of the Niger Bend.[2] Among the Niger-Congo people, however, kings were not considered sacred; instead they served as ritual leaders of clans or lineages (Oliver and Fage 1970; Ehret 2001:240, 249).

The economy of most peoples living in the Sudan was organized around specialization. Starting in the third millennium BCE, fishing and rice farming became the major means of subsistence in the Western Sudan. By the last century BCE, rice cultivation had spread south and west to other Niger-Congo peoples living in the forest where it became the staple crop. When the Bongo-Bagirmi (Chari-Nile speakers) migrated into the Central Sudan from the East during the first millennium BCE, not only did they use iron and were fully agricultural, but they also tended cattle, sheep, and goats and raised a wide range of crops (Ehret 2001:250–251; 2002:220–221).

A second stage of productive specialization, based on occupation, started around 1000 BCE and resulted in a new residential pattern: village clusters or a set of satellite settlements were organized around a larger, central town. Each village became the site of a different kind of manufacturing activity. "One would be the village of the smelters and smith, another the residence of leather workers, another the place of cotton weaving, and still another the potters' abode. The products of each occupation were then taken to the central market in the larger town around which the artisans' villages clustered. There they were bought by local consumers and also by traders, who might carry the items to more distant markets in other localities" (Ehret 2001:259).

Out of this pattern emerged a social system of occupational classes started by ironworkers.[3] When iron metallurgy developed early in the first millennium BCE, the ironworkers protected their activities with taboos and special rituals to ensure the success of their efforts. Whether consciously or not, they managed to secure a monopoly over the production of iron. As time passed, other specialists (e.g., leather workers, weavers, and potters) began to claim the same type of status for themselves and their activities. Their jobs and their skills were passed down from father to son or mother to daughter. People in these occupational groupings eventually began to marry solely among themselves (a practice known as endogamy) (Ehret 2001:259).

The final step in the creation of a socio-occupational class system took place when clan rulers and sacral kings seized power and combined large areas into the first real states of the region. To make their positions of power permanent, the new kings and their followers claimed that ruling was their birthright, just as members of the ironworking classes were born to be smelters and smiths. Among the Mande and Atlantic peoples,[4] an occupational group of professional bards arose under the patronage of nobles. The great majority of the population— who continued to farm and keep livestock—formed by default a residual group consisting of free people who did not belong to any of the groups with more restricted membership. Slaves, who formed the lowest stratum within the social system, originated as captives taken in the wars of the noble class. As more people in the Western Sudan were affected by the class system, the positions of some

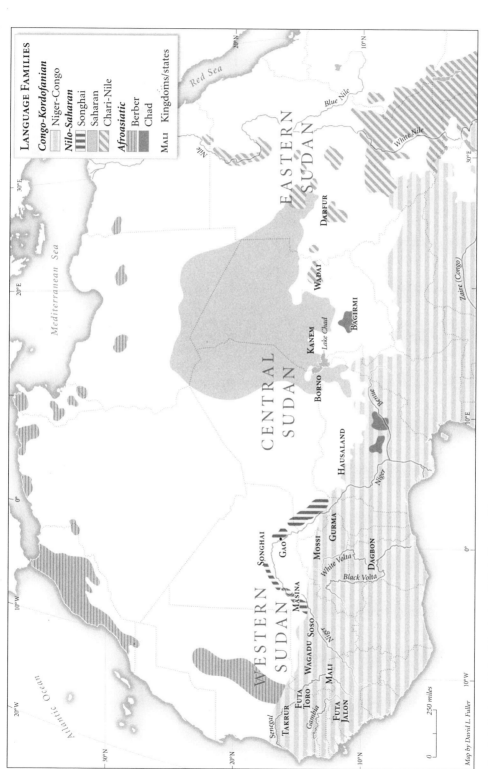

Map 1.1. Sudanic Africa. Map by David L. Fuller. Used by permission.

of the old occupational groups became ambiguous. Originally, their monopoly of certain kinds of production had given them economic power that brought great profit and economic influence. With the rise of a hereditary and powerful noble class, however, the separate status of the socio-occupational groups made it easier for rulers to exert control over them. Gradually, as their relationship to economic and political power changed, they came to be viewed by the majority peasant class as less-esteemed segments of society (Ehret 2001:259–260).[5]

People living in Sudanic West Africa prospered commercially and politically during the first millennium BCE and early first millennium CE because of growth in the long-distance trade of iron products, copper, gold, salt, livestock, grains, and foodstuffs. In the Western Sudan, the fourth century CE marked the first stage of empire building, while, in Central Sudan, trans-Saharan trade and political developments similar to those in the west did not take place until the eighth century CE. The presence of sought-after gold and geographical conditions in the Western Sudan are partly responsible for state development occurring there first.[6] Warfare among groups in the Central Sudan also made routes through that region unattractive to traders (Ehret 2001:270–271). Between the fourth and nineteenth centuries CE, polities that grew in stature included empires—Wagadu (commonly referred to as "Ghana" after its ruler), Susu (Soso), Mali, and Songhai (including Gao or Kawkaw)—and several kingdoms and states—Takrur, Kanem-Borno, Hausa, Fulbe (Futa Toro, Futa Jalon, Masina), Mossi-Gurma, Dagbon, and Wadai-Bagirmi-Darfur.

The Sudan was also a site for interactions with cultures outside the continent. As early as the fifth and fourth millennia BCE, gold and enslaved Africans from the savannah were traded to peoples in the Mediterranean for cloth, copper, and tools. When Egypt and Ethiopia in the third and fourth century CE controlled areas in Southwest Asia, a number of Persians, Arabs, Syrians, Lebanese, and, at a later date, some Indians crossed the Red Sea into the Eastern Sudan to escape famine. The adoption of the camel by some Africans between the second and fourth century CE provided a new mode of transportation that undoubtedly caused even more trans-Saharan travel and migration.[7] By the time Arabs introduced Islam to North Africa in the seventh century CE, many of the cultural groups in West Africa were already clearly differentiated, having evolved separately under different influences. Some were oriented toward Morocco, Tripoli, Egypt, or the Nilotic Sudan, while others in the south developed with minimum external contacts (Trimingham 1970:15). See Map 1.2 on page 15 for a political and geographical landscape of eleventh-century West Africa.

Arabization and Islamization

Contacts with North Africa and Arab culture are directly related to the history of fiddling in Sudanic Africa. The spread of Islam in West Africa occurred in several phases and was accelerated by trade, education, and warfare. Although Mediterranean peoples with the aid of Berbers participated in trans-

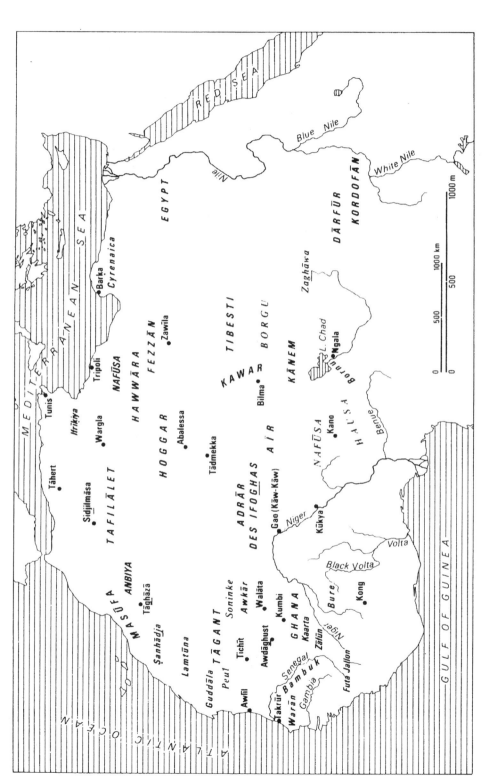

Map 1.2. West Africa in the eleventh century. Source: I. Hrbek (1992:66). Used by permission.

Saharan trade in various parts of the Sudan, Muslim traders developed the industry. Al-Fazari, an Arab astronomer who wrote between 750 and 799 CE, indicates that Muslim merchants were among those in touch with the Sudanic interior (Hiskett 1984:19). By the tenth century, caravan routes fanned out from North Africa in three main directions. In the west, the route extended from southern Morocco to Mauritania and ancient Ghana (i.e., Wagadu) by way of Taodeni, in present-day Mali, and from southern Algeria to Timbuktu via the Tuat oases. In the center, Tunis was connected with Gao (the Kawkaw state) by way of Ghadames (in present-day Libya) and Aïr (in present-day Niger), and from this route subsidiary tracks led toward Tripoli and, in the south, toward Chad. To the east, the Nile valley was connected with Darfur through Assiut, and with Kanem, east of Lake Chad, through Darfur. Another route led from Cyrenaica through Kufra to Darfur (Lewis 1980:20–21).

Prior to the introduction of Islam, some Sudanese heads of state who served as both religious and political leaders had established contacts with North Africa. In addition, some leaders and merchants in the Sudan nominally accepted Islam to enhance their economic contacts with Muslim traders. Although several states were early converts in the tenth and eleventh centuries, indigenous religious practices were, in general, maintained. Nonetheless, interactions between Muslim traders and Sudanic leaders set the stage for the later expansion of Islam. Not only did Muslim traders form settlements in commercial centers where they exchanged goods, some traders married Sudanese and gained political and social power in various communities.[8]

Between the fourteenth and sixteenth centuries, holy men and teachers who accompanied and followed traders greatly advanced the spread of Islam. The presence of Muslim scholars "gave rise to thriving local centers of Muslim learning and scholarship, of which the best known were Djenne and Timbuktu in the west and Harar in the east" (Lewis 1980:28). During this period, more Sudanese embraced Islam, which provided a means for social advancement, especially to those of traditionally low status. In most cases, the Soninke and Mande Sudanese (as well as some others) acted as agents in spreading the religion to non-Muslims.[9] The spread of Islam was successful in Sudanic Africa because of its compatibility with African religions. Thus, instead of abandoning indigenous traditions, the Sudanese combined traditional and Islamic elements to form an African Islam different from that practiced in North Africa and the Arab world.

In spite of Islam's success, many Africans clung to indigenous beliefs between the fourteenth and sixteenth centuries. Although Mande merchants were generally Muslims, other loosely organized groups in Manding were unaffected by the religion. Around the center of the Niger Bend, the Gurma and Mossi kingdoms resisted Islam and blocked its expansion to the south and east (Trimingham 1970:32). In the eighteenth and nineteenth centuries, however, warfare, led by the Fulbe, helped to expand Islam. The Fulbe believed jihads were necessary because not only had Islamic worship declined, but also earlier converts had abandoned moral standards, simple living habits, and the purity of faith of their ancestors (see chapters 2 and 3).

Muslims became catalysts of change and modernization in West Africa (Diouf 1998:6). The wealth produced from selling natural resources (gold, ivory, etc.) to outsiders provided the Sudanese with capital to erect public buildings, maintain well-equipped professional armies, and import raw materials. It also allowed for the development of a unique urban setting that attracted foreign scholars and craftsmen. As a consequence, a schism developed between urban dwellers who were oriented toward Islam and foreign influences, and peasants who lived by agriculture and herding in a very limited economic sphere. On an individual level, the conflation of Islam and Arab culture was responsible for the universal claim to Arab ancestry and the overwhelming currency of Arabic among assimilated Sudanese urbanites (Lewis 1980:5).

European Influence

When Europeans reached West Africa in the fifteenth century, their activities were confined to the coastal areas, with the savannah receiving minimal attention. French and British penetration into the West African hinterland in the late nineteenth century, however, affected the region in several ways. Although Sudanic rulers lost much of their political power, it brought peace to Sudanese who had been living in a perpetual state of insecurity, harassed by Muslim reformists and the raids of slave hunters. European presence also led to the Islamization of many peoples who probably would never have otherwise converted (Trimingham 1970:224–225).

Europeans did not interfere with Muslim religion and education, a circumstance that was interpreted by both parties to mean that Christian missionaries would not be encouraged. Because Europeans regarded African Muslims as members of a higher civilization, they permitted them to establish Islamic law courts and gave them responsibility for European policies through indirect rule. Muslims were employed in subordinate administrative positions, which brought them into close contact with adherents of indigenous African religions. The fact that European officials showed special consideration for Muslims enhanced the prestige of Islam and provided believers with the opportunity to use various forms of pressure to spread propaganda. Africans who adopted Islam during this period included not only the Yoruba and Nupe of Nigeria but also ethnic groups in Sierra Leone, Guinea, Senegal, and Mali. In spite of contact with Muslim agents, however, other societies (e.g., Fon of Dahomey and Asante of Ghana) showed no signs of abandoning their indigenous religions.

When trans-Saharan trade declined in the nineteenth century and European contacts with people who lived on the Niger River opened up, West Africans lost contact with the Muslim world just as it was beginning its modern transformation. Not only were many cut off from the Maghrib and Southwest Asia, Africans in the savannah were not exposed to Western ideas adopted by groups in southern and coastal areas of West Africa (Webster and Boahen 1967: 244–245).

When West African countries gained independence during the 1960s, some African leaders developed policies to re-educate, rebuild, and revitalize savannah culture in a Western mold. Government projects to stimulate the agricultural and economic base were initiated. Children who attended Western schools either gave up their Qur'anic learning entirely or went to Muslim school at an early age before attending a Western primary school. As a result of Westernization, two opposing ideologies came to exist in the savannah: (1) a desire to become progressive by accepting Western values and (2) a subconscious fear of opposing tradition and abandoning Islam. In spite of the changes, Westernization did not disrupt savannah culture to the same degree that it had in the southern and coastal non-Muslim areas in the first half of the twentieth century.

By the late twentieth century, Westernization had made significant gains in the Sudan, but a new surge of interest in Islam had also occurred. With promises of economic aid and development from Arabs in Saudi Arabia, the United Arab Emirates, and other countries in Southwest Asia came greater acceptance of Islamic beliefs. This most recent adoption of Islam has caused a decline in traditional religious practices among some groups, for example, the Sisalaa in northern Ghana and Vai in Liberia-Sierra Leone (see Seavoy 1982, 1994; Monts 1984). These developments have also begun to affect those people who perform the fiddle.

Music of Sudanic West Africa

The music of Sudanic West Africa reveals influences from Southwest Asia, North Africa,[10] and groups that live farther south in the forest, but it is the features identified with Southwest Asia that make the music of the savannah and the Sahel distinct. Ethnomusicologist Ali Jihad Racy indicates that several elements characterize Arab music: (1) the intimate connection between music and language, (2) the principal position of melody and melodic instruments, (3) the modal treatment of rhythm, (4) the predominance of compound formal structures, and (5) the far-reaching influence of Islam and the prevalence of Islamic expressions, such as Qur'anic chanting and the Islamic call to prayer. Despite such unifying features, however, the Arab world remains a land of musical contrasts, and diversity may be observed in terms of geographic areas and repertoires (Racy 1983:130–134).

Commenting on its affective characteristics, music scholar Amnon Shiloah states that Arab music "is identified with the sweet tenderness of love, an emotion it expresses, imprinting its effect on the listener's soul. Among the various definitions of a perfect musician one finds: he who is moved and causes his listeners to be moved. Thus, in addition to a beautiful voice, tenderness and keen sensitivity often recur as basic qualities required from an excellent musician" (1995:16). Eric Charry states that Arab music in Africa "took root in much less uniform ways than that of Islamic doctrine." Whereas Qur'anic recitation, monophony, and melodic ornamentation permeate most Arab-influenced cultures, other aspects of Arab music (e.g., the abstract nature of pieces of music, combining instrumental pieces into concert suites, technical terminology, and the use of certain musical instruments) were rejected or more selectively accepted. West African societies probably did not adopt major aspects of Arab music because of geographic distance and disparities between local traditions and music of the Arabian heartland (Charry 2000b:546).

Although religion plays a major role in the lives of people in the Arab world, music holds an ambiguous position in Islam.[11] Carol Card Wendt has noted, "Since the beginning of Islam, Muslim authorities have disputed the question of whether music should be permitted in worship. Because music, especially instrumental music, was associated with pagan practices and sensual entertainment, early authorities declared the act of listening to music 'unworthy' of a Muslim.... To avoid secular associations, references to music are usually avoided in mention of calls to prayer, Koranic recitations, and other forms of religious expression" (Wendt 1998a:536; also see Anderson 1971:154–155).

In many parts of North Africa, however, pre-Islamic beliefs and the practices of Sufi mystics combined with Islamic canon to produce a unique form of Islam. The veneration of saints and the belief that saints served as mediators between divinity and humanity, and as sources of good health and fortune, became features of Islamic worship in Northwest Africa after the thirteenth century CE (Wendt 1998a:192–193). By the time peoples in the Sudan came in contact with North Africans, much of the musicking of the latter had been strongly Arabized. Not only had some Berbers adopted Arab instruments (e.g., the lute, drum, and shawm) and music terms, but the Arabic language was used in songs and ritual chants.[12]

Just as the people in Sudanic West Africa did not discard traditional religions when faced with the spread of Islam, they did not abandon their indigenous music. Rather, groups combined elements to accommodate various streams of musical ideas. Thus, the music of the Sudanic West Africa may be divided into three music clusters: the Western Sudan (Mande and Atlantic speakers— including the Fulbe who are discussed in chapter 2), the Central Sudan (Chad, Songhai, Saharan, and Chari-Nile speakers—including the Hausa of northern Nigeria who are discussed in chapter 3), and the Voltaic (speakers of the Mossi and Bariba languages—including the Dagbamba of northern Ghana who form the subject of chapter 4).[13]

As noted previously, historians believe the social organization of professional musicians or full-time specialists in the Western Sudan is based on a socio-occupational structure that dates to the first millennium BCE or earlier, and groups in the Central Sudan adopted these ideas during the first millennium CE (Ehret 2001:258–260). In earlier times, musicians who belonged to an endogamous family were born into the profession and received training from kinsmen at a young age. Their repertory was learned and transmitted orally from one generation to another. Because musicians were attached to specific patrons (e.g., royalty, an important official, or another socio-occupational group), they were expected to know details of the history and genealogy of their patrons, sing praises in their honor, serve as custodians of the repertory, and act as advisers and confidants. In addition to offering advice, professional musicians often had a formal political role as well, especially in diplomacy between factions within the same lineage. For their services, musicians received gifts that might include land, animals, houses, cloth, gold, wives, and slaves. The bond between musicians and patrons was close. In precolonial times, we are told, musicians might even have committed suicide when their patrons died. With changes in the sociopolitical system during the colonial and postcolonial periods, there arose full-time specialists who were not attached to a patron or institutions. These individuals normally were self-taught, or they received training through apprenticeship with an established performer within the society. There was no specific age or time period for the schooling of freelance musicians; it began when they expressed the desire to acquire the necessary skills for the profession (DjeDje 1982).

During the precolonial era, professional musicians had specific titles. Musicians in Mande societies—called *jali, jalo,* or *jeli* (singular); *jelilu* or *jalolu* (plural)—were known both by their surname and the instruments they played (Duran 1999:541; Charry 2000a:1). Professional specializations in the Central Sudan, specifically among the Hausa, could be classified into ceremonial music, court praise music, general praise music, entertainment music, music associated with spirits, and vocal acclamation (King 1980a:309–312). Among the Atlantic speakers and musicians in the Voltaic clusters, musicians were known by the instruments they played rather than by the context or type of music they performed. Although some of these categories endure, many have begun to disappear.

When the political power, economic resources, and position of rulers in the Western Sudan were greatly diminished during the European colonial period, the role and status of professional musicians changed. Forced to survive without royal patrons, some musicians resorted to performing for money. Although most remained highly respected, an ambivalent attitude toward them developed. In a position to acquire large sums of money, professional musicians sometimes attracted the resentment of community members of higher social status who did not have wealth but felt obliged by custom to give money to musicians at public events. During the postcolonial era, some musicians have been perceived as "yes-men" because of past close associations with important officials (Charry 2000a:101; Duran 1987; DjeDje 1982).

In the Central Sudanic and Voltaic clusters, the distinctions between musicians and other members of the society are not as rigid as those in the Western Sudan. Because the Central Sudanese and Voltaics did not experience major changes in their traditional political and social structure as a result of European colonial policies, the patronage system was not as dramatically affected. Professional musicians attached to royalty in Central Sudanic and Voltaic areas continue to have a high status, although ambivalence toward freelance musicians in this region also exists.

In precolonial times, performances for royalty and socio-occupational groups (e.g., hunters and blacksmiths) constituted some of the most important contexts for musicking.[14] Even with changes in the traditional political and social structures, musicians continued to perform for important officials and other patrons within the society, singing historical and genealogical praise songs. In modern times, music can still be heard at work, festivals, seasonal events, religious rites, wrestling matches, life-cycle events, and other social gatherings. Ceremonies to celebrate birth and weddings continue to be commonplace in all areas. Differentiation exists, however, in performances for puberty rites and funerals. Because the initiation or circumcision ceremony is one of the most important and unifying institutions in the Western Sudan, music-making at this event is prominent (Monts 1982; *Born Musicians* 1984; Schmidt 1989:245). Yet musicking by professionals during initiation in the Central or Voltaic clusters is either limited or does not occur at all because this rite of passage is not always publicly celebrated (DjeDje 1998). Similarly, few, if any, musicians in the Western and Central Sudan perform music to commemorate death. Music and dramatic display are, however, prevalent at funerals among Voltaic groups. Unlike their neighbors in the Western and Central Sudan who distinguish between the types of music appropriate for Muslim and non-Muslim events, some Voltaics (for example, the Dagbamba in northern Ghana) blur these distinctions; drumming and fiddling as well as Muslim songs and chants are heard at Islamic events.

Differences between the Western and Central Sudanic clusters are most apparent in the types of instruments used. In the Central Sudan, not only are there a larger variety of instruments, but many sound sources are also based on North African models probably introduced into the region by the Songhai and by the Kanembu and Kanuri of Kanem-Borno. Bowed and plucked lutes, reed pipes, and certain types of drums all show influence from Arab culture. The Western Sudan is distinctive because of the prominence of indigenous instruments to be found there. Instruments associated with Mande speakers include the *bala* or *balafon* (xylophone) as well as the *kora, simbi,* and *bolong* (harps); wind instruments from earlier years are rarely performed (Charry 2000a:136, 224; Duran 1999). Among the Atlantic speakers, the *serdu* (flute), one of the few wind instruments now used in the Western Sudan, and *lala* (sistrum rattle) are identified with the Fulbe but not with other groups in Senegambia. Both Mande and Atlantic speakers use lutes (DjeDje 1998:445; Charry 2000a:10). The latter, however, are most often identified with the bowed lute (fiddle), while both perform plucked lutes. Anthony King indicates that the double-membrane hourglass pressure (or tension) drum, used by many people in the savannah, was first noted in North Africa during the fourteenth century (1980a:309). Yet Eric Charry suggests that the *tama* (the term for a type of hourglass-shaped pressure drum played with a curved stick and hands and used among groups in the Western Sudan) and several other instruments date to the time of Wagadu (2000a:19). Other types of membranophones include drums that are cylindrical in shape (double-headed), goblet-shaped, conical-shaped, bowl-shaped, and barrel-shaped. Drums made out of calabash gourd are also prominent.

Stylistically, music in Sudanic West Africa often seems to sound the same because of influences from Arab culture, but minor distinctions are apparent due to differences in instrumental combinations. In many parts of the Sudan, emphasis is placed on solo singing accompanied by one or more instruments and/or a vocal chorus. When melodic instruments are used to accompany singing, monophony or heterophony results. If vocal accompaniment is used with solo singing, the result may be drone-like or ostinato-like in that a short melodic or rhythmic phrase is repeated and varied. Women and men sing with a high-pitched, tense vocal quality. Generally, songs consist of long, rapid declamatory phrases by a soloist. The singer may hold a high pitch for an extended period while the other parts continue their repeated parts. Melodies are generally melismatic with ornamentation.[15] Percussion, polyrhythm, and choral accompaniment tend to be more prominent in areas where there is close contact with groups in the forest region.[16]

The Fiddle in West Africa

Classification and History

Classified as a spike bowl lute that produces sound from bowing, the one-stringed fiddle is believed to have been introduced into Africa as a result of contacts with Arab culture.[17] Although legend suggests that the viol (*rabab*) was known to Arabs before and during the time of the Prophet Muhammad, scholars believe that bowed instruments in the Arab world "can only be definitely traced to the tenth century, when Al-Farabi (d. 950) clearly mentions a *rabab* being bowed" (Farmer 1929b:493, 1960:445; Kuckertz 1980:16). Sibyl Marcuse indicates that the ancestor to the fiddle is the plucked short lute of ancient Persia, which was adopted by the Arabs and became a bowed instrument called *rabab* in the tenth century (1975:432). Roger Blench (1984:171) believes that the present form of the spike box fiddle used by the Arab Bedouins "represents an early savannah-development of the bowed instrument introduced into North Africa in the ninth and tenth centuries." Thus, the introduction of the fiddle in Sudanic West Africa probably occurred some time after the tenth and eleventh centuries because extensive interactions between North Africans and the Sudanese did not begin until this period.[18] In modern times, different versions of this early instrument can be found in both West and North Africa. In West Africa, the one-stringed fiddle is constructed in the form of a long neck connected to a round piece of calabash covered with skin. In Morocco, a comparable single-stringed fiddle, with a round wooden body that is covered with skin, exists and is called *rabab*. Furthermore, in Egypt a two-stringed fiddle (*rabahah*) with a body made from a skin-covered piece of coconut shell is still played (Racy 2006).

It should be noted that ethnomusicologist Kenneth A. Gourlay argues that the use of the fiddle in West Africa, particularly Nigeria, is not due to Arabs or North Africans introducing the instrument to the Sudanese. Rather, he believes the opposite occurred (1982b:225–226). While Gourlay's frustration with the European and Arab bias that permeates much scholarship on African music and history is understandable, overwhelming evidence indicates that the fiddle was introduced into Africa as a result of contact with Arab culture. In any case, this debate threatens to sap scholarly resources required elsewhere. Documenting the history of African music is very important, but, in this instance, too much emphasis has been placed on origin and the role non-Africans have played. What scholars need to do is focus more on what happened to the instrument after its arrival in Africa. In other words, greater attention should be given to the "Africanization" of the instrument and the variety of African fiddle prototypes that now exist.[19] A close examination of performance practice reveals that the fiddle in Africa is no longer an Arab instrument. Without a doubt, it is African.

Distribution Patterns

As noted earlier, West Africans who cultivate the fiddle are located in three clusters of concentration from west to east: (a) Mauritania, Senegal, The Gambia, Guinea, Guinea-Bissau, Sierra Leone, and western Mali; (b) eastern Mali, Burkina Faso, northern Ghana, western Niger, and northern, central, and southwestern Nigeria; and (c) eastern Niger, Chad, northeast Nigeria, and northern Cameroon. Near the Guinea Coast, fiddling occurs sporadically among the Agni of Côte d'Ivoire, the Nago of Benin, and the Yoruba of southwest Nigeria (see Map 1.3).

While most scholars agree that Arabs introduced the fiddle into Africa, there is little consensus among researchers on the reason for the present-day distribution pattern in West Africa. Francis Bebey and André Schaeffner suggest that the instrument is found principally in Muslim areas (Bebey 1975:41; Schaeffner 1955–1956). Yet West African musicians state that fiddling has no connections with Islam and is only occasionally used for Muslim events. Furthermore, some groups that came in contact with Islam did not adopt the instrument.[20] Some researchers believe the fiddle dispersion correlates with trans-Saharan caravan trade routes (see Map 1.4). Other explanations relate to environmental conditions and the mobility of groups in the area. Unlike people in the forest or along the Guinea Coast who tend to be stationary, the Sudanese are mobile, interacting not only with northerners and southerners but also with each other. Thus, constant movement may have led to the borrowing of the fiddle from one group and subsequent adoption by another.

In my opinion, a variety of factors account for the distribution. A factor

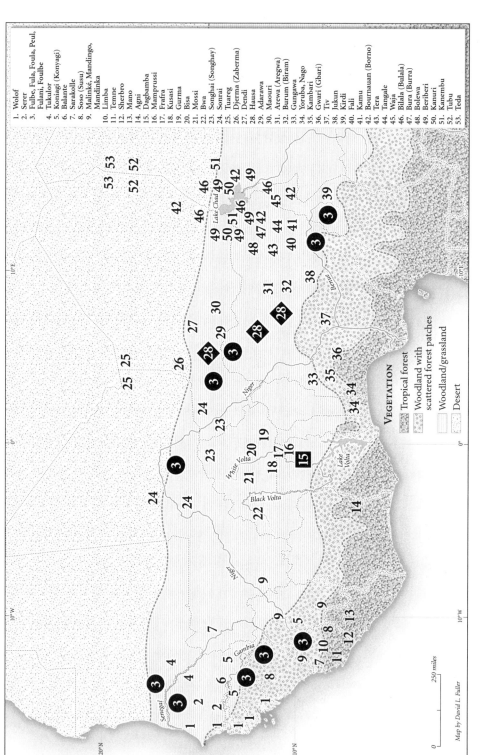

1. Wolof
2. Serer
3. Fulbe, Fula, Foula, Peul, Fulani, Foulbe
4. Tukulor
5. Koniagi (Konyagi)
6. Balante
7. Sarakolle
8. Soso (Susu)
9. Malinké, Mandingo, Mandinka
10. Limba
11. Temne
12. Sherbro
13. Mano
14. Agni
15. Dagbamba
16. Mamprussi
17. Frafra
18. Kusasi
19. Gurma
20. Bisa
21. Mossi
22. Bwa
23. Songhai (Songhay)
24. Sonrai
25. Tuareg
26. Djerma (Zaberma)
27. Dendi
28. Hausa
29. Adarawa
30. Maouri
31. Arewa (Aregwa)
32. Burum (Biram)
33. Gungawa
34. Yoruba, Nago
35. Kambari
36. Gwari (Gbari)
37. Tiv
38. Jukun
39. Kirdi
40. Fali
41. Kamu
42. Bournauan (Borno)
43. Tera
44. Tangale
45. Waja
46. Bilala (Bulala)
47. Bura (Burra)
48. Bolewa
49. Beriberi
50. Kanuri
51. Kanembu
52. Tubu
53. Teda

Map 1.3. Distribution of people in West Africa who use the one-stringed fiddle. Map by David L. Fuller. Based on information in Jacqueline Cogdell DjeDje (1980:40–41). Used by permission.

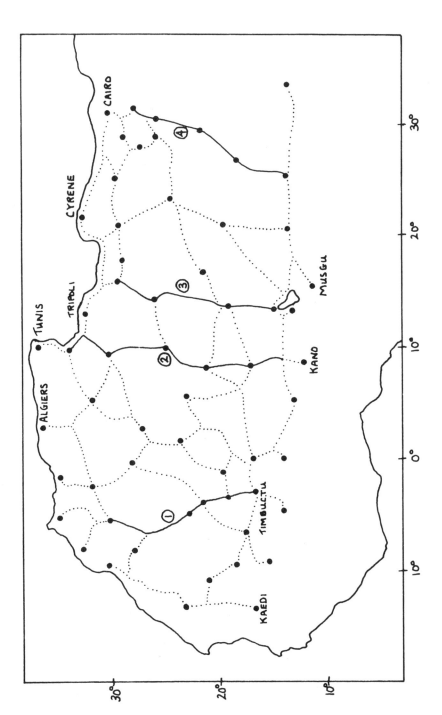

Map 1.4. Trans-Saharan caravan routes. Based on information in George P. Murdock (1959:128) and Jacqueline Cogdell DjeDje (1980:43). Used by permission.

not yet considered, however, has to do with the Fulbe diaspora and migration patterns. Scholars have also overlooked the fact that the homeland for the Fulbe and other northern Atlantic speakers (Tukulor, Wolof, and Serer) is in the Senegal valley where interactions between Sudanic, North African, and Arab cultures were prominent (see Map 1.5 for major concentrations of Fulbe and further discussion in chapter 2).[21] Whether Atlantic speakers in the Western Sudan adopted the instrument directly from North Africans or from interactions with the Tukulor and Fulbe is debatable. I believe, however, that the Fulbe are responsible for the diffusion of the instrument to other locations in Sudanic Africa because they are one of the few groups, outside of the Mande, to have migrated extensively. Unlike the Tukulor who remained somewhat stationary in the Senegal region, Fulbe cattle herders dispersed from the twelfth to the nineteenth centuries throughout West Africa, from the Atlantic Coast to the Eastern Sudan.[22] Some Fulbe settled among Mande, Chad, and Songhai speakers, and others made their homes among Voltaics and Plateau Nigerians who spoke Benue Congo (or Bantu) languages (Rosellini 1980; Nikiprowetzky 1980; King 1980b; Robinson 1985; DjeDje 2001).

The only problem with this hypothesis is that fiddling is not associated with all Fulbe (Fulani) in the Central Sudan. Of the two categories of Fulbe (nomadic and sedentary) in northern Nigeria, only the nomadic Fulbe perform the fiddle, while their sedentary kinsmen do not identify with the tradition. Whether the Nigerian Fulbe's non-identification with the fiddle occurred after the nineteenth-century jihad or earlier is not known. Yet the jihadic period would have been a time for major changes to have taken place. In other words, after urban Fulbe[23] became political and religious leaders of the Hausa states, perhaps they not only gave up participating in public musicking (a decision which caused many Hausa to become the performers of most musical traditions in Hausaland), but also discarded the fiddle as a symbol of Fulbe culture because Muslims considered it to be profane. If this were the case, it would explain why Fulbe cattle herders in the middle belt of Nigeria close to the Cameroon border continue to be the primary performers of the fiddle (King 1980b:241) while urban Fulbe rulers are highly critical of the instrument (see chapter 3).

The fact that fiddling in the Central Sudan is associated with several societies that speak languages classified as Nilo-Saharan (Songhai, Saharan, Chari-Nile) and Afroasiatic (Berber and Chad) suggests that the instrument's presence may also be a result of the interactions of these peoples with the Arab world and each other. By the tenth century, contacts and exchanges between the Kanembu who lived near Lake Chad and Berbers in Fezzan (in present-day Libya) were in full swing. Kanem and Bornu leaders had established diplomatic relations and were sending gifts of slaves, animals (i.e., giraffes), and other items to North Africa. Exchanges between Kanem-Bornu and Hausaland also occurred (Hrbek 1992:222–223; Ki-Zerbo and Niane 1997:110).[24]

The appropriation of the fiddle by the Hausa (who, as previously noted, are Chad speakers) is significant for several reasons. Not only does it force us to think about how the Hausa acquired the tradition and the role they played

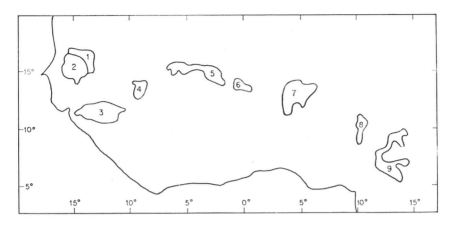

(1–Senegal Valley, 2–Futa Toro, 3–Futa Jalon, 4–Kita, 5–Masina, 6–Liptako, 7–Sokoto, 8–Bauchi, 9–Adamawa).
Map 1.5. Major concentrations of Fulbe. Source: George P. Murdock (1959:414). Used by permission.

in the spread of fiddling to other areas, it helps us to understand the significance of the Hausa in the Central Sudan. I believe the Hausa were introduced to the fiddle through culture contact with neighbors, and after adopting it, became one of the agents in the spread of the instrument. Because they had contacts with a number of groups (Fulbe, Tuareg, Berbers, Kanembu, Kanuri, and Songhai) during the fourteenth and fifteenth centuries, and possibly earlier, all may have played a role in the introduction of the instrument in Hausa culture (see chapter 3). Hausa migrations and cultural dominance in the Central Sudan and Voltaic areas probably account for the use of the fiddle among groups that surround them, particularly among speakers of Voltaic, Kwa, and Benue-Congo/Bantu languages (see appendix).

In summary, the process by which the fiddle was adopted and dispersed is complex. Contact and interaction were not enough to ensure adoption of the fiddle. The selective manner in which the instrument was incorporated into different cultures demonstrates that when foreign elements are introduced, only those aspects that enhance or have some useful purpose to the borrower are voluntarily accepted (Blacking 1977, Racy 1999). The adoption of the fiddle tradition was minimal in forest and coastal areas of West Africa either because musical characteristics there were extremely different or social affiliations with the instrument were unattractive. Because the West Africans who adopted elements from Arab culture integrated them into institutions important in society (e.g., religion or kingship), they came to regard these features as "their variety of traditional African music no matter how 'Arab-influenced' they may appear to the observer" (Nketia 1978:6).

The agents in the spread of Arab/Islamic culture and the type of contact between groups may also account for the exclusion of the fiddle in some areas. When Islam was first introduced in Sudanic West Africa during the eleventh century, a relationship of mutual tolerance was established between the Muslim world and those who were not yet under Islamic rule (Hrbek 1992:24). This may account for the maintenance and fusion of African and Arab traditions by groups who identified themselves as Muslim. The Mande, who were among the first groups to become agents of Islam, maintained many of their indigenous instruments (e.g., the xylophone and harp). The Hausa, however, who became immersed in Islam somewhat later, adopted several instrumental models (long trumpets, the oboe, and drums) associated with Arab culture. The differences in adoption could be the result of timing, the agents, or indigenous cultural practices. Difference in the circumstances of culture contact during the later period, as opposed to the earlier periods, may also have affected the acceptance the instrument. The contacts and interactions that occurred among West Africans in dispersing the fiddle are part and parcel of Stephen Blum's interpretation of culture: a culture should be seen as a series of processes in which people construct, reconstruct, and dismantle cultural materials when they know or suspect that other people have undertaken (or may undertake) such tasks in a different manner (1994:253).

Physical Features and Construction

The fiddle is known by a variety of names throughout West Africa because the term employed to denote the instrument in local languages may most commonly be translated as "to rub." Although *nyanyeru* (or its variant) dominates among the Fulbe and Tukulor of the Western Sudan, most Senegambians use *riti*, a Wolof term. Variants of the word *goge* (e.g., *goje, gondze, guge*) are common among the Hausa and others in the Central Sudanic and Voltaic clusters, but other terms (e.g., *kukuma* and *duduga*) are also used. Among the Tuareg, the fiddle is known as *imzad* in the northern dialect, *anzad* in the southern, and *anzhad* in the western (Wendt 1998b:575).

Most West African fiddles are long necked without spikes and played horizontally.[25] The body resonators of fiddles are made from a hemispherical gourd or calabash of various sizes. Different types of materials are used to cover the body resonators. While most coverings are made from the skin of reptiles (e.g., lizards, alligators, iguanas, or snakes), some are made from the skin of goats, sheep, gazelles, deer, or camel. The placement of the resonator hole(s) is a feature that distinguishes the geographical location of a fiddle. In the Western Sudan, the opening, which may be circular, square, or triangular, is generally placed in the sound box. In the Central Sudan and Voltaic clusters, the circular hole is placed in the skin that covers the body resonator (see Photos 1.1 and 1.2). The number of resonator holes on a fiddle also varies. Although many fiddles are constructed with one hole, two holes are not uncommon.[26]

Photo 1.1. Fulbe *nyanyeru* of The Gambia, with resonating hole displayed. Photograph by Jacqueline Cogdell DjeDje. August 1990.

In most cases, the fiddle bow is made of wood covered with the skin of a goat or left bare. Among the Hausa in Niger, "the bow is considered to be male, whilst the string is female. In the past, it used to be made of a flexible, bow-shaped piece of wood. Now, it is a curved, flat piece of iron" (Bornand 1999:15). The Sherbro of Sierra Leone and the Fulbe in Senegambia use a reed or thin wooden stick for the bow. Several groups (e.g., Fulbe of Sierra Leone, Gurma, Hausa, and Maouri) use a piece of metal; only the end portion of the bow, which is held in the hand by the fiddle player, has a leather covering. While the length of the bow varies even within the same culture, the shape is normally one of two types (see Figure 1.1). Generally, leather-covered bows are made in the shape of Example A, whereas metal, reed, or wooden bows are constructed in the shape of Example B. Musicians who do not cover their wooden bows use either shape.

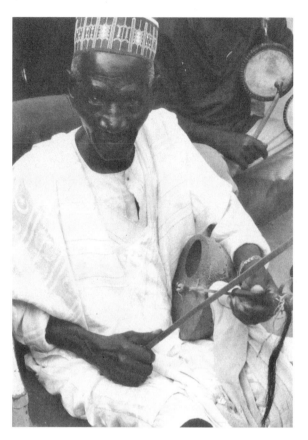

Photo 1.2. Musa dan Gado Saminaka of Nigeria playing the Hausa *goge*, with resonating hole displayed. Photograph by Jacqueline Cogdell DjeDje. July 2003.

The neck or stick fixed through the body resonator is frequently made of wood, but some fiddlers use metal such as chrome (from bicycle bars) or brass (from frames of brass beds). Like the bow, the wooden neck may or may not be covered with leather. Fiddlers prefer metal because of its durability and smoothness to the touch, but also because it symbolizes a higher status or an association with the West. In most cultures, the length of necks varies and is left to the discretion of the performer.

The bridge, placed on top of the membrane and fixed so that the vibrating string passes over it, is also made of different materials. A V-shaped bridge is most commonly used. However, some Tuareg women prefer a rather slender bridge composed of two crossed pieces of wood. The Fulbe in The Gambia use two thin pieces of wood, cylindrical in shape. In Sierra Leone, the bridge

Example A.   Example B.

Figure 1.1. Shapes of fiddle bows used by West African fiddlers.

of some Mande fiddles is made of gourd, while other Mande, Wolof, and Fulbe there use a tuning ring (Lamm 1968:14–15).

The string for the fiddle and the fiddle bow in West Africa is made with hair from a horse's tail. Along the Niger River in the Central Sudan, the instrument is often called "the horse" because its strings are always made of horsehair (Schaeffner 1955–1956). Among the Hausa in Niger, the hair from a living horse is always used, for "the hair of a dead horse would not have had the required sound qualities to reach the spirit world" (Bornand 1999:15).

The tuning of the fiddle is not fixed but left to the discretion of the performer. In some cultures, tuning is controlled by a small wedge-shaped object (the tip of the horn from a bush cow, deer, antelope, or buffalo) inserted between the lower end of the string and body resonator. By inserting or releasing the small wedge to increase or decrease the tension of the string, the performer obtains the desired tuning. Among the Fulbe of The Gambia, several small pieces of wood placed on the resonator underneath the string are moved back and forward to control the tuning. Tuning of the Tuareg fiddle is "achieved by a loop of hair round the string and the neck which may be moved away from or towards the bridge to lower or raise the pitch" (Holiday and Holiday 1960:6).

The type of sound produced on the fiddle is determined by the choice of materials used in construction. In many societies, metal attachments and even reptile skin provide a buzzing that enhances the sound quality of the music (Surugue 1972; Gourlay 1982b). As cultures become more Westernized, other changes are taking place. Some performers place an electrical attachment on the body resonator and hook it to an amplifier. Others use a circular tin box, similar to those used to store tobacco or candy, as the resonator.

The construction of instruments made from gourds takes several days. A spherical gourd, cut in half, serves as the sound box. Before the gourd is completely dried, two holes are cut on each side for placement of the neck, and a short stick, which serves as a brace for the sides of the resonator, is placed inside. If the sound box is to include the resonator hole, it is cut at this time. After the gourd dries, a skin is attached to the open half of the calabash with small tacks or lacings; a leather strip or band made from the skin of a goat is glued around the edges of the gourd to cover the nails (Bornand 1999:15; Wendt 1998b:577). In some areas, a smooth egg-shaped stone or cowry shell is inserted under the membrane covering of the body resonator to increase its tension. In fiddles without resonator holes in the sound box, the hole or holes are cut in the skin and the neck is fixed longitudinally within the two side holes of the body resonator. Strings made from the hairs of a horse's tail and twined together are attached to a ball of cord, connected to a piece of leather twine, and stretched from the fiddle's lower end (the base of the body resonator) to the upper end of the neck and tied or secured with leather binding thongs. Finally, the bridge is placed between the string and membrane of the body resonator. To decorate or add color, some fiddlers attach numerous strips of leather around the body resonator or tie scarves along the neck; others leave the neck bare. In some instances, fiddlers use scarves or handwoven yarn strips tied to the two ends of the neck as straps for holding or transporting the instrument.

Learning and Playing Technique

The manner in which a person is recruited and learns to perform the fiddle varies. In societies where fiddlers belong to an endogamous group or class, they generally learn from kinsmen, and training begins at an early age. With modernity, however, many youths have refused to follow the professions of their parents. Family members or others encourage children to take up other professions, so they might earn more income and prestige and avoid the sometimes negative associations of fiddling. In rare cases, fiddlers do not continue because family members believe it would bring them harm (Bornand 1999). In North Africa and many parts of the Arab world, only men perform the fiddle. In Sudanic West Africa, fiddling is dominated by men, but some women also perform it. In the Central Sudan, in addition to the Tuareg, among whom it is exclusively women who play the fiddle, Hausa and Songhai women perform the instrument.[27]

As professional musicians, fiddlers possess a social distinction different from nonmusicians. Although the Tuareg look down on professionalism as a livelihood for earning money, Tuareg musicians are recognized and admired for their ability to perform (Wendt 1998b:575; see chapter 4 for discussion of social status). Individuals not attached to a family of fiddlers learn to play on their own by observing other fiddlers. Many obtain training by serving as an apprentice with an established musician. Learning generally requires years of lessons and practice, but it may take some individuals less time. The Tuareg believe "that a woman cannot acquire the necessary skill much under the age of thirty" (Wendt 1994:83).

Although fiddles are held in a horizontal position, the resonator may be placed (1) in the center of the abdomen, (2) on the side, (3) on the shoulder, or (4) in the cup of the bent arm, with the neck of the instrument facing away from the performer. The Temne of Sierra Leone place the resonator on the shoulder with handle pointing away from the player (Lamm 1968:16). When playing, the performer either stands or sits and rubs the horsehair on the bow across the horsehair of the body resonator just to the left of the bridge; this is called the performer's position. If the performer is right-handed, the bow is manipulated with right hand while the left hand stops the horsehair string by lightly pressing the finger along the hair of the neck. A left-handed performer would use the same procedure with opposite hands.

Various methods are used to create different tones and amplify the sound of the fiddle. Instead of pressing the string to the neck as is done when playing the Western violin, anzad players, like many fiddlers in other parts of West Africa, lightly touch the string; all fingers, including the thumb, are used in fingering. Wendt explains, "The secondary harmonic, sounding an octave above the open string, is readily accessible by extension of the little finger. Some performers employ additional harmonics; by means of a lighter finger pressure they are able to sound various partials, producing pitches difficult or impossible to attain otherwise. The result is a range beyond the usual octave and a kaleidoscope of tone colors." The type of bowing a Tuareg fiddler uses produces different qualities of sound. "Single bow strokes accompanied by rapidly fingered notes in the left hand can be made to resemble melismatic singing, whereas single strokes paired with single notes produce a syllabic effect. Short, light strokes coupled with harmonics simulate the tones of a flute; rapid strokes in *tremolo* depict animals in flight, while interrupted strokes portray a limping straggler. Such techniques may be used to great effect in musical storytelling or in support of the style and text of a vocalist" (Wendt 1994:86). The volume of sound produced on the fiddle depends on the size of the resonator and thickness of the string. A large resonator with a thick string made from lots of horsehair creates more sound than an instrument with smaller dimensions or fewer strings (Card 1982:89–91).

Performance Contexts and Cultural Significance

In earlier times, most chordophones in Arab culture were associated with magic and the spiritual unknown. Singing girls and stringed instruments (*ma'azif*) not only gave signs about the end of the world, they were considered to be among the most powerful means by which the devil seduced men (Farmer 1929a:24–25). The fiddle in Arab society has also been used for entertainment and continues to serve that function. Not only have Arab Bedouins employed it to accompany epic poems in praise of warriors and other heroic figures, but love songs are also performed with fiddle accompaniment (Racy 1983:134, 140; Reynolds 1993:4–6; Racy 1996).

Selectively integrated by West Africans into the local institutions important to their cultures, the fiddle continues to be widely performed at festivals, social gatherings, and other occasions (sporting events, beer bars, market places, etc.). Fiddlers also provide entertainment at life-cycle events and other contexts. In the past, as now, fiddles were used to accompany work and report on current events. Messages can be transmitted using the fiddle, similar to the way membranophones and aerophones are employed for communication. The people of Niger refer to it as a "talking instrument" (Bebey 1975:44).[28] Among the Tuareg in precolonial times, the fiddle was a powerful force for good. It gave strength to men in battle and inspired them to do heroic deeds. Wendt explains: "Much of the 'power' of the *anzad* was in reality the power of the women who played it. The warrior society required repeated recognition of heroic acts and constant revalidation of the behavioral ideals that motivated them, and the *anzad* melodies and accompanying songs of praise were a potent force toward that end" (Wendt 1994:82). In parts of Sudanic West Africa, the fiddle is still identified with kingship. As early as the eighteenth century, the fiddle was used as a court instrument among groups in the Voltaic areas (e.g., among the Mossi, Gurma, and Dagbamba), but only scattered references are made to the instrument's association with royalty in the Western and Central Sudan, and most relate to activity during precolonial times (see chapters 2 and 3). In fact, Gourlay notes his surprise that a blind fiddler belonged to Sultan Bello's band at Sokoto (Clapperton 1829:286; Gourlay 1982b:229).

The use of the fiddle in religion, divination, and communication with spirits is more widespread among groups in the Central Sudan (e.g., Djerma, Hausa, Maouri, and Songhai) than other areas probably because of the importance of spirit possession in these areas (Nikiprowetzky 1964a; Surugue 1972; Bebey 1975:44; DjeDje 1978b, 1982, 1984b; Besmer 1983; Stoller 1989; Bornand 1999:14; also see chapter 3). An oral tradition explaining the beginnings of fiddling in Djerma and Songhai cultures demonstrates the extent to which the fiddle is related to spirit possession:

> Galankagou lived in *Misra* [Egypt] on a mountain. He had seven vultures, seven horses, and seven blind men. He snatched the hair from the tail of his horses to make the string of the violin *godyé;* to the sound of this music he made the seven blind men dance, *who became possessed* by the spirits carried by the seven vultures. Galankagou is the first *zima* [priest of the possession cult], his violins are the first violins, the seven blind men are the first *kumbaw* (possession dancers *specialized in Tôrou*), and the *rings of feathers that the seven vultures had around* their neck became the rings that all *zima* wear. (Rouch 1960:72–73; quoted in Gourlay 1982b:239)[29]

Paul Stoller, who has conducted much research on spirit possession among the Songhai, indicates that the use of the *godji* during possession ceremonies corresponds to deep themes in Songhai experience. To Songhai musicians, the high-pitched sound or wail produced on the fiddle indicates that the godji is "crying." Because the godji "cries" for all the Songhai, "it is the most sacred of instruments" (1989:109). As Adamu Jenitongo, a Songhai godji player explains:

> The sound of the godji penetrates and makes us feel the presence of the ancestors, the ancients [*don borey*]. We hear the sound and know that we are on the path of the ancestors. The sound is irresistible. We cannot be unaffected by it and neither can the spirits, for when they hear it "cry," it penetrates them. Then they become excited and swoop down to take the body of the medium. (Quoted in Stoller 1989:109)

Stoller states that the godji is so sacred that rarely is it played on secular occasions. "Generally, it is kept in a cloth sack and is placed in a zima's sacred spirit house, a hut in which a zima keeps his or her sacred objects. . . . The sound of the godji is a tangible link between Songhay present and past, for this wailing sound revivifies deep-seated cultural themes about the nature of life and death, the origin of Songhay, the juxtaposition of the social and spirit worlds. These themes, in turn, reinforce Songhay cultural identity" (Stoller 1989:109).[30]

The Hausa of Niger, who are empowered by fiddling and spirits, state that the association began when one of the spirits "whistled his tune to humans and asked them to play it again for him on the *goge,* and all the other spirits did the same. Then they taught the humans how to make the required musical instrument. This is how the *goge* became dedicated to the spirits, and the *goge* player the custodian of their music" (Bornand 1999:14).

Although Hausa influence is prominent among the Voltaics, spirit possession rarely occurs in Voltaic societies. Yet the fiddle's associations with the supernatural or metaphysics is apparent among the Gurma and Dagbamba (see chapter 4). Gourlay uses the religious function of the fiddle to support his argument that the instrument was *not* introduced in Africa as a result of contact with Arabs. While Gourlay's interpretation has validity for societies in the Central Sudanic and Voltaic clusters that believe the fiddle has spiritual powers, his hypothesis fails to explain the cultural significance of the fiddle in the Western Sudan where diviners and seers use primarily plucked lutes for prophecy and healing (Gourlay 1982b:239–241; Coolen 1983:480; *Born Musicians* 1984).

The degree to which Islam has affected fiddling in West Africa depends also on the people's acceptance of the religion (DjeDje 1992b). Those who are strong advocates of the Muslim religion use the fiddle less, particularly at Islamic or royal occasions, than those who are nominal Muslims or live in areas where religious reforms had little impact on attitudes and behavior. (See chapters 3 and 4.)

Among the Tuareg, the meanings surrounding the instrument are complex, not only because of the tensions that exist between Islam and pre-Islamic culture, but also because the fiddle is now basic to the traditional culture. The situation is further complicated by the fact that women "are the custodians of tradition, of folklore and, consequently, of music. No Targi (Tuareg man) plays . . . [the fiddle][31] and his participation in musical emotion is restricted largely to the sensuous and the sensual. His songs are invariable love songs" which are accompanied by the fiddle (Holiday and Holiday 1960). In the past, love songs and musical talents of Tuareg women and men were given full respect by most traditional Tuareg, but this has begun to change (Lhote 1955:328–329; Holiday and Holiday 1960; Baumann and Westermann 1967:429; Gourlay 1982b:238; and DjeDje 1985:67–89).

Tuareg Muslim leaders regard the fiddle as a pagan symbol that distracts the mind from thoughts of Allah and the teachings of the Prophet. In their opinion, not only does the fiddle aggrandize the position of women, it encourages licentious behavior among the youth. They argue that the mystical powers believed to be associated with the music and the instrument "do not derive from the *Qur'an* but hearken back to earlier animistic beliefs." This explains why religious authorities discourage the playing of the anzad and strictly forbid its performance in some encampments and settlements. As a compromise, some women continue to play but pause at the hours of prayer and refuse to play at any time on holy days. A few perform on rare occasions but refuse to keep an anzad in their tents (Wendt 1994:84).

Although lifestyles and traditional values have changed, Tuareg fiddling continues to be a symbol of identity. "The music associated with this instrument . . . embodies the cultural values and ideals of the once-dominated warrior aristocracy. . . . The *anzad,* as a primary ethnic symbol, serves to unify the disparate segments of the society around its cultural core" (Card 1982:3). In modern times, the Tuareg fiddle has different meanings. "On the one hand, the *anzad* symbolizes intellectual and spiritual purity and traditional behavioral ideals; on the other, it signifies gallantry, love, sensuousness, and youth and evokes images of a distant pre-Islamic past. The traditions surrounding it are deeply rooted in and reflect the high status of Tuareg women, unusual in the Muslim world. Yet within this diversity there is no contradiction. . . . The *anzad* is, therefore, a multifaceted symbol of Tuaregness" (Wendt 1994:84).

Contacts with Arab culture may be responsible for the introduction of the fiddle in Sudanic Africa, but the present-day meaning and function of the instrument are based more on indigenous cultural practices than on influence from North Africa. Not only does the fiddle have multiple identities in a variety of contexts, but diverse groups support fiddling. In addition to playing for royalty and noblemen, fiddlers are regularly invited by commoners and religious affiliates to perform at ceremonial and recreational occasions.

Song Types and Performance Style

Fiddle songs can be categorized into several types: praise, political, possession, topical or social comment, and love. Praise songs are the most common because fiddlers regularly sing praises to individuals who hire them. While the praise songs of fiddlers attached to a royal court serve as a historical record for the community, political songs in support of modern political leaders or government agencies aid in propagandizing a political party, its candidate, or a community project. Although possession songs are used to induce trance, some fiddlers perform this music for entertainment at festivals, naming and wedding ceremonies, and other public gatherings. Topical or social comment songs, based on proverbs, folk tales, adages, or current events, educate by referring to values and qualities important to members of a society (Pivin 195?, 1961; DjeDje 1978b:340–342; Johnson 1983; Tomoaki 1988; DjeDje 1999). A Mandinka *susaa* player's story about a man who wanted to marry a woman who was in love with another man demonstrates that greed and jealousy can lead to a tragic ending (Pevar and Pevar 1978:4–5). Love songs performed by Tuareg men during the *ahals* (courtship gatherings) include comments about love for the female whose symbolic representation is the fiddle (Holiday and Holiday 1960).

Examining the performance style of fiddlers is important for several reasons: (1) it reveals the different ways fiddlers create musical identities, (2) it demonstrates the multiplicity of fiddle styles that exist in West Africa, and (3) it forces us to think about the extent to which context affects fiddling. Although performance analysis is central to understanding any musical tradition, few publications include discussions of fiddle musical style. To address this problem, I have analyzed selected examples of fiddle music from different parts of West Africa (see discography). Special focus is given to ensemble organization, form, melody, rhythm, texture, and vocal quality because these features are important in distinguishing fiddle styles.[32]

Bowed string instruments in Arab culture are used primarily to accompany the solo voice. Most often the singer and accompanist are the same person (Racy 1983:134). In West Africa, however, performance styles are more diverse. Fiddlers may (1) accompany their own singing with or without other performers, (2) accompany solo or group singing with or without other performers, (3) perform instrumental solos, or (4) perform as the lead instrumentalist with the accompaniment of singers and other instruments. Whether the fiddle is used as the accompanying or lead instrument also varies. In some traditions (e.g., the Mandinka of The Gambia), the vocalist imitates the sound of the instrument rather than the reverse (Pevar and Pevar 1978:4). Among the Teda, in Chad, the hissing (a sound ornament) produced by the vibration of the bow string on the fiddle string is reinforced when the singer whistles through his teeth (Brandily 1970, 1980).

To understand more clearly the differentiation that exists among groups, I categorize fiddling into three performance styles—Sahelian, savannah, and forest—using geography loosely as a basis for the distinctions. Yet further variation can be made within these categories. For example, Tuareg fiddle music, which I categorize as Sahelian, can be divided into three regional styles (Ahaggar, Aïr, and Azawagh) because musicians within these regions emphasize different elements.[33] Furthermore, the performance style of musicians is not fixed but changes continuously due to cross-cultural influences, individual creativity, and other factors.[34]

The Sahelian performance style includes musical characteristics identified with Arab culture. Not only is there a close relationship between the voice and fiddle, but percussion instruments are rarely used. Most important is the central position of melody and the absence of complex polyphony. Like Arab music, melodies are complex with intricate ornaments and some use of microtonality (intervals that do not conform to the half-step and whole-step division of Western music) (Racy 1983:131).

Ten (23 percent) of the forty-three examples upon which I base my analysis are Sahelian. Seven consist of one fiddler accompanying another person singing, one is a fiddler accompanying two singers, and two are instrumental solos. The Tuareg are the primary performers, but musicians in the Central Sudan

Example 1.1. Tuareg fiddle music. "Le chameau qui boite." *Sahara 1. Chants des Touareg Ajjer* (A4). Le Chant du Monde LDY 4160. 195?. Used by permission.

(Djerma and Sonrai) and Western Sudan (Tukulor, Serer, and Wolof) incorporate Sahelian features in their performances.[35] In the Djerma and Sonrai examples, women sing while men play the fiddle. Among the Tuareg, women perform the fiddle and men sing. The Tuareg *anzad* serves more as an obbligato than a counter melody, providing support not only for the singer, but also creating embellishments that emphasize the main notes of the pentatonic scale (Holiday 1956:51; Nikiprowetzky 1967). When the Tuareg perform fiddle solos, the tunes are "adaptations of a well-known vocal piece" (Nikiprowetzky 1967), demonstrating the importance of the text to fiddle music.

The form of music in the Sahelian style is based on what I refer to as a formulaic structure. Similar to the Tuareg Ahaggar regional style, one or more principal tones, or pitches, are surrounded by a cluster of neighboring pitches (notice that in Example 1.1, which displays music performed twenty seconds from the beginning of the piece, ornamentation is centered around pitches C and D as well as F♯ and G). When the fiddler accompanies the voice, a dialogue takes place between the two. After the fiddler plays the melody (the call), the singer performs the same or a different melody (the response) with or without fiddle accompaniment. In Example 1.1, the *imzad* player performs the call in measure 14 followed by the male vocalist singing the response in measures 15–16. In instrumental solos, which also include lots of improvisation on small motives, melodies are organized into two sections, allowing call and response to take place within the fiddle part (DjeDje 1978b).

Similar to other performance styles, Sahelian melodies are based on a pentatonic scale (see Example 1.2).[36] However, the organization of melody distinguishes the Sahelian style from others. A Sahelian fiddler normally introduces several melodies in a performance that are repeated with variation. Not only are melodies longer, but they are highly ornamented with melismas and other embellishments—grace notes, neighboring and passing tones, anticipatory tones, repeated tones, sliding tones, etc.—demonstrating that ornamentation can be

Example 1.2. Scale pattern used by fiddlers in West Africa.

used as a variable in defining identity (Kimberlin 1989). When the fiddler and singer perform together, a heterophonic texture results because of variations. Although microtonality is rare, improvisatory interludes are common, and drones are also occasionally performed. In Music Example 1.1, the fiddler and singer alternate in performing the drone. After the *imzad* player completes her melodic passage in measure 14, she moves to the pitch C in measure 15, which she sustains while the singer performs an intricate melodic passage. While the *imzad* player improvises in measure 16, the singer remains on pitch C. Rhythmically, the music in the Sahelian performance style is normally free. Although not articulated audibly with percussion or other instruments, an underlying pulse can sometimes be felt.

The vocal quality of singers who perform in the Sahelian style is more tense, strident, and strained than that used in other styles. Performing in a very high pitch, singers use vibrato or tremolo to produce the desired sound quality (Duvelle 1961). A pitch in a high range is sometimes held for an extended period of time (sometimes with the fiddler also sustaining the pitch on the fiddle) similar to the performance of the Muslim call to prayer.[37] The bowing technique used by some fiddlers, particularly the Tuareg, is significant because of the pressure placed on the bow when pitches of the fiddle melody (ascending or descending slurs) are accented.

The performance style prominent among people living in the forest region is distinctive because of the type of fiddle melodies used, the large number of instruments included in the ensemble, and the emphasis placed on polyphony (multipart structure) and rhythm. With greater attention given to the group and the interplay among performers, the fiddle is one instrument among many. In some cases, another instrumentalist or vocalist in the ensemble serves as musical leader while the fiddler complements.

Of the forty-three examples analyzed, the four (9 percent) representing the forest include the Nago or Yoruba of southeast Benin (formerly Dahomey) and southwest Nigeria.[38] The Nago and Yoruba *sakara* (a single head, circular-shaped frame drum) ensemble includes one chordophone (the *godié* fiddle); three membranophones (*sakara* drums—*médjo, yahilou* (*iya-ilu*), and *omélé*); and two idiophones—*aguidigbo* (a lamellophone) and *igba* (a half calabash struck with metal rings worn on fingers). Because percussion dominates in performing groups from the forest, the fiddle is barely heard over other instruments. On recordings of the Yoruba (*Musiques Dahoméennes* 1966), a short melodic phrase performed on the fiddle with little ornamentation complements and enhances the overall sound quality but is not related to the melody performed by singers. The texture of groups from the forest is polyphonic and leans toward polyrhythmic because of percussion. An ostinato (repetitive) pattern played by each musician throughout the piece serves as the basis for organization. Call and response is generally performed between the vocal leader and other instrumentalists, who also serve as the vocal chorus. The vocal quality of singers is open throat and less strident than vocalists performing in the Sahelian style. Whereas Sahelian melodies are long and florid, fiddle melodies in the forest style are short with little variation and few embellishments.

The savannah performance style includes elements from both the Sahel and forest. Like other styles, a pentatonic scale is used. Although the group and percussion are emphasized, the fiddle is the primary and lead instrument, and it plays a central role in the interplay of sounds regardless of the size or ensemble organization. Both melody and rhythm are also important. When compared to the Sahelian style, the vocal quality of singers in the savannah is not as tense or strained. The singer also does not use as many melismas or vary the melody as extensively. Similar to singers in the Sahelian style, however, vocalists in the savannah may sing a pitch in a high range and hold it for an extended period of time for emphasis. Of the forty-three examples, twenty-nine (67 percent) represent the savannah performance style, including groups from the Central Sudanic (Burum, Djerma, Foulbé, Hausa, Kanembu, Maouri, Tangale, Teda), Voltaic (Bisa, Bwa, Dagbamba, Frafra, Kusasi, Mamprussi, Mossi), and Western Sudanic (Fulbe/Peul, Mandinka, Serer, Wolof) clusters (see discography for recordings).

Like fiddling in the forest, a wide variety of instruments are found in fiddle ensembles in the savannah. Yet the combination of fiddle and idiophone (a shaken gourd rattle or calabash drum beaten with hands or sticks) is most prominent. Several groups use membranophones with or without idiophones (Lander 1967:160–161; DjeDje 1978b, 1999; Sulemana 1995b). In addition to percussion, a few societies in the savannah include other melodic instruments (aerophones and chordophones) in ensembles (Duvelle 1961; Lamm 1968:16; Knight 1972:301; Pâques 1964:552–53; Bornand 1999; Pevar and Pevar 1978:5). Contemporary popular musicians such as Ali Farka Touré of Mali combine all types of African and Western instruments with the fiddle, demonstrating how musicians are continuing to fuse the old with the new ("Ali Farka" 1994).

The organization of melody in the savannah varies. Because a multipart structure is used, the texture is polyphonic. Some fiddle melodies are florid, while others contain only minimal ornamentation. In a few societies, the fiddle is played in a percussive manner with little attention given to developing the melody. In the praise song for the ancestors performed by the Frafra fiddler in Example 1.3,[39] the bowing can be described as "sawing" because single strokes are paired with individual pitches. When the same pitches are repeated many times (see measure 9 where pitch E is played five times and measure 11 where the fiddler performs pitch B six times), this produces a percussive sound that corresponds with the syllabic singing. The Frafra fiddler varies his performance by inserting short ornaments at different points in the melody. Placing pressure on the bow at these points allows for certain pitches to be emphasized, but it

Example 1.3. Frafra fiddle music. Song in praise of the ancestors. Field recording from the Institute of African Studies, University of Ghana. n.d. Used by permission.

also creates a rough, percussive sound that complements the part performed by the rattler.

Savannah and forest styles are similar in another way: a set melodic repetitive pattern (cycle or ostinato) serves as the underlying basis for the organization of the music (see chapters 2, 3, and 4). The form of savannah fiddling is also strophic and melodies are performed in a call and response fashion. As stated previously, the fiddle is central to the performance, regardless of the number of instruments included. If several fiddlers are used, one fiddler performs the lead or master role (the call), while other fiddlers and accompanying musicians respond by singing the vocal chorus and/or performing their instrumental ostinato patterns. When one fiddle is included in an ensemble with other instrumentalists and there is no vocal leader, the fiddle serves as the lead and the vocal chorus responds by "stating" what has been performed on the fiddle.

Although it is difficult to make generalizations about fiddling in West Africa, several tendencies can be noted: (1) pentatonicism is prominent in all styles, (2) multiple musical identities exist, and (3) the variations in performance styles are due in part to differences in context and history. Fiddlers living in the Sahel

Fiddling in West Africa 41

are more likely to include elements from Arab-influenced North Africa than fiddlers in the forest where drumming traditions and multipart structures are prominent. Yet fiddlers in all areas fuse elements from the Sahel, savannah, and forest in different ways to create musical identities distinct from others in their local communities.

Instruments included in fiddle ensembles draw attention to markers, symbols, and performance practices that define societies. The fact that several Fulbe ensembles include wind instruments may indicate that flutes are signifiers of Fulbe culture (DjeDje 1998:445, 1999:109). When we find Mande speakers incorporating the plucked lute and occasionally the harp and xylophone in their fiddle ensembles, this reflects both identity and diversity (Charry 2000a:10). Of the groups that use drums prominently, most are located in forest regions or live close to societies with strong drumming traditions. Perhaps individuals who choose drums do so not only because they are readily available geographically, but also because an aesthetic preference for percussion exists (DjeDje 1998). Fiddles were probably adopted when they formed an important part of the musical life of societies during the precolonial era; the same may also apply to performance (Nketia 1978:6). Only when innovation corresponds with the aesthetic qualities of a people will it endure and have meaning.

The general assumption that music in Sudanic West Africa has experienced Arab influence is confirmed, but the process of transmission, adaptation, and integration requires further investigation. While I have proposed some hypotheses, they need to be tested in specific contexts before firm conclusions can be drawn. This is why studies on fiddling among groups in West Africa are so important.

What we know so far is that while the distribution of the fiddle correlates with areas of Muslim concentration, the location of the instrument is linked more closely to the mobility of people, especially the Fulbe and Hausa. Distinctions in construction and terminology also relate to geographical differences. Although several musical features (instrumental types, melodic constructions, rhythmic patterns, and song) show influences from both North African and forest West Africa, other elements (playing technique, musical form, organization of fiddle ensembles, song types, performance contexts and social significance) vary among societies because people choose to integrate fiddling in ways that are locally meaningful.

Instead of debating the issue of Arab influence, which seems evident, researchers would be better served by determining what was appropriated and how these elements have been dispersed and adapted. In other words, more emphases need to be given to the "local" history of musical types, instrumental resources, and stylistic analyses because the physical construction of instruments, social usage, and performance practice of all Sudanic fiddle societies are not the same. Such an approach would enable us to view the history of musical traditions from the African standpoint in terms of what is selected, adapted, or rejected as new musical resources and ideas are integrated into an African experience.

2 An Affirmation of Identity: Fulbe Fiddling in Senegambia

> I learned fiddling because it's what I met. I found that my relatives and other
> Gambians are fiddling, so I joined them. These people fiddled to make old men
> remember the culture. So I find that I also should learn to fiddle so I can make
> those people remember also. Fiddling makes Gambians happy.
>
> —Ngeya Kandeh, 1990

Although several ethnic groups in Senegambia play the fiddle, the instrument is
most often associated with the Fulbe. The Fulbe fiddle, or nyanyeru, is a symbol of ethnic identity.[1] It not only helps the Fulbe to recall their culture, it is a
source of pride. When they participate as performers or observers of fiddling,
they are transformed from Senegambians into Fulbe residing in Senegambia.
This reassertion of identity is particularly important in the Western Sudan,
where ethnic identities are constantly in flux as a result of close interactions,
intermarriages, and overlapping social histories.

The Nyanyeru in Performance

In 1990, after conducting research and writing about fiddling in Hausa
and Dagbamba cultures for nearly twenty years, I decided to visit The Gambia.
I had read and heard directly from Gambian musicians, especially Mandinka
kora player Papa Susso, that several ethnic groups in Senegambia prominently
used the fiddle. On this initial trip I wanted to determine if a fiddle tradition
existed that warranted further study. I was curious about the instrument's construction, and I also wanted to know about the musicians who played it, the
occasions and places where it was performed, and the nature of its importance
to people in Senegambia. I traveled by air from Accra in Ghana to The Gambia's
capital of Banjul on August 18.

Papa Susso had arranged for Mohammed Sissoho to meet me, and he spotted me immediately as I got off the plane. Tall and slender, dressed in a brown
two-piece Western-style suit, white shirt, and brown tie, he approached me and,
in a very serious manner, asked my name. Sissoho was of the Soninke, an ethnic
group culturally related to the Mande and Fulbe. Because he worked as a secret-
service police officer at the airport, he commanded great respect, and I was able
to get through customs and immigration in no time.

Sissoho had arranged for me to work with Tamba Kandeh,[2] a Fulbe fiddler who lived in Lamin, a small town about ten miles from Banjul. I therefore decided to stay in a small motel that was within walking distance of Kandeh's residence. Located along the main highway from Banjul to Basse (the largest city in the upcountry), Lamin served as a stopping-off point for local travelers, and all forms of transportation served the town, making it easy to visit nearby cities. Lamin, however, retained a friendly, rural atmosphere. When I sat on the front porch of the motel, I could see people pushing carts or wheelbarrows filled with wood or bags of rice. Women and children regularly trod alongside the main highway with small loads on their heads, and men rode bicycles and motorbikes. Local vendors could be seen as well, selling fruit and peanuts.

Realizing that there was much I wanted to accomplish on my first visit to his country, Sissoho arrived at my motel on his motorbike the next day. This time, however, he wore a multicolored, tight-fitting, Muslim-style cap and a light-turquoise, long-sleeved flowing gown over matching pants and shirt. He told me that he had already made an appointment for me to meet Tamba Kandeh.

When we reached Kandeh's compound, he had just returned home from working on his farm, and he requested that we wait in the courtyard while he bathed and put on clean clothes. Like homes in northern Ghana, the compound where Kandeh lived consisted of several structures made from wattle and daub, and a large, open yard where a few large trees provided shade. Unlike Ghana, however, the three buildings in Kandeh's compound were rectangular and featured tin roofs. Instead of being encircled by high wattle-and-daub walls, Kandeh's compound was enclosed with a rectangular grass-thatched fence six to eight feet in height. Similar compounds lined the rest of the block.

While we waited, Sissoho explained to me that the three families living in the compound were all Fulbe, although not members of the same family. Rather, two families, one of which was Kandeh's, paid rent to the owner of the compound, who lived on the premises. The structures served as sleeping quarters, and everyone shared an outdoor cooking area and bathroom. Kandeh lived with his two wives, three sons, and two daughters. The atmosphere in the courtyard was relaxed. A few of the women sat on bamboo benches and tended the children while others cooked. Three young men visiting from Senegal (a Pullo and two Wolof) were relaxing and conversing in another area of the courtyard, but eventually they came and sat near us, curious about what was taking place.

When Kandeh emerged, he introduced himself and sat down. Like Sissoho, he was tall and thin. He wore a Western-style long-sleeved white shirt with the wide-legged trousers worn by many men in Sudanic West Africa. Because Kandeh was a well-known fiddler in the area, Sissoho had heard of him, but they had never before met. As a follower of Islam, which associates music with the profane (see chapter 3), Sissoho tolerated music, but no more. His respect for intellectual and scholarly activities was the primary reason he was assisting me with my research.

Because Sissoho had informed Kandeh about my interests, the fiddler had obtained materials to make a fiddle for me, which he began constructing as we talked. He had performed for and interacted with European tourists at hotels in

The Gambia and therefore assumed that I would want to purchase an instrument and eventually learn how to fiddle. The fact that I was female did not matter to him, probably because I was a foreigner. He also indicated that, although most Fulbe fiddlers lived upcountry in the provinces, he knew of several based in the Banjul area whom I could interview and record. Most importantly, he mentioned that he was fiddling at a wedding ceremony (*bangal*) scheduled to begin later in the day and that I could accompany him. We agreed that Sissoho would take me to the wedding on his motorbike and pick me up later that evening.

Kandeh invited us for lunch and asked if he could record and hear his fiddle playing on my tape player. For about six minutes, he performed four praise songs. The first two —"Supere Demba" and "Mamareh Ko Bengel Kaddy Jatou"— were in praise of two of his patrons. They consisted of a melodic cycle played several times on the fiddle without vocal or instrumental accompaniment. Short, intricate ornaments on various pitches helped to embellish the main melody. On the third song, "Jawara Aah Hebe Kodo" (a praise song in honor of The Gambia's former president, Dawda Jawara), Kandeh sang and accompanied himself on the fiddle. The fiddling in "Jawara" was noticeably less florid, and Kandeh sometimes stopped playing briefly when he sang. The final song was a repeat of "Mamareh Ko Bengel Kaddy Jatou," but with vocal accompaniment. After listening to the playback with earphones, Kandeh indicated that he was pleased with the sound, although he was disappointed that there were no speakers so the music could be heard by all.

A Fulbe Wedding

Among the Fulbe, a marriage (*koowgal*) is performed in several stages and consists of two formal ceremonies: the *kabbal* and the *bangal*. During the kabbal (the only ceremony sanctioned by Islam), the cattle (*koowrudi*) used to legitimize the marriage are publicly designated. Because the bride and groom are not present, representatives from both families announce that the man and woman want to marry, describe the koowrudi, and tell the *moodibbo* (man of God) the names of the man and woman to be wed (Riesman 1977: 81, 109–111). The bangal is the act of bringing a woman to the groom's village. It is not a rite of union between individuals or groups, but a rite of passage for the woman—if she has never been married—and a ceremony of welcome on the part of the women of the groom's village. Although one or more years may pass between the kabbal and the bangal, generally the bangal takes place soon after or the same day as the kabbal, particularly when it is not the first marriage for the bride or groom.

The bride's arrival at the groom's home always occurs after sunset, but the villagers who receive her spend the day preparing for her. As soon as she enters the groom's residence, she is passed into the hands of the women. All the women of the village surround her and, having taken milk into their mouths, spew it out on her in a mist. She then enters her mother-in-law's living quarters with her own girlfriends, who have accompanied her from her home. Although she finds no one inside, she stays there with her friends while the young women of the groom's home sing songs of welcome from beyond the now-closed door. Since the men have no role to play in this ceremony, they normally watch it discreetly, observing the girls who have accompanied the young bride. Later, they participate in the dancing and fun, which begin after the official welcome. Even before the songs of welcome have ended, many people play, sing, and dance.

We departed for the wedding around two o'clock in the afternoon and arrived at the home of the groom, Ngeya Kandeh (Tamba's cousin), about an hour later. Ngeya lived in a town called Nema Kundu Combo North, a suburb of Serrekunda, one of the largest cities in The Gambia. I learned from Ngeya's eldest son, Mamma Kandeh, who was about twenty years old, that the wedding ceremony would not be extensive. Ngeya, who was in his fifties, felt that an elaborate celebration was unnecessary as he was taking his second wife. It was, however, the first marriage for the bride, Rabbi Camara, who appeared to be in her late teens (M. Kandeh 1990).

Around four o'clock, guests began to arrive. Most were Fulbe men who had come for an Upper River Division (URD) committee meeting. While the men continued to conduct their meeting in one area of Ngeya's courtyard, four or five women cooked and performed other chores in another area in preparation for the wedding. Around six thirty, I accompanied some of Ngeya's friends and family members to Rabbi's home, even though she was not expected to leave for the groom's residence until late in the night. When the party arrived at the compound where Rabbi lived, they were greeted by her family and offered water and conversation. While the men waited in the yard, Rabbi made preparations for her departure. I was allowed to go inside her room where I found Rabbi sitting among her girlfriends, beautifully dressed in a bright yellow and red outfit consisting of a flowing gown over a wraparound skirt with a matching scarf on her head. Her bundle of belongings had been carefully packed and placed in a corner of her room. She seemed to be afraid or shy because, as her friends surrounded her, talking and giggling, she sat quietly. Among other things, she may have been considering that after she arrived at Ngeya's home, she would have to stay there for one month before being allowed to return to her parents' home.

Although members of the wedding party were dispersed in two locations (both the bride's and groom's residences), all of the musicking took place at Ngeya's compound, where about twenty to thirty people were in attendance on the first day and almost fifty were present on the second. Except for Rabbi, who was not always in public view, no one wore special clothing for the wedding. Women wore wraparound skirts that extended to their ankles with a matching top or Western-style blouse, and a scarf for their heads. Young men, such as Mamma, had on beige or white Western-style cotton shirts with matching pants and no cap. Many of the men thirty years old and older wore flowing gowns over matching pants and a Muslim-style cap.

Intermittently throughout the two-day event, Tamba Kandeh provided entertainment by fiddling as wedding guests ate, danced, and listened to music. On the first day, he performed until three o'clock in the morning. On the second day, musicking began around midday and extended until about seven or eight o'clock in the evening. In addition to the music he had performed at his compound earlier that day, he played songs on all sorts of topics and themes, although few were concerned with people attending the wedding. Some were praise or social comment songs that he had composed or arranged; most were compositions he had adapted from other Fulbe fiddlers.[3]

In most instances, Tamba performed alone. As he played various melodies on the fiddle, he also sang the vocal response. On occasion, a chorus accompanied him. At the evening performance on the first day of the wedding, a group of five to six girls, ten to sixteen in age, sang the response to the fiddle and provided rhythmic accompaniment with handclapping. As Tamba stood and played, he shifted his weight from one foot to the other, moving back and forth slightly to the rhythm of the music. Although he and the singers did not dance, a few of the people looking on got up, stood in front of Tamba, and began moving to the beat of the music, swaying their bodies and taking several steps side to side or back and forth. There did not appear to be any set pattern to their dancing; their movements seemed free and improvisatory. Many people were not actively involved in the performance. Rather, men and women (often separated by gender in groups of three or four) sat on straw mats, small wooden stools, or bamboo benches in various parts of the courtyard and talked quietly with each other as they listened to the music.

After the girls left, Tamba again played and sang alone. A few people at the wedding commented that the girls' singing had not been the best. Some guests believed that the girls did not know the music that well because they had lived in the city too long. The consensus was that if the wedding had taken place in the provinces (the eastern part of the country where most Fulbe lived), or if the girls had been older, the music would have been livelier (DjeDje 1990).

History

The Fulbe in Senegambia

The Fulbe people (also known as Fula, Foulah, Fulani, Ful, Foulbé, Fellani, Filani, Fellataa, Peul, Pullo) live throughout West Africa. From Senegal to Chad, they live in the midst of other populations and rarely constitute a majority.[4] The Fulbe language, Fulfulde (also called Pulaar), belongs to the Atlantic subfamily of the Niger-Congo linguistic family and is closely related to the Serer-Sin and Wolof languages of Senegambia (Greenberg 1970:25). Spoken widely throughout West Africa, Fulfulde can be divided into many regional dialects (Swift, Tambadu, and Imhoff 1965:ix). Writing about Fulbe in The Gambia, Charlotte Quinn states, "Although the Fulbe are often referred to as a homogeneous ethnic and cultural unit, in fact there were wide diversities existing between them arising from differences in origin, period of arrival in the area, and cultural contacts. Fulbe in the Gambia region spoke at least nine dialects within the West Atlantic group of languages" (Quinn 1971:430).[5]

Much controversy surrounds the history of the Fulbe. Boubacar Barry states that "the sedentary populations of northern Senegambia originated from the Sahel. Adrar, in present-day Mauritania, was their gathering site before their southward migration. Reacting to climatic changes, especially the desertification of the Sahel, combined with the political pressure of nomadic Berber encroachments, . . . Sereer, Wolof, Peul and Tukulor communities gradually began moving south. Their north-south migratory movement has continued to this day" (1997:14). Oral tradition and most scholars link the Fulbe and Tukulor to Takrur, an eleventh-century Sudanic state located in the middle of the Senegal valley. The people of Takrur and their descendants are considered to be Halpulaaren (speakers of the Pulaar or Fulfulde language). During the colonial period, scholars began representing the Halpulaaren as two distinct groups—the Tukulor (sedentary agriculturalists) and the Fulbe (nomadic pastoralists). Although the two groups have some customs that differ, researchers state that they are the same ethnically, linguistically, and culturally (Hrbek 1992:68).[6]

Takrur's role in the history of West Africa sheds light on developments among the Fulbe. When the ancient kingdom of Wagadu (Ghana) declined, Takrur became an important power in the Western Sudan. Not only did it take over Wagadu's western territories, it gained control of the trans-Saharan caravan trade and became a flourishing market center.[7] A number of people from Takrur even traveled to Southwest Asia and took up residence (Naqar 1969:370). Takrur's influence waned when the Mali Empire rose to power in the thirteenth century. The Mande eventually dominated Takrur, but as Mali declined between the fifteenth and seventeenth centuries, Takrur broke into three kingdoms: the Wolof kingdoms in the western half of the area enclosed by the Senegal and Gambia rivers were dominated by the central kingdom of Jolof; north of Jolof on the south bank of the Senegal river arose the Denianke kingdom of Futa Toro, which was ruled by a Fulbe dynasty; and, farther south, in the hilly country where the Gambia and Bafing rivers have their source, was Futa Jalon (present-day Guinea), ruled by the Jalonke kings of Mande origin (Hiskett 1984:138–139).

The spread of towns and cities during the formation of Takrur caused some Fulbe to leave. The migration of the pastoral Fulbe into the savannah dates from the twelfth and thirteenth centuries when they spread southward and eastward across West Africa, taking over at first only lands ill-suited to agriculture. For this reason their expansion caused no alarm. Their neighbors, in fact, welcomed the manure the Fulbe cattle provided for the fields and the milk and butter that they exchanged for agricultural products. Few of the pastoral Fulbe were Muslim, and thus religion was not a point of sharp difference with their neighbors. Even when they were Muslim, the pastoral Fulbe were generally tolerant in disposition. They were, however, invariably accompanied in their migration by some of their sedentary kinsmen, who were usually better educated, more sophisticated in political matters, and less tolerant of non-Muslims. It was the sedentary Fulbe who fostered the political influence of the whole group through military aggression, often in the form of jihad. In this way the Fulbe became politically dominant in areas such as Futa Jalon, Bundu, Masina, Hausaland, and the Nupe country (Mabogunje 1976:26–27; Ki-Zerbo and Niane 1997:74).

Fulbe who did not migrate eastward stayed in Senegambia and lived among the Wolof, Serer, and other groups. Oral tradition indicates that when Mande started migrating to Senegambia in the twelfth and thirteenth centuries, some Fulbe were already living there (Sillah 1973; Sidibe 2003). During the fourteenth century, another wave of Fulbe migrants arrived in Mali and established communities in Masina near the Niger Bend. By the mid-fifteenth century, the Fulbe had reached Hausaland, beginning an infiltration into Hausa country that continued through the sixteenth century. In the mid-fifteenth century, a group of Fulbe also settled in Futa Jalon. The Fulbe began to arrive in Adamawa and other parts of the Cameroon during the eighteenth and nineteenth centuries (Adamu 1986:55; Barry 1997:7; Greenberg 1960:479–480; Hiskett 1984:52–53; Murdock 1959:417).

The Fulbe who settled in Masina are important to the history of those in The Gambia, for some later returned to Senegambia. Under their clan leaders in Masina, the Fulbe formed a rigid social structure—serfs, traders, and aristocrats—and an economy based on cattle rearing and agriculture. Originally, they followed their indigenous religion but became influenced by Islam through contact with the Mande and the Tuareg who settled alongside them in and around Masina (Hiskett 1984:151). Fulbe interactions with the Songhai, who by the fifteenth century had more power and wealth than any other West African empire, led to tensions. During the fifteenth and sixteenth centuries, the Songhai Empire extended from the central area of what is now Nigeria to the Atlantic coast. Sonni Ali, a Songhai leader who attacked the Fulbe constantly, was their bitter enemy. After the fall of Songhai, the Fulbe began to have conflicts with the Tuareg. As a result of this pressure, many Fulbe returned to Senegambia during the sixteenth and early seventeenth centuries. Despite their departure, Masina remained an important Fulbe center (Hiskett 1984:152; Spitzer 1987b:592).

While many Fulbe immigrants who returned to Senegambia had embraced Islam, their Mandinka landlords in Futa Jalon and surrounding areas continued indigenous religious practices, even though many considered themselves to be Muslims. Upon arrival in Senegambia, certain Fulbe groups gave up the purely nomadic life for a comparatively regular change of pasturage and settled in one region where they established relations with the non-nomadic farmers on whose lands they spent the dry season. By the early eighteenth century, the Fulbe were in every kingdom along the Gambia River. The exact size of such a mobile population centuries ago is difficult to assess, but scholars know that

Fulbe settlements were scattered throughout the Mande states, ranging in size from clusters of a few dwellings to villages of one or two thousand (Quinn 1972:19).

Although tensions existed, groups in this pluralistic environment learned to tolerate each other.[8] The Fulbe normally bartered their dairy products for rice or millet. The Mande farmers willingly agreed to let the skilled herdsman take charge of the cattle that represented their life's savings and promised to give them protection from slave raids in return for services, taxes, or gifts. Not only were the Fulbe the acknowledged experts in the care of cattle—the accepted form of wealth in the country—they were also in sole charge of this desirable commodity. Both sides profited from this association, but over a period of time the Fulbe were less willing to be treated as vassals, harried, and oppressed. Tensions eventually arose that led to several Islamic reform movements between the mid-seventeenth and late nineteenth centuries (Quinn 1971:428; Suret-Canale and Barry 1976:489; Sidibe 1990). The revolts that took place during the seventeenth and eighteenth centuries were small-scale and did not have as significant an impact as those that would follow in the nineteenth century. Because jihad leaders lacked the support of powerful clan and family networks, no large empires emerged. Mande rule continued until the second half of the nineteenth century before it came under sufficient Fulbe attack and was swept entirely away.[9]

Maba Diakhou Ba (a Fulbe whose family migrated to the Gambian region from Futa Toro) as well as Alfa Molo and his son, Musa Molo (both Fulbe from Kaabu near Futa Jalon), were leaders of the two nineteenth-century jihads that most affected Gambian culture. Although Islam had already been introduced into the area, Maba's greatest achievements were the further spread of the religion and the unification, however briefly, of Mande, Fulbe, and Wolof peoples behind a single cause. Statistics collected in the mid-twentieth century show that by that time 80 percent of the Gambian population was Muslim (Quinn 1968, 1979; Hiskett 1984; Klein 1969, 1972; Curtin 1971; Robinson 1973; Charry 2000a).

Under Alfa Molo's leadership, the Fulbe in other parts of Senegambia and Futa Jalon, as well as the Serahuli[10] and the Mande who were disenchanted with the old Mande aristocracy, combined forces and successfully conquered the Mande landlords. Together the cluster of surrounding chiefdoms became the new Fulbe state of Fuladu (see Map 2.1). Alfa's son, Musa Molo, continued the reforms and carried the Fulbe conquest over much of Gambia's south bank, which included some five thousand square miles near the Gambia River. By the 1870s, the Fulbe state of Fuladu in the east possessed the richest economy along the Gambia River. The state was divided into approximately forty districts administered by Musa's principal followers, who included Fulbe, Mande, Serahuli, and even Wolof from the north banks of the river. Thus, Musa developed a state structure that replaced the pluralistic local institutions that had survived more or less intact from the days of Mande rule. Although both Fuladu and its Muslim neighbor states were superseded by European colonial rule at the beginning of the twentieth century, Musa Molo is considered to be one of Senegambia's most successful leaders because of his attempt to unify the Gambia valley (Quinn 1971:427–440). He was not regarded as a religious man, but his closest advisors were Muslims, and he entrusted his courts to Muslim jurists (Klein 1972:433).

During the nineteenth century, the pastoral Fulbe were egalitarian, other than distinctions defined by wealth and the continued presence of slavery. Sedentary groups, however, were commonly stratified into free men, or nobles, and commoners (Fulbe Foro); slaves (Fulbe Diado); and endogamous *griots* (praise singers), artisans, and fishermen. Normally, slaves were not Fulbe in origin but acquired through capture or purchase. Cultural indicators, such as surnames, first names, body adornment, and scarification, often served as a means of identifying a person as free-born, artisan, or of servile descent. Members of the different groups also spoke distinct dialects, as they do now (Clark 1992:2, 18; Quinn 1971:431; Murdock 1959:419–420).

Prior to colonial rule, while some Fulbe (like their neighbors) cultivated crops, many subsisted by animal husbandry, resorting to farming only under pressure of circumstances. Farming was generally left to slaves (Sidibe 2003). The Fulbe did very little hunting or gathering but involved themselves in trade. In more modern times, nearly all Fulbe kept sheep, goats, dogs, and chickens, as well as cattle, and many had horses and donkeys. Men ordinarily herd cattle, while women often tend goats and sheep (Murdock 1959:419). As more Fulbe have settled in urban locations, some have become involved in business, civil service work, and other occupations associated with life in the city (Sidibe and Galloway 1975).

In the precolonial era, the Fulbe in Gambia were organized into patrilineal groups called *bulundu* that all bore the same name. The bulundu were divided into extended families that served as the units for migration and activities of daily life. In each group, one man held the hereditary leadership position of Ardo (also called Farba) and not only acted as a link between the landlord and the Fulbe population within the settlements, but was also responsible for collecting taxes and settling disputes (Quinn 1971:431–432; Sonko-Godwin 1988:47).[11] In modern times, the largest concentration of Gambian Fulbe live in small hamlets in the eastern part of the country. While the sedentary Fulbe inhabit permanent villages or towns, the pastoral Fulbe wander in nomadic bands and occupy only temporary camps. All Fulbe males practice circumcision. Marriage always involves a bride-price, but the amount tends to be small among the pastoral Fulbe. The household unit is polygynous; co-wives have separate dwellings, and the husband divides his time between them (Quinn 1967).

Senegambia and The Gambia

Senegambians possess a strong cultural cohesiveness that has played a special role in West African history. As Boubacar Barry explains, Senegambia has been the confluence of all the area's migratory streams, from the watersheds of the Upper Niger valley in the east to the Atlantic Ocean in the west; from the

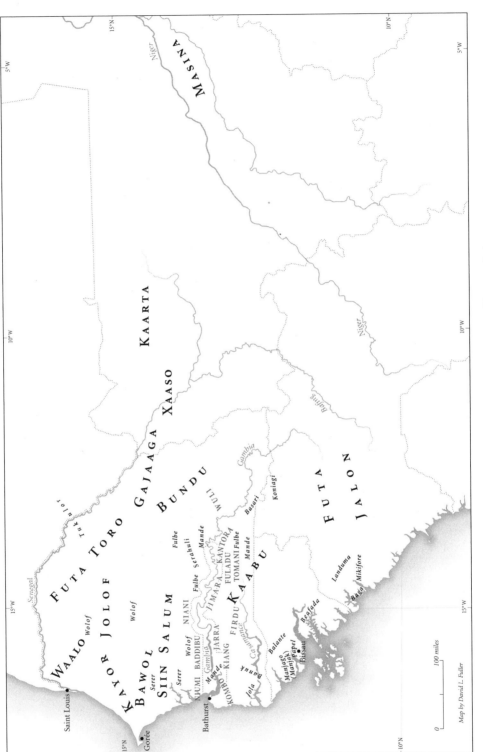

Map 2.1. Senegambia in the eighteenth and nineteenth centuries. Map by David L. Fuller. Used by permission.

Adrar highlands in the north to the Futa Jalon plateau in the south. The result is a blend of demographic and cultural traits dating back to the empires of the Western Sudan with newer influences from the Berber nomads of the Sahara Desert. Therefore, the region deserves its reputation as both a terminus for incoming populations and a point of departure for migrants. With the arrival of Europeans, old continental influences began yielding to maritime currents (Barry 1997:3).

The first European contact with Senegambia occurred in the 1440s when the Portuguese arrived as explorers. Later in the fifteenth century, a Mandinka king named Battimansa established a treaty of friendship with the Portuguese (Barry 1997; Gray 1940). Although the Portuguese took enslaved Africans in their earliest explorations, slave trade did not become important in the region until the sixteenth century with the development of plantation economies in the Americas and Europe. The earliest English and French traders were more concerned with gum arabic, gold, ivory, hides, and spices. By the eighteenth century, however, traffic in slaves was the most important business. In the late nineteenth century, exports included ivory, gum, teak, and gold (Quinn 1972:8; Barry 1997:36).[12]

It was not until 1888 that Gambia was administratively separated from Sierra Leone and a Gambian legislature was established. In the following year, negotiations with France delimited the boundaries between Senegal and Gambia. By 1901, the British had extended a protectorate over all of the major chieftaincies along the river, but did not initiate social and economic changes until after World War II. Although Gambians were given limited representation in the colony's legislative council in 1932, it was only between 1948 and 1963 that the local populace participated in the political process. The Protectorate People's Party, founded in 1959 and led by Dawda Jawara, sought to integrate all ethnic groups. In fact, the party changed its name to the People's Progressive Party (PPP) to ensure that political offices were distributed on an intercommunal basis. The PPP won the 1962 elections that initiated self-government with Jawara as prime minister. In 1965, the PPP led the country to independence as a constitutional monarchy. In 1970, The Gambia became a republic with Jawara as its first president. After a failed military takeover in 1982, the Republic of Senegal and The Gambia signed an agreement to bring the Confederation of Senegambia into existence, but the confederation was dissolved in 1989 (Hughes 1994:392). In July 1994, the civilian government of Jawara was overthrown and a military regime came into power with Yahya Jammeh as leader. When a new constitution was established and national elections were held in 1996, Jammeh became the new president (Emms and Barnett 2001).

The Republic of The Gambia comprises the valley of the navigable Gambia River (see Map 2.2). Except for the sea coast, the country is surrounded by Senegal and extends inland for about two hundred miles. At the mouth of the river in the west, the country is thirty miles wide; it narrows to fifteen miles at its eastern border. Although The Gambia is one of the smallest countries in Africa, it is extremely diverse in population. The principal ethnic groups include the Mande (42 percent), Fulbe (18 percent), Wolof (16 percent), Jola (10 percent), and Serahuli (9 percent); smaller numbers of the Serer (2 percent), Aku (1 percent), Manjago (1 percent), and non-Africans (1 percent) round out the population (Church 1994:392; Elmer 1983:3). The Bainuk, Balante, Beafada, Jola, Papel, and several other ethnic groups are believed to be among the earliest settlers in The Gambia, while the Fulbe, Mande, and Wolof migrated into the region later (Barry 1997:6–7; Sidibe 2003).

Ethnicity and Identity

Ethnicity is central to the sociocultural environment of people living in Senegambia because of the complexity of demographics in the region. In addition to the Fulbe who settled during the earliest migrations from the Senegal valley in the twelfth and thirteenth centuries, those from various Fulbe states—e.g., Futa Jalon (present-day Guinea), Futa Toro (present-day Senegal), Masina (present-day Mali) and Fuladu (present-day The Gambia)—now live in Senegambia. Given intermarriages and overlapping histories with indigenous populations and other migrants (the Mande and Wolof), discerning Fulbe ethnicity and identity is not easy. These issues are continuously in flux and under negotiation.

In the late twentieth century, the concept of ethnicity itself, connoting a sense of kinship, group solidarity, and common culture (including language), generated much debate.[13]

Yet diverse ethnic communities have been present in every period and continent and have played an important role in all societies. Although the impact of ethnic identity and ethnic communities has varied, ethnicity has always constituted one of the basic modes of human association (Hutchinson and Smith 1996:3). As Louis Brenner explains,

> The matter of ethnicity is extremely complex, and in recent years a welcome debate on the precision of its definition has begun to emerge in the West African literature. Ethnicity is primarily a question of identity, and identity is in fact a multidimensional process; it varies with who is doing the identifying and in what context. A Pullo, for examples, has no need to identify himself as a Pullo when he is among other Fulbe; he would identify himself by family, lineage, clan or perhaps village. But if he traveled from Masina to Bamako, he would be seen as a Pullo; and in Paris, among other Africans, he would be a Malian, although to most Europeans he would be an African. This example suggests that one's identity becomes more abstract the further one moves from home; and the same is true of ethnicity. (Brenner 1984:197)

While there are many reasons why issues such as ethnicity, ethnic community, and ethnic identity have been the focus of so much research, two stand out. First, these issues are often associated with conflict resulting from political conditions, economic inequalities, or cultural (e.g., linguistic or religious) differences; yet there is no necessary connection between ethnicity and conflict. Some conflicts in Senegambia during the precolonial period were indeed due to differences in ethnicity (e.g., conflicts between Mande and Fulbe), the basis for

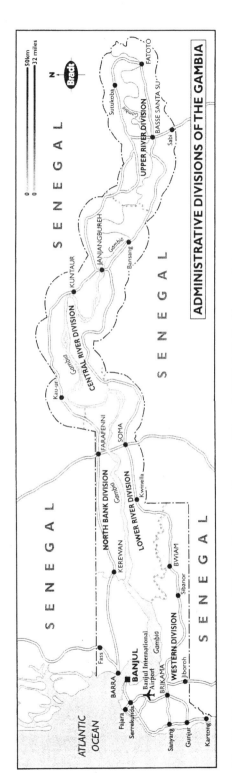

Map 2.2. Administrative divisions of The Gambia. Source: Emms and Barnett (2001:4–5). Used by permission.

much of the tension there was less ethnic than it was religious and political in the Mande's desire to spread Islam and the quest for political power. During the nineteenth century, the Fulbe were the leaders of some of the major struggles. Although tensions among ethnic groups in Senegambia may exist during the postcolonial period, thus far none have developed into armed warfare (Sidibe 2003).

The second factor influencing scholars' research is the fact that ethnicity is used as an argument to justify a dichotomy between a non-ethnic "us" and ethnic "other." Hutchinson and Smith explain, "What these usages have in common is the idea of a number of people who share some cultural or biological characteristics and who live and act in concert. But these usages refer to *other* peoples who . . . belong to some group unlike one's own" (1996:4). In addition to this discourse being prominent in European and some Asian cultures, it is also found "in the English and American (White Anglo-Saxon Protestant) tendency to reserve the term 'nation' for themselves and 'ethnic' for immigrant peoples, as in the frequently used term 'ethnic minorities'" (Hutchinson and Smith 1996:5). For different reasons, the "us"/"other" dichotomy also exists in Fulbe culture, where it not only serves as a major cause for their survival in West Africa, but concerns the essence of being a Fulbe.

I am interested in ethnicity on the individual level; that is, "the individual identification with a culturally defined collectivity" or "the sense on the part of the individual that she or he belongs to a particular cultural community" (Hutchinson and Smith 1996:5). While there are many definitions for cultural community or ethnic group, the one proposed by Hutchinson and Smith is a good working one for our purposes here: "a named human population with myths of common ancestry, shared historical memories, one or more elements of common culture, a link with a homeland and a sense of solidarity among at least some of its members" (1996:5).

Fulbe Identity

Because the Fulbe are so widely dispersed in West Africa, the question that often arises is, What is similar about the Fulbe in terms of ethnicity and culture? Those who have written on the subject give some of the same responses but place emphasis on different issues. In the introduction to *Unity and Diversity of a People: The Search for Fulbe Identity* (1993), Victor Azarya, Paul Kazuhisa Eguchi, and Catherine VerEecke state that most Fulbe favor a cultural approach to ethnic identity rather than basing it on historical origins or lineage. Thus, for the Fulbe, the central markers are: *pulaaku* or *pulaagu* (code of behavior or way of life) and Fulfulde, the Fulbe language (Ogawa 1993:121, 129). Regardless of location, these two characteristics "not only distinguish the Fulbe from other ethnic groups, but also color Fulbe perceptions of themselves and their world and prescribe the way the Fulbe should present themselves, as a sort of moral code" (Azarya, Eguchi, and VerEecke 1993:3).

A very old concept, pulaaku is the one most often discussed by researchers and the one that has adapted to the various conditions in which the Fulbe have lived. Among cattle herders, pulaaku relates to the behavior and character associated with herdsmanship. During the Fulbe jihads, pulaaku prescribed behavior associated with militarism, such as bravery and courage as well as religious qualities such as piety (*njuuldamku*). Specifically, pulaaku

> prescribes how a *Pullo* . . . should act vis-à-vis specific types of people . . . as well as the public in general, in terms of behavior and appearance. Foremost of the many components of *pulaaku* is *semteende,* which may be defined as a kind of shyness, reserve, and even embarrassment when in the presence of relative "others." Other components may include *munyal* (endurance), *hakkiilo* (common sense, care), and a host of others. These values and behavioral prescriptions have aided the Fulbe in their mastery of their precarious physical environment and in their quest to remain distinct from other peoples. (Azarya, Eguchi, and VerEecke 1993:3)

According to Ryo Ogawa, the most "important aspect of *pulaaku* is . . . not as a value system by itself but the fact that it is always defined in relation to other peoples or cultures. . . . When a Pullo thinks or speaks about *pulaagu,* he necessarily has in mind an image of some other people. *Pulaagu* is always defined in contrast with others, and this 'otherness' is of absolute necessity. It is a system of ideas or symbols which makes the Fulbe distinct from others" (1993:130). The qualities of pulaaku can also be explained in negative form. Paul Riesman writes, "In an extreme hypothesis, one would say that the Fulani ideal would be a man without needs, a man capable of living without eating, drinking, or defecating, for example. In other words, a being entirely cultural and independent of nature, a being whose actions are never involuntary" (1977:129).

In addition to being marked by pulaaku and Fulfulde, Fulbe culture is noted for its dynamism because, as a people, the Fulbe are constantly adapting to new circumstances and situations (VerEecke 1993:146). The demographic balance between the Fulbe and other populations in a given location particularly affects Fulbe identity because the Fulbe tend to absorb and integrate the features of other societies into their culture and identity (Azarya, Eguchi, and VerEecke 1993:6–7). Galina Zubko, for example, emphasizes the openness of the Fulbe to contacts with and borrowings from other cultures (Zubko 1993:203). Therefore, much diversity exists among the Fulbe. "It may be stated, with certain limitations, that heterogeneity is one of their most essential ethnic characteristics" (Zubko 1993:207).

Henri Gaden speaks of two categories, or models, of Fulbe—those who are martial and those who are peaceful herdsmen. Whereas the Fulbe in the first category managed to keep their independence but were also open to people and rulers with whom they came in contact, the second category infiltrated West African countries in small, mostly family, groups, attempting by all means to minimize the information publicly available on their actual cattle possessions (Gaden 1931:313). Zubko explains further:

> Among the characteristics of the first model are social and political activity, openness for contacts and outside influence (specifically materialized in active Islamiza-

tion), formation of feudal theocratic states, sedentarization and intermarriage with neighbouring peoples (this could only bring about considerable changes in the anthropological type of the Fulbe). In the second case, the tendency is to preserve their isolation, to adhere to ancient social and religious institutions, and to maintain comparative closeness, avoiding outside influence. Between the first and the second categories of Fulbe there exist complex hierarchical relations: the nomadic Fulbe admit their dependance [sic] on certain families of the sedentarized Fulbe. (Zubko 1993:207–208)

Senegambian Fulbe are both like and unlike their kin in other parts of West Africa. Not only is Senegambia home to a greater variety of Fulbe, but—if the Mande are excluded from calculations—the number of people identified with different ethnic groups is more equitable in Senegambia than in other places.[14] Although Senegambian Fulbe do not constitute the minority as they do in some parts of Africa, the contradictions (e.g., being open to other cultures but also persistent in maintaining their own) often associated with Fulbeness are apparent in Senegambia.

Because of their success in the jihads, some Fulbe in West Africa enjoyed an aristocratic position. After the arrival of the Europeans in the late nineteenth and early twentieth centuries, Fulbe leaders in some regions of the Sudan (e.g., Nigeria and Cameroon) were able to retain their Islamic titles and political offices as long as they assisted European governors in administering the local (Fulbe and non-Fulbe) population. In Senegambia, however, this did not occur. Rather, the Islamic states were disestablished with European colonialization. Some local village rulers exist, but they have little political power (Sissoho 1990). Thus, very early in the twentieth century Gambian Fulbe lost their influence in national and regional political affairs, which led to competition and an ongoing negotiation with non-Fulbe for economic and political power (Azarya, Eguchi, and VerEecke 1993:4).

The strong sense of pride identified with Senegambian Fulbe has caused them to be regarded as conservative and reserved, qualities also associated with other ethnic groups in the region. Bakari Sidibe, whose ethnicity is divided between Fula (the Mandinka term for Fulbe) and Mandinka, explains:

> In the Senegambian region, no ethnic group is as open to change as the Wolof. That's why they are fairly modern, progressive, and outgoing. Mandinkas are conservative. Fulas, because of their background, are very structured and also very conservative. The Fula are praised in Mali, in Guinea Conakry and Guinea Bissau, in Senegal and The Gambia here for their reserve and for their sense of pride. Maybe the wrong kind of pride, maybe the right kind of pride. But pride is there, especially the military Fula from Masina. The wrong kind of pride when you think that you're fair skin, you got a straight nose, you're different from flat-nosed people like us. You're purer; you're closer to the white man, the European, than the rest of us. That's wrong. But they have that. A positive thing is that they would not want to lie or cheat. I don't know about Futa Jalon Fulas. I'm talking about Fulas north of the Senegambia—Futa Toro—and Masina who came and settled. We find them very

honest and decent. They would not provoke. Their sense of reserve and decency has earned many Fulas respect in this region. (Sidibe 2003)

While many Senegambian Fulbe adopted their neighbors' traditions (e.g., farming and bulundu), they were unwilling to accept outsiders into their society. Sidibe states that "drawing other people in their fold is not easy for Fulas of Senegambia. The so-called pure Fulas look down on the impure Fulas" (Sidibe 2003).[15] Since the country's independence and the mass movement of all ethnicities into urban areas, however, many changes have occurred. Not only are there intermarriages among Fulbe groups, relationships with other ethnic groups are common. Sidibe provides some insight:

> The Futa Jalon Fula living in Banjul find their children are changing. They are beginning to drop the Fula language for Wolof. Their parents find this most undesirable. But because of outside influence (peer pressure, their schooling, and so on), there is nothing they can do about this.
>
> Those from Futa Toro and north Senegal near Mauritania are the Fula clerics, the jihadists, the teachers, the Qur'anic scholars. They tend to link together. But to intermarry with Mandinkas is rare. Very rare. They are more politicized, and are more independent also. You find them settled in various areas. Change is coming to them as well, but only in the last ten years. Many of their sons and daughters who are going to the senior high schools are mixing a lot with people in the local areas. We will see intermarrying between Mandinka and Fula more from now on, resulting from their close contact; because in the past they didn't have that kind of contact. (Sidibe 2003)

Fulbe Music in Senegambia

Little scholarly research has been done on Fulbe music in Senegambia, especially when compared to the number of sources available on the Mandinka and Wolof. Except for DjeDje (1999), only brief comments about the music of the Fulbe can be found in general works on The Gambia (e.g., Elmer 1983:15–18) or in publications that include discussion of other ethnic groups who reside in or near Senegambia. A few scholars in related disciplines have devoted attention to the Fulbe in Mali (Bâ 1966), Burkina Faso (Riesman 1977), and Senegal (Sow 1993), but their discussion of music is limited. Even D. W. Arnott's articles on Fulani music (1980) and Fulbe music (2001) in the first and second editions of *The New Grove Dictionary of Music and Musicians,* respectively, contain minimal discussion of traditions in Senegambia. Yet Fulbe groups in other parts of West Africa, particularly the Central Sudan, have been the subject of many scholarly publications.[16] Two of the most valuable studies on Fulbe music are by Henri Gaden (1931) and Christiane Seydou (1972). Although these works do not contain details about Fulbe in The Gambia, their discussion of Fulbe in other areas (Futa Jalon, Futa Toro, and the Nigerian complex) provide valuable insight about Fulbe traditions in West Africa. Commercial sound recordings present a more balanced picture of Fulbe music in various culture clusters, with representative samples from the Western Sudan, the Voltaic area, and the Central Sudan (see DjeDje 1999:113).

Several reasons may account for the minimal research on the Fulbe in Senegambia. First, as noted earlier, Fulbe culture is not confined to a single location. Not only are the Fulbe dispersed throughout West Africa, their migration into Senegambia spans several centuries with different waves of people arriving from the north, east, and south. Upon arrival, rarely did they form themselves into a unified group. Rather, they were divided into a variety of linguistic, occupational, and social groupings (Quinn 1972:21). Confirming this point, Bakari Sidibe indicates that Senegambia is one of the few places in West Africa where *several* Fulbe groups can be found. "The Fulas from Futa Jalon, the Fulas from Masina, the Fulas from Futa Toro, and the Fulas from Fuladu just converged on the valley here. Today you find almost all the different branches of Fulas in the Senegambian region, and they all have their different histories" (Sidibe 2003).

Second, similar to investigations in history and other disciplines, scholars who conduct music research in West Africa have focused on the politically powerful and the most visible in a society. The political dominance of the Fulani (Fulbe) in Hausaland and their large numbers in northern Cameroon and other parts of the Central Sudan have made them prime subjects for investigation. Fulbe leadership in Senegambia did not have a significant and long impact on society when compared to the empires, kingdoms, and states established by the Mande and Wolof. Neither do the Fulbe constitute a majority in Senegambia. The Mandinka are the largest group in The Gambia, and the Wolof are in greater numbers in Senegal. In both places, the Fulbe rank second in population.

Finally, because of the extensive intercultural contacts among groups in Senegambia, some investigators discuss Senegambian music generally without specifying what is unique among the different ethnic groups. Roderic C. Knight (1983:45) states, "it is clear that Fula-Mandinka relations have encompassed a wide range of situations. . . . The most fruitful situation for both parties concerned, that of intermarriage, doubtless went hand in hand with most of the others, and continues to this day, making clear-cut distinctions between the two peoples less and less meaningful." In Saihou Njie's (1970a, 1970b, 1970c) three-part series on music in The Gambia, rarely does he mention the distinctive features of the various societies. Rather, he discusses aspects of music making as if all groups participated similarly.[17] A few scholars suggest that what is found among one group may be applicable to another. Commenting on the Wolof, David P. Gamble, Linda K. Salmon, and Hassan Njie (1985:2) state that when analyzing the details of Wolof culture, one finds little that is not shared with other peoples. Not only have the Wolof adopted Islam from the Tukulor and been greatly influenced by Fulbe religious scholars, but their naming, circumcision, and marriage ceremonies show parallels to Mandinka and Fulbe customs.

While acknowledging these similarities, my research points to significant differences as well. It may be that scholars have overlooked distinctions among groups because the focus of most research in Senegambia has been on non-Fulbe (e.g., Mande and Wolof). The small number of publications on the nyanyeru is a case in point. Also, an adherence to established cultural binaries—openness and isolation, for example—and other stereotypical characteristics associated with Fulbe identity probably limited researchers' understanding of the complex music culture of Senegambian Fulbe.

Musicians and Music Types

In Fulbe culture, several categories of musicians exist, but they are organized differently in various areas of West Africa. Writing about traditions of the early twentieth century, Gaden states that Fulbe and Tukulor musicians in Futa Toro (north Senegal) were divided into three groups: *maabu'be* (plural of *maabo*), who were weavers as well as singers; *wammbaa'be* (plural of *bammbaa'do*), musicians whose instruments were the *hoddu*, a plucked lute, and the *nanoru*, an instrument played with a bow; and *awlu'be* (plural of *gawlo*), singers who played drums (Gaden 1931).[18] The wammbaa'be were the ones "à être venus avec les Peuls, les autres sont d'origine sarakollé, mandingue ou ouolof" [who came with the Fulbe or are derived from Fulbe culture, while the others were of Sarakolle (Serahuli), Mandinka, or Wolof origin] (Gaden 1931:12). To support the common origin and close association of the wammbaa'be with the Fulbe, Gaden relates the following myth:

> There were three brothers who were forced by famine to disperse or separate from each other. The eldest brother took a hatchet, cut trees and obtained an income by making wooden objects. The second brother became a cattle herder. The third brother, supplied with his hoddu, became a singer and received gifts and profit for his activity. After the death of their parents and the famine had passed, the three brothers continued to follow their respective activities.
>
> The eldest was a woodworker (*Labbo*), the junior was a cattle herder (*Poullo*), and the third was a musician (*Bambâdo*). The Pullo, after finding that his two brothers were spending their lives in a degrading way, did not want his children to have an alliance with their children. Thus, the Laobé and the Wambâbé form today the inferior castes with which the Peul do not marry or mix. (Gaden 1931:321, my English translation from French)

Arnott (1980:24) states that the French term *griot* refers to singers in any of the three categories described by Gaden (1931). Both wammbaa'be and maabu'be were, and to some extent still are, associated with chieftaincy. Not only do they sing the praises and genealogies of rulers and other wealthy patrons, but they also sing about the exploits of their ancestors and the epics of the Fulbe past. While some may be attached to individual patrons, others move from one ruler's court to another.

Because Fulbe culture in West Africa is so diverse, discussing it in terms of distinct music types is almost impossible. Arnott writes, "it is difficult to generalize about [Fulbe] music. Nevertheless two important general distinctions must be made: firstly between the music in which the Fulani themselves take part and that of the professional musicians who sing and play for them; and secondly between the hymns and songs (both religious and secular) which have developed from the Arabic Islamic tradition and the everyday songs which are integral to the tradition of Fulani herdsmen" (1980:24).

The music culture of Fulbe musicians in Senegambia is slightly different from that of their neighbors and kin in other parts of West Africa. The Gambian Fulbe I interviewed categorize musicians in two groups: *awlu'be* (plural of *gawlo*) and *jalibeh* or *jali* (plural of *jalijo*).[19] The gawlo specializes in praising or promoting important people through song without instrumental accompaniment, unlike Gaden's reference to the Senegalese gawlo who sings and plays drums. The term *jalibeh* refers to individuals who play musical instruments (strings, drums, etc.) as well as those who sing to the accompaniment of musical instruments. While most Gambian Fulbe musicians are familiar with the terms *wammbaa'be* and *maabu'be,* these words are rarely used in conversation. More importantly, Fulbe musicians in The Gambia associate the maabu'be solely with weaving and not musicking.[20]

Bakari Sidibe indicates that, because of varying histories, Fulbe music culture is not unified. In his opinion, each Fulbe group has distinctive, but overlapping, musical traditions:

> The north Senegalese, the Tukulors who are the politicians, who are the military, they are just like the Serahulis. Islam. Islam. Islam. But they do have their *bambados* and the *gawlos* or their *awlu'be* with their calabash. They do the same sort of singing, they do the same sort of dancing. Otherwise the clerical groups, they have no music hardly.
>
> But in Fuladu, the Fulas are the best musicians there other than Mandinka kora players. Fulas are dominant in wrestling contests, and they have their special music for this. Some of these traditions are not Fula; they are of the local area. The music is played by the slaves.[21] They use drums, fiddle, flute, harp (five strings), and calabash. They are connected to the Manding because they use a set of three drums. Even though the pure Fulas participate, they wouldn't touch the instruments. So they are different from this other group.
>
> Futa Jalon Fulas, we call them Futankes, they have their musicians. When they are here to visit, they are greatly patronized. A lot of people and a lot of Fulas everywhere will attend. They have very fine modern music, Fula music, Futanke music. They use acrobats, flute, calabash, fiddle, and sistrum. But here again, it's mostly the slave group who does the music; the pure ones don't want to touch it. (Sidibe 2003)

When I asked about the prominence of fiddling among the different Fulbe groups, Sidibe stated that all perform the fiddle, even those from Futa Toro (Senegal) and Masina (Mali). "Many Toranka [Futa Toro Fula], because of religion, have dropped certain aspects of their culture like drumming music. The fiddle, they have not dropped. The fiddle is also very popular throughout Fuladu. Some are Manding Puls [slaves], because I know some who are darker. Also, it is in their own [the Lorobe] tradition. They seemed to have brought it from Masina. It's not a Senegambian thing. It came with the migrants" (Sidibe 2003).

As is true of their neighbors, the music profession among the Fulbe in pre-colonial times was hereditary and based on kinship groups that performed certain musical instruments. If a person was born into a family that specialized in the playing of the hoddu, that individual was expected to learn to perform the instrument either from a kinsman or an established musician and continue in the profession as an adult. Some families specialized in several instruments, particularly if the music they played included these in the ensemble. Those raised in a family of fiddlers not only learned how to play the fiddle, they were also taught how to play the tama (also spelled *tema*), the hourglass pressure drum, and in some cases how to sing. With Westernization and particularly since independence, these rules have changed and are not rigidly upheld. In modern times, the distinctions between Fulbe and non-Fulbe musicians are beginning to blur. Many of the musicians I interviewed belong to the Fulbe Firdu dialect group;[22] some also came from areas near Futa Jalon. To my knowledge, however, Senegambia Fulbe do not have family surnames that identify them with the music profession.[23]

The only evidence that the Fulbe in Senegambia served as court musicians is their performances for the nineteenth-century leader Musa Molo. Because they lived in a pluralistic society, with leaders (warriors) who ruled a heterogeneous population, the Fulbe were not the only individuals who served as court musicians. When Fulbe rulers came to power during the mid-nineteenth century, they maintained many of the court traditions that had existed under Mandinka rule, which included the use of Mandinka *jalolu* as court performers. Thus, even though the Fulbe were the rulers, Mandinka, Fulbe, and Wolof performers sang the praises, recited the genealogy, and recorded historical accounts (Innes 1974:7, 1976; Knight 1983; Jobateh 1994).[24] While some Fulbe musicians were attached to royalty and important personages, many were also itinerant musicians, performing for different patrons in various contexts. Therefore, in addition to a core repertory or body of material that served as a historical or permanent record for the Fulbe ruler, Fulbe musicians also had to learn praise songs for commoners.

Instruments

Many instruments used by Senegambian Fulbe are similar to those found among Fulbe in other parts of West Africa. When I asked Tamba Kandeh about the instruments that best represent Fulbe culture, he replied:

"The hoddu, the nyanyeru, and the tama; those are the basic instruments for the Fulas." When I asked him to indicate the instrument that he thought was most important, he elaborated: "The fiddle plays an important role in Fula culture because it is a symbol for Fula. The fiddle was one of the first instruments that the Fulas came with. It's like Fula music has no meaning if the fiddle is absent. With the Fulbe from Guinea, the *fordu* (flute) and nyanyeru are the same. But [for] the Fulas in The Gambia, the nyanyeru has more significance than the flute. The Fulbe

in The Gambia can be without the fordu, but they can't be without the nyanyeru."
(T. Kandeh 2003)

In discussing Fulbe music in The Gambia, Knight (1980:140–141) states,

> The instruments of the *awlu'be* are the *nyaanyooru*, a monochord bowed lute with a horsehair string on both the instrument and its bow; the *hoddu*, a three-string plucked lute similar to the Mandinka *konting* [and Wolof *halam* (*xalam*)]; the *bolon*, identical to the Mandinka *bolon* [arched harp]; and the *serndu*, a transverse flute. The instruments are played alone or in various combinations, with singing. One or two percussive instruments are generally included, the most common of which is the *horde*, a half-gourd percussion vessel [calabash] with a metal rattling-plaque attached inside. The player holds the opening towards his chest and beats the outside with his palms and with rings on some of his fingers. Another percussive instrument is the *lala*, a pair of L-shaped stick-rattles, each with a sistrum with discs of calabash loosely skewered on one arm, while the other forms a handle.

The large number of Fulbe groups in Senegambia probably accounts for the variety of terms used for the flute, which is usually made of bamboo with four to six holes. In addition to *serndu* (*sereendu, serendou, serdu*), other terms include *forrdu, chorumbal* (*tiorumba*), *tambing, neffara, fulannu, poopiliwal,* and *wombere.* While many researchers provide no African term at all for the flute, most indicate that it is associated with herdsmen. In some Fulbe societies, the flute is used as a court instrument.

Two types of plucked lutes are associated with the Fulbe. The *hoddu* (*hodu, hordu, kerona*) has anywhere from one to five strings and is found among most Fulbe groups in Sudanic Africa. The *molo* (*mpolaaru, gambra, jirkil*) is always constructed with one string and more commonly associated with the Fulbe in the Western Sudan and Voltaic clusters (DjeDje 1998). Yet in many parts of Senegambia, it is the Wolof who are associated with plucked lutes. Michael Coolen (1982:74) suggests that the Wolof may have adopted the lute from the Fulbe in Mali who intermarried with the Mandinka. The Hausa of northern Nigeria and northern Cameroon are identified with several varieties of lutes, and the three-stringed molo's use by Cameroon Fulbe dates to the precolonial era (King 1980b; Erlmann 1983b:23; Coolen 1991; Charry 1996).[25]

Most calabashes and rattles used by Fulbe groups in West Africa are similar to those described by Knight (1980:140–141) in The Gambia, but the performance technique differs. In some societies, the horde is not held near the chest; rather, the horde player sits on the ground, places the inverted calabash between his legs and strikes it either with hands or sticks (see chapter 3). The *gedundung* (a water drum), a hemispherical calabash placed in an inverted position in a large gourd filled with water and played with sticks, is normally associated with women. The Fulbe also play other instruments (e.g., the musical bow and the Jew's harp) that different ethnic groups throughout the continent perform (Arnott 1980:25).

Drums used by the Fulbe in Senegambia are similar to those found among their neighbors. Not only do Fulbe perform the *tama*, but the *djembe* (also spelled *djimbe, jembe,* and *jimbeng*), a goblet-shaped drum played with hands and identified with Mande speakers, as well as the *bawdi* (also called *baudi,* plural of *mbahgu*), a set of four cylindrical-shaped drums played with hands, are included in Fulbe music ensembles (DjeDje 1999).

The Fulbe in Senegambia use many instruments, but as scholars and performers agree, fiddling is what signifies and distinguishes the Fulbe from other performances cultures in the region. In the remaining portion of this chapter, I discuss the social and musical role of the nyanyeru in The Gambia to demonstrate how it affects identity.

Fulbe Fiddling

The Nyanyeru

Like the body resonators of other West African fiddles (see photos that follow), the resonator of the Fulbe fiddle is round and covered with the skin of a reptile (lizard). Unlike fiddles in the Central Sudan and Voltaic areas, however, the resonator hole of the Fulbe fiddle is placed in the sound box, not the skin. Although fiddle size varies to suit the taste of the performer, the dimensions of the body resonator used by the Fulbe tend to be smaller—anywhere from five to six inches in diameter, compared to six to twelve inches for those used by the Hausa and Dagbamba. The overall length of the Fulbe fiddle is about eighteen to twenty inches, while other West African fiddles may be as much as thirty inches long (see chapters 3 and 4). The slightly arched bow, generally made from a type of bamboo wood that may or may not be covered with leather, is sixteen to eighteen inches in length. In most instances, the portion of the Fulbe bow that is held in the hand when playing has a leather covering, similar to bows used by Hausa fiddlers. Although made from a harder wood, the neck on the Fulbe fiddle, like the bow itself, is left bare. At least two thin pieces of wood, of different sizes, serve as the bridge and are placed underneath the string in performance (see Photo 2.2 later in this chapter).[26]

The term for the fiddle among Gambian Fulbe is *nyanyeru* (*nyaanyooru, nyanyaru, nyanyur, nanoru, nhènhèru*), but the Fulbe and other people of Senegambia also employ the Wolof term, *riti*. Because the Wolof language is the lingua franca in cities and towns, the use of *riti* is not surprising.[27] Although the Mandinka refer to the fiddle as *susaa,* rarely do they perform the instrument. Rather, *susaa,* like *riti* and *nyanyeru,* refers to the scratching or rubbing of two objects together, which is the action used to produce a sound on the fiddle (T. Kandeh 1990, 1994; Jobateh 1994; Knight 2001).

History

The history of fiddling among the Fulbe has not been documented with an oral tradition or written account. In fact, the majority of Senegambian fiddlers I interviewed indicated they knew nothing about the instrument's history.

Samba Juma Bah (1990), a Pullo fiddler from Guinea, states, "I did not bother to ask my teacher where the fiddle came from and I don't know where the fiddle comes from." However, Tukulor fiddler Majaw Bai (1990) believes the fiddle and plucked lute were introduced into Africa by cattle herders.

As detailed in chapter 1, the history of the fiddle among the Fulbe probably begins with the early interactions with the Tukulor, one of the first groups in Sudanic Africa to have contacts with North Africans and Arab culture. An important feature of Arab music is the performance of melodic instruments, particularly bowed and plucked lutes. Therefore, just as the Tukulor were among the first people in West Africa to convert to Islam, they may have been the earliest performers of lutes, which were subsequently adopted by their kin, the pastoral Fulbe. If this hypothesis is correct, the Fulbe would have been introduced to the fiddle as early as the eleventh or twelfth centuries because this is when Sudanic societies such as the Tukulor made contacts with North Africans. After the initial introduction, the use of the fiddle may have been reinforced through continued Fulbe interactions with North Africans. During their migrations eastward, some Fulbe came in contact and intermarried with Berber pastoralists who were moving south from the Sahara. The Fulbe in Masina (Mali) existed for centuries in contact with the Songhai and Tuareg Berbers before some Fulbe migrated west again to settle in Senegambia. In fact, interactions among the Fulbe, Songhai, and Tuareg may have contributed to the fiddle being adopted and used by musicians in each group in different ways.

If fiddle dispersion in West Africa is closely linked with the movements of the Fulbe, this would mean that the instrument was introduced into Senegambia when the Fulbe first migrated into the region. Thus, other peoples in the Western Sudan (e.g., the Balante, Koniagi, Serer, and Wolof) probably started using the fiddle as a result of interactions with the Fulbe (T. Kandeh 1990). In Sierra Leone, we know that the Temne (Atlantic speakers) have adopted the fiddle, but Fulbe musicians mainly play it (van Oven 1980:302, 1981:10). In discussing Fulbe music in the Futa Jalon mountains of Guinea, Gilbert Rouget states, "In addition to the epic-narrating musicians who are attached to the courts of the nobility, there are also small troupes of wandering musicians who group together round a player of the single-string fiddle. They accompany their singing by striking gourds with finger rings" (Rouget 1980:822). Gamble acknowledges that the Wolof use of the fiddle is derived from the Fulbe when he states: "As they [Wolof] are living in close association with the Fulbe, they are also familiar with the one stringed fiddle (*riti*)" (Gamble 1967:77). Since the Fulbe may have been responsible for the dispersion of the plucked lute (Coolen 1983:481; Charry 1996:5, 2000a:132), the same might be the case for the spread of the bowed lute.[28]

There are conflicting views on the Wolof's current association with the fiddle.[29] When I interviewed Senegalese fiddlers Majaw Bai and Ousainou Chaw, both stated they did not know of any Wolof who played the fiddle (Bai 1990; Chaw 1990). Dieynaba Gaye, a Wolof linguist born and raised in Dakar who has lived in the United States since the early 1980s, indicates that fiddling is identified not with the Wolof, but with the Serer, Peul (Fulbe), and Tukulor (Gaye 2004). Donna Armstrong, a colleague who interviewed the kora musician Moussa Kouyate in Dakar in 1993, learned that some Senegalese musicians regarded the riti as a Peul instrument that was later adopted by the Wolof (Armstrong 1993), and some scholars—e.g., Gamble (1967), Nikiprowetzky (1963, 1966b, 1980), Nketia (1974)—indicate that the Wolof perform the fiddle. However, some Senegalese performers indicate otherwise. During my research in Dakar in 1990, I was not able to find a single Wolof musician who played the instrument. Therefore, the comments by Bai and Chaw are significant because not only were they urban musicians who had lived in Dakar, but they were also aware of the activities of various ethnic groups in the city. That they did not know of Wolof fiddlers suggests that the Wolof in Dakar do not commonly perform the fiddle. Such conflicting information raises several questions. To what degree has Senegalese music culture changed? Was fiddling among the Wolof in Dakar more prominent in the 1960s and 1970s (when scholars conducted their research) only to be abandoned in more recent years due to Westernization or other factors? Did earlier researchers incorrectly assume that the fiddlers were Wolof because they spoke Wolof? Could fiddling among the Wolof living outside Dakar still be common despite the fact that it has died out in the city? People living in rural areas generally tend to hold on to traditions longer than those in cities (Koetting 1975, 1979/1980; Avorgbedor 1998).

Such uncertainty about the Wolof fiddling tradition demonstrates the complexity of ethnicity and identity in Senegambia and perhaps other African societies. Thus, using ethnicity or language to link people with musical traditions should be employed with caution. In addition, since Senegambians use many factors in identifying a musical tradition with a particular ethnic group, researchers need to determine these factors and take them into account when attempting to relate ethnicity to musicking. Although Fulfulde and pulaaku are two of the many characteristics that define Fulbe identity, other aspects of the culture, which are continuously in flux, must also be considered.

Other evidence of the fiddle's association with the Fulbe comes from The Gambia where the media link instrumental sounds with ethnicity. Fiddle music is used to announce the beginning and end of Fulbe news on the radio, while the kora is heard when Mandinka news is broadcast. In discussing the griot tradition in *The Gambia: A Cultural Profile,* Laurel Elmer writes, "Griots of the Mandinka, Fula, Wolof, and Serahule traditions used string instruments to accompany their historical narratives. While all played a type of lute with a wooden resonating chamber and a varying number of strings, the *kora* has become the hall-mark of Mandinka musicians . . . , the Wolof play the *xalam* . . . , the Fulas are known for their fiddles" (Elmer 1983:16). Yet many changes are taking place in the fiddle tradition in The Gambia in the twenty-first century. Although fiddling may still be prominent in the provinces where large numbers of Fulbe reside, the tradition is not as visible in urban areas such as Serrekunda and Banjul. There are many reasons for the decline, but two of the most important seem to be lack of interest on the part of the younger generation and economics.[30] Tamba Kandeh explains:

> The generation changes and there is the introduction of these different musics. In the past, you used to have only traditional music that was very popular. But today, there are lots of Western musics. Reggae is there. Hip hop is there. Swing is there. All types of musics are introduced in Africa now. So traditional musicians are not very powerful like they used to be.
>
> In the past, if musicians go to play (because they are popular), some people offer them cattle and goats or they would have been given some money. Whatever little money you get, it was very valuable. Although they made less money, almost no money at that time, but they were so highly respected. But today, because of their lack of popularity, they don't get much appreciations. So there have been big changes. (T. Kandeh 2003)

Performance Contexts and Social Organization

Fulbe fiddlers perform in a variety of public contexts (e.g., ceremonial occasions and festivals), and they provide entertainment for patrons in the privacy of their clients' homes. Camara (1990) states, "If I am in the house with a few men, without any noise, I can play the fiddle gently and explain about Fulbe warriors." Some musicians play the fiddle to entertain themselves. Tamba Kandeh says he plays after dinner when he is happy (T. Kandeh 1990).

Since people living in Senegambia are culturally related and have such close interactions, many events are shared. At festivals, puberty rites, and Muslim celebrations, musicians representing different ethnic groups in the region generally participate. Kandeh indicates that he is sometimes invited to perform at special occasions: "I play when children go to circumcision in the bush. When they are going, I use the fiddle. When they are coming back, I use the fiddle.[31] When I collect people to go to the farm, I play the fiddle as they work. The fiddler follows them, and they are happy. I play at festivals—for example, Ramadan and Tabaski. As Muslims walked to the mosque to pray, I would move with them. I would not play at the prayers, but just when they go to and from the prayers. When we had festivals to celebrate groundnut harvests, I would be invited" (T. Kandeh 1990). When I asked Mamma Kandeh about the role of fiddling at Muslim occasions, he stated: "When they are playing, all Muslims like it. If it's Fula Muslims, when the fiddlers start playing, you will see them receive ten *dalisis* [at the time, about $1.25 in U.S. currency]. Many, many, many things can happen. If you see people giving money, they feel happy. That's why they give money. When they are playing, everyone is happy" (M. Kandeh 1990).

When The Gambia became an independent country, fiddle performances at political activities became commonplace. Many performances also began to take place at luxury hotels where fiddlers played for tourists, most of whom were from Europe. Although these new performance contexts provided income, Camara believed that entertaining tourists at hotels affected his playing: "One has to play the song the audience seems to appreciate. That is the difficulty in playing music for commercial purposes. One must satisfy the audience. The financial dimension is therefore very important. If one is not financially secure, one would find it very difficult to have enough spare time to develop one's talent" (Camara 1991).

The few accounts in the literature about Fulbe fiddlers provide little discussion about social organization. Fulbe oral traditions in The Gambia include mention of two Fulbe musicians—Mamadou Patah Gawlo (a praise singer) and Yorro Buka (a fiddler)—who performed for Musa Molo. According to Maulday Baldeh,[32] who was born in the provinces in Fula Bantang in the MacCarthy Island Division (MID), Fulbe musicians did not stay in the village (Kesserkunda) with Musa Molo but lived in Basse, a nearby town. When Musa Molo needed musicians to play for him, he sent his servants for them. The servant would ride one horse and travel with empty horses to collect the musicians. When Musa Molo prepared for war, musicians went with him and sang praises and genealogy songs to get him mentally fit for battle. After the battle, they returned to Kesserkunda, where Molo slaughtered bulls for their dinner. Along with other musicians, the fiddler would sing songs to promote Musa Molo. Special historical songs have been composed in honor of Musa Molo, but Baldeh stated that he only knew two "old" songs ("Balla" and "Sorronna") and one "new" song ("Sodahnam Padeh Jelleh"). Fulbe fiddlers in the provinces knew other songs in praise of Musa Molo and still performed them for local chiefs and at rallies for political leaders in the modern government.[33]

Baldeh and other Gambian fiddlers who inherited the fiddle tradition from kin trace their heritage to Musa Molo's court musician, Yorro Buka (known as the "first fiddler"),[34] which suggests that fiddling among Senegambian Fulbe dates to the precolonial period. However, the fact that fiddlers are not aware of court musicians who lived before the time of Musa Molo indicates that the role of court musician probably evolved during the late nineteenth century with the rise to power of Fulbe rulers in the Gambian region. Prior to that time, the position of Fulbe fiddlers in Fuladu was probably comparable to what Isabelle Leymarie-Ortiz (1979) describes for common griots among the Wolof. Although some were attached to families and individuals, most had to move from place to place to find performances; a large number probably had to supplement their income through farming and other occupations.

Like other Fulbe musicians, many Fulbe fiddlers I interviewed refer to themselves as *jali* (or *jalebeh, jalijo,* or *jaliya*) demonstrating the influence of Mandinka culture on Fulbe in Senegambia (Camara 1990; T. Kandeh 1990). Because musicians are identified by the instruments they play, the fiddler as well as the musicians who accompany him in performance are given specific names: *jali nyanyeru* (fiddler), *jali jeymowoh* (singer), *jali tamaaru* (tama player), *jali mbahgu/jalibeh bawdi* (drum player, singular and plural, respectively).

Gambian fiddlers distinguish between musicians who inherit the profession from family members and those who achieve the profession by learning to fiddle on their own or from an established musician. Of the six fiddlers included in this study, three (Maulday Baldeh, Mamadou Baldeh, and Juldeh Camara) became fiddlers because of ascription (inheriting the profession from kinsmen), while the other three (Samba Juma Bah, Ngeya Kandeh, and Tamba Kandeh) achieved the profession.[35] While several of those who inherited the profession state that they trace their heritage to Buka, the fiddlers who learned through achievement know little about the fiddler's association with Musa Molo. Furthermore, unlike the situation among the Dagbamba (see chapter 4), there does not appear to be a formal social structure wherein all Fulbe fiddlers believe they are related to each other or pay homage to one fiddle leader (DjeDje 1978b, 1992). For example, in discussing the fiddlers in URD, Tamba Kandeh (1990) states, "The fiddlers in Basse, they are in groups. You sometimes find one group here, and you go to the next compound and you find another group. There are small villages near Basse. They have many fiddlers in those villages. These fiddlers, they sometimes meet at Basse. Each is with his own group. They don't mix together."

Patrons who support fiddle music can be categorized in two groups. On the one hand, there are persons who maintain a long and continuous relationship with the fiddler and call on him at any time for services because a prearranged contract or agreement between the two parties has been established. On the other hand, clients for whom the fiddler provides services for a short period, such as when he plays a praise song for a person whom he may or may not know at a public gathering, would have to be placed in an entirely different category. The decision to enter into a contract may be initiated by either party—musician or patron (DjeDje 1982).

Rarely are Fulbe fiddlers attached to one patron; rather, they perform services to several people at one time. It is not uncommon for the names of a number of patrons or promoters to be mentioned in one song. For example, in a performance by Juldeh Camara analyzed later in the chapter, the names of at least four of his patrons were called out. On occasion, the praise song for one patron becomes the fiddler's favorite. Tamba Kandeh states that he always begins his performances with a song that he composed in honor of a friend who was a well-known wrestler. Even four years after Kandeh had last seen his friend, who moved to Senegal, he continued to play this song in remembrance. "If somebody tells or asks me to start with another music rather than 'Supere Demba,'" he says, "I would do that. But if I am to suggest, I always need to start with the song 'Supere Demba'" (T. Kandeh 1990).

Because a fiddler's services are crucial to those in politics, long-term agreements are often established between politicians and fiddlers. In the mid-1960s, Tamba and Ngeya Kandeh decided to form a group as a result of their working with Mohammed Cherno Jallowe, one of the first politicians from URD to serve in the modern government. When Jallowe moved to Banjul to serve his term of office, he felt that he needed musicians in his home district to sing his praises both in his absence and when he returned on visits (T. Kandeh 1990, 1994).[36] Juldeh Camara states that when he was performing in the provinces, a politician heard him playing with his troupe and liked what he was doing. So

the politician asked him to travel around URD so that they could campaign together. After the elections, the politician asked Camara to follow him to Banjul
where both stayed and where the politician was responsible for Camara, taking
him to hotels and other places to perform.

Most Fulbe fiddlers believe their profession is a good one. Ngeya Kandeh,
who at one time was considered to be the champion fiddler for The Gambia,[37]
says, "Fiddling is something very high in the country because it's a culture
and it's a remembrance and it makes the Gambians happy" (N. Kandeh 1990).
Commenting on the meaning or significance of fiddling, Tamba Kandeh states,
"Muslims say fiddling is good. Fiddling is good to Allah. Fulbe fiddlers believe
that the fiddle is a music of heavens. If the person did good things here, then
he's going to find good things there [in the heavens]. If he did bad things here,
then he is going to find bad things there. For those who did good things, there
are doors. When opening the doors, the sound it gives, it's the same sound the
fiddles are giving. The sound of the fiddle is similar or is the same as when the
doors of heavens are opening or closing" (T. Kandeh 1990).[38]

Learning, Attributes, and Social Status

In Senegambia, performing the fiddle is a male profession. Before the
1960s, the majority, if not all of the individuals who played the instrument,
were born into a family of fiddlers and began their training between the ages
of seven and ten. In most instances, fiddlers were taught by their fathers. But if
the father had reached an age at which he no longer wanted to fiddle, the child
was sent to a family member or a professional fiddler for training. Fulbe fiddlers
at this time specialized in certain aspects of the fiddling profession. Those who
learned how to play the nyanyeru and tama were not always taught how to sing,
and those who sang were not always able to perform an instrument.

The attributes of a good fiddler in Fulbe society vary because the features
identified with fiddling are not set. In addition to being able to create new
songs, technical virtuosity on the fiddle is a talent that gives a fiddler distinction. Tamba Kandeh states that "when elderly people attend his performances
in the past, what they mostly follow is the tune of the fiddle and the words.
Today, in this generation, they mostly like tunes which are going to make them
dance. They will be very active, like in the nightclub. They are not very interested in tunes which are going to make them try and scan for the meaning"
(T. Kandeh 2003).

Both Maulday and Mamadou Baldeh indicate that their kin learned to perform the nyanyeru by following the same rules that were in place before the
1960s. Maulday states that he began his training when he was nine years old;
his father taught him and his brothers about the fiddle profession. After a small
fiddle was made for him, he was taught how to manipulate the fiddle bow. Later
he learned how to coordinate his dance movements; knowing when to step forward and backward when the women danced in a performance was important.

Maulday indicates that around the same time he learned to fiddle, he received instructions about how to play the tama (Maulday Baldeh 1994).

Mamadou did not learn to fiddle until he was fifteen years old because his father (Nayang Baldeh) had stopped fiddling by the time of Mamadou's birth in the late 1950s. Although Mamadou was born and raised in URD, he learned through an apprenticeship with a professional fiddler, Seidou Windy, who lived in Fula Bantang, a town located about fifteen miles from his home.[39] Mamadou explains that Windy was someone who used to visit his hometown for performances. During one of these visits, Mamadou became interested in learning to fiddle and was allowed to follow the man to his home. Windy already had a spare fiddle, and Mamadou immediately began his lessons. Initially, he was taught how to bow and then move the fingers. During the dry season, he stayed with his teacher, and he returned home during the rainy season for farming. Mamadou says that when he received his training no one knew how to both fiddle and sing simultaneously. In fact, his father only performed the fiddle and did not sing. When Mamadou learned, he was not taught how to play the tama, but tama players who accompanied him knew how to sing. Both Maulday and Mamadou indicate that it took them at least four years before their teachers felt they had learned enough to be recognized as professional musicians (Mamadou Baldeh 1994).

By the mid-1960s it was commonplace for individuals in The Gambia to leave the profession of their family and choose another, although this shift probably occurred even earlier. Musicians I interviewed also stated that the low status or stigma that had been associated with the music profession in earlier years has almost been abolished. Tamba Kandeh (1994) states, "We have started in a new generation whereby everything was accepted." However, fiddlers born into the profession are not entirely pleased with newcomers because it causes them to lose some of their clientele. As a result, they have to spend more time pursuing occupations unrelated to music-making. Maulday Baldeh (1994) states, "I do not like somebody who is not born in the fiddle profession to come and fiddle. This bothers me because that means I got to farm." Baldeh's complaints confirm a trend that began in some parts of West Africa during the twentieth century. Thomas A. Hale indicates that a hierarchy "exists between professional griots and the growing mass of fake griots,[40] including some nobles, who have invaded the profession in search of money. It is a phenomenon probably unheard of a century ago. Today, however, with the economic crises that has descended upon many countries in West Africa, one finds a growing reversal of roles" (Hale 1998:214).

In spite of objections from fiddlers who inherited the profession, many persons during the 1960s and 1970s became fiddlers because they believed it was part of their heritage as Fulbe. For example, although their socio-occupational heritage is Rorobe (cattle herding), several members of the Kandeh family chose the fiddling profession; most began their training in their late teens or twenties. Some received instruction from an established musician; a few learned from kinsmen. Ngeya Kandeh learned to fiddle at twenty-seven years old from an established fiddler in his hometown.[41]

Although many fiddlers state that fiddling is highly regarded, they express some ambivalence about teaching their children how to fiddle because the amount of money fiddlers earn is small in comparison with other occupations. Ngeya Kandeh states that he gave up fiddling in the late 1970s. "I left fiddling because I had three sons and one daughter. I found that we are in a poor country and I have nothing. I have no other technical abilities. So I find that I must leave the fiddling and follow the farm. In farming, there is where I can get money to survive with my family and some of my relatives" (1990).

The lack of patronage has also caused fewer people to choose fiddling as a profession in recent years. When I recorded a group of musicians from Guinea in 1990, the ensemble included flute, fiddle, sistrum rattle (lala), calabash (horde), and drum (djembe). In a performance by a similar group (with the same leader) in 2003, all instruments were represented except the fiddle. When I asked why the nyanyeru was not present, members of the group stated that they had had difficulty finding someone to play it. According to the leader, individuals playing the flute and fiddle were harder to recruit and maintain because it was not easy to learn how to play these two instruments (Jallow 2003).

Ensemble Organization and Performance Style

Prior to the 1970s, most fiddle ensembles consisted of one to three fiddlers and one or more singers. Most Fulbe fiddlers indicate that the tama player was probably added during the sixties and seventies when there was a greater effort to attract a wider audience (Maulday Baldeh 1994; Mamadou Baldeh 1994; T. Kandeh 2003).[42] Kandeh states that including drums made the music sound more "groovy" and stimulated dancing (T. Kandeh 2003). At present, the organization of a fiddle ensemble among the Fulbe in The Gambia is not set. One or more fiddlers may play alone or be accompanied either by calabash (horde), sistrum rattle (lala), or drums—the tama, the djembe, the bawdi, the gedundung, or a combination of membranophones. Sometimes melodic and rhythmic instruments (e.g., fiddle, flute, calabash, sistrum, or one or more drums) are combined in one ensemble. When women are included in the ensemble, they sing and provide rhythmic accompaniment with handclapping. If women are not included, men sing and play instruments.

According to Tamba Kandeh, some individuals have started to add the kora with fiddle. Also, "the Senegalese are playing fiddle alongside these Western instruments" (T. Kandeh 2003). Tamba's son, Buba Kandeh, indicates that popular musicians Baba Maal (a Fulbe), Youssour N'Dour (a Wolof), and Positive Black Soul (a Senegalese group that performs rap) occasionally include the fiddle as well as the tama in their groups. Buba believes that when musicians combine African and Western instruments, they are trying to maintain their African culture. "African instruments make the sound new and special. Something has been changed to make the music different" (B. Kandeh 2003).

Senegambian fiddlers I interviewed indicate that there have been significant changes in the performance of Fulbe fiddle music since the 1960s. Prior to The Gambia's independence, a fiddle ensemble was composed of two or more persons who performed different roles because fiddlers who inherited the profession were rarely taught how to fiddle and sing simultaneously. Mamadou Baldeh (1994) states, "Those who learn how to fiddle do not learn how to sing. When we are fiddling in groups, we have the women singing. Those who sing, normally those people cannot fiddle."[43] In earlier times, the fiddler who served as leader of the nyanyeru ensemble was responsible for performing only the fiddle melodies, while others (possibly women dancers) responded by singing. The tama player provided rhythmic accompaniment and, in some instances, joined in the choral response with the singers.

In a performance by Mamadou (on nyanyeru) and Maulday (on tama) in Tamba Kandeh's courtyard in December 1994,[44] the music was performed in several ways. On the first song, neither the male instrumentalists nor female dancers sang. Rather, Mamadou played different fiddle melodies while Maulday maintained an ostinato rhythm on the tama drum, as will be described below. Emphasis in this case was on the variation of the fiddle melodies while the dancers performed and the rest of the audience clapped their hands. On the second song, which included singing by the dancers and the audience, one eight-beat fiddle melody was repeated throughout with little variation while the drummer played a cyclic pattern. Although Mamadou was the lead instrumentalist, he played a part that was basically an accompaniment to the singing. During the eight-beat melodic cycle, the singers dominated by singing during the first six beats while the fiddler played alone during the remaining two beats. Therefore, in the second song, the fiddler's part seemed to be subservient to the singers. When analyzed in terms of call and response, the singers performed the call while the fiddler played a short response.

Since the mid-1960s, many nyanyeru players have begun to sing and perform the fiddle at the same time. Most Gambians credit Ngeya Kandeh's group and their performance at the country's independence celebration in February 1966 for the change in performance style. Ngeya's group was composed of two fiddlers (Ngeya and Tamba) and five women dancers (Metta Baldeh, Kumba Kandeh, Subbah Jawo, Daddaa Jawo, and Hawa Barro).[45] In addition to wearing traditional Fulbe attire, Ngeya and his group performed differently from other musicians in the provinces—two factors that Ngeya believes account for their prize. As he explains:

> They [members of the group] all performed the same song at the same time. They all possessed the same sound in the fiddles. Secondly, whenever they moved backwards or forwards, their steps always came at the same time, like soldiers marching or policemen marching. [Thirdly], when they were fiddling, they moved the stick [bow], they moved it forward always equal. When they sang and fiddled, their fiddle sound and song matched. No one led the other. Fourthly, when they were fiddling

and when they sang, the ladies who sang after them, when the women started singing, they started and they stopped the same. Nobody led the other. So that's why we were picked as the first champions.

Since making this innovation, many fiddlers have begun to sing and fiddle simultaneously, according to Ngeya. Not only did they master this performance style, but they became more famous than he: "The population came to be high and they came to be champion over me" (N. Kandeh 1994).

When asked why he decided to make changes, Ngeya responded, "The one who taught me, when he is fiddling, there was somebody singing. I learned how to fiddle while this man [my teacher] is fiddling. And secondly, I learned what the person is singing. I said to myself. 'Look at this man singing. He cannot sing and fiddle at the same time.' In my mind, I said, 'This man can fiddle but cannot sing.' Then I decide to take both to make myself popular and famous. I don't know about these places outside. But in The Gambia, I am the first person to sing and fiddle at the same time. I am the first person who learned that" (N. Kandeh 1994).[46]

The Fulbe fiddle can be the lead or accompanying instrument in an ensemble. When a fiddler functions in the primary lead role, not only is he responsible for the sound, but he also plays an active role in all aspects of the performance event. As leader of the group and sole fiddler, he sings the lead vocal, plays the lead fiddle part and fiddle response, and is involved in movement. In instances when a fiddler in the primary role sits and performs with no accompaniment, his physical involvement in the performance is limited, except for the slight movement of the head, shoulders, and feet to the rhythm of the music. On occasions when a fiddler stands during a performance, he tends to shift the weight of his body from one foot to the other as he moves to the rhythm of the music. The sound from this movement and the movement itself help the fiddler to maintain the tempo as he improvises and develops his material, particularly when no accompanying percussion instruments are used.[47] In some cases, a fiddler may dance as he plays the fiddle, turning around to the rhythm of the music or performing small intricate steps with his feet. A Fulbe fiddler's clothing is generally simple and similar to that of members of the audience (a Western-style T-shirt with Sudanic-style trousers). Some fiddlers, however, wear special costumes.

The Fulbe fiddler who performs in a secondary role is generally an accompanying instrumentalist. The music he performs tends to be less improvisatory when compared to that of the lead performer, but he may vary his fiddle part and performance style at moments during the performance. In any case, he is expected to complement and not overshadow the performance of the lead performer. For example, when Samba Bah performed for me, he was the sole fiddler but not the primary or master artist.

Since the Gambian government has placed greater emphasis on developing the tourist industry, more and more musicians have begun to perform at luxury hotels. As a result, performers feel they must do whatever is necessary to entertain this "new" audience because a major part of their income comes from foreign (primarily European) tourists. Although many features of Fulbe fiddle performances remain the same, some things have changed. One of the most significant features of hotel performances is that considerably less emphasis is placed on singing, probably because the audience does not understand Fulfulde, but also because musicians know little about members of the audience and thus cannot create praise songs. In addition, less singing allows each person in a group to showcase his other talents, which musicians believe are more appealing to the new audience. The movement and drama, however, are not innovations. Fiddlers state that "magic" (acrobatics and fire-eating) has always been a part of their performances, even in the provinces. Mamadou Baldeh (1994) explains, "That [magic] even comes before fiddling. That's our magical systems. You did fire. You cut your tongue with a blade, everything such like that. They come even before fiddling and before the tourists come in Africa. You can invite those people who do magic without the fiddle. Sometimes you can do the fiddling without those magics. Some people, if they are fiddling, would like to call these magicians to come to do some magic just to make the thing 'groovy.'"[48] Although fiddlers have always accompanied acrobats and fire-eaters, at present the singing, which was an important feature of some fiddle traditions in earlier times because singers responded to the fiddle, has given way to greater emphasis on movement and theater in this new context and environment.

Songs and Composition

One can learn much about a people by examining the lyrics and meaning of the songs they produce. Not only do song texts reflect the concerns of the person who are performing, but many lyrics deal with issues and themes important to the larger society. Most music played by Fulbe fiddlers can be categorized as praise songs, but a variety of topics and themes may be used. Proverbs, social commentary, historical events, and references to Allah are included with praises. Although fiddlers perform historical songs in honor of rulers, warriors, and heroes (Charters 1975), there does not appear to be a set, standard repertoire of melodies or texts for songs as one would find in a court tradition (see chapter 4). Rather, fiddlers create their own compositions for various rulers and heroes. Juldeh Camara states, "When I am invited somewhere, maybe there will be a lot of people. As I am playing the fiddle, maybe I can explain or tell them the histories of some of these warriors who I know. Maybe people like Musa Molo in the Casamance. Maybe somebody like Bakari Jah, he's also a Fula in Masina, Mali. Now we're in the time of Nelson Mandela. . . . I used to play this [historical songs] normally or enjoyably if I am in the house with a few men without any noise. I play the fiddle gently to explain what I know about these warriors" (Camara 1990).

When fiddlers perform songs that have been composed and made popular by others, most indicate that they change the song and make it their own. For example, Tamba explains that after Ngeya taught him how to play "Tapa Tura" (a song that Ngeya composed during the mid-1960s and which was popular during that period), he always changed the song whenever he performed it (T. Kandeh 1990). In addition to borrowing material from nyanyeru players and musicians who play other instruments, Fulbe fiddlers pride themselves on being able to compose their own songs, most of which are praise songs that include some social commentary. Camara states, "I compose my own songs. This is more creative and inspiring. To repeat what others have composed over and over again is not a demonstration of talent. The true musician must be able to compose his or her own songs" (Camara 1991).

Form and Stylistic Features of Songs

In most fiddle performances by Senegambian Fulbe musicians, two or more songs are performed in a series. When a fiddler moves from one song to the next, he does not stop but uses special techniques (playing in a very high register, sustaining the length of a pitch, repeating a small motive, or playing the basic melody several times) as signals to inform others in the ensemble as well as listeners that he plans to move from one song to the next. Between songs and even before the performance begins, fiddlers play short melodic phrases or long extended pitches to determine if the fiddles are in tune and to make sure that everyone knows the order of songs that will be performed. Tamba Kandeh (1994) states that fiddlers refer to these short melodies, phrases, and extended pitches as *tenandagal* (testing songs).[49]

Fiddle songs in West Africa can be classified into two groups: songs with multiple themes and songs with a single theme. When a piece consists of one or more fiddle themes (i.e., main melodies), oftentimes one or more improvisatory interludes are also included. In songs with a single theme, normally the melody is repeated throughout the piece with variation but no interludes. As with other aspects of Fulbe culture, the form of fiddle songs is not set. Songs with single and multiple themes are used, and several characteristics seem to be common:

1. Three parts—a short opening, a long middle, and a closing
2. One or more fiddle themes that serve as the foundation for the piece
3. Call and response that may occur between (a) the lead fiddle part and vocal chorus, (b) the lead fiddle part and fiddle response, (c) the vocal leader and fiddle response, or (d) the vocal leader and vocal chorus

The three-part organization is significant because fiddlers in other parts of West Africa use a similar structure, but performers include different material in each part. Among the Fulbe, the opening is marked by the lead musician (normally the fiddler) in the group not only introducing some of the themes, but also improvising on melodies and small motives. To establish the song, the leader may focus on the main melody, playing it five or six times before performing the improvisatory material. Some of the accompanying instrumentalists may also enter and perform during the opening.

In the middle section, all themes are introduced (or re-introduced) and developed. This is also when call and response takes place, with dialogue occurring between different parts of the ensemble. The middle section may include several improvisatory interludes similar in performance style to the opening and closing; the improvisatory material may be based on the main melody or other themes and small motives.

In the closing, which is longer than the opening but not as extensive as the middle section, the fiddler continues improvising as he moves to another song in the series. As the music progresses toward the end of a song, more intensity is felt in the performance as the tempo increases and the melodies and rhythms become more intricately patterned. The music becomes less intense at the very end of each song (right before the fiddler starts a new song in the series). Perhaps a change in tempo and mood is another indicator used by fiddlers to demonstrate the move to the next song.

Most Senegambian Fulbe fiddle music is based on an anhemitonic pentatonic scale (five pitches with no semitones). While the ambitus (range of pitches) for some songs can extend to more than two octaves, particularly in the improvisatory sections, the call and response material performed by fiddlers and singers tends to be within a one octave range. Some fiddle melodies are short (extending over a four-quarter-beat time span), but others are long and extended (twelve-quarter-beat time span) with many ornaments (grace notes, neighboring and passing tones, and repeated tones), similar to fiddling in the Sahelian performance style (see chapter 1). Melodies may be based on a duple or triple meter. When the fiddle and vocal parts are performed together, heterophony results with little emphasis on exact unison. Of course, when other instrumentalists are included, the texture is polyphony, and the different timbres and pitch levels of the other instruments create a multilayered spectrum of sound.

To understand how Fulbe fiddlers use these and other features, I analyze one song (but not the same song) by three fiddlers: Juldeh Camara, Tamba Kandeh, and Samba Juma Bah. These musicians were chosen not only because they demonstrate different stylistic tendencies but because each musician is distinct in terms of his recruitment into the profession, birthplace, age, and the type of ensemble in which he performs.

Music and Identity: Profiles of Three Fulbe Fiddlers

Juldeh Camara (Born 1966)

Born in Basse Manasajang, The Gambia, Juldeh Camara moved with his family to Sarre Yala (a village in Casamance, Senegal) when he was a few months old. Thus, his heritage is Fulbe Firdu (or Fuladu). When I interviewed and recorded him in 1990, he had lived in The Gambia since the mid-1980s. Camara inherited the fiddling profession from his family and started playing when he was seven years old. Much of his training occurred when he was a youngster traveling and performing with his father, who was blind.[50] In ad-

Photo 2.1. Juldeh Camara singing and playing the *nyanyeru*.
Photograph by Jacqueline Cogdell DjeDje. September 1990.

dition to the fiddle, Camara played the tama, djembe, and lala. He is also one of the few Fulbe fiddlers I met in The Gambia who had performed on several commercial recordings and traveled to Europe (the Netherlands, Norway, and the United Kingdom) and the United States.[51]

Camara has four brothers and three sisters. All of his brothers, who in 1990 still lived in Casamance, were fiddlers. Camara states that his older sister used to play the fiddle but stopped when he was born. She did not continue in the profession because, by tradition, females do not perform the fiddle. Camara explains,

> For a girl to fiddle and go around the village, I have never seen it. She can sing with women, but not fiddle. I don't do things I have never seen. It's not good for a woman to travel as I am traveling four or five years without going back to their homeland. A woman is to be married. If she has a very good experience on this fiddle, maybe she won't accept to be married. Or the husband wouldn't allow her to go. Maybe there may be a problem between her and her husband. If she is stopped, then there is a problem. Everybody wants a woman. If she became famous, many, many, many people would like to have connections with her. If she became a fiddler and is maybe a pretty girl or woman, looking so attractive to many people, she may be loved by many people. For a woman to travel like that for years on fiddling is not done. (1990)

When I asked if he would teach his wife or children to fiddle, surprisingly Camara stated yes for his wife: "If I'm married, I can teach my wife how to play the fiddle. I can fiddle and I can go with her anywhere she wants to go to perform." While he had no problems passing on the profession to his son, Camara adamantly refused to teach his daughter how to play the instrument: "I can't teach my daughter how to play the fiddle. She can't attend many ceremonies when she arrives there. They will exactly know she's a musician. Maybe her father was a musician. So maybe they give her money for that. But I don't want to teach my daughter how to fiddle, because I've never seen that" (1990).

As has been noted, fiddlers are ambivalent about the profession because of the small amount of money they make. The difficulty that Ngeya Kandeh experienced in taking care of his family on an income earned from fiddling is not unique. In 1991, Camara admitted that he often had financial problems because he was paid so little when he played at public entertainment spots like the Kololi Tavern, the African Experience, or the Kotu Stand in the Banjul area.

> I earn my living by playing music on a contract basis. I am usually paid according to the number of minutes I play. Sometimes I'd earn D170 [US$21.25 in 1991] or less. I never earn enough to be able to sustain myself and devote my attention to my composition. Tourists are willing to pay to receive entertainment, but we the musicians are not organized to be able to create the conditions under which we could benefit from our talent. In other countries musicians have studios to be able to record their music and sell records or cassettes. Here the situation is quite different. Musicians have to be patronized [find patrons] before they can make ends meet. Many of us wake up every morning to look for a place where a naming or marriage ceremony is taking place in order to sing praise to someone to get something. Under these circumstances, the real talent of musicians cannot be realized.

In spite of the obstacles facing fiddlers, Camara encourages young people to continue as musicians:

> Despite the difficulties they are facing, they should continue to develop their talent. Whenever one has time, one should try to compose new songs and new tunes. Whenever one sits down to compose a new tune, even if one is not successful immediately, one is in the process of developing one's talent. One should continue to meet the challenge and sooner or later one would come up with something new. One has to enjoy what one is doing before one can develop it. Every one of us should work hard and try to encourage each other to develop our talent for the common good. Music gives joy to people. It is needed in society. If we continue to develop our talent, sooner or later we will come to enjoy the fruits of our labor. As for me, my major ambition is to develop the riti (violin) so that it will not be limited to our subregion. I want it to be appreciated everywhere in the world. (Camara 1991)

Camara is accomplishing his goal of making others around the world more aware of African fiddling. During the 1990s, he toured several times with established popular musicians outside Africa. His tours to Europe included three to Norway with guitarist Knut Reisersrud and several to Great Britain with Afro Manding Sound and Ifang Bondi. Since 1996, he has been working as a music teacher for ECCO, a Gambian organization supported by the Norwegian Agency for Development that arranges music courses for European students to study traditional African music in The Gambia. In 2003, Camara was in residence in London performing in a play (*Elmina Kitchen* by Kwame Kwei-Armah) at the National Theatre, London. A BBC television broadcast of the play was planned, featuring music by Camara and musicians from Ghana and Australia (Camara and Noble 2003).

Among the Fulbe who lived in Banjul, Juldeh Camara was regarded as an established performer and composer. Mamma Kandeh, Ngeya's son, had commissioned Camara for songs. When I asked Tamba to recommend fiddlers who would be good to record and could furnish material about the history and development of the Fulbe fiddle, he suggested Camara. Although Camara had become well known both in the city and the provinces, he states that he is not sure how he gained fame: "As a small boy, I used to play with my father. I learned some of these songs from my father. I don't know how I got my own group. Maybe it is because people invited me, and I'm famous for that. There are many, many fiddlers who are older than me who used to come to me to ask many questions about fiddling. They would ask about the titles of songs and want to learn songs that I have written" (Camara 1990). When asked what inspires him to compose, Camara (1991) states, "My mind is always in touch with my environment. 'Chemedo,' for example, was composed as I contemplated on the life of young women and their babies. Another composition was an appeal to the whole of Africa to stand firm and struggle for the betterment of the generation. My music talks about marriage, respect for others, and other values, which promote good human relations. I also have a song dedicated to the African youth" (see Song Text 2.1).[52]

In comparison to other Fulbe fiddlers included in this analysis, Camara is the most accomplished, which may be because he was born into the fiddling profession. Not only is his organization of fiddle melodies and improvisatory material much more complex, but the manner in which he interweaves the song texts with the fiddling is more involved. In addition to playing the fiddle and singing, he also dances. His creativity and performance style indicate that he is a professional who strives to be innovative and entertaining, for fiddling is his primary source of income.

The African youth song was one of four songs included in a performance that I commissioned and recorded on September 1, 1990. Unlike Tamba Kandeh's performance on August 19, 1990, described at the beginning of the chapter, the four songs Camara played were much longer: the first song was 8:30; the second (the "African youth song") was 12:21; the third, 12:20; and the fourth, 7:35. In fact, the entire performance took almost forty-one minutes because of Camara's dancing and fiddle improvisations.[53] Although Camara sometimes includes bawdi drums, horde calabashes, and women singers in his ensemble, the sound sources in his performance for me consisted of one fiddle, one male vocal, and one tama. Camara sang and performed the fiddle while Salif Bad-jie played the tama without singing.[54] The performance took place in Tamba Kandeh's courtyard and began around 11 AM. The audience consisted of several of Kandeh's family members and me.

Before his performance, Camara changed from his street clothing (Western-style pants and shirt) into a special costume, thus differentiating himself from the other Fulbe fiddlers I had observed whose clothing matched that of their audience. Camara wore a bright red, white, and blue vest over a white T-shirt and short knee-length pants. The vest was long, extending from his shoulders to his ankles. Around his head was a wide leather-band headdress intricately ornamented with an abundance of cowry shells. A horse tail attached to the headdress appeared prominently above the middle of his forehead.

An analysis of Camara's African youth song demonstrates what is distinct about his music and how his song texts and fiddling differ from fiddlers in Senegambia and other parts of West Africa. In explaining the significance of this selection, which I categorize as a praise song with social commentary, Camara states, "In that song I called on the youth to accept the responsibility of working for a better future" (Camara 1990).

The lyrics for the African youth song (performed in three languages—Fulfulde, a tonal language, Arabic, and English) are straightforward with few proverbs, allusions, or metaphors. Camara probably composed the song in this manner to reach a wide audience, especially the youth who may not under-stand the deeper meaning of song texts with proverbs. In addition to telling the youth what they should do to help The Gambia become a strong country (i.e., "Let us unite and work for The Gambia"—see measures 18–22 of Song Text 2.1), Camara alludes to Fulbe history ("Look at the warriors"—see measures 53–54).[55] When Camara wants to emphasize certain portions of the text, he performs the lyrics sequentially without a break or response, which I refer to as a textual variation (see Example 2.3). With twelve textual variations included in the song, this seems to be a device that Camara uses to describe himself, praise patrons, and comment on issues important in society. The first textual variation occurs in measures 36–38 (after about one minute and twenty-five seconds into song). Here Camara greets me by calling out my name and stating that he wants me to take him to America. The second textual variation takes place about a minute later (measures 53–59). In this instance, Camara refers to Fulbe warriors, formally greets the audience, and introduces himself (he gives the name of place where he was born). Presenting information about his culture is important because the Fulbe are proud of their heritage; they expect musicians such as Camara to recall significant aspects of the culture so those present can establish links with the larger community. In so doing, the Fulbe living in modern times become living products of those who went before them. In this way the fiddle, the fiddlers, and what they perform become symbols of Fulbe identity.[56]

Although the piece was composed to encourage African youth, much of the song, like other praise music by African musicians, also consists of Camara calling out the names of his patrons: Mamma Kandeh and his brother (Lai Kandeh) and Galah Yero (see measures 24, 26, and 55 below). In addition, Camara makes references to me and my daughter (Abiba) probably because I was the person who paid for the performance (see measures 32 and 34–37 below).[57] In using the phrase "sweet neck" (in the sixth textual variation, which is not included below), Camara praises himself, indicating that he is a fiddler who plays music that is "sweet" (or good) and has a nice voice. In other parts of the song, Camara provides more details about his life: his appearances on Malian radio, his aspirations to travel to Europe and the United States, and his religion (he recites Arabic text from the Qur'an and refers to Allah and the Prophet Muhammad).

Song Text 2.1. Juldeh Camara. Song to encourage African youth. Lamin, The Gambia. September 1, 1990.

TRANSLATED INTO ENGLISH BY MAMMA KANDEH (1990) AND
SIDIA S. JATTA AND MATARR BALDEH (2003).

Measure Number	Song Text in English
8	Yes, Gayleh.
10	I am going to The Gambia. I am going to The Gambia.
12	I am going to The Gambia. I am going to The Gambia.
14	The youth should work hard
16	Because hard work is the cutlass to Allah.
18	Let us unite and work for The Gambia
20	And let us work for The Gambia. Let us work for our country
22	Let us work for The Gambia. Let us work for our country.
24	I am greeting my friend, Mamma Kandeh.

26	And his brother, Lai Kandeh.
28	Thank you, thank you.
30	Thank you, thank you.
32	Hello, Juldeh is talking. Dr. DjeDje.
34	Ah, Dr. DjeDje, how are you, how are you?
36	I am greeting you, Dr. DjeDje, it is true.
37	I am greeting you in person, Dr. DjeDje.
38	Then take me along to America to the easy [life].
40	Look at me. See how I work.
42	People look at me when I work. See how I work.
44	Work let me see. I am working little by little.
53	Look at the warriors
54	Look at the warriors.
55	How is Galah Yero [name of a person]? Listen to Juldeh.
56	I am saying hello to you, Fulas, and my relatives.
57	This is a culture for Fulas.
58–59	Juldeh, the famous musician, I did not learn to play the fiddle at Sarre Yala [But I greet the people of Sarre Yala].

In summary, Camara's song texts reflect a performer who straddles both the traditional and modern world. While he is proud of his Fulbe cultural heritage, he wants what the Western world has to offer because his ambitions lie beyond local performances and the limited resources available in Senegambia.

Juldeh Camara incorporates many musical elements discussed above, but they are used in a unique way. What stands out is his ability to improvise, his interest in experimentation, and his efforts to make the musicking exciting on a number of levels. Not only is he an excellent singer and exceptional fiddler, the performance is visually interesting because of his dancing and the costume that he wears.

The African youth song is organized into three sections: opening (:32), middle (9:44), and closing (2:05). The song is based on one main melody: a twelve-beat pattern played on the fiddle with a triple underlying pulse (see Example 2.1). Not only is this melody performed in all three sections, but much of the material used for improvisation is derived from the main melody.[58]

The rhythm performed by the tama is based on a six-beat pattern. Like the main melody, the tama's underlying rhythmic pulse is triple. Salif Badjie, the tama player, performs his rhythmic pattern twice to correspond with Camara's twelve-beat main melody played on the fiddle. During the beginning of the piece, the rhythm for the tama is normally the same each time the pattern is performed. What changes is the pitch. Notice that the organization of the pitch levels for beats 2–5 is different from that for beats 8–11 in measure 12 of Example 2.2 (see tama part).[59] When the music becomes more intense toward the middle and end of the piece, however, Badjie plays in a more improvisatory style by freely changing both the organization and pitch of his patterns.

The manner in which Camara develops the form is what makes the African

Example 2.1. Juldeh Camara. Song to encourage African youth. Main melody (fiddle response) played on the fiddle.

youth song distinct. In the opening, he performs the main melody several times with some improvisation, but the variation is not extensive. The most involved portion of the piece is the middle section, which includes many repetitions of the main melody, improvisatory interludes on the fiddle, and several textual variations in the vocal part. The middle section can be further divided into two parts. The first part (measures 7–59), which is approximately two minutes and thirty seconds in length, includes one interlude (measures 45–52) and two textual variations (measures 36–38 and 53–59). The most significant portion of the first half of the middle section is the call and response that takes place between the vocal and fiddle parts, both of which are performed by Camara. The singing serves as the "call," and the playing of the main melody on the fiddle with no singing represents the "response" (see Example 2.2). The melodies for the call vary because the lyrics influence the melodic organization and contour (compare the "call" melodies in measures 12 and 14 in Example 2.2). The response (main melody) performed on the fiddle remains stable or is performed with slight variation because it serves as the foundation for the piece and is the marker that identifies the song. For example, when the two fiddle responses in Example 2.2 are compared, notice that only the first pitch (one and one-half beats) of measure 15 is different from measure 13; the rest of the melody is the same (see beats 3–12 in measures 13 and 15). The middle section's second part, which is about seven minutes and five seconds long, includes primarily improvisatory material (textual variations and interludes) with little vocal call and fiddle response. The closing is performed almost entirely on the fiddle, for only brief singing is heard at the very end of the song. In the closing, both Camara's and Badjie's playing becomes faster and more intense.

Although all melodies are based on a twelve-beat cycle, Camara varies the internal organization of melodies in different ways. The main melody is significant because of its organization and the role that it plays in the performance. When the main melody is divided into four equal parts (three beats each), the parts can be labeled ABAB′ (see Example 2.1). Thus, a type of call (parts A) and response (parts B and B′) takes place *within* the main melody. Although parts B and B′ look very different, they are really the same because both begin with pitch E and end with B. The only difference is that Camara includes more fill-in material between E and B in part B, which he does not do in B′.[60]

Whereas Arab fiddlers use principal tones (pitches) or phrases as markers

Example 2.2. Juldeh Camara. Song to encourage African youth. Call and response melodies.

to remind listeners about the mode or to bring the piece back home (to its tonal center), Camara uses the main melody for this purpose (see chapter 1). Camara's main melody marks the beginning and ending of sections of the piece. For example, when Camara integrates improvisatory material into the performance, the main melody is used to begin and end the improvisation. He performs the main melody three times to introduce interlude I and one time to end the interlude. At the beginning of the second interlude, the main melody is stated twice, but performed eight times as an ending to interlude II. On occasion, Camara dances while performing the main melody, which is what occurs during interlude III, when he plays the main melody fourteen times.

The melodies used for the textual variation (that is, when Camara states the lyrics sequentially without inserting the fiddle response between the lines) are organized differently from the main melody. Camara performs these sections in a half-spoken, half-sung manner to bring attention to the texts rather than the melody. Although the melody for both the fiddle and vocal parts during the textual variation is simple, the rhythms tend to be more complex. It is here that Camara may include off-beat phrasing and additive rhythms. In Example 2.3, off-beat phrasing appears in measure 36 (beats 2 and 3 of the vocal and nyanyeru parts) and measure 38 (beats 2 and 3 of the vocal and nyanyeru parts as well as beats 8 and 9 of the vocal part). Additive rhythms appear on beats 7, 8, and 9 of the nyanyeru part in measure 38.

The interludes are important because they allow fiddlers to demonstrate their virtuoso skills. Just as some fiddlers use song texts to comment on issues important to society, interludes are employed, I believe, to develop or bring attention to certain aspects of the song. The competence or talent of fiddlers can also be determined by what they perform in the improvisations. Camara's interludes are playful because he not only introduces several ideas but also moves from one idea to another very quickly. In addition to developing small motives (of one or two pitches), he sometimes creates arpeggio melodic patterns and repeats them several times. He likes to perform inversions and repetitions; occasionally these might be played as one pitch or several pitches. Or he may play the pattern in a low register and repeat the same notes in a higher register. When interludes are taken into consideration, Camara is the most skilled of the Fulbe fiddlers included in this study.

Examples 2.4A and 2.4B, which are taken from interlude I (measures 49–50) and interlude II (measures 65–66), demonstrate the manner in which Camara takes small motives from the main melody and develops them. In measure 49, the focus is on the pitch G, the tonal center of the song, which he repeats many times. In measure 50, he develops the pitches E, A, and G, which are performed on beats 2–4 and 8–10 of the main melody (see Example 2.1). However, instead of performing the pitches as they appear in the main melody (G, A, and E), Camara inverts and repeats them several times using a much faster rhythm. Notice that Camara performs the sequence EAGE six times in measure 50 using eighth and sixteenth notes (see Example 2.4A). The material in measures 65 and 66 comes from the B portion of the main melody (see Example 2.1). By repeating E and EDB in various ways and sequences, he brings attention to the response of the main melody.

Camara's skills on the fiddle indicate that he is a virtuoso performer who spends significant time developing his talent. His competence may be due to the type of training he received as someone born into the fiddling profession, yet he is also a product of his historical moment. Compared to Kandeh and Bah,

Example 2.3. Juldeh Camara. Song to encourage African youth. Melody used for textual variation I. Measures 36–38.

Camara is the more innovative—a striking feature when one remembers that fiddlers from fiddling families have in the past tended to be more conservative than those who achieve the profession through other means. Not only does Camara have many new ideas, he presents them experimentally, proof perhaps not only of his unique disposition, but also that in the postcolonial period fiddlers born to the profession have had to become more innovative to compete with newcomers and for audiences.

Tamba Kandeh (Born 1940s)

Tamba Kandeh was born into a family of cattle herders (Rorobe) who migrated from Masina to Senegambia. After his ancestors settled in Fuladu (Kandeh does not know when this occurred), members of the clan became

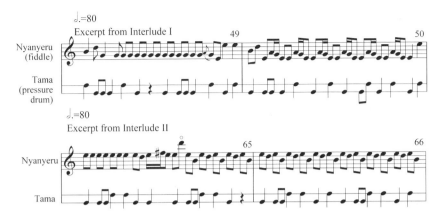

Example 2.4A–B. Juldeh Camara. Song to encourage African youth. Melodic motives developed in interludes. Measures 49–50 and 65–66.

Photo 2.2. Tamba Kandeh playing the *nyanyeru*. Photograph by Jacqueline Cogdell DjeDje. December 1994.

farmers and decided to live in the Jimari District, which is located in present-day URD. Kandeh's grandfather, Dickori Walo, was the leader of the clan. His father and mother, Samba and Dusu Kandeh, were also farmers. Kandeh moved from his birthplace of Sarekokeh (a village in URD) in 1975 and settled in Lamin to be near his patrons, Mohammed Cherno Jallowe and Michael Baldeh, who were both politicians representing the provinces in Banjul. Kandeh's brother, Ngeya, moved to the Banjul area a year later. In addition to traveling in different parts of The Gambia, Tamba has lived in Casamance, Senegal, where he at one time owned a compound (T. Kandeh 1990, 1994).[61]

Unlike Camara who was born into a fiddling family and began his fiddle training as a child, Kandeh was eighteen years old and living in Sarekokeh when he taught himself how to play the fiddle. After three months, he states, he could play the instrument. Learning to bow was easiest for him: "I heard how people fiddle. So I made a small one for myself until I started learning how to form my fingers. Forming the fingers is difficult because the fingers play everything; the fingers give different sounds. Then I went to my brother [Ngeya Kandeh]. When my brother was fiddling, I would also sit beside him and look [at] how he did the fingers. Then I started to follow him" (T. Kandeh 1990).

Although originally cattle herders, other members of Kandeh's family became fiddlers—another older brother who in 1994 still lived in the provinces and a cousin who resided in Guinea Bissau. Before leaving the provinces, Kandeh also taught a younger brother how to play the instrument. Commenting on his children's fiddle training in 1990, he said, "They [my children] are going to school. If they complete their schooling, then I'll teach them how to fiddle because it's a part of our culture." When I interviewed him four years later in 1994, he stated that his children should make their own decisions about an occupation. He was not going to demand that they become fiddlers.

Kandeh depended on fiddling as his sole profession for about sixteen years (1962–1978). During this period, he was well known as a performer, especially in the provinces. Kandeh explains, "I was very popular, famous. I was so occupied. I got lots of bookings because people were just inviting me here and there. That was my mission. Also, I was very popular on Radio Gambia all over the country. Radio Gambia still has my records because I was one of the top musicians in those days" (T. Kandeh 2003). It was during the 1960s that Tamba and Ngeya began performing together. When Mohammed Cherno Jallowe became one of their primary patrons, they gained the opportunity to participate in music competitions at the country's independence celebration in 1966 and 1967, which they won both times. Ngeya became known as the champion fiddler because he was the group's leader, but he was the first one to give up fiddling to become a farmer.

About three years after Ngeya stopped performing, Tamba gave up fiddling as a profession. Increased competition had caused his popularity to decline, which in turn had made it difficult for him to earn an income solely from playing the nyanyeru. Tamba explains, "In the past, I was just like a king, very popular. I had many personalities because of my music. But nowadays, there are lots of musicians where fiddlers are concerned. So fiddlers from the past are not much noticed" (2003). After 1978, Tamba continued to perform for personal pleasure, for special guests (like myself) and for occasions to which he was invited. He made his living, however, by farming and working at the dock at the seaport in Banjul. Since the 1990s, performances at hotels have become important, and he both performs with other musicians (in a group that might be formed on special request) and works alone. He states, "Some [tourists] are just interested in me playing and listening carefully to get the tune. Also, so they can try and learn when I teach them. Then at the end of the day, they pay me" (2003).

Therefore, while Juldeh Camara and Samba Juma Bah were professionals because fiddling was their only means of earning a living, Kandeh would have to be regarded now as a semiprofessional musician, for the majority of his income came from farming. Although Kandeh's performance style (that is, his organization of melody and text) was not as developed as Camara's, the music he performed for me demonstrated that he was a capable fiddler.

Tamba Kandeh's performance of "Jawara Aah Hebe Kodo," one of the songs he played for me while being recorded, demonstrates another song structure used by Fulbe fiddlers. Like Camara, Kandeh sang and accompanied himself on the fiddle; however, no rhythmic accompaniment was used. The entire "recording session" on August 19, 1990, lasted about six minutes, and each of the four songs differed in length: "Supere Demba" (:55), "Mamareh Ko Bengel Kaddy Jatou" (1:15), "Jawara Aah Hebe Kodo" (2:15), and "Mamareh Ko Bengel Kaddy Jatou" (1:20).

"Jawara Aah Hebe Kodo," the song analyzed here, is a praise song in honor of Dawda Jawara, The Gambia's former president. In English, the title means "Jawara has a visitor." The lyrics are very direct (see Song Text 2.2), indicating that Kandeh probably composed the song for the general public. As a musician attached to a politician who represents people from all walks of life, Kandeh felt that he needed to create songs that a wider populace could understand.

In addition to praising Jawara, the names of some of Kandeh's female patrons are called out. Kandeh also mentions Moussa Traoré,[62] the president of Mali. Since the song refers to Traoré as a visitor, perhaps it was composed to commemorate one of Traoré's official visits to The Gambia.

Song Text 2.2. Tamba Kandeh. "Jawara Aah Hebe Kodo" ("Jawara Has a Visitor"). Lamin, The Gambia. August 19, 1990.
TRANSLATED INTO ENGLISH BY MAMMA KANDEH (1990) AND SIDIA S. JATTA AND MATARR BALDEH (2003).

Hello, black person. Hello, black person. Hello, black person.
Mariama, Teneng, and Jabuyel. [names of women]
Jawara has a visitor. (repeated twice)
The visitor is called Moussa.
The Colonel is Moussa Traoré [president of Mali]. (repeated twice)

Example 2.5. Tamba Kandeh. "Jawara Aah Hebe Kodo." Main melodic cycle.

Jawara, I am your visitor.
Hello, black person.
Oh! A black visitor.
Jawara has a visitor. (repeated twice)
Jawara, I am your visitor.
Mariama, Teneng, Jabuyel. (repeated twice)

"Jawara Aah Hebe Kodo" consists of one main melody (cycle) that is re-peated throughout with variations. Based on a four-beat pattern, the underlying pulse is duple (see Example 2.5). The piece can be divided into three sections: opening (:34), middle (1:08), and closing (:39). The opening section consists of Kandeh performing the main melody on the fiddle in an improvisatory manner. The middle section includes call and response, with Kandeh's singing repre-senting the call and his fiddling the response (see Example 2.6A–D). Kandeh does not include any interludes in his performance. Like the opening, the clos-ing is improvisatory and composed of fiddling with no singing. In the closing, he varies the main melody by playing it an octave higher than he played during the middle section. Also, he includes many ornaments. Thus, if the song were longer, the part that now serves as the closing could easily be an interlude be-cause of its organization and performance style.

The call and response between the vocal leader and fiddle serve as the core of Kandeh's song. While the melody and rhythm for the vocal calls vary be-cause of the text (see measures 17, 23, 25, and 31 in Examples 2.6A–D), the fiddle response (or main melody) tends to be stable. Yet the nyanyeru melodies (those used for the call and the response, at least) are melodically similar. The only difference is that the fiddle response (without singing) is ornamented (see measures 18, 24, 26, and 32 in Examples 2.6A–D). The melody played on the fiddle to accompany the calls, however, has very few ornaments and is melodi-cally simpler than the response, probably because it is at this point that Kandeh sings and concentrates more on the text than his fiddling (see measures 17, 23, 25, and 31 in Examples 2.6A–D).

Just as pitches E and B are signifiers in Camara's performance (especially during interlude II), pitches G and A are important in Kandeh's piece. Not only can this be seen in the fiddle response of "Jawara" (when the ornaments are stripped away), it is apparent in the melody used for the texts (or vocal calls) and the music accompanying the texts in Examples 2.6A–D.

Examples 2.6A-D. Tamba Kandeh. "Jawara Aah Hebe Kodo." Call and response melodies.

When compared to Camara, Kandeh's performance is less innovative, possibly because his fiddling was not performed in context but rather as a test to determine how his music sounded on an audio tape. While some ornaments are included in the melodies, their use is straightforward, causing them to have less impact than those performed by Camara.

Samba Juma Bah (1950s–2000)

Samba Juma Bah was thirty-five years old when I interviewed him in 1990, and, in addition to playing the fiddle, he was a fire-eater. Bah's playing

Photo 2.3. Samba Juma Bah playing the *nyanyeru*. Photograph by Jacqueline Cogdell DjeDje. August 1990.

represents the fiddle tradition from Futa Jalon. Originally from Kindia, a city in southwest Guinea, Bah started fiddling when he was seven years old while tending cattle. He states that he learned from Maro Tembo, an "old man" who lived in Kindia. "I went to Maro Tembo for him to teach me because I see what Maro Tembo was playing in town and how he plays. So I liked it. So I tell Maro Tembo to make one fiddle for me. And Maro Tembo asked whether my father would make any problem or not. I said, 'No, there would be no problem.' So Maro Tembo made a fiddle for me and I started to train and learn how to fiddle" (Bah 1990). After two years of instruction, Bah began traveling to various cities in Guinea, including Labé, a town in Futa Jalon. Later he visited Bamako, Mali, and Senegal before settling in The Gambia in 1990. Bah says that during his travels Senegal was the only place, besides Guinea and The Gambia, that he saw the fiddle being played; the fiddlers he saw in Senegal were Fulbe. In Mali, he observed musicians performing only drums and the balafon (xylophone).

Although fiddling had been satisfying as a profession, Bah was reluctant to insist that his children become fiddlers. The explanation that he gives for not wanting his children to learn how to fiddle indicates how much he valued Western education: "I don't want them [my children] to be frivolous. I want them to go to school, for them to learn and get very good jobs. Fiddling is good but since I fiddle, I don't want all of them to be fiddlers. Some of them must get other technical training than fiddling. It was not the aim of my father for me to learn fiddling. My father did not want me to fiddle. So when I learned fiddling, I had to go away from him" (Bah 1990).

The performance on August 23, 1990, by the Fulani Musicians, the name of the group with which Bah performed, took place in the courtyard of Tamba Kandeh's compound. The ensemble included two melodic instruments—the tambing (flute) and the nyanyeru—and four percussion instruments: one djembe, one lala, and two hordes. Galleh Sanneh, the flute player, performed the lead melodic parts and was the primary improviser. Bah (the fiddler) and the four percussionists—Jansewo Jallow (horde and leader of the group), Ousman Barry (horde), Felli Jallow (djembe), and Ebrima Barry (lala and singer)—were accompanists; all performed ostinato patterns with some variations.[63] The group performed three songs: "Churoi Wuro" (11:50), a praise for cattle herders generally played at baptism ceremonies; "Nafa" (10:55), which means remembrance, thanksgiving, appreciation, or profit;[64] and "Wotare" (12:45), a praise of goodwill for the public (Barry 1990). Unlike the performances by Camara and Kandeh, the three songs were not played sequentially without a break. Rather, the performers stopped briefly at the end of each song to give the title and meaning. The first two songs included singing by the vocal leader. The last was entirely instrumental, for it was during this song that acrobatic movements by the performers took place.

In addition to myself, the audience of about thirty people consisted of Kandeh's family members and friends, as well as people in the neighborhood who heard the music and entered the courtyard to observe. The performance began around noon. Because the musicking was done on my behalf, I was the primary patron. Therefore, before playing, the musicians asked me for my name and the names of my close family members. Like Camara, they also changed their clothing. Their attire, which varied, was different from that of most people in the audience.[65]

During the performance, the six performers stood in the center of the courtyard next to each other in a straight line, while the audience formed a large semicircle in front of them. From the perspective of people in the audience, Bah (the fiddler) was located on the far left. To Bah's right was the flute player, followed by the two calabash players, the drummer, and the sistrum player.

When each person performed his special act, he moved in front of the others so he could be the center of attention for that moment. While in front, he improvised not only musically, but also through drama with various types of acrobatic movements.

Bah served in two roles during the performances. During the first two songs, he was an accompanying instrumentalist, playing the fiddle. During the third song ("Wotare"), his role expanded. After fiddling for about two minutes, he placed the instrument on the ground next to where he was standing. Then he went to the front of the group and began to eat fire and perform acrobatic movements for about five minutes.[66] When Bah completed his act, he returned to his place in the line, picked up the instrument, and started playing his fiddle ostinato pattern. Then another person stepped in front of the others and became the focus of attention.

The acrobatics varied, and each person did something special. When Galleh Sanneh (the flute player) stepped to the front, he continued playing his instrument as he performed all kind of movements: he fell to his knees on the ground, stood upside down with his head on the ground, bent backwards until his head touched the ground, and rolled over from side to side on the ground. When the calabash players were the center of attention, the instrument became an integral part of the performance. Not only did they spin the calabash on the tip of a finger, they threw it in the air so that it spun, raised one foot in the air while playing it, stood on top of the calabash (with the open side facing the ground) with one foot and turned around, stood on its rim (with the open side facing upward), turned somersaults, and placed their buttocks inside the calabash and walked around with it attached. In addition to the acrobatic movements, some musicians made grotesque facial expressions. Each time a performer made movements that were appealing, exciting, and interesting, people in the audience indicated their approval by making loud gasping sounds.

Music, dance, and drama are all important aspects of African performance. With the Fulani musicians, however, it was the drama that attracted the most attention. Since this is one of the few examples in this study where extensive emphasis is placed on spectacle, one might ask whether it affected the music and the song texts and whether it enhanced or overshadowed those aspects of the performance. These questions will be addressed below.

The song texts for "Nafa," which include praise and social commentary, touch on a number of topics (see Song Text 2.3). Not surprisingly, Ebrima Barry (the singer) makes references to short- and long-term patrons even though the latter are not present. He identifies those associated with The Gambia's modern government as well as individuals affiliated with traditional politics (measures 41, 56, and 57). Occasionally, he refers to people by their family connection ("Mariama is Binta's elder sister") or the town where they live ("Abdoulie [of] Satina"), as illustrated in measures 35 and 42. In some cases, he just shouts the name of the village or city to praise both the place and everyone who lives there (measure 63 and 64). In terms of gender, he mentions the names of both females (measures 58 and 60) and males (measures 41, 42, 53, 54, 56, and 57).

Not only does Barry refer to himself (as Segalareh, his stage name) in the lyrics (measure 45), he calls out the names of other performers in the ensemble (Felli Jallow in measure 43, Ousman Barry and Galleh Tambin in measure 44) as a way to encourage them in their playing. Even the persons who helped to make the performance possible are praised: Sabally, the person holding the microphone, is mentioned in measure 39, and Tamba Kandeh, the person who hosted the performance, is called out in measure 40.

Some songs by Fulbe musicians, even those performed at hotels, may allude to social themes. In this instance, Barry focuses on prosperity and wealth (a theme that is not only universal but of great importance to most people in The Gambia). Although Barry "cries for profit" (measure 26) or asks for things that will make life better, he also "thanks God" (measure 33) for what has been given. His comments about the world—"the world is a pitiful place" (measure 38), "let us take the world easy" (measure 50), "the world moves in steps" (measure 59)—not only indicate his concern for all humans, but that his message is intended for everyone (both locally and globally). Since some experiences in life are universal, he suggests maxims or precepts for living: "Let's struggle" (measure 37); "Let us take the world easy" (measure 50); "To be wealthy is good when we live, but it is no use to us when we die" (not shown); and "Let's be happy" (not shown). Unlike Camara, who alludes to his personal ambition to travel to the United States and Great Britain, Barry refers to traveling—"traveling is not bad" (measure 36) and "traveling is not bad for a traveler" (not shown)—in a much broader sense. Yet the mention of travel by both artists is significant because the Fulbe have historically been identified as migrants, having moved from the Senegal valley to the shores of Lake Chad over hundreds of years. In short, travel and movement are signifiers of Fulbe culture and identity. The fact that these themes are included in songs performed by modern-day musicians demonstrates the maintenance of tradition within contemporary culture.

Song Text 2.3. Fulani Musicians. "Nafa." Lamin, The Gambia. August 23, 1990.
TRANSLATED INTO ENGLISH BY MAMMA KANDEH (1990) AND SIDIA S. JATTA AND MATARR BALDEH (2003).

Measure Number	Song Text in English
25	Profit.
26	We are crying for profit.
27	[Unintelligible]
28	What are we crying for?
29	What are we crying for?
30	[Unintelligible]
33	Thanks be to God.

34	Gradual steps help.
35	Mariama is Binta's elder sister.
36	Traveling is not bad.
37	Let us struggle.
38	The world is a pitiful place [The world is sad].
39	Hello, Sabally [person holding microphone during the performance].
40	Thank you, [Tamba] Kandeh.
41	Buba Baldeh [name of a former member of parliament].
42	Abdoulie Satina [Satina is a name of a village].
43	Felli Jallow
44	Ousman Barry. Galleh Tambin
45	Segalareh. [Unintelligible]
46	[Unintelligible]
47	[Unintelligible]. What are we crying for?
48	How is the profit?
49	We are crying for profit.
50	Let us take the world easy, easy my friend.
51	It is not all seekers [strugglers] who succeed [It is not every future seeker who succeeds].
52	[Unintelligible]
53	Sulayman Sanseh [a wealthy man from Guinea living in Serrekunda].
54	Sulayman Sanseh
55	[Unintelligible]
56	Yankuba Bojang [son of the former ruler of the Western Division].
57	Hamadi Bojang [son of the former ruler of the Western Division].
58	Fatou Barry [name of a woman].
59	The world moves in steps [The world moves orderly].
60	Haja Lama Barry [name of a woman who went to Mecca on pilgrimage].
61	[Unintelligible]
62	[Unintelligible]
63	Serrekunda [one of the largest cities of The Gambia].
64	Serrekunda
65	Hello, boys.

Like "Jawara Aah Hebe Kodo" by Kandeh, "Nafa" is based on a single theme and organized into three sections: opening (:44), middle (10:08), and closing (:03). One main melody, consisting of eight beats and an underlying duple pulse, is used throughout (see Examples 2.7 and 2.8A–F). In several ways, however, the performance of "Nafa" is distinct from music played by Camara and Kandeh. Not only is the group of musicians larger, but the instrumentation is different. Instead of one melodic instrument being used, two are included, and they have different roles. Each of the four percussionists also has a distinct

Example 2.7. Samba Juma Bah. "Nafa." Main melody.

rhythmic pattern that is repeated and developed. Therefore, what results is a multilayered structure with collective improvisation. Although everyone freely changes and develops his part as the song evolves, each listens to the other so that no one overshadows or performs inappropriately. Not only do the accompanying instrumentalists help to establish the ostinato pattern, but the interplay of parts with different timbres at various pitch levels provides rhythmic interest and a foundation upon which the lead performer improvises.

The most prominent difference in "Nafa" is that the lead instrumentalist is Galleh Sanneh (the flute player) and not Samba Bah (the fiddler), an organizational structure characteristic of ensembles with members from Guinea (T. Kandeh 2003). In the opening, Sanneh demonstrates his virtuoso abilities on the flute by performing an unaccompanied solo for about forty seconds before introducing the main melody, an eight-beat melodic pattern based on a duple rhythm (see fiddle performance of main melody in Example 2.7).[67] After Sanneh plays the main melody once, other instrumentalists (fiddler and percussionists) enter.

Bah's role in the ensemble is similar to the percussionists'. As an accompanying musician, his fiddle performance is secondary to that of the flute player. Throughout the piece, he plays the main melody with some variations but without extensive improvisation. Tamba Kandeh joins the group as a second fiddler after three minutes into the performance, much as he did during songs played by Camara and other music played by the Fulani Musicians. Instead of playing the basic melody, however, Kandeh plays a drone by repeating the pitch C.[68]

The fact that the vocalist in "Nafa" is neither the fiddler nor the lead instrumentalist is another feature that makes this performance different from other Fulbe music examples analyzed in this study. In this case, Ebrima Barry performs the vocal part at the same time that he plays the lala; there is no vocal choral response or singing by other members of the ensemble. Because Barry shouts the text in a declamatory manner, his sound is more rhythmic than melodic, which complements the other layers of percussion heard in the piece.

When Sanneh (the flute player) improvises during the middle section, he develops the main melody (see Example 2.9) and does not introduce other themes. Also, when Sanneh and Bah play the main melody together, Sanneh

Examples 2.8A-F. Samba Juma Bah. "Nafa." Fiddle variations on main melody.

is the one who takes greater liberty in improvising (developing small motives or embellishing the main melody), while Bah only occasionally changes the melody (see beats 5–8 in Examples 2.8A–F for Bah's variations). Although some collective improvisation occurs, rarely do the two musicians perform extensive variations simultaneously. Rather, each person in turn takes the spotlight. Notice in Example 2.9 that Bah performs the main melody with no variation while Sanneh improvises extensively.[69]

Although the form of "Nafa" is similar to Kandeh's performance of "Jawara,"

Example 2.9. Fulani Musicians. "Nafa." Multipart structure.

the call and response is not as straightforward. One could argue that the call and response dialogue in "Nafa" takes place between the flute player and fiddler. But this interpretation does not hold up because not only do the two performers play continuously, they perform (or improvise) on the same melody throughout the piece. Rarely is there an instance in the performance when Sanneh stops performing to allow Bah (the fiddler) to play by himself.

I believe the dialogue in "Nafa" takes place between the flute player and fiddler who both perform the main melody (or call) and the vocalist who responds by shouting short phrases (e.g., names of patrons and members of the group, as well as maxims). If we divide the main theme of "Nafa" into two parts, part 1 would be the music played during beats 1–4 (the call), while part 2 is music played to beats 5–8 (the response). When this division is made, it is noteworthy that while the music to part 1 remains stable (see the first four beats of Examples 2.8A–F), the music in part 2 is varied. Even more importantly, part 2 is the section in which the vocalist performs his text. Similar to the music performed by Camara and Kandeh, the Fulani musicians employ signifiers to identify the song. Whereas other fiddlers used one or two pitches, a short melodic or rhythmic phrase, or a longer theme, the musicians in "Nafa" use the first four beats of the theme.

By examining fiddling by Bah, we discover not only another fiddle style but a different performance role for the fiddler in an ensemble. Although Bah is a professional known for both fire-eating and fiddling, he emphasized the former in his performance because this is his forté. Since fiddling is secondary in importance, he probably does not focus on this aspect of his professional life to the same degree as someone like Camara, which may account for Bah's competence on the instrument being limited. While Bah does well as an accompanying musician, whether he would be able to attract a large number of patrons if he focused only on the nyanyeru is uncertain.

3   Calling the Bori Spirits:
Hausa Fiddling in Nigeria

Some of them, their intention is to go where the *goge* is played.
They fail to return from where drums are played.
In the other world they will pay, for they will be uprooted.

—Shehu 'Uthman dan Fodio, ca. 1770s[1]

Fiddling in northern Nigeria is most often identified with the Hausa, despite the fact that outsiders introduced it to the Central Sudan. Unlike the one-stringed fiddle's roles among Senegambian Fulbe or the Dagbamba of Dagbon, the *goge*, or Hausa fiddle, does not symbolize ethnic identity nor does it represent high social status. The poem "Surely in Truth," quoted above and written by Shehu 'Uthman dan Fodio (1754–1817), a Fulbe scholar who led a jihad in Hausaland in the early nineteenth century, reveals the negative stance of Muslim leaders toward the goge during precolonial times. This, however, did not dislodge fiddling as a prominent musical tradition. While followers of Islam in Hausaland still consider fiddling to be profane, it is essential to the worship of those who practice Bori, a pre-Islamic African religion involving spirit possession. Fiddling is also popular among women and among individuals regarded by some Muslims as social outcasts (Danfulani 1999). A study of Hausa fiddling, therefore, not only demonstrates what happens to a tradition when it comes into conflict with those in authority, but also affirms the resilience of precolonial cultural practices in modern Hausa society. Moreover, although Hausa migration in the Sudan has not been as extensive as that of the Fulbe, Hausa speakers have had contacts with many West Africans. As a result, the Hausa have played a major role in the dispersion of the fiddle among people living in neighboring regions.

The Goge in Performance

Although the goge is performed in a number of contexts in Hausaland, one of the most common is the religious worship of Bori spirits (*iskoki*). Before the introduction of Islam between the eleventh and fifteenth centuries CE, the Bori religion was practiced under the direction of a differentiated priesthood. Islam, however, has been the official state religion since the reign of the Hausa king Muhammad Rumfa (ca. 1463–1499) and most urban Hausa now accept Islamic beliefs—yet some of them incorporate spirit possession in their religious practice (Besmer 1972/1973:1, 1974, 1983; Ingawa 1974), and Bori continues to be the dominant religion in rural areas of northern Nigeria.[2] During the 1960s and 1970s, fiddle music could also be heard in nightclubs in various cities in northern Nigeria.[3] I have had the opportunity to observe fiddling in both contexts, and although the two arenas might initially seem to be nearly diametrically opposed, a close examination of performances in each suggests some interesting connections.

In February of 1974 I attended the Argungu Annual Fishing and Cultural Festival in northern Nigeria. This festival originated to commemorate the first friendly visit of a reigning Sultan of Sokoto—the religious leader of all Muslims in northern Nigeria—to Argungu in 1934. The sultan's visit served as a gesture of unity between the rival political states of Sokoto and Argungu, and its annual celebration attracted fishermen from the two locales, as well as neighboring areas. The Argungu festival initially resembled precolonial festivities marking the ending of the harvest and the beginning of the fishing season, but by 1974 it had become a national cultural event and tourist attraction organized by Nigeria's Commission for Information, Cultural and Social Development.[4] People from throughout Nigeria and beyond traveled to Argungu not only to enjoy the friendly atmosphere, entertainment, and competition at the tourist resort but also to meet and interact with men and women from other African countries ("Argungu" 1974). Unlike religious and cultural festivals that I had observed in northern Ghana—where most of those in attendance were local residents of towns and villages—the Argungu festival was nearly pan-African in its scope and importance in Nigeria.

The festival of 1974 generated special enthusiasm because Nigerian government officials saw it as a prelude to the Second World Black and African Festival of Arts and Culture, scheduled to take place in the Nigerian capital of Lagos from November to December 1975. In addition to music performances by groups from Argungu, other parts of Nigeria, and neighboring Niger, a national motor rally was added to the festivities, with drivers starting in Ibadan in southwest Nigeria and traveling through many of the country's twelve states.

I learned about the Argungu festival from my Ghanaian friend Patsy Dowuna-Hammond who was head mistress of Mensah Sarbah Hall where I was living at the University of Ghana. Aware of my interest in fiddling and my desire to document the role of the goge in Hausa culture, she urged me to attend and arranged contacts for me with Benji Ishaku, a Hausa who taught in the department of electrical engineering at Ahmadu Bello University in Zaria, and Shehu U. Aliyu, the personal assistant to the minister of information in Nigeria's Northwestern State where Argungu is located. In addition, I established contacts with officials at the Center for Nigerian and Cultural Studies (CNCS) in Kano City, who agreed to assist me with my research. Traveling part of the way with friends who were destined for Zaria, I departed Legon-Accra, Ghana, in a private car on January 30, 1974.

We traveled the southern route along the Gulf of Guinea and, after crossing the Dahomey-Nigeria, border, headed straight for Ibadan. After a two-night stay there, we continued our approximately five-hundred-mile journey to Zaria.

When we stopped in Bida (halfway between Ibadan and Zaria), we became aware that the cultural patterns and behavior of individuals had begun to differ slightly from those of the south. Many of the men on the streets in the south wore Western-style cotton slacks and shirts without any head covering. Not only did most males in Bida wear a Muslim-style cap, many wore long-sleeved gowns that reached their knees or ankles and covered matching pants and shirts. Women's clothing, however, did not seem to depart significantly from that worn in southern Nigeria. Many of the women wore scarves on their heads and multicolor wraparound skirts with matching blouses. Unlike southern Nigerian women, however, they decorated their cheeks and foreheads with small geometrical designs and lined their eyes and eyebrows in black, a type of facial decoration unique to the north. They also colored their fingernails and palms orange with henna.

On February 1, I reached the home of my initial contact, Benji Ishaku, who had studied for eleven years in the United States. I spent a night at his house in Zaria, after which his driver took me to Kano, 111 miles to the north. When we left Zaria, it grew cold, windy, and dusty, probably due to the harmattan, the wind that often arrives during this time of the year in Sudanic Africa. The physical landscape also became noticeably different. It was not uncommon to see Fulani herdsmen walking on foot and driving goats and cows along the edge of the highway. Men, women, and children worked on large farms that seemed to extend miles from the main road. The music on the car radio was also unlike anything I had heard since arriving in West Africa. In Ghana and southern Nigeria, the airwaves were dominated by indigenous and sometimes popular African music, or by soul and rock from the United States and Europe. In northern Nigeria, however, where Islam was widespread, Arab and Indian instrumental and vocal music prevailed. In addition to groups that included string and wind instruments performing highly ornamented, intricate melodies with little percussion, men and women sang melismatic melodies using a high-pitched, tense vocal quality.

On arriving in Kano, I was amazed to see remarkable centuries-old buildings still in use. Populated primarily by Hausa, Fulani, and other northern Nigerians, the old city was enclosed by walls fifty miles long and fifteen feet high that had been built between the eleventh and fifteenth centuries. Inside these walls were the emir's palace, the Kano Museum, old markets, the CNCS, and other buildings and homes with adjoining small gardens. Outside the walls was the area known as the Sabon Gari, or new city, where newcomers to Hausaland (southern Nigerians, Asians, Europeans, and North Americans) and some northern Nigerians lived and built their homes and businesses. In general, the architecture outside the city walls was Western, and many buildings were multistory. There was enormous activity throughout all areas of Kano City, which served as the commercial capital and transportation hub not only for the state of Kano and northern Nigeria, but also for the neighboring countries of Niger, Chad, and Cameroon.

Officials and staff members at CNCS in Kano City assisted me in identifying local fiddlers and arranged for a student at Abdullahi Bayero College (ABC), Salihu (Danjume) Y. Ingawa, to assist me in transcribing, translating, and interpreting the texts of fiddle songs. I was therefore able to quickly locate, interview, and record several fiddlers: Ibrahim Mohammadan on February 5, Momman Nabarau on February 7, and Haruna Bande on February 10. Mohammadan and Bande specialized in playing Bori music. Unfortunately, at this early stage òf my research, I was unaware of the significance of Bori as the indigenous, pre-Islamic religion of the Hausa. In retrospect, I wish I had been able to ask these musicians a number of questions in preparation for my trip to Argungu.

As a Hausa-Fulani and Muslim born and raised in Kano City, Danjume provided me with much knowledge about Hausa culture and music. Even though, like the Muslim authorities in Kano City, he considered fiddle music profane because it departed from the teachings of the Prophet Muhammad, he shared with me whatever he knew about fiddling. He respected my research and desire to learn about Hausa culture because he placed a high value on education regardless of the subject matter. When I told him of my plans to attend the Argungu festival, he encouraged me to go.

The scenery to be observed from the bus that took me from Kano City to Sokoto consisted of mountains of rock and vast expanses of sand as we approached the Sahara. Except for the occasional baobab tree, I saw little greenery or vegetation. When we arrived in Sokoto, however, a festive atmosphere was immediately noticeable. Sokoto was not only the capital city of the Northwestern State, it was also the gateway to Argungu. Government officials appeared to have taken extra pains to spruce up the city for the many festival attendees who would travel through. Banners and flags in Nigeria's colors of green and white festooned poles lining both sides of the street leading to the governor's house.

Finding a taxi to Aliyu's house was easy. Upon arriving, however, I learned that he had already gone to Argungu. His wife, children, and other family members welcomed me to their modern Western-style stucco home, and I spent the evening speaking with Sulemana, Aliyu's nephew, before going to bed. On the next morning, February 14, I was able to get a lift to Argungu with friends of the Aliyu family. There I discovered that the festival was divided into several parts: the fishing village located near the river; the village where the agricultural fair took place; the festival village arena where music performances were held; an area for the chalets, or guest rooms; and a large tent for eating food and drinking beverages. Other tents dotted the grounds and were used for visitors to relax in or to peruse items on exhibit. This was clearly an event for tourists who had money to pay for facilities, services, and amenities. Although many of the activities required no admission fee, the fact that several did probably discouraged many local people from attending. VIPs from the federal and state governments were well represented, and later in the day, I saw a few staff members from CNCS. Because the grounds were so spread out, it was difficult to determine the number of people in attendance, but I would guess that there were several thousand.

At about 10 AM, I finally met Aliyu. Like other dignitaries attending the festival and many men in northern Nigeria, he was attired in a light-colored, long-sleeved flowing gown that reached his ankles and was worn over matching pants and a shirt. He also wore the ubiquitous muslim-style cap. When I gave him the letter from my friend Patsy, he welcomed me. In some small measure, my presence indicated that Nigerian government officials had been successful in promoting the festival as a major tourist attraction. At breakfast, he introduced me to some of his Nigerian friends who had lived in the Los Angeles area.

After unpacking my bags, I was able to purchase a festival program, a sign of just how international the event had become. Little information about the names of groups or type of music was given, but the times for different performances were listed. Familiar as I was with some aspects of music in Nigeria from the courses in African music that I had taken at UCLA in the early 1970s, the festival proved an eye-opener and a wonderful opportunity to learn about the enormous diversity of musical traditions in this region of West Africa. The approximately ten different groups that performed were from various parts of the Northwestern State (e.g., Gusau, Argungu, Bida, Minna, Kontagora), other Nigerian states (the Rivers, the Northeastern, Kano, and Benue-Plateau), and Niger. A variety of instruments and dance and music traditions were represented: drumming with stilt-dancing from Niger; Igbo children from the Rivers State singing and dancing to slit-drumming; Fulani women from the Northeastern State singing to drum accompaniment; dancing by masqueraders from Abuja in Plateau-Benue State; Kambari music and dancing from Kontagora (the Northwestern State); praise singing by young girls; praise singing to royalty with drum accompaniment; and flute and drum music from Bida. The high performance quality of all the groups was impressive. I was told by one of Aliyu's assistants that most, if not all, of the troupes had been organized and supported by cultural arts commissions in their states and local communities.

Of special interest to me, of course, were groups that included the one-stringed fiddle and, surprisingly, there were several. On Thursday afternoon, two groups used the fiddle: a Fulani group from Argungu that played farming music and included goge, *sarewa* (flute), *ganga* (double membrane cylindrical snared drum), and *kalangu* (double-membrane hourglass pressure drum) and a Zabermawa group from Niger that played war music using goge, several transverse flutes, a plucked lute, a large calabash drum, and an hourglass pressure drum. On Thursday evening, two other groups included goge in their ensembles: a Bori group from Argungu (see below) and some Kaburu dancers from Minna. Champions of a cultural arts festival that took place in Algiers in 1969, the Minna group included one horn, four flutes, one drum, four musical bows, four goge, and three rattles. On Friday afternoon, there were two performances using the fiddle. The ensemble from Niger included one goge, one flute, three hourglass pressure drums (three sizes), and two cylindrical shaped drums (one small and one large). Another group from Minna used one plucked lute with the goge. On Friday evening, the group from Niger included two fiddles (one goge and one kukuma), one circular frame drum, one cylindrical drum, and one hourglass pressure drum. Because a number of groups would perform during the two-hour performance period, each performance was limited to about five to ten minutes. Professional ensembles that had previously played at festival events, most kept to their time limit.

Of all the groups that included the fiddle, the one that most fascinated me was the Argungu ensemble that performed Bori music. This was the first time I had observed fiddle music used in the context of a spirit possession performance. Among the Dagbamba in northern Ghana, fiddling was often used for entertainment at events celebrating the life cycle and other public gatherings, but never in relationship to spirit possession. I would learn later from my conversations with Danjume and from reading about Bori that possession performances used for entertainment included some of the same elements used in Bori religious ceremonies.

The Bori performance was the first item on the program that evening and the longest; the music and dancing began around nine o'clock and continued for about thirty minutes. For this performance, as for performances by other groups at the festival, the two to three hundred people in attendance were seated in an open-air theater with ascending rows of chairs arranged around a circular ground-level performance area (see Figure 3.1). The ensemble included two goge, two k'warya (calabash beaters), one kalangu, and six female dancers. The male instrumentalists wore Muslim-style caps and were dressed in bluish-green long gowns with matching pants and shirts. The women dancers wore clothing typical of the region with the exception that their skirts, head coverings, and the loose-fitting tops (or *boubous*) that extended to their ankles were all navy blue. The cloth normally wrapped around the waist over the skirts and top was used differently in this performance context. As the women danced, they extended their hands out from their bodies with the cloth draped over their arms in a wing-like fashion. Indeed, their arm gestures recalled the movement of a bird's wings.

The performance started with the women dancing while the men played an instrumental prelude. The dancers performed simple foot and arm movements as they moved all over the dance area. Later, when the tempo increased and the music became more intense, the dancers began to scream. Instead of the small, repetitive dance patterns they had used earlier, their movements became more acrobatic as they seemed to go into trance. Toward the climax of the performance, some dancers fell to the ground, and other women dancers helped them get up. The music ended when the dancers appeared to have reached the height of their ecstatic spiritual state (DjeDje 1978b:259–261; Rhodes 1983:ix). The audience—which consisted of primarily Westerners and Africans from different parts of the country—sat quietly throughout but applauded enthusiastically when the music and dance ended.

After the Bori performance, I began thinking more about my discussions and interactions with Mohammadan and Bande, the fiddlers—both specialists in Bori—I had interviewed in Kano City. More than ever I was anxious to learn about Bori and its meaning for the Hausa. I wished I had been able to iden-

Figure 3.1. Bori performance at the Argungu Festival Village, February 1974. Sketch by Karin Patterson. Used by permission. Based on information in Jacqueline Cogdell DjeDje (1978b:260).

tify the spirit for whom the music and dance was being performed. The fact that Hausa fiddlers were expected to master Bori music before being considered professionals indicates that the religion continued to be central among some groups in Hausaland in the 1970s.

As noted above, fiddling was commonly performed in night spots in Hausaland. In 1974 there was an active nightclub scene outside the walls of Kano City. Clubs were open throughout the week and attracted all types of people. I had the opportunity to attend a goge performance at the Railway Nite Club in the Nassarawa area of Kano City on February 19, 1974, and another at the King's Garden Club in Brigade on February 25. The audiences at both clubs appeared to be middle class. Upper-class Kano Hausa residents preferred listening to music on recordings in the privacy of their homes because nightclubs were off limits to followers of Islam.[5]

The guest artist at both nightclubs I visited was Garba Liyo (also spelled

Figure 3.2. Performance of *goge* music in a nightclub in Kano City, February 1974. Sketch by Karin Patterson. Used by permission. Based on information in Jacqueline Cogdell DjeDje (1978b:274).

Leo), a goge musician (from Funtua, a town located southwest of Kano City) who invited me and Duro Oni to his performance. Liyo was well known in many parts of Nigeria and West Africa and had become prosperous from performing goge. Like most nightclubs in Kano City, all activity took place in the open air. The elevated stage used by musicians was approximately two feet high, circular, and located in the center of the nightclub (see Figure 3.2). When we entered, we saw two people on stage: one was performing a goge that was connected to an electric amplifier and another playing a k'warya. Approximately forty-five people were seated in chairs at tables that had been placed around the stage; most were not listening to the music but engaged in conversation.[6] We learned later that the goge player was 'Dan Sokoto, Liyo's apprentice. Until Liyo arrived, 'Dan Sokoto and the k'warya player were responsible for providing the entertainment.

Around nine thirty, Liyo showed up at the club dressed in a navy blue Western pants suit. An entourage of musicians and followers accompanied him. After sitting and talking with Oni and me for perhaps five minutes, he left our table to converse with others. Over the next half hour, approximately one hundred more people entered the club. Oni stated that they were from all walks of life with different occupations (see Table 3.1). Hausa Muslims would have referred to some as dignitaries who had a middle-class social status (e.g., civil servants, businessmen, and traders), and others would have been regarded as social deviants (e.g., pimps, smugglers, and prostitutes).

'Dan Sokoto continued to play for another forty-five minutes before someone placed another amplifier on stage for Liyo. When Liyo came on, he was accompanied by 'Dan Sokoto playing goge; two drummers (each had two hourglass pressure drums—one 'dan kar'bi and one kalangu); two k'warya (calabash) players; one kuntuku player; five *masu amshi* (or '*yan amshi*); and six marok'a.[7] Except for the marok'a, all performers were seated in chairs placed on stage. As Liyo led the songs on the goge, the masu amshi responded by singing what he played. His playing was very melismatic, intricate, and improvisatory with passing tones and trills. Sometimes he sang the lead part. The rhythm seemed to be in four and was played by the calabash players. The marok'a walked all over the stage platform, shouting praises for the distinguished persons in the club (Cogdell 1974a). People in the audience did not overtly respond to Liyo's music by singing, handclapping, dancing, or going on stage to indicate their approval. Rather, most sat in chairs at their tables, talking with the other guests and paying little attention to the performance. Only when one of the marok'a interrupted the music to announce a gift of money did people listen attentively.

When Randall Grass visited Kano City during the seventies, he also attended a nightclub performance by Garba Liyo. Because aspects of Grass's experience differ from mine, the full description of his nightclub visit is worth including here:

On the night of the performance by Garba Leo in Kano you will likely find Alh. [Alhaji] Leo seated on a mat outside the Niger Club. He will sit conversing with friends and well-wishers, take some food, and sometimes drink *magani* (local "medicine" for strength).

Around ten o'clock, he will enter the club and have some drinks at a table. Some of his drummers and a student of goge will be playing in a tentative way, as if flexing musical muscles. People in the club will be sitting and drinking, greeting friends and sometimes doing little spontaneous jig-like dance steps in the large open space of the open-air club. The shrill sound of the amplified goge is like a call to the faithful as the initiatory tunes are played. By ten-thirty, Alh. Leo himself will begin to play with all his musicians, the drummers, calabash players, singers clustered around him, his student at his immediate left with his own instrument. The music has little momentum as yet—he will stop in the middle of songs to smoke, drink or be greeted (people will bow before him according to their status in Hausa society). He begins to improvise praise songs as the singers praise people in the audience.

Table 3.1. Categories and Characteristics of Nightclubs in Kano City, February 1974

Basis for Categories	Category A	Category B	Category C
Number of Fights and Disagreements between Guests	High	Low	None
Closing Hour	2:00 to 3:00 AM or later	2:00 to 3:00 AM or later	12:00 to 1:00 AM or later on weekends
Socioeconomic Status of Guests	Lower	Upper-Lower and Middle	Middle and Upper
Ethnicity in Attendance	Northerners	Northerners and Southerners	Foreigners (Expatriates or Westerners), Southerners, and a few Northerners
Occupation of Guests	Manual laborers and other traditional occupations	Clerks, civil servants, teachers, chauffeurs, etc.	Well-established businessmen, politicians, civil servants, teachers, and clerks
Type of Music Used for Entertainment: Northern Nigerian (Hausa *kalangu* and *goge* music); Southern Nigerian (highlife, Yoruba *juju*, Igbo music, etc.); African-American popular music; Other (music from other African countries)	Northern Nigerian music is most popular; local performers are usually the guest artists	Mixture of Northern Nigerian, Southern Nigerian, and African-American music; performers are well-known musicians from various parts of Nigeria and neighboring countries	Western or African-American music dominates; some Southern Nigerian music; no Northern Nigerian music; few live performances; most music is played from discs
Dancing by Guests	Rarely done	Occasionally done on Southern Nigerian and African-American music	Club divided into two sections: one for listening and another for dancing

Some of his supporters will dance in the middle of the open area and then rush over to sing in front of the person being praised. This person is expected to contribute money to keep the music going. Anyone who contributes money will have music played for him—whether the contribution is 20 kobo (30 cents) or ten naira ($15). As soon as money is contributed the supporter will rush in mock haste to the musicians—waving the money high in the air—seize the microphone from the singers and stop the music. He will shout into the microphone, telling Alh. Leo who has contributed, how much, and why. Then the musicians explode into action after a short invocatory phrase from Garba Leo.

As the contributions become more frequent, the music becomes more intense. By 2:00 AM, the contributions are dwindling. There is a short break and then the six dancers appear, sometimes in stage uniforms, sometimes in ordinary clothing, with bright cloths, head ties, and waist sashes on the women. The music begins in a medium tempo and the dancers (men and women in separate groups) begin to walk rhythmically in a big circle. Little-by-little, the dancers begin adding movements—turns, twists, undulations—which increase as the music develops. After some time, the male dancers begin leaping high into the air and making fast turns while the women begin to vibrate their bodies and shake their hips as they skip around the circle. By now the musicians are playing hard, the drummers' eyes wide with excitement, and Garba Leo lost in a kind of dreamy trance, rocking back and forth in his chair, trading progressively faster, higher, more complex licks with his student. The rhythm becomes climatic and some of the dancers are literally rolling on the ground, shaking, with the musicians sweating and playing hard and fast. Then suddenly it's over as the music stops and the spell is broken. (Grass 1976)

Although many of the activities Grass observed took place when I attended Liyo's nightclub performances, there were noticeable distinctions. During my visits, Liyo did not sit outside the club before the performance, nor was there any dancing on the part of the performers or guests. Furthermore, the comparison of the music and behavior of goge performers at Bori and at nightclub performances is instructive. While nightclub musicians are able to perform songs freely for patrons and guests in whatever order they choose, Bori entails a ritual structure to facilitate the entrance of the spirits. Despite this, there are some striking similarities between the behavior of musicians at the Bori ceremony performance in Argungu and the nightclub performances in Kano. At both, the goge player served as the event's leader and conductor. On occasion, Liyo sang a small portion of a song, but only when chorus members made mistakes or did not understand the fiddle melody. Otherwise, he did not speak or sing but controlled the group by playing the fiddle while the other musicians responded accordingly. Since Liyo's marok'i indicated that the group did not perform with Bori initiates, it is of note that Grass describes male and female dancers falling to the floor and behaving in a trance-like state, as performers would do at Bori ceremonies. The suggestion seems to be that the features distinguishing one performance tradition from another in Hausa culture are blurred, and if this is the case, it reveals the maintenance of traditional practices in a modern setting.

History

The Hausa

The history of the Hausa people is commingled with the oral traditions of other Africans, but several historical accounts exist. One of the most well-known narratives suggests that the ancestors of the Hausa were Arabs from Baghdad who arrived around 900 CE and introduced the horse into Hausaland. When Bayajida or Bayazid, the legendary figure from Baghdad, received an "ambiguous" reception from the Mai (king) of Kanem-Borno, he fled westward where he came to Daura, a town ruled by a queen and terrorized by a snake. After killing the snake, Bayajida "married the queen who gave him a son, Bawogari, while a concubine gave him another son, Karbogari. Bawogari had six sons who became the kings of Kano, Daura, Gobir, Zazzau (Zaria), Katsina, and Rano. Together with Biram [also spelled Berom, Birom, or Burum], which was ruled by the son of a Borno princess, these seven states were called the *hausa bakwai*. The sons of Karbogari founded another seven states: Kebbi, Zamfara, Gwari, Jukun (Kwararafa), Yoruba, Nupe and Yawuri, the so-called *banza bakwai* (the 'seven bastards')" (Ki-Zerbo and Niane 1997:106).[8]

Although most versions of the history focus on the foreigner, Bayajida, historian Mahdi Adamu prefers to highlight the indigenous aspects of the tradition, which indicate that "the ancestors came out of holes in the ground" but benefited greatly from the immigration of the Wangara and Dyula (Mande Muslim merchants and missionaries) and Fulbe. This interpretation emphasizes that the original home of Hausa speakers included parts of the Sahara, particularly Aïr (Azbin), and it was not until the Tuareg (Berbers) conquered them in the fourteenth and fifteenth centuries that they were pushed south toward Gobir (Adamu 1986). In fact, "Hausa," which does not appear until the sixteenth century (Ki-Zerbo and Niane 1997:105–106), was at first primarily a linguistic—rather than religious or cultural—category (Meek 1921:27). As noted previously, Hausa belongs to the Chad subfamily of Afroasiatic languages (Smith 1965:122–123).[9] Just as there are several oral accounts documenting the origin of the Hausa, there are several for the history of the area now known as Kano, the setting for my research on goge traditions.[10]

Although oral tradition suggests that the Wangara introduced Islam into Hausaland from Mali in the fourteenth century during the reign of Yaji dan Tsamiya (1349–1385), scholars believe Islam appeared earlier because it already existed in Kanem-Borno in the eleventh century (Ki-Zerbo and Niane 1997: 114). In its earliest beginnings, privileged urban minorities (traders, jurists, and aristocrats) were the primary practitioners, as in other parts of West Africa, while Hausa of lower status continued their indigenous religious practices. After the Wangara, Fulbe, and Berbers entered the region during the fourteenth and fifteenth centuries, Islam took firmer root with the introduction of its ritual, theology, and law. More Arabic loanwords were adopted and given Hausa forms (a fourth of Hausa vocabulary is of Arabic derivation), adding to the

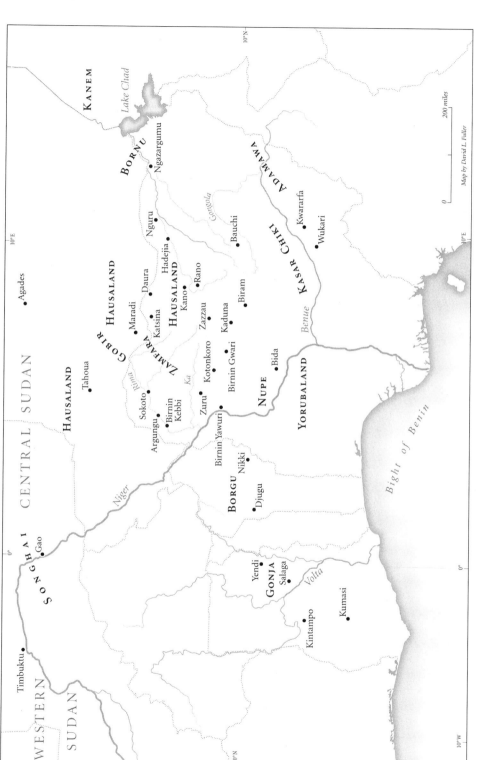

Map 3.1. The Hausa and neighboring peoples. Map by David L. Fuller. Used by permission.

layer already acquired through contact with Borno. Newly converted Hausa also adopted Muslim names (Hiskett 1984:73; Smith 1965:122–123).[11]

Because of its location politically and commercially, Kano was one of the most powerful states in the Central Sudan during the precolonial period. From the fourteenth to the eighteenth century, it warred with neighboring states (e.g., Kwararafa [or Jukun], Zaria [Zazzau], Borno, Songhai, Katsina, Zamfara, and Gobir), which helped to expand its power (see Map 3.1 for locations). Economically, the region had considerable resources. Deposits of iron ore were to be found near wooded areas, providing necessary firewood, and the rich soil made agriculture one of the most important activities in the state. The geographical position was also excellent for international and regional trade, causing a considerable volume of merchandise to be circulated. Although several groups (Arabs, Kanuri, and Wangara) were involved in commerce, foreign trade from the sixteenth to the eighteenth centuries remained primarily in the hands of the Hausa with Kano playing a central role (Ki-Zerbo and Niane 1997:107–108, 116; Ogot 1999:232–237, 243).[12]

Not only did the economic prosperity attract religious figures, the end of the fifteenth century witnessed several innovations. Under Muhammadu Rumfa (1463–1499), the city walls were extended, eunuchs were appointed to political offices, the great market was founded, and a council of nine leading state officers was established. Some innovations—the construction of a new palace, the use of long trumpets and ostrich-feather fans, and marking the end of the Ramadan ('Id al-fitr) with major festivities—suggest copying of Borno's practices (Ki-Zerbo and Niane 1997:107–108).

As noted in foregoing chapters, the spread of Islam in West Africa took a militant turn in the nineteenth century. Under the leadership of 'Uthman dan Fodio as Sarkin Musulmi (chief of Muslims), the Fulbe in Hausaland launched a jihad between 1804 and 1810 that was successful partly because of the assistance from Hausa and Fulbe Muslims already settled in the region. 'Uthman dan Fodio's successors, as sultans of Sokoto, maintained the empire until the British under Lord Frederick Lugard established the Protectorate of Northern Nigerian between 1900 and 1903. Throughout the nineteenth and twentieth centuries, the ruling Fulbe justified their dominion over the Hausa by maintaining, extending, and strengthening Islam, the same motives that had underlain the jihad (Smith 1965:151; Johnston 1967).

Like other jihadists, 'Uthman dan Fodio saw the jihad not only as an opportunity to reform Islam as it was then practiced, but as a way to redress political and social abuses and alleviate the economic burdens of society. The goal was to create theocracies, kingdoms administered according to Islamic law and injunctions. In the end, the jihad brought changes in political, social, and religious practices. Politically, it led to the creation of large empires like the Sokoto Caliphate and to major shifts in political authority. Not only were the old Hausa kings replaced by new Fulbe emirs, but the old rulers of Borno, the Sefuwa, were replaced by a new and reforming dynasty that revised the fortunes of the empire. Socially and religiously, the jihad led to a better knowledge of the Qur'an and the works of leading Islamic jurists and discouraged traditional religious practices that continued to be mixed with Islam. Most importantly, it transformed Islam from a religion of the court and rulers into that of the whole community, resulting in improved Islamic scholarship and mass literacy in the nineteenth century. In some cases, compromises were made. Because many people refused to abandon former practices completely, reformists allowed some of the existing sociopolitical institutions to continue functioning, which brought about the amalgamation of Hausa and Fulbe cultures (Ajayi 1998:15–16; Lewis 1980:228).

The history of language use in the region provides but one example of compromise. Because Hausa identity was based primarily on language (and religion), it was not difficult for Hausa-speaking persons of Fulbe origin in Kano to accept Hausa identity (Paden 1973:355). While rural Fulbe continued to use Fulfulde, urban Fulbe in Kano "substituted Arabic for Fulfulde as a religious language and Hausa for Fulfulde as a language of daily discourse" (Paden 1973:50). After the Nigerian civil war in the mid-1960s, one could speak of a Hausa-Fulbe identity representing the fusion of Hausa and Fulbe peoples in Nigeria. Yet some Fulbe continue to regard themselves solely as Fulbe; these include (1) those from Adamawa, Cameroon, who migrated and settled in Kano City, (2) rural Fulbe who are culturally and linguistically distinct from the Hausa, and (3) some high-status Fulbe families (Paden 1973:22–23, 355).

When Nigeria returned to civilian rule in 1999, Islamic law became a political issue in the country's northern states.[13] Many Muslims in Hausaland supported Shari'a because they saw it as a return to the laws introduced by 'Uthman dan Fodio and a way "to prod Nigeria's Muslims to return to clean living in a decadent society" (Maier 2000:176); many also thought Shari'a would bring peace to Kano and force corrupt politicians to reform their ways ("Nigeria's Kano State" 2000). The degree to which Kano Muslims support Shari'a can be seen in the results of the 2003 election for governor in Kano State. Some Kano City Hausa residents believe the reason that Rabiu Musa Kwankwaso (the governor of Kano State from 1999–2003 who was responsible for the revival of Shari'a) lost his bid for re-election to Ibrahim Shakarau is that he did not fully implement Shari'a in the state (Hassan 2003; Zubairu 2003).

In traditional culture, many Hausa see their society as an association of rulers and ruled, nobles and commoners, or in ethnic terms, Fulani and Hausa. Before the 1960s, there existed a social stratification based on occupational specialization within these dichotomies. *Sarautu* (ruling) was an occupation that outranked all others. *Mallanci* (Qur'anic learning) and *kasuwanci* (successful trading), which had universalistic emphases, ranked next. Below these came the majority of traditional Hausa occupations; ranking lowest of all were butchers, praise singers, drummers, blacksmiths, house servants, and hunters (Smith 1965:139). Although few Hausa have followed in the profession of their families since the 1960s, the social order of the society still correlates with Hausa distinctions between the rich and powerful (those who are economically independent and observe Islam) and the economically unstable (the poor, powerless, nominal Muslims). Dandatti Abdulkadir's comments about the status of the oral singer in Hausa society are insightful because they explain how stratification affects musicians, including fiddlers, who are among the powerless:

> Most of the musicians, however, are clearly near the bottom of the social pyramid. It is interesting to note that the singers are still subjected to certain kinds of restrictions that the society does not impose on the upper class. For example, a singer is not allowed to marry into a royal or learned family. He has to marry within his own group. . . .
>
> The singers' social rank is highly visible. . . . Even at naming and wedding ceremonies, we find that singers and other musicians are segregated. While the rest of the people sit inside the entrance hall where the ceremony is performed, singers sit outside the entrance and do not enter unless called or invited. When they visit their patrons they do not sit in the same room with them; rather they will sit outside the room or in the *soro* (entrance porch). Furthermore, people who are not singers will never agree to share the same dish with a singer. Economically, singers depend largely on their profession or *sana'a* (craft) as they call it. (1975:52–53)

As in earlier times, the Hausa continue to subsist by agriculture, animal husbandry, some hunting and fishing, occupational crafts, and trade. Those living in cities may also work as civil servants, office workers, teachers, businessmen, and in other professions. Apart from a few cattle employed in farming, livestock raised by Hausa consists of horses, donkeys, goats, sheep, turkeys, and other poultry. For meat, milk, and butter, the Hausa depend on the Fulbe who graze their herds near village markets. Hausa women process foods for local sale; weave and sew local products; raise some livestock; trade in small commodities of medicines, vegetable oils, and cigarettes; and maintain Bori by serving as the main devotees and exponents. A *karuwa* (any woman of childbearing age who is not married) may become a praise singer, female messenger, or prostitute, in which case she either enters the local guild or works independently (Smith 1965:124–125; Ajayi 1987:419–420).[14]

The number of villages and towns in Hausaland during the precolonial era suggests that most states were densely populated and the population was evenly distributed. With little change in modern times, the Hausa classify their settlements as cities, towns, or hamlets. Residence in cities carries the most prestige, in hamlets the least. Each state has one pre-eminent city, the *birni* (capital) where the ruler (Sarki or emir) and senior officials live, the main administrative and economic institutions of the state are located, and learning, crafts, and communications are most advanced. The Hausa living pattern is based on the extended family structure where two or more men and their wives and families live in the same compound and work a common farm. The patrilineal system of kinship is used for inheritance and other titles (Smith 1965:129).

Many of the basic principles of Hausa government established during the sixteenth century continue to exist. Traditional as well as modern governments proceed through a system of titled offices (plural, *sarautu;* singular, *sarauta*), each having definite rights, powers and duties, special relations to the throne and to certain other offices, special lands, farms, compounds, horses, praise songs, clients, and, formerly, slaves. Before the British occupation of 1900–1903, the principal offices of any Hausa state were distributed among the dynasty, noble lineages (most of which were Fulani), certain clerical groups, the ruler's clients, eunuchs, and throne slaves. An order of occupational officials, mainly reserved for commoners, had little direct political importance, though they were of value administratively (Smith 1965:132–133).

At an early age, Hausa children attend Qur'anic school.[15] During the precolonial and colonial period, children in northern Nigeria were often trained as apprentices to work in family occupational crafts (Oppong 1966a:19). However, since independence, not only have a number of Western primary and secondary schools been made available in the north, but several colleges and universities have been constructed. More northern Nigerians receiving Western education, "has meant that alongside the more traditional patterns of status and rank there are now complex sets of interlocking criteria by which sometimes conflicting statuses can be ascribed and utilised; money, military rank, bureaucratic position, religious affiliation and status, educational attainment and 'classmate' status, all overlap with social class or genealogy. Twentieth-century northern Nigeria is now a society in which old social distinctions are overlaid with new social formations" (Furniss 1996:5).

Kano State and Kano City

Located in the Northern High Plains region, Kano was one of the largest states in northern Nigeria in 1968. It covered an area of approximately 16,630 square miles. The population during the late 1960s was approximately 5,774,842, and the number of persons per square mile was 347. By 1972, the state's population had increased to 7.4 million. During the 1970s, Kano State was divided into four emirates (Gumel, Hadejia, Kano, and Kazaure), and each emirate had its own capital. After the country was reconfigured and divided into thirty states in 1991, Kano became the second largest state in Nigeria with a population of approximately 5,632,040 (Smith 1994:660). In 1996, the country was reorganized again, this time into thirty-six states. With an estimated population of 8,077,751 in 2005, Kano State continues to be the second most populous state in the country ("List of Nigerian States" 2006).

Kano City, the *birni* of Kano State, is one of the oldest surviving cities in the Sudan. As noted above, it is a large, complex, and important commercial and administrative center and has been so since precolonial times (*National Atlas* 1978). By the end of the twentieth century, it was the second-most populous city in Nigeria. Throughout its history, its multi-ethnic and heterogeneous populations have shaped the city's culture and character. Because of its ethnic diversity, some Nigerians describe Kano City as the "Lagos of the North," implying that it is a setting with many peoples and ideas. In recent years, elements from the precolonial past have combined with colonial and postcolonial modernization. Instead of discarding Islamic laws, many Hausa are attempting to fuse the new with the old as a strategy for coping with and controlling the myriad changes taking place in the modern world. As shown below, these conflicts and innovations play an interesting role in the development of Hausa fiddling.

Religion

John Mbiti, an authority on African religion and philosophy, indicates that not only are Africans notoriously religious, but each society has its own religious system. Because religion is the strongest element in traditional life and exerts the greatest influence on the thinking and living of Africans, to ignore indigenous beliefs, attitudes, and practices only leads to a complete misunderstanding of African behavior and problems (1989:1). Religions permeate all aspects of African life; there is no "formal distinction between the sacred and the secular, between the religious and non-religious, between the spiritual and the material areas of life." Although changes in society may modify religious practices, traditional African religions do not become extinct. "In times of crisis they often come to the surface, or people revert to them in secret" (Mbiti 1989:2). Instead of choosing between indigenous and foreign religions (e.g., Christianity or Islam), many Africans practice both. However, "[u]nless Christianity and Islam fully occupy the whole person as much as, if not more than, traditional religions do, most converts to these faiths will continue to revert to their old beliefs and practices for perhaps six days a week, and certainly in times of emergency and crisis" (Mbiti 1989:3).

Among the religions practiced in Hausaland, Bori and Islam are the most prominent. While no one takes issue with the fact that Islam is a religion, this is not the case with Bori, which is often referred to as a "cult." Bori is probably regarded as a cult by most urban Nigerian Muslims because it encourages veneration of and sacrifices to spirits, which runs counter to the teachings of Islam. Others may consider Bori a cult because it is not a world religion comparable to Christianity, Islam, or Judaism.[16] I refer to Bori as a religion, however, because its purposes and functions for those who practice it are no different from other belief systems (Mohammadan 1974; Bassa 2003; Mayani 2003; Saminaka 2003; Cole 1988).

Ethnomusicologist Fremont E. Besmer, who has written one of the most authoritative works on the subject, *Horses, Musicians, and Gods: The Hausa Cult of Possession-Trance* (1983), states that Bori has two meanings. In a general sense, it refers to the religion, while in a specific sense, the term indicates supernatural spirit or "mediumship." When someone says, "He is able to do bori" or "He has bori," this means, according to Besmer, that he is a competent medium. Although *iska* (plural, *iskoki*) is the common term used to refer to a supernatural spirit, its primary meaning is wind. In urban Hausa settlements, *aljan* or *aljani* (feminine, *aljana;* plural, *aljanu*)—derived from the Arabic *jinn*—is frequently substituted for *iska* or Bori (Besmer 1983:3–4). Possession-trance, which may or may not occur at Bori ceremonies, is an altered state of consciousness that is institutionalized and culturally patterned (Erlmann 1982a; Besmer 1983: 3; Rouget 1985). Initiates (mediums) who become possessed, or enter an ecstatic state, are expected to behave in certain ways as a learned skill. Their personality disappears under trance because their gestures and speech belong to the possessing world (Besmer 1983:3). Yet Harris warns that a very clear distinction should be drawn between genuine and false Bori. The latter, seen in barracks and prostitutes' quarters, is a dramatic presentation of the real thing and looked upon with abhorrence and scorn by true devotees of the Bori (Harris 1930:333).

The Maguzawa, or non-Muslim Hausa, with whom Bori originated were rural agriculturalists organized in patrilineal descent groups. With the coming of Islam, however, their clans became more endogamous and less exogamous (Besmer 1983:113). Umar Habila Dadem Danfulani, a scholar who has written several studies on religion in Hausaland, indicates that spirits are central to the Hausa worldview, which accounts for the tolerance and acceptance of Bori among some Hausa Muslims. He notes that

> [t]he Hausa world view exhibits a strong belief in the existence of spirits and their interaction with human beings. It is this strong belief among Hausa people in the influence of spirits on human affairs that forms one of the bedrocks upon which the survival of the *bori* cult in a predominantly Muslim environment hinges. . . . When spirits appear, the phenomenon is referred to as *Ikon Allah!*—"God's power/ miracle!" They are thus tacitly accepted in an Islamic environment as coming from Allah, God himself. This paradox serves to emphasize the existence of the institution of *bori* as a contemporary cult in the predominantly Hausa-Muslim societies of Northern Nigeria. (Danfulani 1999:414)

Bori activities in urban areas fall into two categories: (1) those connected with entertainment for social events such as weddings, naming ceremonies, and festivals; and (2) those concerned with the ritual healing of maladies or ill-fortune caused by iskoki. The first category is divided into two parts: *ki'dan Bori,* which includes possession by Bori initiates (*'yan Bori*) and *ki'dan waasaa* (drumming for play), which does not include possession (Besmer 1973:27–28). To call a spirit, the musician plays through a series of praise songs or special melodies and rhythms until one of the 'yan Bori, usually someone who is already dancing, becomes possessed. After arrival, the spirit controls the selection of tunes (Smith 1973:564–565).

As noted, Islam was a religion of the privileged when it was first introduced into Hausaland; the masses never seriously embraced the faith nor followed its tenets. Therefore, there was justification for 'Uthman dan Fodio's complaints in the early nineteenth century that "most so-called Muslims in Hausaland were half-hearted in their allegiance to Islam, and while making a lip-profession of the faith, still believed in other gods whom they called upon in their shrines and at their sacred rocks and trees" (Lewis 1980:134).

Historically, Islam has been attractive to Africans because of its catholic recognition of the multiplicity of mystical power. Lewis explains, "Of course, Islam insists on the uniqueness of God as a single omnipotent creator deity, and rigorously excludes all conflicting sources of power which could in any way impair His absolute dominion. But once this is said, and as long as God's lofty preeminence is not compromised, the Qur'an itself provides scriptural warrant for the existence of a host of subsidiary powers and spirits. These may not all be equally legitimate, but their existence and effectiveness, whether as malign or beneficial agencies, is not disputed" (Lewis 1980:60). Thus, as long as indigenous beliefs are adjusted so Allah remains unquestioned, Islam does not ask its new adherents to abandon confidence in their mystical forces. Rather, many of the traditional powers find a hospitable home in Islam, and passages from the Qur'an are cited to justify their existence as real phenomena (Lewis 1980:60). The degree of tolerance and acceptance shown these mystical forces is an issue of much debate among Muslim clergy. In Hausaland, what was acceptable and not acceptable in Islam was put forward and preserved in the writings of 'Uthman dan Fodio and members of his family.

In earlier times, overt defiance of Islam in Hausaland tended to be limited to the Bori religion, which drew support mainly from women, butchers, hunters, blacksmiths, praise singers, and prostitutes, the latter providing the continuous organization on which religious activities and survival depends. In the present day, many individuals still do not feel fully accepted in dominant religions such as Islam, which accounts for the popularity of indigenous African religions with women and the association of these religions with prostitution. By appealing to spirits, women not only seek benefits or personal relief, but Bori also provides entertainment. The spirits' appeal, however, is not limited merely to those who are subject to regular discrimination and for whom it offers some sort of compensation. Spirit possession religions also attract those who seek relief from afflictions that the orthodox rituals and prophylactics of Islam have failed to remedy (Lewis 1980:64–65; Smith 1965:151–152).

Danfulani believes that females are attracted to Bori because it provides an avenue for them "to find freedom and escape from a chauvinistic, male dominated world.... Lack of love in marriage, maltreatment by the husband and lack of satisfaction in marriage may force a woman to leave her husband. This may partly be responsible for the fairly high divorce rate among Hausa Muslims" (1999:430). When women are possessed, they reject male dominance by freely expressing their feelings and frustrations, as well as by making demands on their husbands. A woman may ask the husband for forgiveness or rebuke him for ill-treatment and cruelty. Under normal circumstances, a woman would not approach her husband in this way. "However as a medium under possession, it is a spirit that is speaking to her husband, not the woman herself. The husband must listen to and obey the divine voice of the spirit. Hence *bori* is not only a symbolic, but an actual way for women to break through the 'macho-like' male dominance of Hausa Muslim society" (1999:432).

When all is taken into account, one understands both why Bori and Islam continue to be important in Hausa society and why they remain in conflict. Not only is Islam used to validate the social order, it justifies the subordination of specific groups. Muslim leaders criticize Bori because they recognize the power of the spirits and how they might interfere or impair the absolute dominion of Allah. For practitioners, Bori serves as a form of resistance, a means to escape, and a mechanism for protesting the social injustices made against marginal groups (Danfulani 1999). When initiates call on the spirits, most feel that they are being healed immediately and their problems dealt with posthaste. Since the goge is the medium used to call Bori spirits, its nonacceptance by followers of Islam is not surprising. By the same token, the fiddle's power is one of the reasons goge music is central to Bori initiates. As Nketia explains, "it is the instrumental ensemble that provides the required energy levels for movement expression and more especially for trance and spirit possession" (Nketia 1987:173).

Besmer's findings suggest that the extremely low status of Bori musicians in Hausaland has two main sources. One is the fact that music has no official role in Islamic ritual. Except for unaccompanied chanting of religious poems and Muslim hymns and the playing of the drums (*bandiri*), musicking does not take place in the mosque (Ames 1973b:141; Besmer 1983:34; Hassan 2003). Not only do many Muslims in Hausaland and other parts of the world refer to melodies produced on the chordophone as music of the devil, some believe fiddle music causes people to perform immoral acts against their will. In earlier times, string instruments were viewed as signs of the end of the world (Farmer 1929a:24; Erlmann 1986:10). Thus, the fiddle's association with pre-Islamic rites, including possession and spirits, made it especially taboo. Muslim scholars, teachers, and religious officials in northern Nigeria believe that many kinds of Hausa music are evil. As goge is one of the main instruments used to venerate Bori spirits, it is understandable that fiddlers are not received with much enthusiasm. The second explanation points to the behavior of musicians and the belief that Bori performers keep bad company. Many in Hausaland believe musicians are lazy, dishonest, deceitful, adulterous, and obsequious. The fiddle's association with intoxicating beverages and "provocative" dancing by women in nightclubs and houses of prostitution does not help matters (Ames 1982:137). Since Bori initiates are treated as deviants, the musicians who play for them must share the religion's social stigma. "In other words, it is bad enough to be a musician, but inexcusable to practice one's craft in support of this heathen cult" (Besmer 1983:34).

In spite of such obstacles, Bori continued to be popular in northern Nigeria through the late 1970s. In the late twentieth century, it declined in prominence. Malami Buba and Graham Furniss explain:

> The campaign against *jahiliyaa* "ignorance" was conducted through compositions, treatises and even wars, but it never succeeded in abolishing the *bori* belief system among 'yan cikin gari . . . . And until the late 1970s, *bori* performance remained the high point of any communal gathering, including those which were celebrated as part of the Islamic calendar. In the minds of people at the time, *bori* was a transgression and not apostasy. Nowadays, *bori* is largely ceremonial, and is only prac-

tised publicly in the more remote areas of Islamic Hausaland. (Buba and Furniss 1999:34–35)

By the early twenty-first century, Bori practices in Kano City were not strongly visible.[17]

Whether practiced widely or in restricted areas, Bori is likely to continue to be important to many Hausa, especially during this crisis period occasioned by the revival of Shari'a. Not only does Bori include aspects of traditional culture, but people are able to adapt it to their life experiences. Danfulani explains: "With the planting of Islam in Hausaland the *bori* spirits were exposed and introduced to Islamic religious practices. The *iskoki* conversion to Islam thus fitted properly within the context of Islam. With the conquest of Fulani jihadists from 1804, *bori* spirits adopted Fulani names, making it possible for Fulani Muslim spirits to fit well into the cult. The cult again adapted itself to the coming of Europeans, a characteristic reflected in their interaction with other ethnic groups" (1999:434).

Beliefs associated with Bori also reflect the Hausa's attitudes and interactions with foreigners. In traditional culture, the Hausa value and protect strangers in their midst. Kings sometimes quarrel among themselves because each would like an important visitor to settle in his town, for the power of a Hausa ruler is often symbolized by the number of people he rules. This is illustrated in Bori as all spirits—Muslims and Christians, Fulbe and European, Biram and Yoruba—find accommodation. Thus Bori "symbolises a part of the historical process, philosophy and growth of the indigenous religion of the Hausa. It emphasises the continuity of the Hausa cultural heritage of hospitality, warmth, friendship, accommodation and cheerful acceptance of visitors no matter where they come from, in its total innocence of pure Africanness" (Danfulani 1999:440).

Hausa Music

Hausaland's location at a crossroads in the Central Sudan with numerous contacts, borrowings, and cultural fusions has not only helped the Hausa to become a powerful political, commercial, and religious force, it has also produced one of the richest music cultures in West Africa. When compared to the Dagbamba in Ghana and Fulbe in Senegambia, the Hausa of Nigeria have been fairly well documented. Yet in comparison to other major groups in Nigeria (e.g., the Yoruba and the Igbo), far less research has been done. Furthermore, the number of music sources on ethnic groups that live in northern Nigeria is small relative to those for southern Nigeria.[18] Of the few ethnic groups in northern Nigeria that have been investigated (e.g., Birom, Jukun, Nupe, and Tiv), research on Hausa music dominates.[19]

As is the case in many non-Western societies, there is no word in the Hausa language that means "music" or "musician." The closest term for "music"—*rok'o* (begging)—reflects social attitudes towards musicians rather than their occupation or product. A man participating in music is known as *marok'i* in Hausa, while a woman is called *marok'iya* or *zabiya* (Ames and King 1971:ix, 62, 67; Besmer 1998:519). Five major categories of professional musicians exist in Hausa culture: (1) musicians attached to butchers, blacksmiths, hunters, farmers, and other socio-occupational groups; (2) court musicians of the emir, high officials, and district heads, as well as famous singers and their bands who played for modern political parties before they were outlawed in January 1966; (3) freelance musicians of recreational music who play for the general public (including titled nobility, high officeholders, wealthy merchants) at dances, boxing and wrestling matches, and youth plays, and at brothels, hotels, and gambling places; (4) musician entertainers and comedians who perform at markets and other large public gatherings; (5) Bori musicians who play for spirit possession and naming and marriage ceremonies, and who played for modern political party functions before they were abolished (Ames 1973b:134–141; DjeDje 1982:117).

Hausa society is enormously rich in material culture. As many as nineteen idiophones, twenty-two membranophones, seven chordophones, and nine aerophones are identified with the Hausa (see Ames and King 1971; Ames 1973b), representing a diversity of instruments that far exceeds that found among the Fulbe and Dagbamba (see chapters 2 and 4). As is true among the Fulbe, many of these instruments were appropriated from non-Hausa. In some cases the Hausa acknowledge the borrowing; in other cases, instruments have been integrated into the culture to such a degree that individuals regard them not as foreign, but as Hausa. The Hausa categorize instruments using "terms such as *bushe-bushe* (singular, *busa;* blowing), *ka'de-ka'de* (singular, *ki'da;* beating, shaking, plucking, or bowing), and *wak'e-wak'e* (singular, *wak'a;* singing)," which refer to performance technique rather than sound (Ames and King 1971:ix). Instruments that are blown and beaten, which tend to be associated with royalty, have a higher status than those shaken, plucked, or bowed. Similarly, instruments identified with recreation, entertainment, and Bori are ranked lower. See below for instruments identified with different occupations, occasions, and social contexts.[20]

Instruments Associated with Socio-occupational Groups

Occupation	Instruments
Blacksmiths	*dundufa* and *'yar dundufa* (daughter of the *dundufa*)—two long single-membrane drums
Butchers	*kalangu* (also spelled *kalengu*)—hourglass-shaped pressure drum
Farmers	*gangar noma*—large double-membrane drum accompanied by a *kazagi*, a smaller, single open-ended drum
Hunters	*komo*—two-stringed plucked lute or *babbar garaya*

Musicians and　　*kalangu* (also spelled *kalengu*)—hourglass-shaped pressure
Praise Shouters　　drum

Instruments Used at Court

algaita—reed pipe
banga—small single-membrane cone-shaped drum covered with pieces of
　　cloth
farai—horn made of bamboo and wood about two and one-half feet long
gangar algaita—small double-membrane drum played with the *algaita*
gangar saraki—large double-membrane drum
jauje—double-membrane, hourglass-shaped pressure drum
kaho—roan antelope horn
kakaki—long trumpet made of tin or brass
kalangu na sarki—similar to the *jauje,* but smaller
kotso—single-membrane, open-ended, snared hourglass-shaped drum with
　　tension cords
tambura (singular, *tambari*)—large single-membrane kettle-shaped drums
　　also called "royal drums"
taushi—large single-membrane cone-shaped drum

Instruments Used for Recreation and Entertainment

gangan 'yan kama—single-membrane open-ended hourglass drum, no tension
　　cords
goge—large single-stringed bowed lute (i.e., fiddle)
kalangu (large) and *'dan kar'bi* (small)—double-membrane, hourglass-shaped
　　pressure drums played for young females and males
kukuma—smaller version of the *goge*
kuntuku or *kuntukuru*—single-membrane cone-shaped drum that accompa-
　　nies the *kalangu* and *'dan kar'bi*
kwairama—double-membrane drum often made of metal
k'warya—calabash drum that accompanies the goge
tallabe—double-membrane cylindrical drum
tandu—narrow-necked leather flask

Instruments Used for Bori

caki (*buta, duma, galura, gora,* or *gyan'dama*)—gourd rattles that may accom-
　　pany the *garaya*
garaya—two-stringed plucked lute accompanied by *caki,* gourd rattles
goge—one-stringed bowed lute accompanied by *k'warya, kalangu,* and *'dan
　　kar'bi*
kukuma—smaller version of the goge
k'warya ki'dan ruwa—calabash placed inside a half gourd filled with water and
　　beaten; normally associated with women

Hausa Fiddling

The physical features of the Hausa goge serve as a model for other fiddles in the Central Sudan (see photos below). In terms of size, the body resonator (about eight to ten inches in diameter) tends to be larger than those used by the Fulbe and Dagbamba.[21] Like most fiddles in the Central Sudan and Voltaic areas, the resonator hole for the goge is placed in the skin that covers the body resonator. A three-pronged piece of wood on the membrane near the resonator hole serves as the bridge (called *jaki*, which means donkey) for the horsehair string. The length of the goge, including the fifteen-inch vibrating string, is about twenty-six inches. Before the 1960s, the goge neck was shorter but was extended because longer necks allowed performers to produce a more melodious sound. During the 1970s, most Hausa fiddlers used a metal chrome bar (similar to a straight bicycle handlebar) as the neck rather than leather-covered wood because the former was more durable. Liyo states that he also liked the chrome because it gave the fiddle a modern, Western appearance (1974). Although the size and shape of the Hausa bow (eighteen to twenty inches in length and slightly arched) are similar to those of the bows used by the Fulbe, most goge bows are made of iron. The end portion, the part held in the hand when playing, is generally covered with leather (DjeDje 1978b:121). In the early twentieth century and possibly the precolonial period, Hausa bows were made from wood or giraffe bone (said to give "added sweetness"). For decoration, a fiddler would ring his bow with silver and copper rings or attach cowries given to him as presents by grateful Bori initiates (Harris 1932: 122–123).

When Harris served as a British colonial officer in northwest Nigeria during the early twentieth century, he noted that the Hausa used three types of fiddles: the *babban goge* (the largest of the three with a sound board, called *kwachiya*, of ten inches); the *kannen babban goge* (the large fiddle's younger brother with a sound board of six inches); and the *kukuma* (the smallest of the three) (Harris 1932:122). While the large fiddles were used out-of-doors because of their loud volume, the kukuma, which Harris refers to as a "chamber" instrument, was performed indoors "at weddings, naming ceremonies, and convivial meetings of Bori devotees" (Harris 1932:123). Having three fiddles is significant and distinguishes Hausa fiddling from other societies. Except for fiddlers who make use of instruments of different sizes for learning (e.g., children in Dagbon use a small size instrument when they begin their fiddle lessons but change to a larger one when they grow older), no other people in West Africa, to my knowledge, have several fiddle prototypes.

History

Unlike the Dagbamba who have several oral traditions documenting the introduction of fiddling in Dagbon (see chapter 4), there appears to be a lack of interest in the history of fiddling in Hausaland. This may be related to several factors: the association of the goge with the profane, deviance, and institutions (e.g., Bori, nightclubs, and other recreational activities) not highly regarded in Hausa society may have led Hausa speakers to think that such a history is unnecessary or unimportant; because Hausa fiddlers have never been organized into a social unit that bonds them together, no pressure has been placed on them to legitimize their founding; the goge musicians' view of fiddling as essentially an occupation that leads to an income rather than a tradition of historical importance may have caused them to focus their energies on learning to play the instrument (DjeDje 1992:154–160). In the absence of an oral tradition documenting goge history, several culture bearers and scholars have debated the issue with little general consensus, except that nearly everyone agrees that fiddling is not indigenous to Hausaland.

Except for publications by DjeDje (1978b, 1992), Kenneth Gourlay (1980, 1982b), Sanusi Mohammed Yakubu (1981), Junzo Kawada (2001), and scattered references to fiddling in other works (see below), few scholars have written on the history of the goge. Most Hausa fiddlers I interviewed in 1974 also had little to say.[22] Neither Haruna Bande (a resident of Kano City who had been playing the fiddle for about eight years), Mamman Landi (a resident of Panshekara, a town about twelve miles from Kano City), nor Momman Nabarau (a forty-nine-year-old native of Kano City who had been fiddling for about thirty years) knew anything about the history. In fact, Nabarau's response to my question "Do you know when the goge was first brought to Kano?" was "By that time, I was not born" (Nabarau 1974).

Other Hausa fiddlers I contacted in 1974 had somewhat more to say about the instrument's history. Ahmadu Samunaka of Wudil (a town located about twenty-five miles southeast of Kano), but a Kano City resident at the time of the interview, was forty-two years old and had played the instrument for about twenty-eight years. Like many Hausa who believe that all historical data can be found in Islamic writings, he stated, "Only a person educated in Islam culture knows. Muslims believe that whatever is in the world is written in the Qur'an [and is] already predestined by God. So mallams can look in [the Qur'an] and find out" (1974). Ibrahim Mohammadan, fifty and the eldest fiddler interviewed, commented, "The fiddle was introduced quite a long time—as far as seventy years ago. The people of Damagarau [north of Kano] in the Niger Republic are the people who introduced the instrument into Hausaland. They have been playing goge before Islam was introduced into the culture" (1974). Born in Patika (in the former Zaria Province), Mohammadan had performed the fiddle for almost thirty-five years and was well known in Kano City during the 1970s. As an established Bori musician, he also performed widely in northern Nigeria and Niger where Bori practitioners were prevalent.[23]

Garba Liyo, who provided the most extensive history, stated that he acquired details about the fiddle's origin as a child from his father when he was learning to play the instrument:

The Maguzawa people who lived in Dala, probably one of the oldest sections of Kano, had a king whose name was Bagauda. During Bagauda's reign, which was before the introduction of Islam into Hausaland, the people worshipped a *juju* [spirit] called Tsumburburai [also spelled Tchunburburai]. In worshipping the juju the people used a musical instrument called the *sunsuma*.

The *sunsuma* was made of a calabash gourd. The gourd was so large that two men played on the calabash simultaneously. A rattle, called the *sham'bara,* was used to accompany the sunsuma. The sham'bara, known today as the *sam'bara*—an accompaniment for the garaya instrument (the two-stringed plucked lute)—is made from guinea corn stalks and is rolled in the hands to make the vibrating sound.[24]

When the sunsuma was played, the music caused a spiritual communication between the god and its priest. The god would give messages through the king [priest] about farming practices and other activities within the life of the people. After harvesting of the farm crops, the people would honor the juju by playing the sunsuma.

During the course of time, another instrument evolved to replace the sunsuma. This instrument was called the *gyandamma.* The gyandamma was much smaller in size and different in physical appearance from the sunsuma; this instrument was in the shape of a lute or violin.[25] Horsehair was used for the vibrating strings rather than leather. A bow, also with horsehair strings, was rubbed against the string of the calabash.

After the gyandamma, the goge appeared in somewhat its present size; the neck, however was longer than today's goge. Gradually the instrument developed to its present physical appearance. (Liyo 1974)

After the narration, Liyo stated that he believed stringed instruments had spiritual powers. In his opinion, the goge is used in Bori because a trance could not be obtained without fiddle music.

Liyo's account is important for several reasons. First, it parallels the oral tradition concerning the founding of Kano, including references to the spirit Tsumburburai (see Palmer 1928; Smith 1976:187; Danfulani 1999:419). Yalwa states that oral narratives about Hausa history are common knowledge: "Most Hausa know about this [Bagauda and Bori], and there are so many versions. The Bagauda story is one of the first stories taught by elder people. . . . I first heard this story from my grandmother and later I was taught it in primary school." Because Liyo's account resembles other oral narratives that he had heard, Yalwa believed it was reliable, but added, "Nowadays goge and Bori are two different things. You don't call the spirits with goge nowadays. Goge is just music; you play it, sing, and praise people and other things. They use garaya for Bori" (1989).

The uneven development of historical detail in Liyo's narrative also resembles other oral traditions. While Liyo provides details about the instruments' beginnings (in his discussion of the sunsuma), the middle part of the history is vague (little data exist on the gadangama and its transformation to the goge). For the Hausa, the presentation of the narrative in this manner does not discredit its validity, particularly when other information supports the account. In explaining the structure and selection of material used by oral narrators, Miller states:

> Like their western counterparts, they [oral narrators] are historians and as such are concerned with what they understand as change. . . . Whereas western historians perceive change in terms of refined and lengthy series of gradual increments, the constraints of orality lead narrators to conceive of and to present change in the form of abrupt, dichotomous transformations. [This] . . . sometimes lends their narratives a "magical" quality. (Miller 1980:35–36)

Finally, by stating that the sunsuma was not played with a bow (implying that the strings were probably plucked) and was accompanied by the sam'bara (an instrument normally used with the garaya), Liyo's narrative confirms the opinions of those Hausa who believe that the garaya was the original instrument used at Bori ceremonies (see below). Since Bori is the religion of the Maguzawa (the first inhabitants of Hausaland), this suggests that the goge evolved later in history, which supports the argument that the one-stringed fiddle is not indigenous to Hausa culture.

The fiddlers I interviewed in 2003 offered different opinions about the goge's history. Musa dan Gado Saminaka, a fiddler in his fifties or sixties from Saminaka, a small town in central Nigeria,[26] says, "It originated in northern Nigeria with a very small instrument called *kwambilo*. It's similar to the goge. The people who perform this, in those days, they used to give them a penny. It's an instrument used by beggars." When asked about the ethnicity of the people and the time period that the instrument was introduced into Hausaland, Saminaka explained: "The Zaberma [Djerma] people from Zamfara State brought it here. I can't tell how long ago because it's beyond my age. The Zamfara came here, and the Hausa decided to try it. I have seen these people play it" (2003). The fact that Saminaka introduces the term *kwambilo* into the discussion is noteworthy because Babba Mai Goge, one of the three fiddlers Yakubu (1981) profiles, states that he became interested in learning how to fiddle after observing "some Adarawa people from Niger playing something similar to *goge* called *kwambilo* as they sang" (Yakubu 1981:12).[27]

Balan Na Bassa and Umarun Mayani, two fiddlers I interviewed in Jos, agreed that the kwambilo was played by people from Niger but did not believe it was the first fiddle to be used in Hausaland. Rather, both emphasize that the kwambilo referred to a bow used to play the fiddle: "It's like a goge bow, but it's smaller. Any instrument that uses a curved bow is what is known as kwambilo" (Bassa 2003; Mayani 2003). Concerning the history of the goge, Bassa states, "It originated from Ethiopia. When you go to Ethiopia, you find different types of fiddles." Yet he adds, "It is difficult to get the true history of goge from any person" (2003).[28]

I also consulted individuals who were not involved in fiddling but who had knowledge about musicking in northern Nigeria. The director of the School of Music in Kano State believed that the fiddle was brought from North Africa during the caravan trades and other interactions between the Hausa and northerners, because the materials used for the construction of goge were not indigenous to West Africa. He emphasized that the horse, whose hair is essential to the sound production of goge, was introduced into Sudanic Africa by Berbers. One of the first printed references concerning goge is found in the eighteenth century writings of 'Uthman dan Fodio (see above; Erlmann 1986:38). The manner in which 'Uthman dan Fodio references the fiddle implies that the instrument and activities surrounding its performance were familiar to people in Hausaland. Since string instruments from other parts of Africa (e.g., the molo) were known among both the Fulbe and Hausa, this suggests that fiddling was introduced into the region before the late eighteenth century.

Sanusi Mohammed Yakubu indicates that the people he interviewed believe "the origin of goge is as old as the existence of Hausas because it is . . . not only used in the worship of Bori, it is used for communal work on the farm to stimulate men to work" (Yakubu 1981:2). Regarding the kukuma, Yakubu argues that "it came after the advent of goge." To support his position, he references Ahmadu Doka, a well-known kukuma player from Kaduna, Nigeria, who gives two explanations for the instrument's presence in the country. Doka explains:

A group of people called Zabermawa from Niger first brought the *kukuma* [to Nigeria] after the Second World War in 1945. The men played the *kukuma* while the women did the dancing. When *kukuma* could be found almost everywhere, the prostitutes then used it for praise songs for their male friends. Secondly one could say *kukuma* emanated from eastern countries like Borno and Chad from a group called Shuwa Arabs. When they came with the *kukuma,* the usage was restricted to their men and women only. The men did the playing of the *kukuma* while their ladies danced and clapped their hands, at the same time shaking their behinds. This proves the point that probably they got or inherited it from Arab countries because the people of Borno embraced the Islamic religion before the people of Hausaland. (Yakubu 1981:5–6)

In *The Northern Tribes of Nigeria,* C. K. Meek includes a detailed discussion of the names and physical characteristics of chordophones used in northern Nigeria and his belief that the fiddle originated among hunters. Meek states:

Stringed instruments of the fiddle and lute type have a widespread distribution, and are notably found among the Hausa and Gwari. The fiddle is sometimes, as among the Kamu and many other tribes, only used by hunters, and this fact might appear to confirm the belief that the fiddle originated among hunters who converted their bows into music-producing instruments. . . . The ordinary fiddle is made with a calabash resonator and a membrane of a monitor's skin. . . . The Beri-Beri have a two-stringed fiddle known as the *kukuma,* which has a membrane of red leather. The bow-string is always made of horsehair. The fiddle-strings are attached to the handle by binding, no tuning-pegs being used. (Meek 1921:156–157)[29]

Henry George Farmer (1939) and Helen Hause (1948) argue a North African origin for the goge because the terms *goge* and *ghugha* are similar and because they assume that influence in this instance went from north to south. Yet historical and linguistic evidence reveals that instead of the Hausa adopting a North African term, the reverse occurred. After enslaved Hausa speakers, during the precolonial era, were taken to North Africa, they changed the term for the instrument from *goge* to *ghugha*. Junzo Kawada also emphasizes that the construction of the goge in North Africa is distinct from other fiddles in that region. The spike fiddle (e.g., the North African rabab or kamanje) with its unique body resonator and vertical performance position differs from the Hausa goge in North Africa, which is constructed from a calabash gourd body resonator and held horizontally in performance. Whereas fiddles similar in physical appearance to the rabab can be found in many parts of the world, the construction used for the goge is unique to West Africa (Kawada 2001:6; Blench 1984; Schuyler 1979).[30]

Fremont Besmer seems more confident about the origins of goge than the history of the garaya:

> The case for the origin of the goge is much clearer than that for the plucked lute [garaya], but again the chronology is problematic. . . . The date of its borrowing is probably coincident with the spread of Islam to northern Nigeria. The goge is not an instrument generally related to either Islamic ritual practice or court ceremony, however, so it was most likely borrowed when the contacts between north Africa and northern Nigeria had been firmly established rather than with the earliest of the Muslim travellers. We might suggest the sixteenth or seventeenth centuries as a period during which the goge could have been brought to northern Nigeria—Islam having been established as the official state religion in Kano for example, during the reign of Muhammad Rumfa (AD 1463-99) . . . but no confirmation of this exists in the Hausa chronicles. Further, no mention is made of any role musical instruments might have had in pre-Islamic religious worship. (Besmer 1983:55-56)

Although Besmer's suggestion that the fiddle's introduction into Hausaland occurred during the sixteenth or seventeenth centuries, after Islam had been firmly established rather than with Muslim travelers who arrived in the fourteenth and fifteenth centuries (and possibly earlier), seems plausible, other issues need to be considered before settling on this hypothesis.

Kenneth Gourlay is one of the few scholars to oppose the argument that the goge originated in North Africa. Instead, he believes that fiddling began in Hausaland and suggests that ethnocentrism and bias (by Arab and Western scholars) have prevented the Hausa from being acknowledged for this invention (1982b:225-226). While bias should not be overlooked or dismissed, too much evidence supports the thesis that fiddling *is not* indigenous to the Hausa or any people in West Africa. When examining the Africanization of the fiddle, I believe such a debate distracts from more important questions: what happened to fiddling after its introduction in West Africa? how and why was the instrument dispersed? what types of changes took place in the tradition before West Africans, including Hausa speakers, began to regard it not as foreign but as their own?

Like Besmer, Kawada places the introduction of the fiddle in the Central Sudan around the sixteenth and seventeenth centuries because he links the instrument's arrival in Hausaland with the Ottoman occupation of North Africa (Kawada 2001:5). But Kawada goes a step further by indicating that the influence came from the Maghrib (or northwest Africa) instead of through Borno and the east (or northeast Africa).[31] Yet Nigerian Hausa (e.g., Doka [quoted in Yakubu 1981]; Bassa 2003; Yalwa 2003a) think otherwise, which forces us to consider reasons why a dispersion from the east should not be discounted. Not only does oral tradition suggest that some peoples now living in Nigeria migrated from the east (Euba 1971), many Hausa believe that the introduction of Islam and other cultural traditions in Hausaland is due to interactions with Borno (Erlmann 1983b). Furthermore, traditions concerning Bayajida and Bagauda lend support to influence from the east. Just as a dispersion from the east should not be discounted, arguments by Nigerians supporting influence from the west and northwest should not be dismissed either; see Mohammadan (1974); Doka (quoted in Yakubu 1981); Saminaka (2003).[32] Since fiddling is not identified with the Mande (see Charry 2000a; Kawada 2001:4), the only peoples west or northwest of Hausaland who were knowledgeable about fiddling and in a position to introduce the tradition into the region were the Fulbe, the Songhai, and the Tuareg because all, by the fifteenth century, had made contacts with the Hausa (Greenberg 1960:479–480; Adamu 1986:55; Hiskett 1984:153; also see chapters 1 and 2).

While speculation may exist on how fiddling reached Hausaland, the arguments supporting the Hausa and Fulbe as agents in the dispersion of the instrument in the Central Sudan are compelling (Sulemana 1995a). As noted above, Hausaland sat at a crossroads where many musical ideas, practices, and aspects of material culture were shared. Furthermore, the Hausa were traders who traveled and introduced others to their way of life. Not only does this account for the widespread use of the term *goge* (see chapter 1), it may also be the reason that the fiddle construction employed by the Hausa (i.e., the placement of the resonator hole in the skin) dominates in Voltaic and Central Sudan and the eastern forest regions of West Africa (DjeDje 1998).

Of the three Fulbe groups—pastoral nomads or cattle herders, rural settled Fulbe, and sedentary urban Fulbe—that Paden (1973:32) proposes for Nigeria, the first and second most likely continued to play the fiddle, while the third abandoned fiddling because it was never important to them. Not only were the urban Fulbe better educated and more politically sophisticated, it was they who promoted the jihads and were orthodox in their Islamic beliefs; thus, the instrument, in their eyes, was profane (see King 1980b and chapters 1 and 2). The goge's identification with the Hausa and not the sedentary Fulbe probably became doctrine during the late eighteenth and early nineteenth centuries when 'Uthman dan Fodio and his followers were promoting Islamic reforms. In fact, the abandonment of fiddling may have coincided with the dwindling use of Fulfulde among urban Fulbe in Kano (Paden 1973:49–50). As Fulbe Muslims in Kano City disassociated themselves with musicking and fiddling, Hausa musicians, fusing Fulbe traditions with their own, became both court performers and the major exponents of fiddling.[33]

When the political structure in Hausaland was transformed during the first half of the twentieth century to serve the needs of British colonialists, social distinctions from the precolonial era were replaced by two status groups: a ruling class of new rich merchants and the rest of the population, who were impoverished. Changes in class structure and modes of subsistence did not, however, affect musicking in Kano. Although professional musicians such as fiddlers were socially inferior, fiddling continued to be important. Some musicians even switched from performing other instruments to take up fiddling.[34] With Nigerian independence in the 1960s, the goge's role in Hausa society expanded beyond traditional contexts to new occasions and patrons (see below). By the end of the twentieth century, however, fiddling in Kano and other cities in northern Nigeria was on the decline due to changes in sociopolitical and religious institutions in postcolonial Nigeria. Because of the importance of fiddling to Bori and other aspects of Hausa society, however, I doubt that goge music will disappear completely. Just as Bori has been re-invented at different points in history to satisfy the needs of its practitioners, the goge will most likely adapt to a new set of circumstances.

It is my own belief that the fiddle was introduced into the region by Fulbe cattle herders and reinforced as a result of interactions with the Songhai and Tuareg who had more direct contacts with Arab culture. My hypothesis that fiddling came from the west does not dismiss interactions with easterners who played the instrument and had contacts with the Hausa. In fact, influences from both directions may explain why the fiddle is known by *goge* (a Hausa term) and *kukuma* (a term identified with Borno).[35] But regardless of the origin of fiddling, the role of Africans in the distribution of the fiddle should not be minimized. Just as the Sudanese were agents in the spread of Islam in Hausaland, I argue that Africans and not Southwest Asians were responsible for introducing the fiddle in the Central Sudan. While no documented evidence is available to support my position, this argument does not differ from what we already know about the culture history of Sudanic Africa. As researchers continue to conduct research on African music history, their investigations will, I hope, shed light on such issues.

Performance Contexts

Because goge musicians are eager to earn money, the contexts for fiddling in Hausaland have been varied. During the 1960s and 1970s, fiddlers performed at events of the life cycle (naming and wedding ceremonies), Bori, nightclubs, beer bars, houses of prostitution, political rallies, and other public gatherings (festivals, parades, town square, markets, hotels, dramas and plays for youth, national holidays, harvest seasons, celebration of the first rains, etc.). In these contexts fiddlers obtained clients from different backgrounds. Before independence, fiddlers also regularly visited the homes of so-called "big men" uninvited, but they became more cautious about such performances after the 1960s (Landi 1974; Bande 1974).

Although fiddlers are not attached to Hausa royalty, the emir occasionally invites them to perform at the palace for special events, a practice that continues to the present day.[36] Goge musicians in Kano, Zaria, and other cities in

Hausaland also perform annually for high-ranking officials and clients at *hawan salla* (a royal cavalcade from the palace of the emir to the praying grounds outside the city walls or to the central mosque and back again). Besides goge, court musicians (many of whom are mounted on horseback to distinguish their rank from other performers) and other low-ranking performers (popular male and female singers and musicians who patronize socio-occupational groups and Bori initiates) participate in the event (Ames and King 1971:120; Mohammadan 1974; Hassan 2003).[37]

In spite of the fiddlers' acceptance in a number of contexts, goge musicians rarely perform at occasions that include Islamic worship. Wedding ceremonies, for example, are generally divided into two parts, the first a sacred portion conducted according to Islamic laws and attended by the imam who sometimes presides, and the second a festive occasion, not strongly supported by religion but accepted by traditional laws. During the second part, goge music may be performed because neither the imam nor other religious leaders are present.

Although Kano fiddlers used to visit rural areas when invited to naming and wedding ceremonies, cities traditionally provided a greater opportunity for performances. With the revival of Shari'a in the late twentieth century, however, fiddle performances have become scarce at urban public events. When I visited Kano City in 2003, all nightclubs had been closed and Bori ceremonies, if held, took place in villages on the outskirts of the city. Mohammad Kassim Hassan, a Kano City resident, explains:

> Since we are in the democratic society now and governed by democratic [leaders], our religion, Islam, forbids the way that [fiddlers are] playing. They formerly played for hotels and clubs where they used to drink alcohol and play this thing [the fiddle]. After drinking the alcohol, you'd see some free women going with them. Our religion forbids that. That is why they are just driven away. The only [ones left] went into villages and play on the outskirts of the municipals. Even though they play in Kano now, it's just in the hidden places. No one [is supposed] to know, but they still play inside the Kano City. But it is very rare to see them open because of the introduction of the Shari'a. (Hassan 2003)

Although the instrument's visibility at public gatherings was diminished when I visited the region in 2003, fiddle music continued to be heard in films, on radio and television,[38] and in private homes in Hausaland. Hassan says, "People who are inclined, patronize them [fiddlers] at their weddings and naming ceremonies" (2003).

Social Organization, Patronage, and Popularity

Unlike Hausa court musicians or Dagbamba fiddlers who belong to the same family and are attached to rulers, Hausa fiddlers have not formed a social kinship unit. To show respect, a Hausa fiddler may be called *Baba* (a term that refers to a father or elder) because of his age or experience, but the title confers no status within the Hausa social system. Similarly, when a fiddler is called

Sarkin Ki'dan (chief of drummers) at Bori or political rallies, this relates to his position within the group and not kinship.[39]

Goge musicians, to my knowledge, have never had a patron or socio-occupational group that supports them exclusively. When politicians and business people hire fiddlers for advertising or public relations, other instrumentalists may be employed for the same purpose. Although Bori practitioners are among the oldest patrons of Hausa fiddlers (Tremearne 1914; Harris 1930), two other performance traditions, equally effective in calling spirits, are associated with possession: the *k'waryar kidan ruwa* ensembles (which use hemispherical calabashes for beating on water) comprised solely of women, and the garaya ensembles comprised of men. In some places, goge ensembles are preferred; in others, garaya groups predominate because Bori ceremonies are subject to regional variation (Besmer 1983:53). The Hausa of Niger use the goge at Bori and rarely, if ever, use a plucked lute for possession (Erlmann 1982b:51).

Goge musicians rarely fall into trance during ceremonies, but they are intimately involved in nearly all phases of the religion and play an indispensable role in both public and private religious performances (Besmer 1983:2). The musician-patron relationship in Bori is complicated. When goge musician and Bori practitioner Haruna Bande played "Ki'dan Barahaza," a song in honor of the female Fulbe spirit Barahaza (also spelled Barrahaza or Barhaza), for me in a private recording session, the song text included information about the occupation, family genealogy, and spirit association of at least three of his clients, suggesting that the people cited were Bori initiates who had established agreements for Bande to mention them whenever he played the song. Thus, the fiddler can provide services for several clients simultaneously: the spirit and the medium(s) for the spirit.[40]

Business agreements between fiddlers and clients are critical for their livelihood. Goge performers earn a substantial income from short-term contracts. Lesser-known artists (who have not become established enough to attract wealthy clients) and famous musicians rely heavily on such relationships. Therefore, at public gatherings where likely clients are seen, fiddlers immediately create music in praise of such persons. Because the Hausa feel obliged to show their appreciation for such gestures, they pay the musicians. The amount that individuals give fiddlers for an unsolicited praise varies and depends on their access to income, circumstance, and status. While the total amount for someone of low income may be less than one dollar, the total for someone of a higher income and status may be as high as fifty.

To enter into a long-term agreement with patrons of importance or prosperous individuals is one of the ultimate objectives of goge musicians. Not only does this provide fiddlers with continuous support, but as the patron rises in social status, adding titles to his name, fiddlers are similarly ranked higher. The relationship that fiddlers have had with politicians could be regarded as long and continuous. Prior to the 1966 coup, goge musicians were noted for their performances at political party activities. In hotel beer gardens of cities in Hausaland, fiddlers played for the various political parties while dancers performed *rawan kashewa* or *rawan banjo* (popular dances of the day). The goge player was always the group's leader, assuming the title *Sarkin* and appending the name of the political party: Sarkin Ki'dan of the NPC (chief of drummers of the Northern Peoples Congress). When Liyo performed for candidates, for example, he provided not only entertainment for prospective voters, but also praises in honor of politicians, interjecting party slogans, platform messages, and details about the candidates' personal lives. After being identified with a party candidate, Liyo no longer needed to be seen with the client to provide services. Members of the community were reminded of the politician just by seeing the fiddler.[41] Wealthy merchants establish agreements with fiddlers for similar reasons; musicians who are mobile can perform in different communities throughout the country. What better way could a businessman find to advertise his goods than to be identified with a famous artist? The contract between the two would stipulate that no matter where or when the fiddler performed, he was obliged to mention the name and sing praises in honor of the businessman (Liyo 2003).

Gift-giving, an important aspect of the Hausa music profession, constitutes a major source of income for goge performers but rarely covers the performer's expenses. Some musicians, however, are satisfied with an expensive gown because fashions constantly change, and the production and wearing of clothing are forms of artistic expression. Ames explains, "In gift-giving, a fine gown is valued more highly than other goods of an equivalent value—perhaps only the gifts of a wife, a horse, or in former times, a slave, would be appreciated more. Emirs and other persons of rank and wealth constantly give gifts of clothing" (Ames 1973b:143). While patrons who enter a short-term contract with musicians often give money (another acceptable form of payment), performers maintaining a permanent relationship with patrons may receive clothing, money, and other support, such as recommendations (Ames 1973b:143).

Gift-giving is also extremely important in Bori, for the amount and type of gift that fiddlers receive is often decided upon and paid by the sponsor of the event before the ritual begins and determines if the performance will be with or without a trance. If musicians accept the payment (kola nuts, cash, or hard candy), they are obliged to reciprocate with services. Customarily, gifts are slightly larger when trancers are asked to demonstrate possession at the event than when they do not enter trance (Besmer 1983:136–137).

Because fiddlers depend heavily on gift-giving for an income, they have to be innovative to attract patrons. Maintaining popularity, however, is not easy because of the diverse range of patrons of fiddle music. While some goge musicians are known for a distinct performance style or repertoire of songs, others attract clients by modifying the physical appearance of their instrument or adding new instruments to the ensemble. By the 1970s, goge music had become a popular medium for radio and recordings, providing fiddlers with even wider exposure and appeal and an additional source of income. Goge musician Balan

Na Bassa from Jos, who was born into a family of fiddlers in the 1920s, explains some of the preferences of both goge musicians and patrons during the twentieth century:

> When my forefathers (my grandfather and father) wanted to know a real, good goge player, they distinguish him on how well he plays Bori songs: either "Ki'dan Sarkin Rafi" or "Ki'dan Barahaza" or "Ki'dan Wanzami." Those are the distinguishing songs that they will be able to know if one is really a good fiddler.
>
> During the time of my reign [ca. 1940s to early 1960s], there was nothing like "Ki'dan Banjo." "Banjo" is from recent times. It is actually a praise song. [Now] almost everybody knows of it and everybody knows how to play it. At a certain time, politicians got advantage of them [goge musicians] and invite them [to play "Ki'dan Banjo"]. Whenever [politicians] want to have a rally, they invite them. The sound of their [fiddle] music, it's a force for inviting people.
>
> If you could get my songs from Radio Kaduna, you would be able to distinguish between the songs. If someone plays "Ki'dan Barahaza" and "Sarkin Rafi," it's the older people that would be able to recognize what he's saying and that he's a very good goge musician.[42] But youngsters may not know what the goge is saying. At the same time, if you play "Ki'dan Banjo," youngsters will understand it. But then the older people may not understand what is being played. (Bassa 2003)

Bassa's comments indicate that prior to the rise of political parties in the 1950s and 1960s, a goge musician's ability to perform Bori songs was primary. While knowledge of Bori continued to be important in the second half of the twentieth century, some fiddlers felt that, because the social backgrounds and socio-economic levels of clients had become more diverse, changes needed to be made. In the postcolonial era, not only did fiddlers add dancers, a new repertoire, and different instruments to their ensembles, some began performing in new contexts (hotels and nightclubs modeled on those in Western societies).

Beginning in the 1960s, varying reasons accounted for the popularity of fiddlers. Young people discovered that because goge musicians desired to attract new patrons, they were more receptive to innovations than other performers. The fascination of youth with Western ideas, particularly African-American culture, led to a dance called the *tuwis* or *tiwis* (twist) and a song performed in honor of James Brown called "Jabula," which was associated with goge performance. Several musicians referred to the goge as a guitar or banjo, and the song entitled "Ki'dan Banjo" that Balan Na Bassa mentions was composed for the fiddle (Bande 1974; Ingawa 1974). Noteworthy, too, was the incorporation of music elements from East India. The showing of East Indian films resulted in young people adopting East Indian dances, dance rhythms, and songs. Goge musicians capitalized on this fad by creating a unique amalgam of Hausa and East Indian music utilizing their own instruments and performance style (Ames 1973b).

In addition to being inventive, fiddlers and their performances are expected to stimulate the audience's intellectual interest and emotional response (Ames 1973b:145–146). To do so, some fiddlers develop a large repertory of songs on topics that can appeal to diverse audiences. During the 1960s, for example, some patrons preferred social commentary songs and others wanted performers who fused Hausa music with that of other cultures. Knowing the genealogy and details of patrons' lives was also important for both praising and criticizing clients.

As with certain African-American musicians (e.g., James Brown, Isaac Hayes, or Teddy Pendergrass), sex appeal and charisma were important attributes for goge musicians in the 1960s and 1970s. Some fiddlers gave up the profession because they no longer had youthful good looks to attract female listeners. Older goge performers also mentioned that they could not play the new tunes and rhythms popular among young people (Ames 1973b:151).

Because many Hausa admire a virtuoso style of fiddle playing, a fiddler's musical creativity and ability to improvise with technical competence are essential to his popularity. Not only are goge performers expected to know variations that can be integrated into new and old fiddle songs, they must also develop their own, unique and distinctive performance style. After listening to the performance of a fiddler at a political rally in 1964, Ames stated: "I was impressed with his ability to improvise endless variations on any tune and at the same time to produce a variety of unusual tones and percussive effects. The nearest parallel to the Hausa fiddle music in Western music are the 'hot violins' of Joe Venuty and Eddy [sic] South, who played with American hot jazz ensembles in the nineteen twenties and thirties" (Ames 1973b:151).

When fiddling in Hausaland began to decline during the latter part of the twentieth century, most nonmusicians in Kano City believed the decline was due to the revival of Shari'a, while others felt that differences between generations and the socio-economic level of patrons were factors. Mohammadan Hassan states: "These goge musicians, they are for elderly people and the middle class. The generation that goes on now don't look for that. That is why it [goge's popularity] is medium. Hausa youth are more inclined to be Western. But the same Hausa youth that like jazz and reggae also like kukuma and kalangu" (2003). When asked why the youth preferred kukuma over goge since both are one-stringed fiddles, Hassan stated: "This goge, you cannot dance to it. It's only a few people that can dance to goge. But for kukuma, anyone can dance to it." (Hassan 2003).[43] When I asked thirty-year-old Shehu Garba Liyo, who was not a musician but had studied math in school with the hopes of becoming an accountant, about his musical preferences, he stated: "I like to hear it [goge] through the radio, but I don't like to play [dance to] it." In addition to "break dancing," Shehu liked "music from other African countries and abroad" (2003). While rap music and the music of Michael Jackson were his favorites, his youngest sister, who was fourteen, liked kuntigi, kalangu, and gurmi music (Liyo 2003).

Most Hausa fiddlers believe their decline in popularity is due to generational differences. Goge musician Saminaka states that music played on the gurmi and garaya is heard more often on the radio in his village than goge. Yet in spite of the popularity of other instrumental traditions in the twenty-first century, Saminaka indicates that he would continue to fiddle if he were a young, active musician: "I would still want to play goge. I still believe that goge is more interesting than garaya" (2003). In fact, Yusuf Isa, one of Saminaka's fans who resides in the village where Saminaka lives, agrees that fiddling is more exciting: "If you have two people playing—one person playing garaya and the other playing goge—at the same time, you will find more people listening to and watching the goge musician than the garaya. And each time the goge player is playing, you will feel as if there are a hundred people playing. The sound appears as if there are hundreds of them" (2003). When I questioned him further, I discovered that it was the improvisational character and complexity of the fiddle playing that Isa believed attracted the listener's attention and made the goge sound like a hundred people performing.

Innovation has thus been one of the primary reasons Hausa fiddling has thrived over the centuries. Just as the Hausa political states during the precolonial era survived as important cultural centers because of their willingness to adapt to change, goge musicians similarly made adjustments. Instead of rejecting new ideas because they clashed with the norm, fiddlers believed embracing innovation and features from other cultures gave them a competitive edge. When Hausa fiddlers introduced new ideas from the East, West, and other parts of Africa into their performances during the 1960s and 1970s, fiddling was at the height of its popularity, and even though the public performance of goge has declined considerably in northern Nigerian cities in the latter part of the twentieth century, the tradition has not been completely abandoned. Fervent Muslim practitioners such as Hassan believe that goge has no place in Muslim life, but he also thinks knowledge about fiddling should be preserved. When asked how he felt about my writing a book on the Hausa goge at a time when Muslims in Hausaland viewed fiddling negatively, he stated: "Since you are writing a book on goge music, I'll ask you to include everything on it so that our generation coming can know about it and the usefulness of it, and how it comes to be. To Islam, [fiddling is] bad. To myself, now it's bad. But I would like them [my children] to know what is good and bad, but not actually to work on [participating in] it" (2003).

Contemporary Social Status and Attitude toward Fiddlers

The current social status of fiddlers and the attitude of the Hausa toward fiddling are determined to a large degree by views held by Muslims in Hausaland. Since most Fulbe-Hausa, particularly those who consider themselves to be deeply religious, condemn and do not want to be associated with music, fiddlers have had a low social status in spite of their popularity (Erlmann 1983b, 1983b). Most Hausa regard musicians and the music profession, with the exception of court performers, with disdain. Whereas several types of idiophones, membranophones, and aerophones are attached to the emir's court, those who perform chordophones are not represented. Many Hausa parents would also disapprove of their daughter's marriage to a fiddler. Even during the 1960s when fiddling was popular, Ames observed that the lack of social acceptance could be seen in the refusal of many nonmusicians to eat of the same bowl with musicians or to lodge in the same dwelling (Ames 1973b:154).

The attitude that members of a community have about a musical tradition is sometimes reflected in their oral literature. The proverbs and jokes listed below indicate how some people in Hausaland regard the goge:

Proverbs

Hairs of the dead horse, not even a religious teacher can say you are not sweet to the ear, he can only say you are not edifying.

Goge who silences the mob (i.e., it is louder). [Fiddle, which deadens the sharpness of molo.][44]

Goge is the music of worldly people.

Goge is the source of heresy. (Ames and King 1971:43)

Jokes

The goge fiddler to the hourglass drummer: "You only play for the girls to dance and [they] give you pennies."

The drummer replies: "You only play for the harlots to dance and [they] give you a half-smoked cigarette to finish up." (Ames 1982:14)

Because fiddlers are freelancers with substantial incomes that exceed the monies received by court musicians and other occupations, goge performers have not been overly concerned about the Islamic communities valuation or restrictions. When I asked Saminaka if it concerned him that Muslims regarded fiddling negatively, he responded: "When I was young and playing the fiddle, it did not bother me what other people said because it was my means of livelihood. I was actually getting money" (2003). On the subject of Islamic laws prohibiting fiddling, he says: "Islam does not stop the playing of goge. I know that even with the enactment of the Shari'a law [in earlier years] that there was a time when the government of Kano State gave them [fiddlers] the permission. Anybody who wanted to perform could come and see the officer to gain permission. So as far as I'm concerned, the Shari'a law has nothing to do with the stopping of goge music" (2003).[45]

While most goge musicians regard their performances simply as a means for earning income and providing entertainment at recreational activities, some view their profession as necessary to Hausa society. On the one hand, fiddlers believe they help maintain social control because nonmusicians rarely comment publicly on moral or social issues. If community members are displeased with government policies, administrators, and officials, or if a person needs to be honored, musicians are hired to sing praises or express opposing opinions (Landi 1974). On the other hand, goge musicians also feel they are among the few in Hausa society who respond to the spiritual and emotional needs of those ostracized by Muslims. Not only are Bori practitioners healed from harmful diseases through listening to fiddle music, but they are advised on what to do about the wrongs they experience (Mohammadan 1974; Saminaka 2003).

The poem at the beginning of this chapter by 'Uthman dan Fodio indicates that conflicting attitudes about the goge profession have existed for many centuries. Whereas some community members believe that fiddling and everything associated with it should be banned, others continue to participate in and patronize fiddle performances. Such dynamics are not uncommon in other global cultures, even as the reasons for the disparity between musicians' low status and the vital roles they play may differ (see Merriam 1982a, 1982b; Conrad and Frank 1995b; chapters 2 and 4).

Recruitment and Training

In Hausaland, a person does not have to be born into a goge family (i.e., be "ascribed" to the profession) to become a fiddler.[46] Any individual who wants to perform goge may enter (i.e., "achieve") the profession. Although females sometimes play the goge and are invited to perform at the emir's palace, the profession is dominated by males (Hassan 2003). Women are more known for performing the kukuma because some listeners prefer their playing, but men also play the instrument (Ames and King 1971).[47]

Most fiddlers in Hausaland are Muslims, despite the fact that Islam wants nothing to do with fiddling. Mohammadan explains: "Goge musicians do not connect religion and work. It [the goge profession] is a business; it is what you do at work" (Mohammadan 1974). Mohammadan's statement confirms what most researchers have learned. Individuals become goge musicians for economic reasons. When David Ames surveyed some Hausa in Zaria about reasons for being a musician, the greatest number of respondents identified the need to earn a living. Pleasure and prestige came in a poor second and third (Ames 1973a:257–259). In another publication, Ames reports that "most informants indicated that they would not play for their own pleasure if they shifted to another occupation, and some asked, 'what would be the use of it?'" (Ames 1973b:152).

Although ascription and kinship do not determine who becomes a fiddler in Hausaland, some goge musicians do enter the profession because their family members play the instrument.[48] Several performers I interviewed (i.e., Balan Na Bassa, Mamman Landi, and Garba Liyo) learned to play at a young age from kin. Yet those who learned from relatives did not expect their children to become fiddlers. In most instances, fiddlers encourage their children to attend a Qur'anic or Western school that leaves little time for fiddling (Landi 2003; Liyo 2003).[49] Others do not become fiddlers because family members believe doing so would bring them harm. Sandra Bornand, who found such a situation in northwest Nigeria, explains: "Sanaye Oumarou, a Hausa originating from the village of Koko, in the region of Birni Kebbi, in Nigeria, was a goge-player himself, but he did not want his son [Harouna] to play the instrument for fear that other musicians, his rivals, might put a curse on the boy. In the past, competition was fierce" (1999:12). Although his father did not want him to become a fiddler, Harouna was determined to learn fiddling because he believed the spirits called him to do so. To satisfy his father, however, he delayed learning the fiddle until after his father died. When he started training, he had to learn on his own, playing with friends who recalled how his father performed. After studying with an established fiddler, Harouna's performance improved to such a degree that he became a "renowned musician" in his home and surrounding areas (Bornand 1999:13).[50]

Because fiddlers who achieve the profession are eager to be known as celebrities, they carefully select the person from whom they will receive training, for along with acquiring basic fiddling skills, they must be concerned about their future as professionals. Fiddlers who study with non-kinsmen normally start their training in their teens or twenties. Two fiddlers I interviewed fit the profile of those who achieved. Momman Nabarau, who was forty-nine years old when I interviewed him in 1974, started playing the goge when he was about nineteen, and studied with a non-kinsman who was an established goge performer. After becoming a professional fiddler (playing primarily in beer bars), Nabarau taught his younger brother how to fiddle. However, none of Nabarau's children learned to perform the instrument (Nabarau 1974). Bori musician Mohammadan indicates that his experience was slightly different: "My father taught me how to play garaya [when I was a young child]. But the time came that I found I enjoyed goge and felt that people liked goge more than garaya. So I went to learn goge [between the ages of twenty and twenty-five] from Chautan Baya of Mina."[51]

While their social status may be low, most fiddlers are financially well off because, in addition to receiving gifts from performances, they participate in farming, trading, and other occupations. Although profitable, fiddling is highly competitive. Not only must fiddlers appeal to different age groups, patrons expect them to continuously create new material. Thus, attaining success is not easy, and training varies widely depending upon which type of music a fiddler wishes to perform and which type patrons wish to support. Some believe that training to become a Bori performer is more demanding than other specializations because fiddlers must learn both the Bori ritual and the possession songs for all spirits. Fortunately, the repertoire of songs for spirits rarely changes (Besmer 1983; Bassa 2003). Bori specialists also do not feel inferior about their lack of inventiveness when they are compared with fiddlers who regularly create new songs. While new compositions in Bori music are avoided, great value is placed on embellishment and improvisation. Song texts and melodies are subject to recomposition, allowing performers to incorporate their own distinctive features into the music (Besmer 1983:42, 58). The training to become a successful performer of recreation music is so varied that any creative and ambitious individual can develop a new and interesting performance style that attracts clients. Musicians can also easily cross over from another specialization to recreation music, for the material and skills already learned can be adapted to new performance contexts. Knowing the different songs popular with the public is the only major concern of those who focus on recreation (Bande 1974).

Once goge performers have obtained sufficient training, most form their own ensembles. The length of time from initial instruction to the formation of a group varies. Some musicians play for more than thirty years and never acquire the necessary skills to become a person of great talent, while others who have studied for only six to eight years are able to become successful. After students become professionals, they are expected to avoid competition with their former master, seeking engagements in parts of the town in which the master does not play or waiting until he sends prospective clients to them (Besmer 1983:43).

In recent years, few young people have chosen fiddling as a occupation not only because they believe the goge is a difficult instrument to learn but also because of the length of time it takes to become an established musician (Bassa 2003). Several fiddlers noted that other musical styles and instrumental types have become more prominent. Bassa states, "As far as I'm concerned, what is at the root of [the decline of fiddling] is that many of the goge musicians have died, and some of them are too old. Some [fiddlers] lack others to support them in the performance of their art" (2003).

Ensemble Organization and Performance Style

Similar to the Fulbe in Senegambia, the size and type of instruments included in Hausa fiddle orchestras vary and have changed over the years. Prior to the 1950s, most fiddlers in cities such as Kano and Jos performed only the fiddle without any instrumental accompaniment except for perhaps the k'warya. By the late 1950s, dancers had been added because of their popularity among patrons who attended performances for political parties. Musicians and nonmusicians indicate that the use of drums did not become common until the early 1960s (Ingawa 1973; Bassa 2003; Hassan 2003; Mayani 2003; Yalwa 2003a). Bassa, whose family members were involved in fiddling during the nineteenth century, explains: "Initially, when I started, we used to play only goge. Then gradually as I kept playing, I began to add the k'warya. Then later on I had dancers. I used to go to places like Kano, Lagos, Kaduna, and people would appreciate me. I have traveled to almost all parts of Nigeria, and each time I go around with my dancers" (Bassa 2003). By the mid-1960s, most goge ensembles in Kano were composed of several instruments: one or more goge, two k'warya, one kuntuku, one or more kalangu and 'dan kar'bi, two or more chorus members (masu amshi), and two or more praise singers (marok'a).[52] Female and male dancers (three to four of each) also occasionally performed with the group.

Regional variations may also account for differences in the organization of fiddle ensembles. Evidence from the early nineteenth century indicates that in the northwestern part of the area now known as Nigeria (south of Sokoto), fiddles were included in ensembles with drums, wind, and other string instruments (Lander 1967:160–161).[53] During the 1930s, Harris writes that a fiddler in the Sokoto Province was usually accompanied by at least one *chekki* (gourd rattle), and the largest orchestra consisted of nine instruments: two large fiddles, four gourd rattles, two inverted calabashes beaten with thin sticks, and one kalangu drum (Harris 1932:123). While conducting research in Kano in 1974, an officer in the Ministry of Information in Kano City provided me with audio recordings of goge music from several parts of Nigeria with ensembles that included not only fiddles, drums, and calabash beaters, but also wind instruments.

Performance context also affects the size of ensembles. When fiddlers know the patrons' expectations as well as the amount and type of payment they will receive from an event, they make adjustments in the organization of their group. For example, if spirit possession is expected, fiddlers invite individuals who they know will fall into trance. Because drums help to stimulate dancing, fiddlers used drummers with choreographed dancing at political rallies and nightclubs.

The spatial arrangement of members of a fiddle ensemble during a performance is based on rank. With the goge player in the leadership position, the accompanying rattle or gourd players are divided into principal and secondary members. The principal member of the chorus, a buta or k'warya player, sits closest to the fiddler, while other members place themselves in descending order of rank, down to the group's most junior member, who sits to the fiddler's extreme left or right. When the ensemble uses a vocalist who does not play an instrument, he sits near the fiddler if he is especially proficient and near the lowest-ranked chorus member if he is undistinguished. His proximity to the fiddler therefore represents his social position in the group. Praise singers and shouters wander about outside the group of seated musicians and hold the ensemble's lowest positions (Besmer 1983:37).

The role and behavior of musicians in performance affect the group's sound as well as what they play. As musical conductor, the fiddler introduces themes and phrases on the goge while the vocal chorus responds by singing the same material with minor changes. Harris observed in 1932 that when two or more fiddles played together, they were invariably tuned by the senior player. "This does not mean that they are tuned to a common known note, but that they are all tuned to the note of the tuner's instrument" (Harris 1932:122–123). Goge musicians do not dance and rarely sing while playing (except when chorus members make mistakes or do not understand the fiddle part) because they believe that performing the fiddle so that it "talks" demonstrates greater talent and skill. Bassa explains:

> For the fiddler to think up words and play it with the fiddle like you're speaking, and for the k'warya players and the chorus singers to understand what the fiddler is playing and then sing it out, it's more difficult than [the fiddler] playing and singing at the same time. It invites more people's attention and makes you [the fiddler]

greater. People tend to wonder how is it that you play the fiddle and others [can] understand what you mean. It is not an innovation. It's been happening a long time. (Bassa 2003)

Bassa also indicates that in earlier times only a few performers played the fiddle and sang at the same time: "Even in the days of my grandfather, there were some goge musicians that play their goge and at the same time sing. They didn't have a chorus, only k'warya. I can remember just three persons during all my days of playing. But they are dead now. So this goes to show you how few there were, if at all" (Bassa 2003).

The role of percussionists in goge ensembles corresponds to their role in Fulbe and Dagbamba fiddle groups. In addition to playing a rhythmic timeline (a repetitive pattern) that accompanies and helps define the melodic cycle, they establish the tempo and sing the chorus (especially when a vocal chorus is not included in the group). Seated on the ground with legs spread apart and slightly arched, the calabash rests between their legs with their feet resting lightly against its sides. Since the arches of their soles rest against the gourd, k'warya players often tap the sides of the gourd to place emphasis on accented beats of the rhythm. Although kalangu and 'dan kar'bi (hourglass pressure drum) players do not perform the rhythmic timeline, their cyclic patterns, which are derived from the k'warya's part, enrich the texture and provide rhythmic density (DjeDje 1984a:94).

The masu amshi (vocal chorus) interpret or translate into words what the fiddler performs on the instrument by either supplying the refrain as a stanza marker or extending and completing the solo section before stating the refrain (Ames and King 1971:132). The call and response that takes place between fiddler and chorus necessitates that performers coordinate their utterances, either through nonmusical gestures (nod of the head, movement of the eye, arm, etc.) or a clue or hint in the melody. When I interviewed Usman Garba (a calabash player who played with Balan Na Bassa[54]) about the interplay between the fiddler and chorus members in performance, he explained, "We don't have prior knowledge of what the fiddler is going to say [play]. When we're performing, we tend to know the individual that he knows. He will just play the song or hit his fiddle. In view of the fact that we're familiar with the sound of the fiddle, we will be able to tell if it is a song or whether it's somebody name he's calling on the fiddle. So we will be able to voice it out" (U. Garba 2003). A chorus's lead singer performs several functions. Not only does he shout praises of encouragement to the goge player and indicate when the chorus should begin and end, but, in the absence of the marok'a, he sings praises to patrons who may or may not be present at the event. Thus, in performances, the lead singer has a more intimate relationship with the fiddler than with other members of the group.

The marok'a (praise shouters) serve as links between the audience and the orchestra. During a performance, the marok'a move about on stage or in the audience shouting praises to individuals. If an important person arrives or is already present, a marok'i publicly introduces him to the audience and orchestra by shouting acclamations in the person's honor. In recognition of this act, the individual gives the praise singer a gift of money for the fiddler. The marok'i then cries out to the audience and orchestra, and the music stops. The marok'i announces the name of the donor of the gift and the amount given, mentioning also the additional small "tip" that the donor may have personally given him. Afterwards, the goge player creates a song and performs it in honor of the donor. If the donor is a patron, the fiddler performs the patron's praise song. The marok'a add or detract from the performance depending on their ability. They are important to the goge player because a witty marok'i is able to encourage the audience to give generously. Because of the marok'i's personal contact with the audience, he is also able to gauge the general ambiance and mood of the listeners and advise the goge player on which songs to perform.

Fiddlers I interviewed indicate that the mode of presenting goge music has changed. Emphasis during the early years (when fiddlers played primarily for Bori or were itinerant performers who made a living singing praises to individuals at markets and other public gatherings) was on developing the music and song texts rather than presenting a visual spectacle with professional dancers. Most fiddlers believe that changes began to occur during the 1950s and 1960s with the rise in political parties and expanding audiences. While more well-to-do goge musicians introduced dramatic innovations (e.g., including professional dancers and different instruments in their ensembles), other fiddlers made only modest changes by either creating new songs or focusing on one aspect of the tradition: Bori, topical songs, or nightclub entertainment. Mamman Landi (1974) and Ahmadu Samunaka (1974) state that they did not add dancers to their ensembles until the 1960s when other performers had incorporated them, and goge performances became more commercial and competitive.[55]

Dance

Different types of dances have been created to accompany fiddle performances. Expert fiddlers have an endless repertoire of dance rhythms, but because of fads, they play only a limited number during any given year. The urban young are leaders in innovation, with their rural counterparts lagging and playing older rhythms. Several dance styles were popular during the 1960s and 1970s: *tuwis, rawan kashewa* or *rawan banjo, soja* (soldier), and Bori. The tuwis is a Hausa variation of the twist, an African-American dance borrowed from the cinema.[56] Performed by professional dancers, the tuwis was sometimes included as an adjunct to a choreographed routine. Couples (male and female) paired off to do the tuwis in free form. The basic movements consisted of twisting or moving the entire lower portion of the body back and forth (shoulder and hips moving in opposite directions). When the arms, held slightly away from the body, and shoulders were twisted toward the left, the hips, thighs, legs, and feet were twisted toward the right. Normally dancers stood on the ball of their feet with knees slightly dropped. Because this was a free style of dancing, dancers did as they wished by adding more intricate movements to the basic steps, such as doing splits, jumping, sliding across the dance floor, or moving up and down while standing in place and twisting the body (Ames 1973b:150).

Believed to have originated in the city of Jos in the 1950s by several youthful traders who danced to goge music for pleasure (Ames 1982:134), rawan kashewa or rawan banjo became popular with the growth of modern political parties in northern Nigeria during the 1960s.[57] Most large cities in Hausaland had professional dance teams hired by political parties. Composed of young men and women, the teams traveled around the country and competed with one another, performing in outdoor courtyards of hotels. Although admission was charged to view the competitions, the same dance was also done in combination with other forms of entertainment at pre-election campaign meetings (*wasan* NPC or NEPU). A dance team consisted of separate lines of female and male youth (identically costumed in Western dress) who danced a series of intricate steps in unison. Occasionally male and female dancers paired off to dance the tuwis. Soja, the least known of all the dances, is also of local derivation and reflects some of the modern ideas and changing attitudes developing in Nigeria during the 1970s (Ames 1973b:150; Ames and King 1971:124).

Bori dance is a dance drama enacted by dancers (trancers) and musicians and is not a simple formation of organized or free movements. When fiddlers play special melodies and rhythms for the iskoki (spirits), the trancers perform prescribed bodily movements associated with the spirits. Dramatic movements by the dancer and melodic and rhythmic phrases played by the musicians must relate to each other. Thus, communication between both groups is essential. On occasion a fiddler can regain control over the arrival and departure of spirits by changing the melody or selecting a new tune for a different spirit.

Songs and Composition

As I have stated elsewhere, one can learn much about a people by examining the lyrics and meanings of the songs they produce because the themes and symbols used in song texts often deal with issues that reflect deeper concerns not articulated in other settings. The songs performed by Hausa fiddlers included in this study fall into several categories: entertainment (*wak'ar nasha'di*), possession (*wak'ar bori*), praise (*wak'ar yabo*), and politics (*wak'ar siyasa*). Although the entertainment category encompasses all songs used for recreation, two types were used by fiddlers I interviewed: (1) topical or social comment and (2) dance. Topical songs are used to satirize, ridicule, or censure individuals, and dance songs accompany dances such as banjo or tuwis. Possession songs are performed in praise of iskoki either as part of entertainment or to invoke the possession of male (*'dan Bori*) or female (*'yar Bori*) dancers. Most songs played by fiddlers can be regarded as praise, which is similar to the music in the entertainment category. Although the subjects may vary, everyone is praised: traditional rulers (emirs and their officials), important commoners (wealthy merchants, owners of transport companies), and lesser-known individuals (members of different socio-occupational groups). By an extension of the meaning, wak'ar siyasa includes any song in praise of a governmental authority other than those of the traditional emirate. Before the January 1966 military coup, political songs were popular because of their use as propaganda for political parties (Ames and King 1971).

The creation of new songs, an important aspect of the goge tradition, can be the result of inspiration from the audience, specific patrons, or members of the community. Thus, the fiddler's role is similar to that of the oral singer. In addition to entertaining and informing the community about current events and ancient historical accounts, he instructs new generations about traditions, custom, history, folklore, and the culture of their ancestors. Depending on the situation and circumstance, he can also praise, warn, condemn, or advise (Abdulkadir 1975:37). During the 1960s and 1970s, not only did musicians compose topical songs concerned with national unity and moral issues, but also protest and social comment songs that dealt with local, national, and world problems (Landi 1974).

Although metaphors, similes, allusions, innuendoes, satire, and other figurative forms of speech are commonly used in Hausa oral tradition and performed by many oral singers (Abdulkadir 1975:36), the song texts I collected are straightforward and do not contain extensive word imagery or philosophical aphorisms. Singers who accompany goge performers employ a language readily understood by their patrons. Even when proverbs, such as those found in Haruna Bande's performance of "Ki'dan Banjo," appear, they tend not to be embedded in ancient terms, phrases, or formulae understood by a few. In the following song texts, for example, listeners would readily comprehend the figurative language used.

a. Shoot of the deleb,[58] you didn't come out until you were ready. (Performed in praise of Staff Sergeant Mamman Gusau, this means that the Sergeant is a man of his own will; he is well off.)

b. The name of God, the remedy of fetish (God is the ruler of all.)

In general, only the specific praise names for individuals and/or spirits used in goge lyrics risk being unfamiliar to audiences.

Goge song texts also provide evidence of contact with Western and Arab cultures in addition. In the songs "Ki'dan Banjo" and "Jabula" by Bande, for example, *Sataf Saje* refers to Staff Sergeant; *Samanja* indicates "sergeant major"; and *soja* refers to "soldier". In the Hausa language, *Jabula* is the name for James Brown, and *shime* means "show me," something that James Brown might say while performing. Referring to Allah as the Being who can solve all problems is common in fiddle music. The phrase *Idan kana nema nemi ga Allah* (If you are searching, want, want from Allah) is repeated several times in "Ki'dan Barahaza," a song performed by Bande. In "Wakakai," the singer accompanying

Landi's fiddling states, *Ya Allah kai mana arziki* (Oh, Allah make us wealthy). The song, "Ki'dan Kanawa," includes the statement *Sarki Allah, Allah gyara mana Kano State* (Allah, repair Kano State for us).

Some lyrics reveal why many Muslims in Hausaland have such negative views of Bori practitioners. The inclusion of both Allah *and* the names of Bori spirits in goge song texts not only demonstrates the influence of Islam in Bori but also that aspects of the pre-Islamic religion have not been abandoned (Danfulani 1999:434) and that Allah is not omnipotent in the lives of Bori initiates. For example, the statement *Allah ne ya baka, aljana ta baka* (God gave you, the jinn gave you) in Bande's performance of "Ki'dan Barahaza" implies that both Allah and *aljana* (the Hausa term for spirit used here in reference to Barahaza) can give or take away good fortune (money, clothes, luck, life, or a profession). Salihu Ingawa states that some Bori initiates believe that spirits serve as a mediator between God and man (Ingawa 1974).

Song texts also demonstrate that class distinctions continue to be important in Hausa society. Not only is religion used for differentiation, but a person's occupation and access to income affect social status. Because most Hausa believe profession, a gift from God, determines status, a person's occupation is often cited. In Bande's performance of "Ki'dan Barahaza," the names and professions of two of his patrons (Yakubu and Juma) are mentioned:

a. Yakubu, owner of the grinding machine, Yakubu of Ladi.
b. Call Juma, the mechanic. . . .

Nation building and nationalism, important issues for Nigerians when the country became an independent republic in 1960, were popular themes of songs created in the 1960s and 1970s. In several of Landi's performances, he implores people to do something positive for the well-being of the community. Similar to Senegambian Fulbe fiddler Juldeh Camara, the singer in Landi's "Maginin Zaman Banza" warns Nigerian youth not to be idle. To stimulate them to action, the singer advises, gently insults, and counsels the youth about their behavior (see Song Text 3.1).

Song Text 3.1. Mamman Landi. Excerpt from "Maginin Zaman Banza." Kano, Nigeria. February 22, 1974.
TRANSLATED INTO ENGLISH BY SALIHU Y. INGAWA.

Youth of the world, stop sleeping.
Youth of the world, let's wake up and stop sleeping.
For if the world gets loose, we will regret it.
Youth of the world, let's wake up and stop sleeping.
Sleeping doesn't pay; we better take [action].
The time has all changed, idle stay has ceased.
We must farm, pray, and go back to school. . . .

The song text for "Alhaji Balan Gwaggo, Sarkin Shanu," by Garba Liyo is different from the lyrics of other fiddlers (see Song Text 3.2).[59] Not only does it include several proverbs, but allusions are also made to animals (e.g., cattle and elephants). Since references to animals rarely appear in goge songs (see DjeDje 1978b), the use of such lyrics by Liyo alludes to the personality traits of the person being praised (an owner of cattle) rather than implying an aspect of Liyo's performance style.[60]

Song Text 3.2. Garba Liyo. Excerpt from "Alhaji Balan Gwaggo, Sarkin Shanu." Folkways FW 8860. Recorded April 11, 1976. Radio-Television Kaduna Studios.

TRANSLATED INTO ENGLISH BY RUSSELL SCHUH AND LAWAN DANLADI YALWA.

Tethering post of the land, binder of elephants,
Tethering post of the land, binder of elephants,
Trees are the food of an elephant.
If it refuses to eat, it will spend the night hungry,
Gyara, Alhaji the chief of cattle.
Oh Lord, God, leave us the chief of cattle.
Oh Lord, God, leave us the chief of cattle.

Since songs performed at different occasions cover a variety of themes, fiddlers must be attuned to how their audiences will respond to messages in texts. Mohammadan states that he knows the audience finds his performance pleasing when they sit, listen attentively, and give gifts.

Form and Stylistic Features of Songs

Of the three fiddle traditions considered in this study, Hausa fiddling is the most complex structurally. Most goge music has multiple themes (as many as six or seven) with one or more interludes. In spite of the complexity, however, goge music is similar to fiddling by other West Africans, especially in its division into three sections: a short opening introduces themes and other material, a long middle section establishes and develops themes, and a short closing further develops melodies and rhythms.

In the opening, the one or more themes introduced by the fiddler are generally performed unaccompanied in a highly embellished style, including grace notes, neighboring and passing tones, anticipatory tones, repeated tones, and glissandi. In some cases, fiddlers do not present complete themes but perform short melodic phrases (unrelated to themes), which are developed in the improvisatory interludes and closing. The tempo of the opening is slower and freer than music played in the middle and closing. When the percussion enters (either during the latter part of the opening or beginning of the middle section), the rhythm becomes stricter and the fiddler plays *a tempo*. The middle section not only includes the presentation and development of all themes, but call and response between the fiddler and vocal chorus and improvisatory interludes by the fiddler also take place (while the marok'i shouts praises in honor of patrons and members of the group). Normally, the vocal chorus performs the response without fiddle accompaniment. A goge performer, however, may use the fiddle accompaniment to aid chorus members in remembering their parts, to further develop fiddle material, or to cue musicians that he plans to enter another section of the piece. The closing is improvisatory and performed in a fast tempo with much intensity; the fiddler either restates material presented in the middle section or develops phrases introduced in the opening and interludes.

To some degree, Hausa fiddlers also conceptualize the structure of their songs into sections. Before one of Haruna Bande's interludes in "Ki'dan Banjo," the *marok'i* states:

> I wish you a peaceful journey to and from Haru, the beloved of Dije.
> (twice)
> I wish you a happy journey, that of Umma, Agadasawa Kano State.
> (DjeDje 1978b:819–820)

Ingawa suggests that "journey" refers to Bande beginning his improvisatory interlude. To mark this transition, the marok'i interjects a note of encouragement by telling Bande to have both a "peaceful journey to and from" and a "happy journey."

Hausa musicians place great emphasis on the fiddle and the sounds produced on it, which accounts for several features that make Hausa fiddling distinctive: (1) using the fiddle (instead of the voice) to perform the call, (2) playing long fiddle themes with lots of embellishments, and (3) incorporating extensive improvisation throughout the piece. Because a goge musician's talent is determined by how well he can make the fiddle "talk," rarely do Hausa fiddlers sing. The fiddle's "talking" also affects the varying lengths and complexity of goge themes. Most fiddle themes are based on a duple or triple eight-, twelve-, or twenty-four-beat pattern, but one of the themes in "Ki'dan Barahaza" by Haruna Bande is ninety-six quarter-note beats in length, which means that Bande's theme extends over eight twelve-beat melodic cycles because his goge melody is based on a twelve-beat pattern (see theme C—measures 30–37 for fiddle part and measures 38–45 for chorus part—in the transcription for "Ki'dan Barahaza" in DjeDje 1978b:859–864).

However, fiddlers organize their themes differently when emulating the music of other cultures. When Bande, for example, integrates elements from African-American popular music into his performance of "Jabula," not only is the length of the melodies shorter (eight beats), but a more percussive performance style is also used (DjeDje 1978b).

Similar to the Fulbe, the Hausa use improvisation to demonstrate virtuosity. Melodic and rhythmic motives in improvisations are also used as markers or cues either to unify the piece or let members of the group know what they are planning to do. When fiddlers want to begin or end an improvisatory section or bring the song to a close, they often give musical cues to indicate this.

Like Fulbe and Dagbamba traditions, the percussion section of Hausa fiddle ensembles is based on a cyclic rhythm with a time span that relates to the length of goge themes. Although twelve- and twenty-four-beat patterns are most prominent, the length of time spans varies. For example, in Bande's performance of "Ki'dan Banjo," "Ki'dan Barahaza," and "Jabula," a twelve-, twenty-four-, and eight-beat time span are used, respectively. Landi uses an eight-beat pattern for "Wakakai," but a twelve-beat cycle is employed in "Ki'dan Kanawa" (DjeDje 1978b).

Most goge music is played within a range of two octaves (even though the ambitus for a goge extends to almost four octaves), but the choral part accompanying Hausa fiddling is usually sung within one octave (see DjeDje 1978b). Like other fiddle traditions in Africa, goge performers use an anhemitonic pentatonic scale. Since Hausa fiddle music is generally accompanied by percussion, the texture is always polyphony. Occasionally, incidental harmony (or homophonic parallelism)[61] can be heard in vocal parts.

Hausa fiddlers do not use a distinct performance style for specific occasions or music events (DjeDje 1984b), although there are some exceptions (see DjeDje 1978b). In other words, what a goge musician plays at a wedding would be acceptable at a beer bar, just as the mode of presentation at a Bori ceremony could be used at a festival. The only distinguishing feature is the type of songs used. At a nightclub or beer bar, the fiddler performs praise songs for individual patrons, whereas at a Bori ceremony songs in honor of the different spirits are emphasized (DjeDje 1984b). Yet using aspects of Bori at nightclubs, beer bars, houses of prostitution, or naming and wedding ceremonies is not uncommon when the audience prefers (see foregoing description of Garba Liyo's nightclub performance).

To demonstrate how these general characteristics are employed, the music of three Hausa fiddlers (Haruna Bande, Mamman Landi, and Garba Liyo) is analyzed with attention given to form, melody, and rhythm.[62] The personal backgrounds and specializations of the fiddlers are also presented to determine not only if, but how, sociocultural factors affect performance style.

Music and Identity: Profiles of Three Hausa Fiddlers

Haruna Bande (late 1930s–late 1990s)

Haruna Bande was born in Damagarau, Niger.[63] At the age of twenty-seven, he began his fiddle training with an established goge specialist (a non-kinsman). After serving as an apprentice with this person for a short time, Bande formed his own group, which in 1974 had been together for eight years. Most of his performances took place at beer bars and Bori ceremonies. Bande was not born into a family that specialized in goge, nor did he expect his children to become fiddlers.

Photo 3.1. Haruna Bande holding the *goge*. Photograph by Jacqueline Cogdell DjeDje. February 1974.

Bande's performance was recorded on February 11 and 12, 1974.[64] The group, called Haruna Yaron Goge, included five persons: Haruna Bande (goge), Garba Sokuato (marok'i), Shehu Babayo (marok'i), Bala Rano (k'warya), and Ali Sankara (k'warya). On the first day, Bande performed two songs—"Ki'dan Banjo" (8:17) and "Ki'dan Barahaza" (7:02)—with his entire group. On the second day, he continued the recording session by performing four songs—"Sarkin Rafi" (1:05), "Gagara Sarki" (2:05), "Jabula" (4:53), and "Wanzami" (7:35)—with himself on goge accompanied by one marok'i. The songs fall into several categories: entertainment or recreation ("Ki'dan Banjo" and "Jabula"), possession ("Ki'dan Barahaza," "Sarkin Rafi," and "Wanzami"), and praise ("Gagara Sarki").

Haruna Bande was the youngest and least experienced of the fiddlers chosen for analysis. While his performance technique was not as developed as that of Mamman Landi or Garba Liyo (e.g., his use of ornaments and the range of pitches used for fiddle melodies and improvisations were less developed), the type of songs he performed was more varied. The way in which Bande performs songs from different categories is also unique. For example, his performance of recreation music is simpler than the possession song. To understand the performance characteristics of Bande's fiddle playing, I decided to analyze "Ki'dan Barahaza," a well-known Bori song in the repertoire of Hausa fiddlers.

"Ki'dan Barahaza" is organized into three sections: opening (:17), middle (6:26), and closing (:19). The call and response in the middle section is based on four themes that are melodically similar. While the beginning of each theme is slightly different, the endings, except for one, are based on the same one-octave descending phrase. The most distinctive feature of each theme is the length. Using the quarter note as the unit of measurement for beats, theme A is composed of roughly sixteen beats; theme B, twenty-one to twenty-four beats; theme C, ninety-six beats; and theme D, twenty-four beats (see Example 3.1).[65]

Because the calls in "Ki'dan Barahaza" are highly ornamented, the vocal chorus does not repeat exactly what Bande performs on the fiddle (see DjeDje 1984a). Whereas the goge part is more involved, including quarter, dotted eighth, and sixteenth notes, the chorus response is rhythmically simpler with notes longer in length (half, whole, and some quarter and eighth notes); see Example 3.2.

The improvisatory sections in "Ki'dan Barahaza" are distinct from other songs by Bande. The material presented in the opening has nothing to do with the rest of the song and is never heard again, but the themes presented in the middle section are central to the improvisations. While theme B is emphasized in interludes I, II, and IV, theme A serves as the basis for improvisation in interlude III. In the closing, not only does Bande improvise on all themes, he also introduces new material. The song ends with the k'warya performing the first half of the rhythmic cycle accompanied by the marok'i who shouts the phrase *Hakane da kayu. Haruna Yaron Goge. To!* (That is good, Haruna, servant of Goge!).

Since Bande does not sing while fiddling, the marok'i plays a major role in shouting praises when Bande performs either a call or an interlude. The first statement by the marok'i occurs during the performance of theme C when he encourages Bande by shouting *Dai dai ne Harun Yaron Goge* (Correct Haruna, servant of goge) and then comments on the importance of having a profession: *Sana'a sa'a rashin sana'a rashin sa'a* (Profession is life; without a profession there is no luck). At the moment Bande plays a melody that references the patron, the marok'i calls out the patron's name, Yakubu of Ladi, and states that the patron is the "possessor of Barahaza." Then the chorus sings its response that consists of statements in praise of Yakubu of Ladi. During the long interludes, the marok'i's statements are more extensive, for then he has time to praise several persons and recite proverbs.

Although fiddle melodies in "Ki'dan Barahaza" are based on additive rhythms (durational values of notes extending beyond the regular division of the time span),[66] the rhythmic patterns of the calabash beaters are divisive (accented pulses articulated during regular divisions of the time span). The k'warya's rhythmic timeline in "Ki'dan Barahaza" is based on a twenty-four-beat pattern, encompassing two twelve-beat timelines or six groups of four (see Example 3.3). The first beat of each group (see underlining for beats 1, 5, 9, 13, 17, and 21 in Example 3.3) is generally played to emphasize the pulse, although rests may appear on other beats in the cycle. Not only does the rhythmic timeline reinforce the melodic statements, which are all based on twenty-four beats, the rhythmic pattern also aids choral members in their point of entry. So there is no confusion about the beginning or ending of each theme.

Example 3.1. Haruna Bande. "Ki'dan Barahaza." Themes A, B, C, and D.

Example 3.2. Haruna Bande. "Ki'dan Barahaza." Theme B fiddle statement and choral response.

Example 3.3. Haruna Bande. "Ki'dan Barahaza." Rhythmic pattern used by *k'warya*.

The role of performers in any ensemble naturally affects their music. For example, the simple, almost skeletal nature of the rhythmic pattern performed by the k'warya when the chorus sings in "Ki'dan Barahaza" (see k'warya part for Example 3.2) is probably due to what the percussionists are doing at that moment. When the k'warya performers sing, they stop playing the calabash. Not only does this allow the choral part to be heard more clearly, but it gives the percussionists the opportunity to think of the words they need to sing.

Several elements serve as markers to unify "Ki'dan Barahaza": (a) the five-pitch descending melody performed at the end of most themes (Example 3.4) and (b) the last four beats of the twenty-four-beat rhythmic pattern performed by the k'warya. Although the time value for pitches in Example 3.4 may vary or there may be extensive ornamentation (see measures 19 and 21 of Example 3.2 and themes B and D of Example 3.1), the phrase (the descending melody of an octave) is always played melodically the same way. Even the final statement that Bande performs at the end of the song is based on a modification of the phrase (see measures 158–159 in DjeDje 1978b:902). The rest in the last four beats that ends the twenty-four-beat pattern (see beats 21–24 in the last measure of themes A, B, C, and D of Examples 3.1) is important because this lets everyone

♩=126

Example 3.4. Haruna Bande. "Ki'dan Barahaza." Five-pitch melody at end of themes.

in the group know where they are in the cycle. In many ways, the descending melodic phrase as well as the last four beats link because they both serve as cadences.

In comparison to Bande's other songs and the music performed by other Hausa fiddlers, "Jabula" is by far the simplest. In fact, the melody and rhythm of the song in honor of James Brown are so simple that they appear out of character for goge music. Not only is the fiddle melody performed in a limited pitch range, the rhythm is based on a very strict duple meter and the musical utterances by the marok'i are unusual for a goge chorus. With the fiddle repeating many short melodic phrases and rhythmic patterns (which he produces with motives that are performed on strong beats) and the marok'i shouting stock phrases in English (e.g., "Come on baby") and Hausa (*Cido, Dai dai, Shime, Anko*), Bande performs what he believes are the salient features of African-American popular music (see the song text for "Jabula" in DjeDje 1978b). Or one could say these are features that most impressed Bande about the music of James Brown.

More research needs to be done to determine if there is actually a close relationship between song type and performance style in Hausa fiddling. Yet when comparing "Ki'dan Barahaza" (a spirit possession song) with Bande's performances of entertainment songs, certain differences become apparent. In my opinion, the melodic and rhythmic organization of "Ki'dan Barahaza" is the more complex: the majority of melodies are longer and encompass a wider pitch range; the k'warya's rhythmic timeline is based on groups of four quarter notes and extends to twenty-four beats; and multipart organization (homophonic parallelism) is evident in the vocal parts. Because fiddlers judge a goge musician's performance skills by his competence in playing spirit possession songs (Bassa 2003), this is significant. All factors lend weight to the hypothesis that within the limits of a given individual's performance style, certain differences become apparent when the same individual performs different song types.

Mamman Landi (mid-1930s–1999)

A native of Panshekara (a town on the outskirts of Kano City), Mamman Landi began his fiddle training at the age of fifteen. Unlike many fiddlers in the Kano area, he inherited the profession from his father, who also taught him how to play. When I interviewed him in 1974, he was thirty-five years old and had

Photo 3.2. Mamman Landi holding the *goge*. Photograph by Jacqueline Cogdell DjeDje. February 1974.

been fiddling for about twenty years. His uncle, who lived in Zaria, also played the fiddle. Although fiddling was a family profession, Landi had not encouraged his own children to learn to play the instrument.

During the 1970s not only was Landi known for his performances at naming and wedding ceremonies, he had achieved fame as an ambassador of goodwill for performing songs with patriotic themes on the government, education, and the attitudes and moods of the Nigerian populace and its youth. Landi believed that the young "must not totally forget about the good of the past just to accept the ways of the 'new society' " (Landi 1974). In addition to frequent appearances at government-sponsored arts festivals, he was one of the few musicians from northern Nigeria and the only goge player chosen to represent Nigeria on tour in Europe in the early 1970s. His notoriety was responsible for him becoming a member of the Northern Nigerian Musical Troupe that played at FESTAC, an international festival held in Lagos in 1977.[67]

My recording session with Mamman Landi took place on February 26, 1974. For his performance, he brought only one percussionist to accompany him.[68] Landi performed four songs: "Wakakai" (3:59), a welcome song to the people of Kano; "Ki'dan Kanawa" (2:03), a praise song for Kano State; "Ki'dan Sarki Kano" (2:45), a praise song for the emir of Kano; and "Maganin Zaman Banza" (6:05), a warning song to the youth of Nigeria. All four songs fall into the praise category. I have chosen to focus on the first because it best represents his play-

Example 3.5. Mamman Landi. "Wakakai." Excerpt from introduction.

ing. As an established artist, his focus is on improvisation and virtuosity regardless of the type of song he performs.

"Wakakai" is, like so many fiddle songs, divided into three sections: opening (1:14), middle (2:10), and closing (:35). However, what Landi includes in each section is distinct from the music of other Hausa fiddlers in this study. During the first twenty seconds of the opening of "Wakakai," Landi performs unaccompanied, in a very free rubato style, some of the most intricately ornamented melodic phrases on the fiddle that I have ever heard (see Example 3.5). Not only are there many grace notes and sixteenth and thirty-second notes,[69] his melodies cover a wide pitch range (two octaves and a fifth).

Immediately after the rhythmically free passage, Landi continues with the opening by performing three themes on the fiddle *a tempo* that are repeated several times with no accompaniment. While playing the fiddle, Landi introduces himself by shouting:

> I am Mamman Landi Panshekara Kano.
> It is me who is going to play for Kano people as much as possible.
> Gee up, Mamman of A'i, Mamman the chief of Goge in Kano.
> Gee up, Muhamman Landi, chief of Goge in Kano.

After the fiddle melodies are performed for about thirty seconds more, the percussionist joins in the opening by playing his rhythmic ostinato.

Whereas other fiddlers generally perform a short opening (anywhere from five to twenty seconds), Landi's opening is longer. He does not start playing the middle section until he is one minute and fourteen seconds into the song. Furthermore, in the middle section, he performs themes totally unrelated to material that he performs in the opening. Like Bande, though, Landi varies the length of the themes in the middle section, probably as a way to build to a climax. Theme A consists of eight beats; theme B, sixteen; theme C, twenty-four; theme D, eight; and theme E, forty beats (see Examples 3.6A–E). In theme A, the text is reminiscent of prayer; Landi implores Allah to make the people of Kano

Example 3.6. Mamman Landi. "Wakakai." Themes A, B, C, D, and E used in chorus.
Continued on the next page

wealthy (*Ya Allah kai, mana Arziki* [Oh God! Make us wealthy]). However, by the end of the song (theme E in measures 60–64), proverbs and the names of patrons are included, making the textual statements and fiddle melodies longer and more involved.

Several features make Landi's performance of "Wakakai" distinctive. The call and response (by fiddle and chorus) is always the same length, which is not the case in his other songs (DjeDje 1978b).[70] If the "Wakakai" fiddle part is twenty-four beats in length, the chorus responds with a twenty-four-beat melody. Like other goge musicians, Landi includes more ornamentation in his performance of the call than the chorus response. He also plays a fiddle accompaniment to aid the percussion in singing the chorus. Each theme ends with a similar melodic phrase, which creates a cadential formula within the piece (com-

Example 3.6. *Continued*

pare Example 3.7 with the endings for themes [see bracketed material] in Example 3.6). Only one interlude is included. Similar to other Hausa fiddle songs, "Wakakai's" closing is short. However, a portion of the closing serves as a bridge to the next song. In other words, the closing twelve-beat melody at the end of "Wakakai" (about five seconds in length) is a connecting statement to "Ki'dan Kanawa," the next song performed. Since "Ki'dan Kanawa" is based on a twelve-beat melodic cycle, the concluding phrase of "Wakakai" is also based on a twelve-beat pattern.

The percussionist's divisive rhythmic timeline used to accompany "Wakakai" is composed of eight pulses and corresponds closely with the rhythm used for fiddle themes; quarter and eighth notes are prominent in rhythm for both parts (fiddle and percussion); see Example 3.6. To unify "Wakakai," not only does Landi use the same melodic material for his improvisations in the opening, interlude, and closing, which differ from themes in the middle section (see Example 3.6), the improvisatory sections begin and end with the same melody. In other words, the music in Example 3.8 appears at the beginning *and*

Example 3.7. Mamman Landi. "Wakakai." Melodic phrase used at end of themes.

Example 3.8. Mamman Landi. "Wakakai." Theme used in opening, interlude, and closing.

ending of (a) the *a tempo* part of the opening, (b) the interlude in the middle section, and (c) the closing (DjeDje 1978b:937–961). Thus, not only does this melody unify the song, but Landi uses it as a marker to let members of the group know what he is planning to do.

In summary, the greater emphasis on virtuosity sets Landi apart from other performers in this study. This can be seen both in the improvisatory material that he employs and in the amount of time he devotes to improvisation. Although the structure of "Wakakai" is similar to other goge songs, Landi makes the form reflect his playing style.

Garba Liyo (1933–1995)

When I interviewed Garba Liyo in 1974, he was forty-one years old. Originally from Hadejia (a large town about a hundred miles northeast of Kano City), Liyo's permanent residence was Funtua, a town about eighty miles to the southwest. Liyo began his fiddle training around the age of nine. He and his brother inherited the profession from their father who taught them how to fiddle. During the 1960s, Liyo focused on playing for activities associated with Nigeria's new federal government. When the existing political parties were banned in the mid-1960s, however, he had to change his specialization. By the 1970s, he had become a celebrated entertainer and recording artist noted for performances in nightclubs, hotels, and other established entertainment venues frequented by middle- and some upper-class Hausa. His popularity throughout Nigeria and in countries such as Niger, Chad, Benin, and Côte d'Ivoire gave him an opportunity to attract a diverse clientele of patrons.

When I observed Liyo at the two nightclubs in Kano, I made audio recordings of both performances, but the background noise at the clubs was loud, and

Photo 3.3. Garba Liyo (seated, second from right) playing the *goge* with his group. Photograph by Randall Grass. 1976. Used by permission.

the sound quality of these recordings is not clear enough to use for musical analysis. Therefore, the discussion here of Liyo's music is based on selections from a commercial recording produced by Randall Grass for Folkways Records. Grass writes in the liner notes that Liyo's performances include someone playing kalangu, "a drummer playing a small, ordinary drum" (*kuntuku*), two calabash percussionists, and six singers (Grass 1976).[71] Except for the music on side one, which is described as "instrumental improvisation of the type used for dance performances" (Grass 1976), all selections on the recording fall into the category of praise songs. For the analysis here, I shall focus on "Ali Mai Sai da Mai a Shal Bipi," the last of the five songs on side two.[72]

Of all the Hausa fiddlers considered in this study, Liyo was the most commercially successful. Perhaps this is the reason his music, in my opinion, sounds more polished or mainstream. By this, I mean that most characteristics identified with Hausa fiddling are present, but they are handled with moderation and without too much deviation from the norm. While Liyo includes some improvisatory material, his use of ornamentation is not as extensive as Landi's. Liyo also only slightly modifies the different sections (opening, middle, and closing) of his songs, suggesting that he prefers not to experiment with the form. One of the few ways he makes his music stand out is by including a variety of percussion instruments. The inclusion of a drum orchestra not only causes his music to be organized similar to the drumming traditions of both northern and southern Nigeria, this instrumentation produces a sound distinct from ensembles consisting of solely fiddle and calabash.[73]

The form of "Ali Mai Sai da Mai a Shal Bipi" (5:40) is no different from songs by Bande and Landi even though Liyo includes several instruments in the ensemble. "Ali Mai Sai" can be divided into three parts: a short opening (:46), a long middle section (4:52), and a very brief closing (:02). Similar to his improvisatory interludes, Liyo's opening is florid but not as intricately ornamented as openings played by some goge musicians. Nor is the slow, free portion of the opening extensive; the percussion accompaniment begins almost immediately (six seconds) after the fiddling. Liyo unifies the middle section by using the same descending motive, which corresponds with the text ("*d'an Sulaimaanu*"; son of Sulaiman) at the end of each of the four themes (see bracketed parts in Example 3.9). Unlike Landi, Liyo does not introduce new material in the interludes; rather, he develops music that is familiar, theme A. The closing is what makes "Ali Mai Sai" most distinct. Instead of the chorus stopping fifteen to twenty seconds before the end, the call and response between the fiddle and chorus continues almost to the very end. Right before the end, Liyo, accompanied by kuntuku and k'warya, performs a short (eight-beat) improvisation based on theme B as the volume gradually decreases. Because the closing is so different from other songs, it is most likely that studio technicians manipulated the fading.

Like other goge performances, the themes used by Liyo have different lengths. Theme A consists of twelve beats; theme B, six beats; theme C, sixteen to eighteen beats; and theme D, fifteen to twenty-one beats. Regardless of the length of melodies, however, the chorus always repeats what the fiddler performs. In a few instances, Liyo performs the fiddle along with the chorus, which may have been done either to develop the melodic material or cue the chorus that he wants to begin another section (DjeDje 1978b:495–496).

The masu amshi in Liyo's group includes one member who serves as leader. Instead of shouting praises when Liyo performs his fiddle themes and improvisations (like the marok'i does in Bande's performance), Liyo's vocal leader distinguishes himself by singing a melody at a higher pitch than other choral members. In doing so, he creates harmony in the response (see the choral part on beats 3–5 of measure 13 in Example 3.9).

The rhythmic organization of "Ali Mai Sai" is denser and more complex than other songs because of the interlocking (i.e.,when percussionists start and stop at specified points in the rhythmic timeline) and patterns played by the three parts in the percussion section: (1) k'warya, (2) kuntuku, and (3) kalangu. Similar to some songs by other performers, the rhythmic timeline is composed of twelve beats organized into four groups of three pulses:
1   2   3 | 4   5   6 | 7   8   9 | 10   11   12.

Example 3.9. Garba Liyo. "Ali Mai Sai da Mai a Shal Bipi." Themes A and B. Used by permission.

Continued on the next page

Actually, the k'warya players, who are responsible for the timeline, play a six-beat pattern that is repeated twice within the twelve-beat time span. The rhythmic cycle for the kalangu is a five-beat pattern that begins on beat 4 and ends on beat 8. The kuntuku performs a two-note pattern (an eighth note and a quarter note) throughout the performance. While the music played on the k'warya and kalangu is based on divisive rhythms, rhythms played on the kuntuku are additive.

Example 3.9. *Continued*

Liyo's performance of "Ali Mai Sai" demonstrates how percussion instruments interconnect to produce a complex, thick, layered sound. Rhythmic patterns and melo-rhythms (melodically conceived rhythmic organizations) can be distinctly heard because each instrument has a distinguishing pitch, timbre, and performance technique (Nzewi 1974:24, 1997). While the kalangu performs the highest pitches and the kuntuku the next highest, the k'warya performs the lowest pitches. Instead of beating their calabashes with sticks, k'warya players use the palms of their hands to create a bass sound that contrasts with the higher-pitched instruments. With the volume decreased considerably, the muffled calabash sound does not overshadow the performance of the other percussionists. In addition to interlocking rhythms, the time values of the patterns played by instrumentalists add to the complexity. Percussionists (as accompanists in the performance) use primarily quarter and eighth notes, while the fiddler (as the leader and primary improviser) uses eighth, sixteenth, thirty-second, and even sixty-fourth notes, giving the goge a much more elaborate and fuller sound, as Yusuf Isa described above.

Garba Liyo's music demonstrates another way in which a goge performer mixes basic characteristics to create a distinct performance style. As an artist born into the profession who decided to specialize in playing for audiences from different cultures and class levels, Liyo knows how to use fiddling to maintain a livelihood. His music excites many Nigerians because he integrates percussive instruments into his ensemble that contrast with his fiddling. Nonetheless, although he is an exceptional fiddler and his ensemble organization is innovative, in my opinion, the inventiveness apparent in the music of other fiddlers is not prominent in his Folkways performances. Perhaps the lack of innovation can be explained by incidental factors: the music was performed in a studio without an audience to provide inspiration; his desire to be accepted by Western listeners caused him to be less creative; a lifetime of experience had taught him that performing in a straightforward, polished, and professional manner is a better way to be successful than being too experimental.

4   In Service to the King: Dagbamba Fiddling in Ghana

> The *gondze* are a special clan that are second to none because you must be schooled from infancy. You just don't get up and pick it up. One is gifted from the source of the *gondze*. Because in misery or in times of need, *gondze* music can advise you on how to improve your life.
>
> —Salisu Mahama Gondze, 1994

The Dagbamba fiddle, or gondze, is a court instrument that is considered to be the most beloved of the king (Ya Naa) of Dagbon,[1] a small but politically important kingdom in northern Ghana. Performed by professionals who belong to the same family or clan, Dagbamba fiddlers are highly valued and have a high social status because the instrument they perform symbolizes political authority. Thus, the history of fiddling is widely known by the musicians and others in the community. In many parts of Sudanic West Africa, ambiguity surrounds the music profession. On the one hand, many nonmusicians regard professional musicians (oftentimes called *griots*) as social outcasts who live on the margins of society because of what they do and represent. On the other hand, community members consider musicians "to be the respected keepers of the heritages of families, clans, and societies" (Hale 1998:193). The situation among fiddlers in Dagbon is unique because such ambivalence does not exist.

The Gondze in Performance

I left for my first field research trip to northern Ghana on January 13, 1973, hoping to document a Dagbamba festival called Tsimsi Tsugu. Held in Yendi, the traditional capital of Dagbon, Tsimsi Tsugu not only commemorates the Muslim Great Feast, it reveals how the Dagbamba, who are nominal Muslims, have uniquely combined Islam with indigenous cultural practices. In 1973, the celebration was scheduled to take place over three days from January 15 through January 17.[2] I was fortunate that Salisu Mahama, a master Dagbamba fiddler with whom I took lessons at the Institute of African Studies (IAS) at the University of Ghana (see introduction), and M. D. Sulley, a Dagbani language teacher and researcher at IAS—both of whom were born and raised in Dagbon—agreed to become involved in the research. Not only would they accompany me, they would serve as my hosts.

We traveled separately, and I flew to Tamale, the commercial capital of Dagbon, some 404 miles north of Accra. There I met Sulley, who had come by bus. While waiting for my plane to arrive, Sulley met some friends, government officials, who offered to drive us to the local transport station for the trip by van to Yendi. The weather in northern Ghana was cool and very dry. The harmattan season was at its peak, and the air was choked with dust. This was markedly different from the high humidity, high temperatures, and clear skies I had experienced in southern Ghana. Our sixty-mile trip to Yendi took nearly three hours, allowing me to view the northern landscape and housing, as well as to observe farming practices. Situated some distance from the main road were compounds consisting of three or four round structures made from wattle and daub with grass-thatched roofs. In most cases, six-foot-high walls, also of wattle and daub, encircled the compounds. Between them were expanses of two or three miles of open land where farming was carried out. Sulley explained that the primary food crops in northern Ghana were yams, maize, rice, millet, guinea corn, ground nuts (peanuts), and grain. During this time of the year, however, most farmers started brush fires on their lands, the traditional method for fertilizing the earth.

By the time we reached Yendi, it was dusk. Fortunately, three or four young men recognized Sulley when he got out of the van at the transport station. Because his late father had been a leader of the warrior clan (a socio-occupational group called *waluna* or *wulana*, literally "chief spear bearer and senior adviser" to the Ya Naa), the townspeople greeted Sulley with great respect. Following the elaborate greetings, we walked to Sulley's family home, a few yards from the transport station, with the men carrying our bags on their heads. When we arrived, everyone in the compound was excited—children jumping up and down, turning around, and yelling at the top of their voices. First, Sulley introduced me to his mother, a small woman who appeared to be in her sixties or seventies. After greeting her himself, he introduced me to others living in the compound: his smiling sisters and their children, who continued to be excited about the arrival of guests. (I was not introduced to Sulley's brothers until the next day because all of them lived elsewhere; they had built compounds in other parts of town where they lived with their wives and children.) Because of their high social status, Sulley's family owned a large compound with an expansive inner courtyard (like that of a king) with a number of rooms or structures encircling it. Sulley explained that Dagbamba social organization and customs were part of the reason why so many women lived in the family compound. Once a Dagbamba woman gave birth, she was expected to return to her parents' home and live there for two years before going back to stay in her husband's compound. Several other women were living there because they had been widowed, and others were old and could no longer bear children (women also returned to their parents' compound when they were no longer fertile). At the time of our visit, about seven or eight of Sulley's sisters lived in the compound with his mother. Because she was the eldest of her husband's wives, Sulley's mother lived in a structure in the center of the compound.

After visiting with his family for about twenty minutes, Sulley decided that we should go to the Guest House where he had made reservations for us. On the next day, Sunday, January 14, he took me on a tour of the town. Life in Yendi was what many Ghanaians described as "traditional." Except for the town's main mosque, a very large white structure made of wood, and government buildings that had been constructed of stone blocks, most homes in Yendi were of wattle and daub with grass-thatched roofs and were encircled with a wall. Compounds and buildings sat closer to one another than those I had observed in villages we passed along the road during our travel. Yendi appeared to be urban but was uncongested. Almost everyone traveled by foot, although a few men rode bicycles. There was also more vegetation than I had seen during the van ride. In fact, one street, starting about a mile from the main entrance to the town, was lined with a row of tall trees on each side, providing a beautiful entrance into the traditional capital that made it distinct from the landscape of Tamale and other Dagbamba towns I visited in northern Ghana. We also strolled through the open-air market among many stalls and vendors selling foodstuffs, clothing, meats, wood, and other items, and later that afternoon met Salisu Mahama walking down the street on his way to the Guest House with his traveling bag. With a smile on his face that indicated that he was in good spirits, he said that he had just arrived.

On the afternoon of January 15, Sulley and I had arrangements to visit the Ya Naa. Upon arriving at the royal palace, I saw several of the king's elders seated on straw mats outside the palace grounds. In addition, several young children and young women with babies on their backs milled around the palace entrance. What struck me most when I arrived, however, was a white horse standing in a circular enclosure (eight to ten feet in diameter) made of rocks. Grass was scattered inside for the horse to graze on, and a long orange-colored streak had been painted along its back. Its lower legs had also been painted orange. I was told that the horse belonged to the Ya Naa and was used when he participated in royal processions. Like most buildings in Yendi, the many structures of the royal palace were constructed of wattle and daub. The building that served as the entrance to the palace, like a few other structures inside the compound, was painted white. The door of the entrance was bordered with embedded shards of white and blue china.

One of the seated elders rose and came toward us, at which Sulley immediately bowed and spoke greetings because his social status was lower. The elder greeted us in return and led us inside the first building of the palace, where we took off our shoes and left them. As we moved through various rooms before entering the area where the Ya Naa received visitors, Sulley continued to bow before all of the elders he met. Entering at last the large, round room where the Ya Naa received visitors, however, both Sulley and our guide bowed as each expressed his greetings to the king. After the salutations, the elder who had led us into the palace joined six or seven others seated on mats scattered throughout the room. I was told to sit in a chair (the only one in the room) that had been placed six to eight feet in front of the Ya Naa, while Sulley sat on a mat slightly in front of me to my left.

Mohamadu Abudulai IV, the Ya Naa, was dressed in a large *kente* cloth (a type of strip-woven material identified with the Asante of central Ghana), which he wore over locally made light blue pants and a matching long-sleeve shirt. His head was bare. Although the Dagbamba refer to their king's throne as the "skins," the Ya Naa usually does not sit on the skins at all times. On this day, he sat on a dais covered with several pillows.

The Ya Naa was a young man perhaps in his early twenties. When Sulley and I paid homage to him by giving him two *cedis* (Ghanaian currency worth about one U.S. dollar at the time), he seemed surprised and touched by our gesture. Our visit was short, only about ten minutes. During that time, however, Sulley expressed—through the king's "mouthpiece," one of the elders who sat in front of the Ya Naa and mediated all his audiences—our desire to document the festival and conduct research and our hope to receive the Ya Naa's blessing. When told that our request had been granted, Sulley thanked the Ya Naa and we soon departed. During our walk back to the Guest House, Sulley explained in more detail what to expect during the festival. He indicated that activities would take place in three locations: the Ya Naa's palace in the central part of town, the praying grounds on the outskirts of Yendi, and other parts of the community (DjeDje 1978b).

Although I observed most of the festivities, I focus here on what transpired during the first two days. The activities held on Monday evening show how the fiddle was used at court and demonstrate the different ways members of the community respond to the playing of the gondze and *lunsi* (singular, *lunga*)[3] drummers. The public events at midday on Tuesday provide an opportunity to examine how the fiddle is used in both indigenous and Islamic ritual, and the performance at the palace later on Tuesday afternoon reveals the intimacy that exists between gondze musicians and the Ya Naa.

Monday evening's performance took place immediately outside the Ya Naa's palace. The musical activities occurred in a circle with musicians and other performers (dancers and praise singers) located in the middle. The royal flute players, however, stood on opposite sides of the door to the palace entrance (see Figure 4.1). At about eight thirty, fourteen lunsi, led by the head drummer, began playing to announce the official commencement of Tsimsi Tsugu. As they performed, members of the community, dressed in everyday attire, began to gather near the palace. By nine o'clock, three to four hundred attendees had arrived. After forty-five minutes of lunsi drumming, Ya Naa Mohamadu Abudulai and his elders entered the gathering and took their reserved seats. Drumming and the blowing of wind instruments accompanied their entrance. With the Ya Naa's arrival, the lead drummer began performing the *lunsarigu*, or recitation of the royal genealogy, starting with Naa Yanzoo, the eighteenth Dagbamba king (ca. 1538). As the lead drummer sang about each king, other drummers performed a repetitive rhythmic response on their lunsi; no vocal choral response was performed. During the drumming, the audience sat attentively, listening to the recitation with occasional comments, laughter, nods of the head, or other sounds of approval or satisfaction (e.g., saying *naa* or performing ulu-

Figure 4.1. Performance setting during Tsimsi Tsugu at the Ya Naa's Palace, January 1973. Sketch by Karin Patterson. Used by permission. Based on information in Jacqueline Cogdell DjeDje (1978b:282).

lations). At ten o'clock, however, the Ya Naa, accompanied by a few of his elders, left the gathering, went inside the palace, and returned fifteen minutes later. During the king's brief absence, the gondze musicians arrived and sat on the ground in their reserved space inside the circle. At eleven o'clock men, carrying long sticks symbolizing bows and arrows, and women, with heavy loads on their heads and backs, entered the circle for the victory dance, which continued for twenty to thirty minutes to the accompaniment of drumming. As the dancers moved counterclockwise inside the circle, screams and hollers were heard to signify Ya Naa Luro's successful battle over the Gonja people (Sulley 1973; Chernoff 1985:111).

Around midnight the gondze musicians, approximately ten fiddlers and ten rattlers, started performing the gondze *kpebu* (praise songs in honor of Dagbamba kings). With the entire group standing in a semicircle and facing the Ya Naa, Sulemana Iddrisu,[4] the fiddler who led the gondze ensemble, began singing the praises of Naa Yakuba I, the thirty-fifth Dagbamba king who came to

In Service to the King 173

power in the nineteenth century, and continued up to Naa Mohamadu Abudulai, the forty-fifth and reigning king in 1973. The fiddlers played ten songs. While the longest ("Nantoh" in honor of Ya Naa Yakuba I) was three minutes and twenty seconds, the shortest ("Allah Gaba" in honor of Ya Naa Mahama II) was one minute. The entire gondze presentation took fifteen to twenty minutes to complete.

Although the gondze musicians did not dance or make any unnecessary movements, their performance stimulated a jovial atmosphere that was not as serious as the presentation by the lunsi. Instead of sitting quietly, individuals in the audience began to disperse, and a few danced outside the musicians' circle. Yet no one entered the circle to place money on the foreheads of the players, a typical manner of presenting gifts to musicians in Dagbon. After the final song, the elders showed appreciation by snapping their fingers, a Dagbamba form of applause. Then processional music ("Taaka Sannu") was played by the gondze as the Ya Naa, surrounded by elders and court attendants, returned to the palace. When the king entered the palace, the ceremony officially ended and everyone returned to their homes.

The Tuesday afternoon festivities took place on the outskirts of Yendi. At three o'clock, participants in the royal cavalcade gathered in front of the Ya Naa's palace for the procession through town to the prayer grounds. Naa Mohamadu Abudulai, along with his royal courtiers (carrying the throne, umbrella, and fans—part of the royal regalia), elders, Muslim officials, and musicians (lunsi, gondze, bell, and flute players) were included. Royal and religious leaders rode on horseback behind the musicians while members of the community stood alongside the road or walked near the cavalcade.

After the dignitaries and musicians arrived at the prayer grounds, the one thousand or more people in attendance formed a circle. At one end, the Ya Naa sat on his throne underneath a large umbrella, while the elders sat on the ground in front of him. The royal courtiers stood beside and at the back of the king. The gondze musicians stood to the right of the Ya Naa, and the lunsi were on his left.

The ceremony began with prayers by the Yidan Moli, the imam in charge of festivals in Yendi, and the muezzin (who chants the Muslim call to prayer), who knelt facing east. After the prayers, people paid homage to the king by walking near him and throwing money on a small Persian rug placed in front of him. The elders counted the money as it was given. A ram was then sacrificed in the middle of the circle.[5] After the rituals were completed, the king, religious leaders, and elders mounted their horses and returned to the palace while courtiers, musicians, and members of the community made their way along the return route, dancing and moving to the sounds of gondze and lunsi music. Some people stood along the road and looked on as participants passed.

Upon arrival at the palace, members of the community formed a semicircle. The king dismounted his horse and sat on his throne near the palace entrance with the elders. Music-making continued from the gondze (who were seated underneath a shelter) and wind players (who stood on either side of the Ya

Naa). Facing the king, the drummers performed at another location approximately twenty to thirty feet away on the other side of the circle. Community members entered the circle to dance as the king watched the performance.

Around 4:45 PM, Naa Mohamadu Abudulai left the large gathering and went into the inner courtyard of the palace, dancing to "Taaka Sannu" performed by the gondze. While community members continued celebrating to the accompaniment of drum and bell music outside the palace, the fiddlers and flute players went inside with the king, elders, and members of the royal family. The king continued to dance to gondze music after he entered the inner courtyard. When he retired to his private chambers to change into more comfortable attire, the gondze and flute players kept playing, and the queen mother (the king's eldest sister),[6] other family members, and gondze musicians danced. As each person danced in the circle that had been formed in the courtyard, the twenty-five to thirty people in the audience showed appreciation by placing money on the forehead of each dancer or of Sulemana Iddrisu, the lead gondze singer.

When the Ya Naa returned to the courtyard, he moved among those present, giving gifts of money to those in attendance, stirring up much excitement. Relatives and flute and gondze players knelt before the king as he placed money on their foreheads. During the course of the gift-giving the gondze continued playing. Honoraria given to Iddrisu, the lead gondze, created the most excitement because of the drama that was enacted between him and the king. Before presenting the money, the Ya Naa danced in the circle but then indicated he wanted special music for his dance. When Iddrisu did not play the correct tune, Naa Mohamadu Abudulai stood still and shook his head in disapproval. This exchange continued between the king and the lead gondze for several minutes until the fiddler started playing the desired song. When this was done, the Ya Naa began dancing again and members of the audience either screamed, ululated, clapped hands, or danced in place with excitement. As a reward, Iddrisu obtained his honorarium. He knelt on the ground while Naa Mohamadu Abudulai danced and placed the money on his forehead, the largest amount given to anyone. As the coins fell to the ground, other fiddlers and rattlers picked up the money and gave it to Yamba Naa Salifu Issah (the head of the gondze in Dagbon) who looked on.

Around six o'clock, the Ya Naa's feasting ended when he went into his private chamber and everyone left the courtyard. Festival activities for members of the community, however, did not cease. Young children and adults gathered around the fiddlers and drummers as they performed in the streets until later in the evening.

History

The original inhabitants of the Dagbamba kingdom were organized around families and clans. Earth priests (*tindamba,* plural; *tindana,* singular), who had authority over particular areas but did not have any secular political functions, controlled the land. As a priest who mediates between the people and their god, the tindamba continue to be important in indigenous religious practices in Dagbon (Staniland 1975:15; Hiskett 1984:122; Mahama 1994). The Dagbamba people speak Dagbani (Dagbane), which belongs to the Mossi or Mole-Dagbe subgroup of the Gur language of the Niger-Congo linguistic family, and their culture has many features in common with other groups of the Voltaic cluster (DjeDje 1998; Ki-Zerbo and Niane 1997:87).

According to oral tradition, Dagbon was formed by migrant cavalrymen who moved south and imposed themselves as a ruling class on the indigenous people some time between the eleventh and thirteenth centuries when West Africans were experiencing invasions from North Africa. Tohajiye (also spelled Tohazee), the mythical figure identified as the head of the ruling family of Dagbon, lived in Tunga or Kanga, a village located to the east of Lake Chad on the road to Wadai. From Wadai, Tohajiye migrated to Hausa country and lived among the Zamfara. After moving to Mali around 1119 CE, he married a daughter of the king of Mali and had a son, Kpogonumbo. In 1150, Kpogonumbo left Mali and settled in Fada N'Gurma (also spelled Fadan Gurma). In Grumaland (also known as Gurma), Kpogonumbo married two women and had seven sons, five of whom became Ya Naas of Dagbon. Naa Gbewaa, one of Kpogonumbo's sons, is believed to be the common ancestor of the related Mossi, Mamprussi, and Nanumba royal dynasties, while Naa Sitobu, another son, is the founder and first king of Dagbon. Some of Sitobu's sons settled in Sunson, Karaga, and other villages, while Nyagse (also spelled Nyagsi), the son who succeeded him, conquered the indigenous groups. The first capital of Dagbon was built near the town of Diare (also spelled Diari or Dabari, located about thirty miles northwest of Tamale) during the reign of Ya Naa Nyagse in the fourteenth century. The move eastward to Yendi, the present site of the capital, occurred some time between the sixteenth and eighteenth centuries (Osumanu n.d.:1; Tamakloe 1931:3–5; Staniland 1975; Hiskett 1984:122; Ferguson 1973; Ki-Zerbo and Niane 1997:106; Pilaszewicz 2000:69).

Although the Dagbamba were involved in several military conflicts, two of the most significant were wars with the Gonja and the Asante, who lived to the west and south, respectively. When Sumaila Jakpa, a Mande, invaded and dominated the Gonja in the late sixteenth or seventeenth century, he came into conflict with the Dagbamba because he took control of Daboya, a town northwest of Tamale that was commercially important to Dagbon. The war led to the death of Ya Naa Dariziegu (the nineteenth Dagbamba king). The final release from Gonja dominance did not come until the early eighteenth century, during the reign of Ya Naa Zangina. In addition to conquering the Gonja, Naa Zangina is given credit for introducing Islam into Dagbon, some time during the late seventeenth or early eighteenth century. According to oral tradition, Zangina, as a young man, traveled to Timbuktu and Hausaland, where he came in contact with the religion (Staniland 1975; Osumanu n.d.).

Soon after the Gonja were expelled in the eighteenth century, the Dagbamba fell victim to raids by the Asante, a large and important kingdom located to the south (Fynn 1971:19–20). The conflict came to a head when political rivalries within Dagbon and other problems led to the Asante's capture of Ya Naa Gariba. In return for the king's release, Dagbon was required to send cloth and a fixed number of slaves, cattle, and sheep to the Asante capital of Kumasi each year. In addition, an Asante representative was stationed at Yendi. The payments continued through the mid-nineteenth century. Historians believe that economics were a driving force in both the Gonja and Asante wars. The Asante hinterland was the meeting point of two important caravan routes: one went northwest to Djenne on the Niger River and the other went northeast to Kano. According to Martin Staniland, "These routes were linked at their northern ends to the trans-Saharan caravans and along them passed kola nuts, gold, salt, and other goods, not to mention the creed of Islam" (1975:5).

The nineteenth century was a period of internal conflicts, as well as of economic and political challenges for Dagbon. In addition to the pressure to provide the annual consignment of slaves for the Asante king, the system of indeterminate succession of Dagbamba kings led to disputes and factionalism. When Asante involvement in the trans-Saharan trade declined, Salaga and Yendi lost their prestige as commercial towns, which led to decreased revenues for the kingdom. In addition, Dagbon had to deal with the growing presence of Europeans (Staniland 1975:8–9).

Because the Asante had shielded the Dagbamba, their contact with Europeans did not commence until the 1890s when the German, French, and British made several military expeditions to Dagbon. The Dagbamba were defeated by the Germans in December 1896. The actual partitioning of the kingdom did not occur, however, until November 1899. Lines were drawn so that Gambaga and all Mamprussi territories went to Great Britain, while Yendi and all Chakosi territories fell to Germany (Staniland 1975:11); see Map 4.1 and Map 4.2. During the fifty-year colonial rule, Dagbon was affected by two major political decisions. The first was the reunification in 1919 of the German and British sections after World War I. The second involved the introduction of indirect rule in the 1930s, which led to a single Dagbamba district with headquarters at Yendi and boundaries that closely fit those of the kingdom during precolonial times (Staniland 1975:11–12).[7] Lying in a fairly wooded plain of the savannah, watered by the White Volta River and its tributaries to the west and the Oti River and its tributaries to the east, the kingdom of Dagbon covered an area of approximately eight thousand square miles of the northern region of present-day Ghana.

Because the north offered few assets, the British focused their resources on the wealthier Asante and coastal regions. Economically, the northern region during the colonial period was a satellite of the southern economy. Martin Staniland explains: "the relationship of north and south was marked more by indifference than by aggressive exploitation.... The British administration adopted a philosophy of explicit isolationism, which, under the title of 'indirect rule,' was intended to dissipate any tendency which might have existed towards an assimilation of the north into a southern-dominated Gold Coast. The doctrine of 'indirect rule' was highly effective in keeping northerners outside the main

Map 4.1. The partition of Dagbon. Source: Martin Staniland (1975:40). Reprinted with the permission of Cambridge University Press.

currents of politics in the Gold Coast, at least until the 1950s, when they were pushed abruptly (and, in some instances, over protest) into a wide and dazzling world of polling booths, election manifestos, and parliamentary procedure" (Staniland 1975:41).

Due to growing initiatives for self-determination by Africans in the Gold Coast during the 1940s and 1950s, the British gradually relinquished some of their political control. By 1952, Kwame Nkrumah had formed a cabinet and become prime minister. When the Gold Coast achieved independence from Great Britain in 1957, British Togoland became part of the new nation called Ghana (a name taken in remembrance of one of the precolonial West African

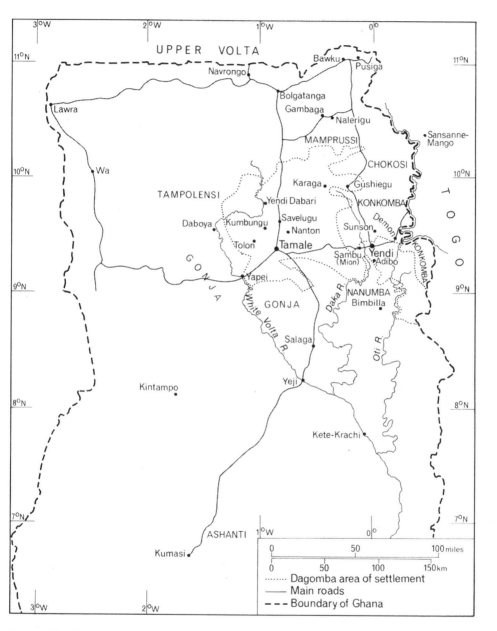

Map 4.2. Northern Ghana, 1965. Source: Martin Staniland (1975: facing p. 1). Reprinted with the permission of Cambridge University Press.

empires). In 1960, Ghana became a republic with Nkrumah as its elected president. When he was overthrown in 1966, the country went through a series of political leaders, both military and civilian (Wallerstein 1988:178–180). At the time of this writing, a civilian government controls Ghana.

Dagbamba Society

Dagbamba society is based on a patrilineal system of kinship. A household is made up of two or more men with their wives and other dependents. The senior man acts as head of the household exercising authority in agricultural work, negotiations over marriage, and prayers to the ancestors (Oppong 1967; Staniland 1975:14). As agriculturalists, the Dagbamba depend more on their crops than on their livestock for food. Selling surplus foodstuffs provides a cash income. In earlier times, professional occupations practiced by exclusive groups that required extensive apprenticeship and training included drumming, fiddling, smithing, divining, barbering, and butchering. Professions that did not require a specialized and lengthy apprenticeship or membership in an exclusive kin group included tailoring, pito brewing, shea butter-making, and trading. Westernization and modernization have brought job opportunities in mechanics, nursing, teaching, and positions in clerical and administrative fields. Although many adults in earlier times preferred that their children obtain a traditional education, which prepared them for occupations in local communities, this thinking has changed in favor of a Western education. In spite of increased opportunities, most Dagbamba are poorer than ethnic groups residing in southern Ghana. Thus, young Dagbamba men commonly move south to gain employment (DjeDje 1978b).

The Dagbamba kingdom is organized into several hierarchically ranked divisions composed of a number of villages. The village community, a fairly compact nucleated settlement of circular compounds in which the king's house is the center, is usually subdivided into several wards or quarters (*fona* or *fondi*), each characteristically inhabited by one large interrelated social, professional, or religious group: king's quarters (*nayili fong*), mallam's quarters (*limam fong*, quarters for teachers of Islam), earth priest's quarters (*tindan yili*), and so forth. Territorial divisions also exist for those involved in trade and crafts. For example, lunsi drummers, butchers, barbers, and blacksmiths live in special wards. Occupational groups that are too few to form a separate ward—gondze, leather workers, weavers, or *timpani* drummers[8]—either live near the king's quarters to serve him or within the wards of other occupational specialists (Staniland 1975).

The Dagbamba social system is not as rigidly stratified as that of the Fulbe, Hausa, and other West African societies. Anthropologist Christine Oppong states that the different social groups in Dagbon, "which may be termed 'estates' (including royals, Muslims, and commoners) trace their origins to different regions and that they became welded into the social organization at different points in time" (Oppong 1973:15). The original inhabitants of the land form the commoner estate and their priests officiate at the land shrines. The Ya Naa and other traditional leaders who comprise the ruling estate are descendants of the cavalrymen who invaded the region hundreds of years ago. Some members of the third estate of Muslims are descended from Wangara (Mande) and Hausa traders, but their numbers have increased with conversions to Islam (Oppong 1973:15–16).

While external influences in Dagbon have been minimal in comparison to other areas of the Sudan, some outside contacts nonetheless affected the Dagbamba. One of the most interesting transformations has taken place in the people's belief system. Like other people in the Volta basin, the Dagbamba resisted the early spread of Islam during the eleventh to fourteenth centuries. When Islam was finally adopted between the seventeenth and eighteenth centuries, royalty and commoners continued to practice the indigenous religion that fits into a four-fold classification of supreme being (Naawuni, also spelled Naawine), nature spirits, lesser gods, and ancestral spirits (Seyire 1968:i). Compared to its role among the Hausa and Fulbe, Islam has not been as fully integrated into the spiritual life of the Dagbamba, but the religion brought about several political and social developments. Muslim officials became an integral part of the royal courts, the personal attire of royalty and commoners changed, and the reading and writing of Arabic texts became important avocations for those who practiced the faith. According to Staniland (1975:16), "Islam is strongest in the towns and at the courts of the king and his chiefs; it has not penetrated village culture to the same extent, and even within the ruling class the two forms co-exist and blend." In the late twentieth century, roughly 80 to 85 percent of the Yendi population was Muslim while the rest either adhered to traditional beliefs or were affiliated with Christian denominations (including Catholic, Presbyterian, Anglican, Baptist, Methodist, Assembly of God, Jehovah's Witness, Pentecostal, and Apostolic) that had spread throughout Ghana. Within Ghana, the country, 10 percent of the population were Muslims, 40 percent Christians, and 45–50 percent traditionalists.

The leader of Dagbon, the Ya Naa, always resides in Yendi. Before colonial rule, not only was he the commander of the army and highest judicial authority, but he also appointed rulers and elders who conducted the administration of the state. The Ya Naa was also the lineage head of the dynasty, head of the royal patriclan, and a figure surrounded by rituals of avoidance and deference (Staniland 1975:16–17). The next in the hierarchy were the three divisional rulers of Savelugu, Karaga, and Mion.[9] Although the Ya Naa does not have as much political power and influence within Ghana's civilian government, the Dagbamba regard him as the leader in local affairs. During the 1960s and 1970s, a major political dispute regarding royal succession engulfed Dagbon. Known as the Yendi Skin Crisis, the dispute became so inflamed politically that Ghana's government, during the tenure of Colonel I. K. Acheampong, took over the responsibility for deciding if the Ya Naa should be someone from the Abudulai (or Abudu) or Andani family line. A final decision was made when the government, in April 1974, published a white paper that "stated that Mohamadu Abudulai had not been correctly selected or enskinned and that, as a result, his appointment was null and void. . . . The White Paper prescribed that the funeral of Andani [the former king] should be carried out at Yendi at the end of May and that a new paramount [king or Ya Naa] should then be selected from the Andani side of the royal family" (Staniland 1975:175). After the proper rituals were performed, the traditional kingmakers met and consulted the diviners. They then announced that the new Ya Naa was to be Yakubu Andani, who took the title of Yakubu II when he was formally enskinned in May 1974 (Staniland 1975:176).[10]

Although most Ghanaians believed that the government's decision resolved the crisis, the people of Dagbon knew differently because tensions between the Andani and Abudu families escalated over the years. The situation came to a head on March 27, 2002, when fighting between supporters of the two families resulted not only in the death of Naa Yakubu Andani II and forty other people, but severe damage to the Ya Naa's place and other homes ("Ya-Na Killed" 2002; "President Declares" 2002; "Yendi Crisis" 2002). To resolve the crisis, Ghana's federal government established a commission to investigate the deaths and burning of the palace. To date, no one has been brought to justice. The government also formed the Committee of Eminent Chiefs, composed of three of the most prominent traditional rulers in Ghana, to create a "road map to peace in Dagbon." The committee decided that in addition to reconstructing the Gbewaa Palace (its formal name), the formal burial of Naa Yakubu Andani should take place and a regent (interim ruler) and new Ya Naa be installed. On April 10, 2006, the former king was buried, and on April 21, 2006, his son, Kampakuya Naa Yakubu Andani, was enskinned. All parties agreed that the regent would reside in a temporary place that had been constructed following the 2002 incident; the old Gbewaa Palace would remain unoccupied until a formal burial had been held for Naa Mohamadu Abudulai, who died in 1989 without a burial. Because both families—the Abudus and the Andanis—are claiming rights to the next kingship, a new Ya Naa has not been chosen. A seven-member Council of Elders comprising members of both the Andani and Abudu royal gates has been inaugurated to manage the affairs of Dagbon until a new Ya Naa is enskinned ("Yaa Na Goes Home Finally" 2006; "Andanis to Enskin Regent on Friday" 2006; "More Progress in Dagbon" 2006).

Social Status of Musicians

As has been shown, most musicians in the Sudan are organized into a socio-occupational group, based on a highly stratified West African social system that dates to the first millennium BCE (Ehret 2001:258–260 and chapter 1). Although highly regarded, musicians in Sudanic West Africa normally have a low social status, a contradiction that distinguishes them from other socio-occupational groups. Some researchers attribute the ambivalence to the unique social structure that exists in West Africa, while others believe it is the result of the musicians' behavior.

Without understanding the history and complexity of social systems, some researchers refer to professional musicians in the Sudan as "caste" people, suggesting that their social status corresponds to one of the hereditary social classes in Hinduism (the untouchables), which restricts associations with members of other castes. Yet West Africans do not conceive of their social organization in the same way as castes are understood in India (Tamari 1991). Researchers who have examined the subject more closely, also argue that no relationship exists between West African and Indian social structures. Thus, to use "caste" in the context of Africa contributes to a simplification and distortion of the complex situation of professional musicians in Africa (Hale 1998:215).[11]

The low status accorded some West African musicians is not unique; musicians in many parts of the world are ostracized because members of their society consider them to be different. Bruno Nettl states, "In Europe, throughout history, musicians were of low status. One expected foreigners to take the roles of musicians, and there is folklore in which the musician is somehow associated with the supernatural, in league with the devil. His ability to be creative and virtuosic was ascribed to the supernaturally tinged concept of talent. He was permitted and even expected to engage in unconventional social, sexual, and even religious behavior" (1997:52). The situation in Southwest Asia corresponds in some ways to that of West Africa in that musicians have not always had a low status. Ammon Shiloah indicates that before the advent of Islam, Persian court musicians "occupied an elevated status in the king's retinue and were represented in three hierarchic classes of courtiers" (Shiloah 1995:8). In modern times, the music profession in Southwest Asia is complicated because while some musicians are treated with great respect, others are not.

Musicians (especially fiddlers) in Dagbon are unique because they are highly regarded, and *have never* had a low social status. The Mande term *siya* probably best explains the social organization of Dagbamba fiddlers. According to Barbara Hoffman, *siya* "is sometimes translated as 'race,' sometimes as 'kind' or 'lineage' 'genotype' or 'seed,' 'origins,' or 'ethnicity'" (quoted in Hale 1998:205). Unlike the situation in the Western Sudan where the family name identifies a person as a musician, such distinctions do not exist in Dagbon. Although gondze musicians do not have distinct family names,[12] the Dagbamba consider fiddlers to be a separate group because their origins and lineage are associated with kingship. Dagbamba fiddlers acknowledge and accept the separation with pride, although they are sometimes discriminated against by other members of the community because of the rewards they receive from royalty. The gondze are what Hale considers "a distinct but symbiotic component of a complex whole made up of both noble and griot [professional musician]." Thus, the relationship between the Ya Naa and gondze is "interdependent and complementary" (Hale 1998:215).

For researchers who continue to insist that the term *caste* should be applied to West Africa, the Dagbamba situation demonstrates that factors used to determine a caste do not apply. The gondze are not of captive origin (slaves), they are not endogamous, and they are not considered to be inferior by members of their community. Social status is another issue that needs to be examined with greater scrutiny. While many commonalities may exist among musicians in the Sudan, there are also distinctions. As Conrad and Frank state, learning more about the past and present historical narratives of musicians in societies promises to encourage the rethinking of our notions of collective status and identity (1995a:16).

Dagbamba Music

Scholarly interest in Dagbamba music and culture did not begin until the 1960s and coincided with the founding of the Institute of African Studies (IAS) at the University of Ghana at Legon. During the 1960s and 1970s, researchers on the staff at IAS and in the language and history departments at Legon produced a number of works that appeared in the Institute's journal, *Research Review,* and other Ghanaian publications. The pioneering contributions of these researchers served as the foundation for studies by later scholars.[13]

As has occurred in other areas of West Africa (see chapters 2 and 3), most music research on Dagbon has focused on traditions associated with royalty, with the largest number of publications dealing with instruments and performers. Drumming has received the most attention, and only a few studies are concerned with other instrumental traditions.[14] Christine Oppong's work is particularly noteworthy because of her discussion of the social organization and training of professional musicians. Other issues and topics that have served as the basis for investigations include history, musical style (specifically rhythm and melody), music and language, patronage, women, religion, and the performance event (e.g., the festival). In many ways, the research topics on the Dagbamba are similar to issues explored in investigations on Hausa music, but considerably less has been done on religion in Dagbon. Instead of an interest in the creation of *new* songs, the focus in Dagbon has been on proverbial and praise name songs used to record history.[15] The difference obviously lies in the fact that many occasions for musicking in Dagbon, which are not as extensive as those found in Hausaland, are closely associated with royalty and "pithy wisdom that is linked to social history" (Locke and Lunna 1990:12).

As in other societies in West Africa, professional musicians in Dagbon pursue other occupations (farming, weaving, trading, etc.) in addition to performing music. Although there are some itinerant performers, professionals become musicians because of their obligation to continue the family tradition. The hereditary system that exists prevents access to the profession by outsiders unless they are married into the musician's family. Some of the categories of professional musicians found in Hausa culture—(1) musicians attached to socio-occupational groups, (2) court musicians and famous musicians who played for modern political parties, (3) freelance performers of recreational music who play for the general public, (4) musician entertainers who perform at markets and large public gatherings, and (5) Bori musicians—are applicable to Dagbon, but differences exist. Although Dagbamba performers compose songs to honor government officials—such as Kwame Nkrumah, who was popular among the Dagbamba—or to encourage the public to become involved in government projects, they have never been attached to modern political parties. In Dagbon, there are not many freelance performers or musician entertainers. Some young gondze or lunsi musicians may leave their families to perform on their own, but this practice is much more developed in Hausaland. A few Dagbamba musicians are aware of the music and spirits associated with Bori, but they do not perform at spirit possession ceremonies (DjeDje 1978a; Lali 1973; Chernoff 1985:106; Sulemana 1995b).[16]

In terms of their functions, most songs in Dagbon are used for praise, recreation, or historical purposes. While not played by professionals, music accompanying work, play (by adults and children), and festivals (e.g., Fire Festival) can also be heard. Some restrictions are placed on what is performed at court but, as is true of Hausa and Fulbe performances, different types of songs may be used at Dagbamba occasions. A praise song in honor of a Ya Naa or another ruler can be performed at other ceremonies or the market.

Also like the Fulbe and Hausa, musicians in Dagbon perform a variety of instruments, although not so many as the Hausa. Dagbamba instruments fall into four categories:

Membranophones

batani—gourd drum
bindili (*binduli* or *binigu*)—gourd drum
daligu (also known as *dalugu, doalga* and *dalbihi*)—single-membrane cylindrical-shaped drum
gungon (plural, *gungona*)—cylindrical-shaped drum the size of a Western snare drum
lunga (plural, *lunsi*)—double-membrane hourglass-shaped pressure drum in three sizes: *zagtitali* (large), *lunga* (medium), and *lung-bila* (small) (Sulemana 2003).
timpani—single-membrane goblet-shaped drum played in pairs

Chordophones

biegu—three-stringed plucked lute with gourd resonator covered with the skin of a monkey
gondze (also spelled *gonje*)—one-stringed fiddle or bowed lute with gourd resonator
jinjelin (also spelled *gingeli*)—two-stringed musical bow with gourd resonator
kuntunji—three-stringed plucked lute with resonator made from sardine can
moglo—three-stringed plucked lute with gourd resonator

Aerophones

aligaita—reed pipe
bani (also called *kikoya*)—horn from a bush animal (i.e., duiker)
kalamboo—cane flute made from a stalk of guinea corn
kate—cane flute made from a stalk of maize or guinea corn
kikaa—a transverse wooden flute with a small gourd attached to the end
kikoya (also called *bani*)—horn from a bush animal (i.e., duiker)
lugunyini (also known as *lugu*)—horn made of ivory
nakpagu—stalked cane flute
yua (also spelled *yuya*)—wooden notched flute

Idiophones

anangbo—lamellophone (wooden or metal strips arranged on a flat sounding
   board and mounted on a box, gourd, or tin resonator)
dawule—double bell
feenga (plural, *feensi*)—castanets
gagle—gourd rattle
kushihi—bell made from the blade of a hoe
sayalli (or *sayeli*)—rattle

Several instruments originally reserved for royalty are now played for commoners at nonroyal occasions. Some of the most prominent court instruments are drums: *lunga, gungon, timpani, daligu,* and *bindili* (Nketia 1968:4). The *moglo,* the only string instrument besides the gondze used for royalty, is normally performed in private sessions with the king. Called the "reciter" because of its use in reciting history, which is similar to that of the lunsi, the moglo was created by the sons of rulers to aid them in learning Dagbamba history (Mahama 1994).

Wind instruments associated with chieftaincy include the *aligaita, bani* (or *kikoya*), *kikaa, lugunyini, kate,* and *yua.* In precolonial times, performers attached to the *kambonse* (local warriors or musketeers) used the bani to praise and encourage warriors before, during, and after a battle. During peace and in modern times, bani music is heard at festive occasions commemorating the victories and successes of the kingdom. Performers who play the kikaa always travel with the king and stand beside (or on each side of) him when he sits in state. Musicians who perform the lugunyini are associated with the Ya Naa's close elders—Kuga Naa, Kpati Naa, and Tugri Nam—and play an important role in the selection and enskinment of Ya Naas. The kate "is of chiefship origin," while the yua is played at festive occasions with drums (e.g., lunsi and gungon) and rattles (*sayalli*) (Mahama 1994; DjeDje 1978a). The aligaita is identified primarily with the Karaga Naa (Phyfferoen 2006).

Other sound sources are identified with earth priests (*kushihi*) and recreation (*biegu, jinjelin, feenga, anangbo, nakpagu,* and *kuntunji*), or are used to accompany drum and wind instruments (*dawule,* sayalli, or feenga). Towards the end of the twentieth century, however, some fiddlers had begun to perform the dawule bell with gondze (Mahama 1994; Sulemana 1994).

Dagbamba Fiddling

The Gondze

Although the physical appearance of the Dagbamba gondze more closely resembles the Hausa goge than the Fulbe nyanyeru, the gondze differs from both. Like the goge, the size of the gondze resonator (six to ten inches in diameter) is larger than that of the nyanyeru. The bridge for the string on the gondze, a three-pronged piece of wood, is also placed on the membrane. In addition to influencing the volume of sound produced on the fiddle, the Dagbamba's placement of the resonator hole in the skin has a practical purpose: during a performance, fiddlers can use it to place gifts of money inside the resonator. The hole also allows easy access to the inside of the resonator where parts of the fiddle (bridge and rosin) and other objects are stored—for example, twine or thread used as a strap for holding the instrument, and scarves, which are tied around the fiddle's neck for decoration.

The shape and size of the bow used by the Dagbamba are different from those employed by the Hausa and Fulbe. Not only is the Dagbamba bow shorter (ten to twelve inches), but it is curved in the shape of an arch (see Figure 1.1 in chapter 1). Like the Fulbe, the Dagbamba use wood for the bow and neck of the instrument. Whereas the Fulbe bow is thin, however, the bow used by the Dagbamba is thicker and the same size in diameter as the neck. Some Dagbamba fiddlers (like the Fulbe) use bows that are bare, but most gondze bows and necks are covered with the skin of a goat, which is dyed black and decorated with white trimming. In length, the gondze is longer than the nyanyeru and goge. Constructed with a fifteen- to twenty-inch vibrating string, the gondze extends anywhere from twenty-two to thirty inches in length (see photos of musicians later in chapter).

Except for some decorative additions, gondze musicians indicate that Westernization has not affected the construction of their instrument, and all tend to use the same instrument throughout their lives. When parts (e.g., the skin, horsehair string, the bridge) wear out, they are replaced. In 1973 when I asked Salifu Lali, the head gondze in Bimbilla (a town in eastern Dagbon located south of Yendi), how long he had owned his instrument, he stated: "I have handled this instrument for the past thirty-seven years. I can boast of keeping this instrument without any disturbance on it for another ten years at least." When I conducted another interview with Lali in 1995 and asked about changes, he indicated: "The instrument has remained the same. The decorations on it have changed. To beautify it, a metal [brass] object [in the shape of a ball] has been placed at the end of the neck. Scarves hang loose from the neck to the main bowl [resonator] to make it beautiful." By comparison, Lali implied that the fiddle used by the Frafra was not as beautiful or well constructed: "The Frafra don't take much care to construct their instrument. They use the skin of a goat or sheep to cover the resonator. Sticks can be seen piercing through the gourds" (Lali 1995).[17]

When no instrument has been inherited from a kinsman, most Dagbamba fiddlers construct their own gondze (it takes three to seven days) and are expected to take great care of their instrument because the fiddle identifies who they are (Mahama 1972–1974). Abubakari Salifu Meiregah, the son of Salifu Lali, explains: "It is against our law of the gondze to ever break it unless it falls. If you break it, you've put a hole in your stomach because it is you yourself who plays the music. You've broken it just because you feel proud; you get annoyed and hit it. So we don't do that" (Meiregah 1990).[18]

History

Because knowing the history of institutions, officials, and important individuals is critical in many West African societies, professional musicians are expected to record such traditions (DjeDje 1998; Wachsmann 1971), yet the Dagbamba are one of the few people in West Africa to have an oral tradition documenting the history of fiddling in their culture. This is significant for, as noted elsewhere, Fulbe and Hausa musicians know little about the history of fiddling in their societies, and most people in their cultures do not believe this information is important. The fact that an oral tradition exists for the Dagbamba fiddle not only reveals the importance of history in Dagbon, it indicates the value of the gondze in the culture. John Chernoff has studied the relationship between history and drumming in Dagbon, and much of what he says about the lunsi also applies to the gondze: "A sense of history is central to the integration of Dagbamba culture and to the Dagbamba musical heritage. . . . Dagbamba tradition is transmitted through artistic specialists, that is, musicians. A Dagbamba drummer is a political figure whose influence extends from conferring varying degrees of respect on rulers to discriminating the status of individual lineage identities at social gatherings. As such, drummers acquire high respect not only for their historical erudition but also for their detailed knowledge of the kinship patterns of their local communities" (Chernoff 1997:102).

For the Dagbamba, history legitimizes the fiddle by explaining how and why gondze became linked to chieftaincy, and it helps people in the community to understand the value of the instrument by signifying its continued importance in society. It is only after a high status has been achieved that the institution, person, or object becomes highly valued. Furthermore, anything of value in Dagbon must have a history (DjeDje 1992b:171). As Hale explains, "The genealogy [or history] can represent both a virtue and a challenge to the individual in the present. To understand and appreciate the full measure of someone today, what he or she represents to other members of society, one must place the individual into a long-term perspective that includes the ancestors. The individual is part of a lineage and can win a permanent or higher-profile place in it by his or her actions in the present. But that lineage is also one of many others" (Hale 1998:19).

Most fiddlers and members of the community have a basic knowledge of the early history of gondze.[19] Although most Dagbamba agree that the fiddle is not indigenous and was introduced into Dagbon as the result of contacts with the Gurma, there is disagreement on when this occurred. Mahama argues that the first Gurma fiddlers arrived during the reign of Ya Naa Andani Sigli (1710–1736), while Abu Gondze of Nyohini-Tamale credits Naa Ziblim Naa Saa (1764–1778), Naa Sigli's son, with the introduction of the fiddle in Dagbon (Sulley 1971; Abu 1973; DjeDje 1978b, 1992b).[20] M. D. Sulley first documented Mahama's version of gondze history in writing during the early 1970s. Because this version of the tradition is so well known by gondze musicians, I present it here in its entirety:

> Goondze (violin) playing started in the Grumaland in a town called Yambi, and was introduced in Dagbon by Naa Sigli, son of Naa Zagali [and Naapaga Gorigu Lana, Zagali's wife]. The originator of goondze is called Yantsebli [also spelled Yenchebli]. He was the first to introduce and to start playing the violin.
>
> Yantsebli as a child always chose to sit and converse amongst his colleagues.[21] On one of such days whilst he was seated with his other colleagues, there was a strong whirlwind which took him away into the bush and the inhabitants of Yambi searched for Yantsebli days upon days all in vain.
>
> For almost seven years Yantsebli was nowhere to be found and it was later on revealed that he had been carried away by fairies. These fairies had their own music which they played and danced, shaking small gourds filled with pebbles and playing on a designed musical instrument later to be known as the violin. These fairies it was further told played and danced to this music on Mondays and Fridays at dawn.
>
> It was also told that the fairies could use their music to treat madness. So throughout the seven year period Yantsebli was staying with the fairies, they taught him how to play the goondze and how to use it in treating madness. He was also taught all the taboos.
>
> The inhabitants of Yambi were just seated one day when Yantsebli arrived home holding a violin and a gourd [gagle].[22] During his period of absence from home his father had died and he happened to be the father's first or oldest issue. Yantsebli's hair had not been shaven for the seven years he was away, so the elders of Yambi summoned a local barber (wanzam) and he came and shaved all the hair from his head and he then looked like a normal person.
>
> Yantsebli father's funeral was then performed and he was installed Yambi-Naa to occupy the vacant post of his late father. Yantsebli then took his violin into his hands and said that from that day any of his descendants who would learn to play the violin should make it a point to praise the wanzama or local-shavers for it was only the wanzam who loved him so well. Yantsebli always played upon his goondze each Monday and Friday. Anyone who became insane and was brought before Yantsebli, the Yambi-Naa, was cured of his madness.[23] Soon many other lands got to hear of his power. At one time the chief of Gruma himself became insane and Yantsebli was well informed.

When Yantsebli arrived, he found the madness to be a very serious one and he prepared certain talismans (*saba*) of *juju* for wearing around the neck of the chief of Gruma. When the madness descended upon the chief of Gruma [again], Yantsebli was summoned and he gave him some medicine and played his violin at the same time. Soon other charms in the form of waist bands (*guruma*) were also prepared and worn around the waist of the insane chief. He also put certain charms into a large hat and the insane chief wore this whilst Yantsebli played his violin majestically.

This was how he played it—*Burusoo-burusoo,* and he sang a particular song.

When the chief of Gruma recovered, he gathered all his descendants and told them that if ever Yantsebli and his descendants did any wrong or committed any offence they should not be beheaded nor should they be asked to labour for any chief by way of farming. [Since that time] their clothing has remained the burden of the chief and his descendants.

From that time onwards, the violinists went every Monday and Friday at dawn to wake up the chief by way of playing their *goondze* and later brought him out amidst the same music after sunrise to receive homage from his people.

It was at one time that Naa Sigli, paramount chief of the Dagbamba traditional area travelled to the Grumaland. On arrival he soon got to enjoy the strange music played at the palace of the chief of Gruma and had to confess before the chief that his instruments produced very good music so it would be very proper for the *Ya-Naa* to have that type of music in Dagbon.

He therefore brought one of the violinists on his return to Dagbon and he always played at his palace on Mondays and Fridays whenever the elders and subjects went to pay homage to the *Ya-Naa*.[24]

After the death of the violinist in Dagbon the people of Yambi delegated one Abudulai to trace him without knowing of his death. On arrival he neither met the violinist nor did he meet Naa Sigli again. He only met the successor of Naa Sigli in the person of Naa Saa Lana Ziblim.

Naa Saa Lana Ziblim therefore told him of the death of the violinist and of his father Naa Sigli. So all the *Yenni-kpamba* were assembled and told the mission of Abudulai. It was therefore agreed that the violinist's funeral be performed in Dagbon and information sent home to confirm it. So Abudulai remained in Dagbon to continue the work of his uncle—that is to play the violin.

For many years Abudulai remained in Dagbon until it was his turn to occupy the *Nam* of Yambi. The kingmakers in the Grumaland sent bearers to escort Abudulai home customarily to occupy the vacant post. This compelled the *Ya-Naa* [Yakuba I] to summon all his elders and inform them of how the kingmakers of Grumaland had sent for Abudulai to occupy the skin of his ancestors, but he was objecting to it. Therefore he would enskin him with his father's title, the chief of his place, and send back bearers to inform the kingmakers of the Grumaland about his action.[25]

Abudulai was therefore installed the *Yamba-Naa* in front of the shed of the *Ya-Naa's* palace and actually became the first *Yamba-Naa* in Dagbon. Now that he had been installed the chief of the violinists, all young lads were trained or taught how to play on the *goondze*. Each Monday and Friday, they actually went to the *Ya-Naa's* palace to perform as well as festive occasions and other days when the *Ya-Naa* sat in state in receive homage. (Sulley 1971:48–53)

Although the gondze oral tradition dates to the eighteenth century, the first printed reference to Dagbamba fiddling appears in a nineteenth-century manuscript entitled "History of the Dagomba People," by Mallam Alhasan, a Dagbamba Muslim scribe who obtained the information from Mallam Kundu Gunda, a grandson of Ya Naa Yakuba I.[26] Written in the *àjàmi* Hausa script some time before 1899 (Pilaszewicz 2000:32), the text makes references to the fiddle in the context of the circumstances surrounding Naa Yakuba's appointment of Kundu Gunda (his younger brother who is also known as Yahaya Sunson) to the position of Karaga Naa. Because the people of Karaga refused to accept Naa Yakuba's appointment, he personally escorted his younger brother to Karaga to install him as the new ruler. When Naa Yakuba arrived, many of the people of Karaga fled. "Only a few servants and some women remained in order to draw drinking water for him. He stayed there and rejoiced. People played the fiddle [*gooro*][27] for him, and he kept on giving them kola nuts" (Pilaszewicz 2000:229). The mention of fiddling in the script provides documentation that gondze musicians were not only prominent (otherwise they would have not been included in the discussion), but they had become established as court performers by the late nineteenth century.

The history of the gondze after Abudulai was installed as Yamba Naa has been maintained through songs that fiddlers have created in honor of the different gondze leaders. Because the Yamba Naas are identified with specific Ya Naas, in theory one should be able to link the names of head gondzes with specific time periods. However, only a few Dagbamba fiddlers can recount the development of fiddling from the beginning to the present. The reason for the difficulty in reciting a complete history, including information about the genealogy of the various Yamba Naas, is that fiddlers have different interpretations about who served as Yamba Naa and when each person was installed. During my research, I collected two versions of the complete history: one by Salisu Mahama and another by Alhassan Sulemana. The different versions of gondze history are not unlike variations that occur in the historical record of other societies (see DjeDje 1992b:152–153). History is not what has happened but rather "what has been recorded of what happened. There has to be a synthesis and interpretation of all pertinent records, of whatever kind they may be. This is the essence of saying that heroes and conquerors do not make history; historians do" (McCall 1969:1). Because Mahama and Sulemana have opposing views on politics in Dagbon (Mahama supported Andani and Sulemana and his family aligned with Abudulai), it is to be expected that their synthesis of facts would result in different interpretations.[28]

Unlike many Hausa fiddlers, the Dagbamba are aware of other people in West Africa who perform the fiddle. When I asked gondze musicians about other fiddlers, generally they mentioned the Frafra, the Fulbe (Fulani), the Gurma, the Hausa, the Kusasi, the Mamprussi, and the Mossi. While all gondze musicians acknowledge that the fiddle is not indigenous to Dagbamba culture, there is much debate about the ethnicity of the people who first introduced the gondze into Dagbon. The majority of Dagbamba musicians believe that it was imported into Dagbon from Grumaland and that other ethnic groups in the region acquired it from the Gurma. My 1973 interview with Salifu Lali, who elaborated on fiddling in the Voltaic region, reveals how closely the Dagbamba identify with the Gurma.

> All the three ethnic groups—the Mossi, the Hausa, the Fulani—their instrument originated from Grumaland. When our great-grandfather came from the Gruma-land and settled in Dagbon here, he married Dagbamba women and brought forth children with them. They taught us how to play the instrument. But while playing, we were equally encouraged to sing by ourselves in accompanying the instrument. This is not so with the Hausas. The player goes on playing whilst the singer, a sepa-rate man accompanies him. So with the Fulani, and so with the Mossi too.
>
> Here in Dagbon, it is no different with regards to our way of playing and that at the Grumaland. We play to honor chieftaincy in the Grumaland and in Ghana here. Besides these two ethnic groups [the Dagbamba and the Gruma], we do not know of any other group who play to accompany the chief or to sing praises to the chief. All that I know is that in the Hausaland, they have a particular figurehead which is known as the Magajia[29]—she's a female. They do all their playing in praise of the Magajia. The Fulani, they play and drink. Where the drinking goes on is where they go to feature, that is in bars. The Mossi, they equally play for some sort of merri-ment. They don't play in particular to worship or play to sing praises to their chief.
>
> All three ethnic groups [Mossi, Hausa, and Fulani] go to play when it is on oc-casion of wedding or naming ceremony. But all that I emphasize is that they do not have anything to do with the chieftaincy or traditional ruler. (Lali 1973)

Although many reasons may account for gondze musicians linking their his-tory with the Gurma, I believe two stand out. First, Dagbamba oral tradition indicates that when members of the ruling family of Dagbon migrated from the north to their present location, they maintained close ties with Grumaland (Swanson 1985:15–17; Pilaszewicz 2000; Obichere 1971:12–13). Not only did the Dagbamba summon aid from the Gurma in dealing with the Asante's de-mands during the mid-nineteenth century (Staniland 1975:9), but the Gurma and Dagbamba also had trade contacts, for "Gurma was of considerable im-portance in the commercial activities of the Dahomey-Niger hinterland" (Obi-chere 1971:12). Second, included in the gondze song repertory is praise music in honor of Bantchande (also spelled Banchendi), a Gurma ruler who lived during the nineteenth century. No songs for leaders from other ethnic groups are in-cluded in the repertoire.[30]

The fact that the Fulbe are mentioned is significant in light of my argument that the Fulbe may have been responsible for the dispersion of the fiddle in Su-danic West Africa (see chapter 1). When I spoke to Lali in 1995 about the Fulbe, he reiterated how their use of the instrument differed from that of the Dag-bamba: "I know Fulani fiddlers in Mali who came to Ghana. They do not play their instrument or sing praises for chieftaincy. They play it when they come together with a particular ritual. Or it could be a particular recreational period. They put some sort of firewood, burn it, and while it's burning they make some merry. They don't cross over the fire, but they enter into the fire. It's part of their rituals to test their supernatural power or belief. It's not easy walking through fire. That's the time they do that" (Lali 1995).[31]

In a 1995 interview, Mahama indicated that he knew about Fulbe fiddlers in other regions of West Africa and had seen them perform in Ghana. Concerning where they resided, Mahama states: "Some are in Burkina Faso. Some are in Niger. Some are in the north of Ivory Coast. Some can be found in Togo. They move because they are tending to their cattle. They are in Zaria. Jelgoji is their principal land where they migrated from. Jelgoji is noted for Fulani settlement in Mali." To demonstrate how their music sounds, Mahama played two songs that he identified as Fulbe and noted: "I have seen Fulani perform several times at Tampion. When they come down, they pay homage to my elder uncle and at times they will sit around and perform. If the Fulani is seated, you will think that he's possessed. One song 'Sambo Yariga' is in praise of a Fulani king, and 'Jam Tara' is a praise song for any Fulani" (Mahama 1995). Concerning the differences in Fulbe and Dagbamba music, Mahama states: "The difference is principally the language. The Fulani sing in their language, while the Dagomba sing in the Dagbani language. If it is the gondze itself, it is almost the same model. The difference is that theirs is smaller. When I perform for the Fulani, I don't use a big instrument like this. I was playing for them when I was doing an outdooring.[32] They call their fiddle *goge*" (Mahama 1995).

Sulemana indicates that Fulbe living in northern Ghana often interacted with the Dagbamba. In explaining his interaction with them, he notes how Fulbe and Dagbamba fiddles differ:

> On Fridays, it is very difficult to get fresh milk from Fulani herdsmen because a lot of people want the fresh milk to perform sacrifices. So I went to Ali, a herdsman, on one Thursday to give him money so that on Friday morning I could come for the milk. It was when I went there that I saw this small fiddle hanging in one of the straw huts (rooms). Their calabash is smaller than ours. The bow of the fiddle was like an arch or a semicircle. Another difference was the bridge. The bridge of the Fulani fiddle was not high and placed close to the base of the calabash. The way we play is different from the way they handle theirs. We put the calabash here [he makes a gesture toward his lap and abdomen], but they put the calabash here [cupped inside the arm where the elbow bends]. Then they play like this [he gestures the up and down movement of the bow on the fiddle string]. (Sulemana 1995b)

Many Dagbamba fiddlers emphatically disagreed with the possibility that the Hausa were involved with or responsible for the introduction of the instrument into Dagbon. Although few Hausa fiddlers knew other ethnic groups that played the fiddle, gondze musicians knew that the Hausa performed the instrument because some Hausa had settled in Dagbon. Certain factors, however, must be considered before completely dismissing Hausa involvement. First, the text of most Dagbamba fiddle songs is composed of three different languages: Dagbani, Gourmantché, and Hausa. If the Hausa have no links with the fiddle in Dagbon, why is the Hausa language included in Dagbamba songs?

Why are the terms for the fiddle in both cultures (*goge* and *goondze*) similar? When Dagbamba fiddlers were asked these questions, few gave an explanation. However, several believed that because the Hausa language is so widely spoken throughout West Africa, gondze musicians simply incorporated the lingua franca of the region into their songs. Lali states:

> The Gruma migrated and they came with their language. But as the time progressed, the Dagomba chiefs did not understand the Gruma language and even the Dagomba well-to-dos who liked to listen to the music accompanied with various praise chants did not understand the Gruma language. So the best way for them to do [solve the problem] was to try and mix it up with Dagbani so they would understand the praise singing better. Just as the Grumas came and settled in Dagbon, so did the Hausas come in. And when the Hausas came, they didn't come in with their instruments. Rather they came and married some of the Gruma women and the Gruma men married some of the Hausa girls. So this was a case of [an] inter-ethnic mixture of Gruma taking Hausa, Hausa taking Gruma, and vice versa. (Lali 1995)

Sulemana is one of the few who believes that the Hausa were more deeply involved in the history of gondze than people realize. He explains:

> You can ask many fiddlers about the history of gondze. They may tell you that the gondze performers are Grumas and that they are from Fada N'Gurma. However, it doesn't necessarily mean that if you come from Accra [the capital of Ghana] that you are a Ga [the dominant ethnic group in Accra]. Coming from Yambi doesn't mean that the gondze people are Gruma people.
>
> If you look at the name gondze, you will know that it is not of Gruma origin. The name of the fiddle in Dagbani is gondze, which is a derivative of the Hausa word goge that means friction; two things that are rubbed together. The bridge that raises the *zum* (horse hair) when the instrument is played is called *zaachi*, a derivative of the Hausa *jaaki* (a term for the bridge in Hausa and a donkey that carries loads).
>
> The rosin used to rub the horse hair to produce clearer music is called *kaalo,* which is a derivative of *kaaro* (Hausa term for gum). Kaalo is rolled from gum of a savannah tree. The tuning horn that tightens or loosens the horse hair string of the instrument is called *kafu.* Again this is a derivative of the *kaho* or *kafo,* a term for horn in the Hausa language.
>
> What I am saying is that I do not know the source of the instrument itself before it came to the Hausa people. But what we know is that the gondze instrument was brought from Hausaland. Yes, it is true that our people settled at Fada N'Gurma before coming to Dagbon, but that does not mean that we are Gruma people. If we were, then almost all the gondze songs composed or played in the 1700s would be in the Gourmantché language. Most of the gondze song texts since 1710 when the fiddlers arrived in Dagbon have been in the Hausa language. Praise song texts in honor of Dagbamba kings from the Naa Saa Zimblim (1786) to Naa Mahamadu IV (1968) are in Hausa except those in honor of Naa Yakubu ("Nantoh") and Naa Abdulai IV (1953–1967) ("Ninsali nim bori Naawuni nyebu").
>
> Another point to support the Hausa origin of our fiddle tradition is the type of materials used to robe a Yamba Naa during his enskinment. These include a gown, a red cap and a turban: a robed Yamba Naa is dressed exactly like a Hausa chief [*sarki*].[33]

Lastly, only the gondze musician uses the epithet *toron giwa* (herd/bull elephant) or *goron giwa* (bull elephant) for the king, which is the exact epithet used by the Hausa to salute their kings. I wonder whether Gruma fiddlers use the same epithet to address their chiefs. (Sulemana 1994, 1995b)

Sulemana's observations have credence. As indicated in the previous chapters, the Hausa had extensive contacts with groups in West Africa. Not only were they a dominant political force in the Central Sudan, but the Hausa states were also centrally located, facilitating trade contacts with many people (DjeDje 1992b:165). If the Hausa and Gurma had an opportunity to exchange commercial and possibly cultural ideas, the former could have introduced fiddling into the culture of the latter, which would explain why several Dagbamba fiddle songs are performed in three languages and Hausa terminology is used for parts of the fiddle. Whether the Hausa could have played a more direct role in the development of the Dagbamba fiddle tradition is a matter that needs investigation (also see Schlottner 2004). Envy and an unwillingness to forget minor hostilities between the two ethnic groups may account for the Dagbamba's reluctance to associate their use of the fiddle with the Hausa. Dagbamba musicians prefer to recognize the contributions made by the Gurma because of previous political, commercial, and ancestral ties. Yet it is significant that the text of most Hausa fiddle music is comprised of only Hausa and Arabic. Until a textual analysis of Gurma fiddle songs has been completed, these issues cannot be resolved.

To complicate gondze history further, some Dagbamba drummers argue that the introduction of the fiddle into Dagbon did not occur until the early nineteenth century, which is much later than the time period (the early eighteenth century) documented by Mahama and Sulemana (Mahama 1990a; Sulemana 1995a). Yet the drummers interviewed by Chernoff believe, like Mahama, that the Gurma introduced the fiddle in Dagbon. This is noteworthy because drummers believe "they know more about people than the people themselves know" (Chernoff 2001). Presenting the perspective of lunga drummers in the liner notes to the recording *Master Fiddlers of Dagbon* (2001), Chernoff writes: "the goonji [*sic*] is a recent introduction, at least, in relative terms given Dagbon's lengthy existence. According to the Tamale drummers, the goonji was introduced in the early nineteenth century during the reign of Naa (Chief) Ziblim Kulunku [the thirty-third king]. The ancestors of the Dagbamba goonji players originally came from the Guruma traditional area in southeastern Burkina Faso. When some Gurumas moved from their original area to the south and west, Guruma goonji players settled in the Mamprusi traditional area to the north of Dagbon in northern Ghana. They intermarried and brought forth Mamprusi children who were playing the goonji. It was from the Mamprusi area that they went to Dagbon, where they also intermarried, and their descendants became Dagbamba." Thus Dagbamba drummers believe the gondze to be "strangers" and suggest that "some Dagbamba do not even consider the goonji to be a part of Dagbamba custom because the goonji was not there at the beginning of the chieftaincy tradition that Dagbamba consider the center of their culture" (Chernoff 2001). The rivalry that exists between fiddlers and drummers must be kept in mind when considering this interpretation of gondze history. The fact Dagbamba kings not only allow their children to marry fiddlers but also permit them to enter their inner compounds on a regular basis suggests that the gondze have greater importance in Dagbon than drummers would like to admit (Sulemana 1995b).[34]

In addition to inquiring about the oral tradition and identifying other fiddlers in the region who played the fiddle, I was also interested in the fiddlers' perspectives on changes in the gondze tradition. In one of my last interviews with Mahama in 1995, he elaborated on transformations since the fiddle's introduction in Dagbon. Speaking very eloquently, his response touched on demographics, the material culture, and the impact of politics on musicking. Because it is important to understand how culture bearers regard and are affected by change, I include much of Mahama's commentary here:

> There have been some changes. I feel as we progress, we get new ideas that can be transferred to not only the model of the instrument but also the playing of the instrument as well as the song texts.
>
> In the beginning, those who were involved in the gondze playing, there were not so many who migrated from the Grumaland. There were just a few players and a rattler. While the performance was going on in those days, the female rattler would be the one singing whereas the two males might be leading songs and playing the fiddle. Gondze were not scattered all over Dagbon. Because of growth and increase in the population, the gondze family has expanded. They have married within their own families, [and] they have married outside the gondze clan. So we can now boast of so many players and so many rattlers. I can approximate the fiddle players in the entire Dagbon state to be between two hundred and three hundred.
>
> At that time, my great-grandfather's instrument was not so big as it is today. The main resonator was a small gourd. Even the rattles were small. The neck wasn't as long as we find it today. Some of these decorations, like the tail end of the neck with round metal, they are improvised.
>
> The alligator skin has been used from time immemorial. We came and met this from our great ancestors. Since then, we've maintained it. One of the old fiddles that was handled by one of my great ancestors is still available but we don't expose it because it is reserved for ritual purposes. It's in Nanton in western Dagomba.
>
> Now you've seen this goat skin covering the entire circumference of the gourd. But this is not how it looked [before]. It wasn't common to obtain a skin and decorate or bind the resonator. It was mostly a type of local loin cloth that they used for the cover. Because they were mostly weavers, they wove their cloth.
>
> This string or twine [that is used as a strap for the fiddler to hold the instrument while performing], it wasn't common. It was a piece of leather that you used after having cut it into the shape you want. Then you tie it. Such skins are reserved for preserving animals which are not common here. So that alone tells you the changes within the instrument.
>
> These head gears [scarves] or handkerchiefs are decorations, which weren't common in those days. It was the same piece of woven cloth, which was tied so that if

you should be performing and so much sweat settles on your face, you will wipe it with the cloth. But today, you have so many head gears and handkerchiefs aligning the neck end of the instrument. All these are decorations just to attract. Also, it is some sort of gift from the ladies who come in and participate in the performance. When they are filled with joy, one can remove it from their head and come and tie it around.

Most fiddlers believe that the chieftaincy dispute seriously affected Dagbamba fiddling. As in the rest of the community, the dispute divided gondze musicians into two camps. While one group supported Andani's claim to the skins (and this included Mahama), the other (represented in this study by Sulemana) supported Abudulai. What made the situation contentious was the fact that Salifu Issah, the reigning Yamba Naa, and his family aligned with Mohamadu Abudulai. Even when Abudulai was deskinned in 1974, Issah continued to support him and never recognized Ya Naa Yakubu Andani. Although Issah's decision had serious repercussions on fiddling in Dagbon, as will be discussed below, he felt strongly about his position for several reasons. First, Mohamadu Abudulai IV was the king who enskinned him as leader of gondze in 1971. For this reason alone, Issah believed that he should remain loyal. Second, as Yamba Naa, Issah was regarded as the "wife" of the king. Therefore, just as a wife is expected to be faithful to her husband regardless of the circumstances, Issah felt that he should maintain ties with Mohamadu Abudulai. Third, Issah did not want to be forced into an association with Ya Naa Yakubu Andani.[35]

As a result of the Yendi Skin Crises, modernity, and Westernization, Sulemana suggests that fiddling in Dagbon is not as important as it used to be:

Actually, people's interest in traditional music, including gondze music, is dying down. It's unfortunate. There is little we can do about it. The gondze was played and loved by a lot of people. That was the time everybody was happy and attended all festive occasions in their colorful attire. But it is certain that people are not happy, either due to the worsening economic situation or the effect of the protracted chieftaincy disputes of Dagbon, or even both. The introduction of Western music into the society is another reason people's interest in gondze music has declined. Western music is gaining [popularity] among the youth as compared to traditional music. People who loved gondze music are aging, and the younger generation that is coming up does not appreciate it. (Sulemana 1994)

Instead of placing emphasis on innovation, most gondze performers believe it is the responsibility of Yendi fiddlers to maintain the tradition, so other fiddlers in Dagbon can use performances at Yendi as a model for what they should be doing in their local communities. Mahama also believes the chieftaincy dispute caused interest in the tradition to decline:

Presently, gondze has been politicized to such a level that there is not much truth in it. How come that where the king of Dagbon resides, that is Yendi, none is prepared to go and play the fiddle for the Ya Naa? How come? The Ya Naa has not condemned them or put them to task because before the gondze, the chiefship was there. Whether they go to perform or not, he's still the Ya Naa. Because they don't have the time and they don't have the courtesy to go and play before the king, they are not going to learn the proverbs. They rather concentrate on recreational activities. That is not why it [gondze] was principally introduced. They who taught us, the majority of them are dead. And we will also pass away. Now when we have gone, what will the present youth or young men do or say? How will they progress? (Mahama 1995)

As a result of the death of Ya Naa Yakubu Andani and severe damage to the Ya Naa's palace (the symbol of Dagbon's monarchy), many questions surround the future of gondze in Dagbon. In March 2002, all festive occasions and musical performances in Dagbon were banned for fear that the musicking would incite further violence. Ghana's president, John Agyekum Kuffuor, made this decision when he declared a state of emergency in Yendi following the death of Ya Naa Yakubu (Sulemana 2003).[36]

Performance Contexts

As court musicians, Dagbamba fiddlers perform for the king in a variety of contexts: biweekly paying of homage to the king; naming, wedding, and funeral ceremonies; festivals, parades, and meetings attended by community members, regional and national heads of state; installation ceremonies; travel to other kingdoms; and other events associated with chieftaincy. As noted above, fiddlers also perform for the king's private enjoyment. At the paying of homage on Mondays and Fridays, fiddlers go inside the royal palace and awaken the king before dawn with their playing. Other musicians do not enter the inner courtyard but wait and perform for the king when he appears in public. On festive occasions, fiddlers entertain the king and his family inside the palace at the end of each day.

Dagbamba fiddlers regularly perform at Islamic events such as Ramadan, Tsimsi Tsugu, and Damba. The only restriction is that they should not perform when the chanter (muezzin) sings the call to prayer or when there is singing of Muslim hymns and chants.[37] During the parades that take place at Muslim and other festivals, gondze musicians accompany official cavalcades to and from the prayer grounds. Upon return to the palace, fiddlers, along with other musicians, perform out front while community members dance. Along with lunsi drummers, fiddlers also perform royal genealogy songs at the palace for the Ya Naa and members of the community on the eve of any important festive occasion.

The contexts for gondze performances have expanded. Gondze musicians in recent decades perform at all types of occasions for commoners and other groups: events of the life cycle (naming, wedding, and funeral ceremonies), festivals, pito houses (bars where locally-brewed beer is sold), and other public gatherings. Although young musicians who are in training often use the marketplace as a context for performances, Dagbamba fiddlers never perform at nightclubs or houses of prostitution.[38]

Since the early 1990s, fiddling at community rallies, dramatic plays, and dances has become more widespread to assist the country's government officials in informing the public about new programs and policies. When I interviewed Sulemana in 1994 and inquired about new contexts for fiddling, he stated:

> We decided to come together (to form a drama and music troupe) and perform traditional dances, acts, and role plays to educate the public on civic, health, and other issues. We acted role plays so citizens would know about taxation and the proper relationship they should have with importers and personnel of the Customs Excise and Preventive Service. We also acted plays on the guinea worm in our effort to eradicate the guinea worm pandemic in our community. If there is a community-initiated project like a tree planting, sanitation (clearing of refuse or the construction of public toilets), we are invited by government officials to perform to attract people to come participate in the voluntary communal work. During such gatherings, some royals who happen to be around may reward the fiddlers with money if the fiddlers praise them. (Sulemana 1994, 1995b)[39]

Because the government regarded Ya Naa Yakubu Andani as the traditional leader of Yendi during the 1990s, most performances involving community projects took place at the palace. When I asked Sulemana if he was hesitant about performing at the palace, considering his family's position on the chieftaincy dispute, he indicated that his position as a public figure demanded that he work closely with the Ya Naa so programs could run smoothly. Yet the public relationship did not change his personal feelings about the king: "I discuss a lot of issues with him, but when it comes to fiddling in his honor, that is a private matter and I do not do that" (Sulemana 1994).

Social Organization, Patronage, and Social Significance

In Dagbon, as previously noted, the social system is divided into three categories: royals, commoners, and Muslims. While stratification exists, the rigid hierarchy apparent in other parts of the Sudan is not strongly evident. In some cases, Dagbamba musicians have the same status as other occupational groups, and, in other cases, music performers are even more highly regarded.

In each Dagbamba village, gondze musicians comprise a family composed of two or more households living adjacent to each other in a section of town near the ruler's palace. Usually the eldest male is the head of the extended family. His sons, brothers, and their wives may live within his compound or build a home nearby. As a closely linked kinship group, all relatives remain in the family unless one moves to another village. Although gondze musicians are found throughout the Dagbamba kingdom, the leader of the group is always predetermined by prescribed rules and customs. The highest title of Yamba Naa (head of gondze in Dagbon) is always held by the person in Yendi and chosen by the Ya Naa. Usually the eldest person in the gondze family in Yendi is appointed (Mahama 1990a). As a symbol of the position, the Yamba Naa uses a fiddle with a metal neck. Sulemana states that "the neck of the fiddle of any ordinary gondze player is wood, but that of the Yamba Naa is always metal [normally obtained from the frame of a brass bed]. It looks very nice and is a symbol of status among fiddlers. He is the only person entitled to use a fiddle with a metal neck" (Sulemana 1994).[40] In addition to the honor and prestige that surround the title, monetary benefits make the position attractive. The Yamba Naa collects customary dues (*saliya*) during funerals of the Ya Naa and other rulers. When festivals, installation ceremonies, and other events take place, the Yamba Naa is given a portion of the money received as gifts from the audience.

The head gondze of other towns in Dagbon are chosen by the Naa (or ruler) of those areas according to the same procedures used in Yendi. Musicians in other areas, however, are not given a formal title, but the term *gondze* is attached to their names to signify that they belong to the gondze occupational group. They may be referred to as Abu Gondze, Alhassan Gondze, or Iddrisu Gondze. A gondze outside Yendi also receives many of the same monetary benefits from members of the local community. Although some people refer to their local head gondze as "Yamba Naa" as a title of endearment, the title has nothing to do with the position held by the Yamba Naa in Yendi.

When Ghana's government officials intervened in the Yendi Skin Crises, a major issue for the gondze family was who would serve as Yamba Naa since Salifu Issah, the head gondze in Yendi, refused to recognize Ya Naa Yakubu Andani. Sulemana explains: "There was a chieftaincy problem. What happened was that most of the [occupational] chiefs [e.g., the head of drummers, the head of butchers, and the head of warriors] who refused to recognize the new Ya Naa were replaced. Within the fiddlers, it was not possible to enskin a new Yamba Naa because of the blood relations" (Sulemana 1994). Instead of choosing the next eldest person in the gondze clan to replace Issah, Abu Gondze, the head fiddler in Karaga who was also Issah's younger brother, persuaded Ya Naa Yakubu Andani as well as other gondze musicians to allow Issah to keep the title of Yamba Naa even though he was being disobedient. To avoid further confusion among the gondze, in the end Ya Naa Yakubu Andani did not enskin a new Yamba Naa but merely chose someone to perform the services without giving him a title (Mahama 1990b; Sulemana 1995b). Interestingly, the gondze musicians who were chosen to perform for Yakubu Andani without official titles—Ziblim Napari, who died in 1980, and his replacement, Iddrisu Osumanu—maintained relations with the Yamba Naa, but Issah never participated in performances with them.[41] When Napari accepted the position, his family eventually moved to Yendi to support his work with the new Ya Naa. Osumanu, however, was not fortunate. During my visit to Yendi in 1995, he did not have any fiddlers to accompany him on a regular basis when he went to perform for the Ya Naa.[42]

In earlier times gondze musicians obtained a large portion of their income from royalty, receiving gifts of clothing, money, food, land, cattle, and slaves. Because they were so close, it was not uncommon for the king to give the gondze his daughter to marry (Sulemana 1994).[43] Commenting on the king's responsibility to fiddlers, Mahama states: "In the past . . . the gondze knew nothing besides going to sing praises to the Ya Naa or to the ruler. Having performed this, the very aims for which the gondze was introduced had been fulfilled because the gondze did not go on the land to farm. The gondze involved in certain of-fences was not to be punished. The gondze, on the clothing side, was not heavily taxed as an individual. All these were the burden of the chiefs of the land" (Ma-hama 1972–1974).

Because the royal family, by tradition, is expected to care for their well-being, gondze musicians are not overly concerned about economic trends or popu-larity. Generally, gondze musicians do not aggressively hunt or beg for money in the same manner as some Fulbe and Hausa musicians. Sulemana indicates that there have been instances when a patron has no money to give, but fiddlers do not ridicule such individuals: "Sometimes you see somebody, a client, and you sing his praise song. If he does not have money, he will dip his hand in his pocket, and then bring out his hand and act as if he has given you, the fiddler, something. The fiddler also acts as if he has received some gift from the client and pretend to put it in his gondze resonator" (Sulemana 1995b). Since gondze musicians never demand more payment than is offered, there is no extensive competition or rivalry among members of the profession.

Beginning in the colonial period, fiddlers in both rural and urban areas of Dagbon began to receive less royal support. When the Ya Naa and other rulers could no longer levy taxes on members of their community, they were unable to take care of the expenses of the gondze family, which had grown in size and needed even more financial help. Fiddlers, including those resid-ing in urban areas in and outside Dagbon (e.g., Tamale, Accra, Kumasi, and other large towns in Ghana), began to supplement their income through other endeavors—farming, trading, and playing for other patrons at nonroyal oc-casions. Although practices may have changed in recent years, performances with commoners or non-Dagbamba were generally not permitted without the gondze first obtaining permission from the king to whom they were attached. If conflicts arose, fiddlers either forwent their private appointments or arranged for younger members of the family to perform at the royal function. Despite performing for other patrons and receiving substantial payment from guests attending nonroyal functions, most fiddlers still regard themselves as court musicians rather than performers of recreational music or simply entertainers. However, "once a nonroyal patron tells the fiddler his praise song [or proverbial name], it becomes permanent so that any time, any place the fiddler sees him, and his fiddle is with him, he [the fiddler] will play the song to praise him" (Sulemana 1995b).

In addition to pursuing other occupations to supplement their income, gondze musicians gradually became more careful about their visits to the Ya Naa's pal-ace. In earlier times, fiddlers may have spent their entire days at the palace or visited the king's residence uninvited on festive days or whenever there was a special ceremony. Repercussions from the Yendi Skin Crises as well as the se-rious economic challenges that the entire nation of Ghana experienced during the 1980s and 1990s have had a dramatic impact on patronage. As a result, fid-dlers now wait to be invited to performances.

Dagbamba fiddlers believe their relationship with the Ya Naa and members of the community is different from that of other musicians in Dagbon. When comparing the patronage of drummers and fiddlers, Sulemana explains: "If you observe the drummers of Dagbon, you will notice that they are present at every small function, even without their drums, looking for money. Today, the drummers appear to be a nuisance to people in public gatherings where they are always present in their numbers hunting for money. Fiddlers do not do that. Even when a royal has a function, for example, an outdooring, marriage, or any occasions that will attract many well wishers, he will have to formally invite fiddlers to perform at that function. If he does not invite the fiddlers, they will not go to the occasion. On the contrary, the drummers, the lunsi, will go there whether they are invited or not" (Sulemana 1995b). Unlike the situation among the Fulbe or Hausa, there is no evidence of "fake" fiddlers (persons who represent themselves as "professional" musicians without acquiring any training or having any affiliation with the gondze family).

Not only have the Yamba Naas been regarded as members of the royal family, they were considered to be the most beloved of the king's wives.[44] As Mahama explains: "The gondze is regarded as the chief's wife because he is exclusively permitted to walk into the private courtyard of the chief, divisional, or paramount chief. At occasions (festive, ritual or any other), all musicians who attend to the court of palace would be dismissed. But the gondze can even sit with him and still entertain him; that is why the gondze is a real different culture from other clans" (Mahama 1994). In addition, the gondze are the only ones permitted to wear their slippers (sandals) in the king's bedroom; others have to take their shoes off (Sulemana 1995b).

When I asked fiddlers about the deeper meaning of their profession, responses varied. The most interesting comments came from Mahama and Sulemana. Mahama states:

> Gondze is a special performance created for the Dagomba to enhance them from misery, to promote chieftaincy, and to actually improve upon the custom and the traditions of the Dagomba people. The song text of the gondze is actually very educative. It gives advice and makes one grow up into a real adult life. In misery or in times of need, gondze music, the text alone, can advise you on how to improve upon your life. It actually gives some sort of education that is not common with the other instrumentalists.
>
> When you are given food to eat and it's the meal that you enjoy most, you don't look at the amount of meat on the food. Your pleasure is the meal itself. So I look at the gondze like a sort of meal for enjoyment. Because of this, gondze has penetrated through the rank and file of almost every ritual within the Dagomba state to the extent that it has taken precedence over other instruments. Whenever there is any ceremony—a funeral, a wedding, a naming ceremony—the gondze are invited. They are not just invited by word of mouth. They call us and we go and perform. Some yam, some guinea fowl, and kola nuts are sent to us. That's the procedure. When we have accepted it, then we will go and render our services.
>
> It is because of the sweetness that one enjoys from the instrument; the listening and participating. That's why they invite us. And they who invite us make us feel

proud because when you're being invited to come and perform, then you are recognized. (Mahama 1994, 1995)

Sulemana's response touched on several issues. I present excerpts from the interview here:

DJEDJE: *What do you think is special about fiddle music? Why do people like it so much?*

SULEMANA: The gondze music is sweet and melodious and has numerous tunes that suit many occasions. It touches the spirit. The text and melodies for dirges are sometimes sorrowful enough to cause the listeners to break down into tears. In times of happiness, the melody can stir people into a state of ecstasy, joy, and frenzy. When a client is in a state of hopelessness (dejected and empty), the gondze music is able to bring inspiration and stir him or her up into a state of hope and happiness. Because gondze music is sweet and soft, it is the best music for recreation and relaxation. The song texts are proverbs (a spoken language of Dagbamba wise men) for people who prefer to express their state of mind, relieve themselves of stress, or remind themselves of special events and experiences in their lives. The music carries some sort of sensation into the human body. It makes you feel the soul. When it is music for dance, it excites. It's a pulling object; it attracts people. When you hear the music, it sends some inspiration right down to your feet up to your brain. I don't know how I'm going to express it. I'm already a musician, and I know how it feels. But if you're not a musician, there is a sort of an inner feeling or satisfaction within you.

DJEDJE: *How would you compare fiddle music with lunsi music? Do people have different reactions when they hear the two?*

SULEMANA: People react differently to both lunsi and gondze music at occasions. For instance, people normally will listen attentively to the song texts of lunsi music, particularly when the drum history is being performed. Otherwise, people normally prefer gondze music to lunsi music. It is generally believed that the lunsi music is very noisy and does not have a variety of melodies. People will dance to gondze music at the slightest opportunity. Maybe because the tunes of gondze music are many, and many people can have many tunes for themselves. Gondze is patronized better than lunsi music.

DJEDJE: *Do you think people really listen to the words with fiddle music or is it the feeling that's more important?*

SULEMANA: In fiddle music, both the words and melody interest people, particularly when people understand the text. Most gondze song texts are in the Hausa language. Since some fiddlers do not speak Hausa fluently, they tend to mispronounce the texts, especially when fiddlers do not take the pains to properly learn the texts from their teachers. In such cases, the people cannot understand the song and may be interested only in the melody. If a performer knows the song text, people will very much like to listen to the text. If you take my music, for instance, you will hear the words clearer as I pronounce them and repeat them quite often. This is why several people want to have tapes of my performances (see below).

DJEDJE: *How does the music make you feel when you perform as a musician?*

SULEMANA: It depends upon the occasion or the mood I find myself in at the time I am performing. When I am excited and I play my music, I feel very happy and I may dance to the music while performing. On the other hand, when I feel lonely or upset, the music that I play can console me or inspire me to move on.

DJEDJE: *Why do you think the Ya Naa likes this music?*

SULEMANA: First, we came with their ancestors and we've always been with them all of these years. Secondly, it is not noisy. The melody is so sweet. It's so sweet that even when the king becomes angry and there is the need to calm him down or offer an apology, the fiddlers are called in to perform for him. All the parties will come out. Then you bow on your knees and you play from the courtyard into the palace. Besides all these, the song text is philosophical and contains words of wisdom which serve as pieces of advice for him. In times of crises, the music infuses courage into the Ya Naa and puts him in a better state of mind to deal with the situations. (Sulemana 1995b)

The rank of a fiddler depends upon the member of the royal family to whom he is assigned. Whether a fiddler's rank changes when his patron's position changes is debatable. Mahama indicates that a fiddler achieves a higher rank when his patron, normally a *na bihe* (a royal prince), is assigned more responsibilities in the kingdom (Mahama 1972–74). When a prince moves from a small village to rule a larger one, his fiddler normally accompanies him. Similarly, if the royal leader is demoted or relieved of certain duties to take on a lesser assignment, the fiddler also looses his rank and status (Oppong 1973:57). Sulemana, however, states that "[w]hen a Savelugu chief moves to Yendi, the fiddler doesn't automatically come with him. If he had fiddlers at Savelugu and he moves to Yendi, that fiddler who was attached to him at Savelugu doesn't automatically come to Yendi to help the fiddlers" (Sulemana 1995b).[45]

In contrast to the fiddling vocation in Hausaland, fiddling in Dagbon is so respectable that not only do few people publicly ridicule or ostracize gondze musicians but parents sometimes encourage their children to marry fiddlers. The only disadvantage is that musicians never settle permanently in one place. And though fiddlers are highly regarded, some members of the community disapprove of their behavior. Fiddlers are thought by some to be lazy, lacking in good character, and too proud. Yet their behavior is tolerated, not from fear that they may withhold praises, but out of esteem held for the king and the royal family.

Recruitment and Training

Dagbamba fiddlers inherit their profession from family members and become gondze musicians because of their obligation to continue the tradition.

Unless one is born into the family, a person is not allowed to perform the fiddle or gagle. Similar to Fulbe and Hausa fiddlers, Dagbamba gondze and rattlers are not required to be a Muslim although most are nominally associated with Islam. Unlike the Hausa and Fulbe, however, the Dagbamba do not regard economics as the essential concern of the profession. Few gondze attempt to commercialize the occupation or concern themselves significantly with popularity. Many indicate they would continue to play the instrument simply for personal enjoyment if no payment were received. Thus, competition and individualism are not as prominent as in other Sudanic areas. While rivalry exists, the basis for it tends to be politics rather than economics. Gondze musicians are, however, highly critical of non-Dagbamba fiddlers and not reluctant to boast verbally of their superior skills. When the discussion turns to Hausa fiddlers, this competitive attitude becomes apparent. Because the Dagbamba believe the song text is the most important feature of the gondze tradition, they cannot see any worth in fiddlers (i.e., Hausa goge musicians) who do not sing and fiddle simultaneously.

In Dagbon, fiddling is a male profession. Females play the rattle and provide vocal accompaniment. When I asked gondze musicians why women did not play the fiddle, most stated that it was not part of their tradition. Yet Yamba Naa Salifu Issah indicates there is no reason for females not to receive training: "It has been our experiment to let them learn or to encourage them to learn how to play the instrument. But it's surprising that anyone who is given the go-ahead fails" (Issah 1973). On the other hand, Abu Gondze of Tamale indicates that females did not play because they had not been urged to learn (Abu 1973).

Nineteen-year-old Aruatu, one of the Yamba Naa's married daughters, began rattling when she was six years old and planned to continue as long as she could. She stated that she did not perform the fiddle because she did not think she was physically fit to play such an instrument: "Since the men are well built for that, they are good at playing. I still become happy when I'm rattling alongside my parents. I can't stop rattling until I'm actually very old and can no more feature prominently amongst the other performers" (Aruatu 1995). After women marry, they are not compelled to continue rattling but "because of economic reasons, they do perform" (Sulemana 1995b). When a woman marries and decides not to perform in an ensemble, at least one of her children is expected to replace her. Her other children, however, are free to enter the profession of their father (Mahama 1972–1974; Oppong 1973). In earlier times, male gondze were not relieved of their duties once they married. Not only were all their children expected to become either fiddlers or rattlers, they were not allowed to pursue the occupation of the mother's family. With social changes occurring in Dagbon, however, many rules have been altered or abandoned.[46]

Although women are allowed to lead gondze songs, they only perform in this role when they are exceptional. Mahama recalls "his grandmother who was a rattler but was good in [the] composition of song texts. So she would lead even for the rattlers and fiddlers to answer or respond. Ever since she passed away, no one has been able to fill that vacuum" (Mahama 1995). Sulemana explains that female lead singers tend to be "older than any of the fiddlers who are performing." They most often lead in singing at funerals and outdoorings and only occasionally perform at the Ya Naa's palace (Sulemana 1995b).

When a male child receives fiddle lessons, he also learns how to play the rattle. A few males decide to focus on rattling even though they are able to play the fiddle, but a female normally does not have this choice. Mahama explains: "Previously, rattling was reserved for only women or females. If a boy chose to rattle and they found that he was out-doing the females, he remained with it. That is why if you see a male rattler, then he must be an excellent one. The other thing is traveling from one place to another. You need to be on the bicycle to cover some distance of ten, twelve, or eighteen kilometers to go to the next place to perform. It's not easy going with a woman. It's inconvenient. The male rattlers fit in better" (Mahama 1995).

Because the gondze is a court instrument, the material that Dagbamba fiddlers are required to learn demands that they begin their training at an early age, usually between five and eight. Taught by a kinsman, students may be given a rattle to perform, which gives confidence and encourages them to participate. Meiregah states that when he began on the rattle, he was allowed to play it freely: "I began playing the accompaniment with the rattle. We always played whatever we wanted until the time you can also listen to the correct beat of what is going on. Then they will start correcting you, 'Do like this'" (Meiregah 1990).

When students are slightly older, they are given a small fiddle. After mastering the smaller size, a bigger one is provided. Training on the gondze involves imitation. The first step is simply to learn to move the bow up and down with the right hand, while the teacher performs the finger movements with his left hand. After the student learns the left-hand movements, then actions in both hands are coordinated. Words and music are always learned simultaneously because of the close structural relationship between the two. Even if a student does not sing aloud while he plays, he is expected to mouth the words at the same time. Students are encouraged to practice when they are free. If the teacher is around and hears the student playing badly, the teacher demonstrates the correct way. Meiregah explains that he was subject to different expectations in his training as he grew older:

> They gave me a small one [fiddle]. That is the one I could play any time. And sometimes when people asked my senior brothers to play the gondze, I [would] also bring mine. But my father say I should be just listening to what they are playing. So they [would] be playing, and I [would] be listening. There came a time when I could also play. I just took it the way I wanted. I was taking it as a joke.
> Between eight and nine years old, I knew what I was doing. It became compulsory whether I liked it or not. They can wake you up any time of the night and you should play gondze. And the places I was going before, I was now forced to go there, like the chief's house on Mondays and Fridays around three or four o'clock in the morning. Three o'clock up to 5:30 or 6 am you'd be playing for the paramount chief. At that time, I didn't like it because I felt like sleeping and my father would wake me

up to go. Sometime I would cry and I wouldn't like to go. But I have to go. Sometimes they have to beat me. Before I knew, I could also play the gondze. (Meiregah 1990)

Fiddlers play an important role in all activities involving the royal family, including installation, naming, and funeral ceremonies. The praise songs they have to remember not only relate to the history of the kingdom, but praises in honor of the leaders are vital to the continuity of the traditional social and political system. In addition, the gondze must learn their own history as well as the praise songs for other members of the community. Learning this massive oral body of historical material requires long hours of patient application and practice on the part of the teacher as well as the pupil. Learning the history as well as the order and texts of the genealogy songs is not as straightforward as learning to perform the instrument, and Mahama indicates that teaching methods and student motivation affect this part of the training:

> It depends upon who gave you tuition and how well you're able to grab it because there are some who are taught this. And when you don't put it into practice, you will continue to forget it. But if you put it to your zeal and your whole mind, then you grab it and will be able to build upon it and even polish it up.
>
> For instance, whenever we were given these lessons in song texts, it so happened that after this lesson, we would go and sit by ourselves or sit on our own. The best time to sit would be early morning or dawn around 3 to 4 am. Then you might start singing the beginning of the chiefship, the Ya Naas, recount that this was the first Ya Naa, second Ya Naa, because you are learning. You must be able to recount all of the Ya Naas through the present. After which, you will go [to perform] over to the chief of the town of which you are settled or resident. If you dare make a mistake, the chief on hearing it can question you: "You jumped over this particular chief or that particular chief. Wasn't he one of the chiefs? Or wasn't he related to me?" (Mahama 1995)

The method that Sulemana's teachers (who, before 1974, were court musicians for the Ya Naa) used to pass on knowledge about the gondze song texts differs somewhat:

> The problem is for the learner to know praise names for the various families and clans in the community. The easiest way to do that is to accompany the adult fiddlers to occasions when they perform. These occasions may be for royals or nonroyals. The learner pays much attention to the praise names for the people who patronize the occasion. As the fiddlers perform and praise the clients, they may include praises of the fathers and grandfathers of the clients. The profession of the clients may also be mentioned. The learner takes note of all this and as he improves upon his performances, he simultaneously learns the praise names of others in the community and sings praises in their honor if he sees them at other occasions. So this exercise normally takes some time. The teachers do not just sit a learner down and teach him everything. The learner must accompany the adults on their trips to occasions like the wedding and outdooring ceremonies, to market places, to the royal houses to get exposed to the praise songs of a cross section of the families and clans in the community. (Sulemana 1994)

The abilities and talents of Dagbamba fiddlers differ. While one may have a good memory for songs and praises, another may have a sweet voice, and a third may be a skillful player. Some students are able to learn to play in a matter of months; others may take years and become only mediocre performers. By the age of nine or ten, however, students were expected to be competent players able to perform with other musicians at events. Some males, of course, never learn to play the fiddle.

Rarely are gondze musicians taught to become virtuoso fiddle players. Improvisation on the fiddle is not emphasized because the textual material is more important. Because they are expected to record and interpret history as well as comment on important events in the culture, gondze musicians must continue to train and practice after their initial instruction. Occasionally fiddlers gather together and rehearse certain songs before performances. The rehearsal, which is not formal, may take place during the children's instruction time at the end of the day or whenever fiddlers feel the need to come together (Issah 1973).

During the course of his education, a student is allowed to travel and obtain further training from a relative or friend of the family. During this period, he is free to play at various social occasions. A student may decide to follow an experienced player on his travels or go on his own, combining itinerant trade with his music or attaching himself to a royal patron as he finds it expedient. A fiddler's kinship relationship with other fiddle players in the kingdom and his ready supply of musical entertainment to suit any occasion make him welcome wherever he goes. This high degree of mobility leads to a wide dispersal of kin and may be associated with the high divorce rate and small size of compounds found among some fiddler's households (Oppong 1973:57).

Since young people in Dagbon now receive a Western education, they have greater choice of profession. A few continue to follow tradition, but even before the Yendi Skin Crisis others had begun to abandon it. Sulemana believes that "the youth [who dismiss fiddling as a viable profession] have a wrong mentality. They just feel that once you are educated, there is no need to go to the fiddle again, which I feel is wrong. When I showed interest in that [fiddling], they were teasing me. But I didn't mind. I still kept on" (Sulemana 1994).[47]

In the long run, Sulemana suggests that Western education helps the gondze tradition because information can be preserved and taught in different ways. "For instance, this is how I got my information. Sometimes in the night when my father is resting, I'll go to him and massage his body. And as I am massaging him, he would ask me a question: 'Do you have the praise song for this particular chief?' And I would say, 'No.' And he would teach me. Now when he teaches us, what I do is at the end of the day or before I go to sleep, I go write it down. Then the following morning I have it. And it's documented. So that is why I have an advantage over the other fiddlers. And then sometimes, they will talk to you about some historical things, you go to write it down" (Sulemana 1995b).[48]

The Yendi Skin Crisis, however, has affected the learning and the transmission of knowledge about gondze. Since few fiddlers perform for royalty, there is no one to train and pass on the repertory of praise songs. Sulemana explains that some of the information is in danger of being lost: "When Naa Mohamadu was at the palace, we went there every Friday and Monday between 3 and 5:30 AM to perform. At mid-morning, between 9:30 and 11:30 AM, we went back to perform for him. During these visits my father performed the praise names of past kings of Dagbon and these were opportunities for us to learn the song texts and praise names. In 1974, when Naa Mohamadu was deskinned, the palace performance which had served as a school for the young fiddlers ceased and therefore we had to now constantly inquire from the elders to document the song texts so they do not get lost." Commenting on the same problem, Mahama states: "When I look at the youth of today, few of them can perform the gondze and accompany themselves because they have not devoted much time to the song texts and the rituals involved in the song text tuition" (Mahama 1995). Since all musicking in Dagbon was banned as a result of the death of Naa Yakubu Andani in 2002, only time will tell if the gondze tradition can be maintained. Sulemana indicates that his family is now prepared to perform for the new Ya Naa when he is enskinned; it will not matter to them if the person is from the Abudu or Andani family (Sulemana 2003).

Dancing

Although dancing is an integral part of a gondze performance, no professional dancers are included in ensembles. Rather, audience members are encouraged to dance, and when this does not occur, fiddlers and rattlers normally dance. In earlier times, however, gondze musicians did not dance while they played the violin. Like the Fulbe and Hausa, Dagbamba fiddlers used to remain stationary while members of the audience danced. Dancing by the gondze began during the early twentieth century when Seidu Gondze, the head fiddler for the Kumbungu ruler (in western Dagbon),[49] started dancing and playing the fiddle at the same time. Mahama explains:

> Seidu Gondze used to perform and create some laughter with his antics. He had this sort of style added to his performance. So anytime he was entering a village or a particular town, he would start playing and creating this movement. So people admired him that way. This was one single instrumentalist who could play his instrument and dance or accompany himself whilst dancing. This was how he became famous. (Mahama 1995)

When other fiddlers saw that Seidu's dancing pleased his audience, members of the gondze family began to emulate him. Eventually, dancing became a part of the performance culture (Mahama 1995).

In modern times, fiddlers play an integral part in the performance through free and improvisatory dancing. By demonstrating the dance movement, gondze musicians encourage others to dance, creating greater excitement in the performance. When I asked Mahama why he sometimes shook his buttocks when playing the fiddle, he stated: "Gondze can teach someone to dance with the music. So if I don't perform it myself to other people's taste, how will I convince them to dance? You can tell who is a good dancer by the foot work and the body swerves"[50] (Mahama 1995). When some Dagbamba dance, they hold a horse tail (whisk), towel, or scarf in their hands or around their necks. Sometimes these items have a utilitarian function. Other times they are used for decoration, and as symbols of prestige and power (Mahama 1995).

Similar to other African performances, the interaction and communication between people participating at the event are critical. Mahama relates: "It's a combination of the gondze player and the dancer. I look at the dancer. When the dancer is getting tired, then it means that he needs either a vigorous song or the one which will give him a rest. Take it that you're dancing a slow number and he wants you to pick up. He can even say near me, 'Pick up with a fast melody.' When I'm on a fast melody dance and he feels like cooling down, then I get it [the message] through his leg movement" (Mahama 1995).

Dancing also increases the gift-giving. Sulley states that "when a dancer gets to the dancing floor, you've got to dish out some money. You just don't look at him dancing throughout, if you're being satisfied with his dancing and you want him to dance more. Of course, to compensate the fiddlers as well, you've got to dish out some money. When there is a performance, you don't go with less than ten thousand cedis [ten U.S. dollars] or more" (Sulley 1995). Sulemana explains:

> We do not have special dancers who go with us during our performances. Rather, the clients are encouraged to come out individually to dance to their praise music. Normally during a performance, one fiddler and a rattler will approach a dancer sitting in a special place reserved for dancers at that occasion. The fiddler will kneel before the person and begin to play his music of praise song, if he knows it. If the fiddler does not know him, he asks the client the song or tune he wants to dance to. The tune is played and the dancer will then follow the fiddler into the space reserved for dancing. The other dancers and spectators may then come out to show their appreciation by giving some money to the dancer who in turn gives the money to the fiddlers when he finishes dancing and then goes to take his seat. There are times when a patron may not dance but will only give money to the fiddlers. (Sulemana 1995b)

Sulemana explains most of his family members learn to dance through observation and imitation:

> During performances we watch and observe several people dance, and during our leisure at home we imitate the dancing styles of the dancers. Through the imitations, young fiddlers learn to dance. The imitations can sometimes cost the fiddlers in future performances. If bad dancers get to know that the young fiddlers are imitating or ridiculing their style of dancing, they may refuse to dance. The fewer people that dance during performances, the less honorarium the fiddlers will get. In other words fiddlers are not trained to dance. Rather, the princes and other royals are taught/trained to dance during our biweekly visits to the palace to perform for the king. (Sulemana 1995b)

Ensemble Organization and Performance Style

The organization of Dagbamba fiddle ensembles is similar to that used by Fulbe and Hausa groups; both melodic (gondze) and percussive (gagle) instruments are employed. Gondze ensembles, however, do not include membranophones, while drums are prominent in Fulbe and some Hausa groups. Although the number of people in a gondze ensemble may vary from two to twenty-five, it normally consists of one to eight fiddlers and one or more rattlers, regardless of the context or occasion. In special cases, a fiddler may perform alone without rattle accompaniment.[51] In small villages where the gondze family unit is not very large, only one fiddler may be included in the ensemble. The leader of the ensemble is the head gondze within the town or village.

In a performance, the responsibilities of the leader of the gondze ensemble are quite varied. Constantly moving and guiding the entire event, he sings the lead vocal part, leads the fiddle playing by selecting the repertoire, gives cues to start or stop a song, and controls the tempo. As vocal leader of all songs, not only must he have wit and a pleasing voice, he should know how to organize and perform the text to attract the attention of the audience. On occasion, he momentarily stops fiddling to sing improvisatory textual phrases or dance for and with members of the audience. He also serves as the main actor in the musical drama that unfolds between musicians and audience during gift-giving. For example, the bearer of gifts may reward the group by placing coins and bills on the forehead of the lead singer or on the forehead of members of the audience who enter the circle to dance.

Occasionally, the head gondze in a town allows others (a son, nephew, or younger brother) to assume the leadership role. In a 1973 interview, Sulemana Iddrisu explained why he sometimes took over the role of leader of the fiddle ensemble in Yendi: "Since the Yamba Naa is of age, it's the custom that his deputy, who is still younger, should lead all songs or whatever functions the gondze will feature. It is equally the practice that when the head of the family has a farm, the boys, young men, and even the females in the house all go to farm for him. He will only accompany them to the farm when he feels like doing so. If he's at the farm, he's there just to inspect or help guide them, and give them some sort of company. So the Yamba Naa, since he's of age, he sits down while I lead all the songs" (Iddrisu 1973).

The other fiddlers in the ensemble serve as the vocal and fiddle chorus, responding to the lead vocalist by performing a repetitive vocal and fiddle melody throughout the performance. Sitting or standing, they tend to be more stationary during performances than the lead gondze. Some, however, may occasionally sway to the rhythm of the music and dance. The zaabia (adult women, young girls and boys, and some adult men who play the rattle) serve two functions. Not only do they perform the vocal chorus along with the fiddlers, they are the time keepers. The rattle accompaniment is critical to a gondze performance for several reasons: it emphasizes the pulse to produce the desired rhythm and

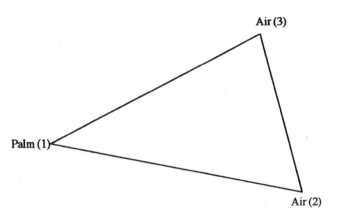

Figure 4.2. Rhythm A. Diagram for performing the *gagle*. Source: Jacqueline Cogdell DjeDje (1978b:546).

mark the movement of dancers;[52] it helps to establish the time span; and it adds percussive sounds that enrich the texture of the music. Playing the rattle involves a three-step kinetic motion. The rattle is struck in the palm of the hand, moved diagonally to the lower or upper right, and raised perpendicularly (see Figure 4.2) before the entire pattern is started again. In very fast tempi, the second step is sometimes omitted: the pattern would then consist of only two motions as shown in Figure 4.3.

Because many members of the audience at a Dagbamba event do not understand the language of the song text but are moved by the music, there is much dancing at gondze performances. When they do not overtly respond, the gondze leader may use gestures to stimulate more reaction. Sulemana Iddrisu (1973) states that he knows that a performance is a success when the audience actively participates by dancing, ululating, or clapping hands. Performance context, however, dictates what takes place at an event. When praise songs in honor of royalty are performed at festivals and the paying of homage at the palace, fiddlers do not include as much movement and dancing as would be evident when they play music to entertain guests at naming and wedding ceremonies. At a royal performance, songs related to chieftaincy would be emphasized. At ceremonies for commoners, not only would fiddlers perform praise songs in honor of the invited guests, but recreation and royal praise songs popular among commoners would be heard.

When money is given to gondze (either by a dancer or member of the audience), no one announces the amount of the donation or the name of the donor. During the gift-giving, however, some communication is evident between donor and dancer. A female dancer may cup her hands below her abdomen to catch the money as it falls from her forehead to the ground. She then smiles and

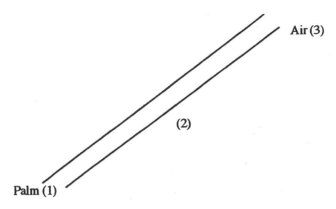

Air (3)

(2)

Palm (1)

Figure 4.3. Rhythm B. Diagram for performing the *gagle* (fast tempo). Source: Jacqueline Cogdell DjeDje (1978b:547).

lowers her eyes to show appreciation. Because male dancers move vigorously, it is difficult to give them money. So the donor gives the money directly to the lead fiddler as the male dancer performs.

Just as new performance contexts have come into being, the organization of the gondze ensemble has begun to change. The cultural troupe formed by Sulemana and his relatives includes not only fiddle and rattle; they have added the lunga drum and dawule bell. Although most people believe that this was the group's innovation, Sulemana insists that the former Ya Naa initiated the new instrumentation. Sulemana explains: "On festival occasions after the festivities outside the palace, Naa Mohamadu IV would retire to his inner court to re-move his big gowns and reappear in his private compound to dance to the fiddle music accompanied with one lunga and a double bell (dawule) performer. This was how it all began" (Sulemana 1995b). In 1992, when Sulemana and his group made a cassette recording using the new instrumentation, the response was en-thusiastic but the financial rewards for his efforts were small. Sulemana ex-plains: "When I recorded this cassette with the new instrumentation, the music producers did not treat me fairly at all. The cassette attracted a lot of market when they [producers] produced it for sale and yet I got no money from them.[53] The cassette was also played over the airwaves of the Ghana Broadcast Corpora-tion [GBC] and yet I got no honorarium from the GBC. The cassette was played everywhere in Dagbon, in shops, commercial vehicles, etc." (Sulemana 1994).

When innovation is initiated, the response by various individuals in the community will determine if the change becomes permanent. When asked if he thought Yamba Naa Salifu Issah would ever include the bell and drum in a gondze ensemble, Sulemana did not answer the question but stated: "He is old and does not play fiddle music anymore. However, at the time this new in-strumentation was performed for Ya Naa Mohamadu IV's personal relaxation, the Yamba Naa was active and did not oppose it. Also, he did not say anything against the new instrumentation when we recorded our cassette. He did not object to it" (Sulemana 1994). When asked if Osumanu, who served Ya Naa Yakubu Andani, had used the new combination of instruments, Sulemana responded: "No, maybe because it doesn't suit his tastes or the tastes of the new Ya Naa" (Sulemana 1994).

Members of the community who have responded most positively to the innovations are the youth. Sulemana states that over time, the youth of the community learned about the new sounds being created at the palace. Therefore, when Ya Naa Mohamadu Abudulai IV died, many people thought that the 1992 recording had been made earlier. Sulemana explains: "People even misconstrue this cassette and claim that it was recorded at the time of the burial of Ya Naa Mohamadu IV in 1989. This cassette was not recorded at the time of internment of Naa Mohamadu. The reason people attribute the recording to Naa Mohamadu may be due to the fact that he liked the new instrumentation so much" (Sulemana 1994).

Songs and Composition

Among the Dagbamba, song texts are important because they help in socializing and controlling the behavior of individuals in the society. Furthermore, some gondze musicians believe that the song texts are what make them special in the eyes of patrons, especially royalty. Mahama explains:

> When gondze was introduced into Dagbon, it wasn't the instrument they [the kings] were interested in. It was the song text. Song texts contain proverbs that give you so much advice and wisdom. Song text is not just for listening pleasure. It's actually instructions the fiddlers give to the king and the entire chiefdom. Instructions about life accompany the song text. While the song texts of the gondze are real educational, the song texts of the lunsi are mainly historical of past chiefs. Some recreational song texts could be fused into the gondze text, but that doesn't carry the real meaning of the gondze. Other musicians are trying to pick some of the song texts from the gondze to blend into their type of music. Because of the richness of the song text, when they're playing alongside with the drummers, the chief said, "You let the drummers make their noise. And then you will take over." So because of the special performance by the fiddlers, they were allowed into the main palace of the king. No other drummers or instrumentalists were allowed in at that time. (Mahama 1994, 1995)

In many African cultures, the themes, symbols, and language used in songs both deal with everyday life and have deeper meanings that are not expressed in other contexts. J. H. Kwabena Nketia notes that, "the themes of songs tend to center around events and matters of common interest and concern to the members of a community or the social groups within it. They may deal with everyday life or with the traditions, beliefs, and customs of the society" (Nketia 1974:189). Songs performed by gondze musicians can be placed into three categories: historical, praise, and recreation. Because of the importance of history and praise in Dagbamba culture, references to historical figures and elements of praise dominate in most song texts. Recreation and topical songs that concern current events are occasionally performed, but the playing of possession songs is rare.

Of the three fiddle traditions considered in this study, gondze song texts are the most difficult to understand because of the proverbs and the language used. Although historical songs are important because they remind people of the past and of the values of a society, they require some knowledge of oral tradition before they can be understood. What they generally provide is not detailed narration of events but brief allusions to significant incidents and genealogies. The cultivation of historical songs finds its highest expression at the courts of rulers. Here, chronicles of kings and genealogical references that link the present generation of royalty to their ancestors help to strengthen the position of those in authority or to legitimize their claim to power. But such songs are also intended to exhort the king, to encourage him to emulate his predecessors, and to share in their glories and learn from their defeats; they may also be intended as praise songs (Nketia 1974:196–197). While they are not performed as often, recreation songs in Dagbon are just as important as history and praise songs because all music has educational value.

Although song texts are essential, an irony exists in that most Dagbamba do not understand the literal meaning of the lyrics. According to Mahama, not only do commoners have difficulty in understanding the texts to gondze songs, but Dagbamba kings and court officials are also unable to understand them as well. Yet this is not unique to Dagbon. Writing about the Mande in the Western Sudan, Barbara G. Hoffman states: "In my attempts to discover what it is about praise genres that is so powerful, I found that most nobles could not decipher the referential content of *jelikan* [griot language]" (Hoffman 1995:41). Yet this did not matter because the layers of obscure sounds added power to the griots' performance. According to Hoffman, the images associated with the name of a great warrior or the name of a famous village can evoke entire histories heard upon countless occasions in innumerable contexts. What is heard is not merely what is said by the griot at the time, but what has been heard on the same topic at different times, in different places. "The griot has called the weight of extraordinary achievement from the distant past into the living present of the noble 'descendant' a juxtaposition which invites comparison, thus encouraging the noble to swell with pride at the thought of being on a par with such heroism, or to sink with shame at the thought that his/her own reputation will not stand up to the scrutiny—in either case, the emotion thus stirred is literally dripping with *nyama* [power]" (Hoffman 1995:42).

In Dagbamba society, people relate to music in different ways, by dancing, observing, and listening. Instead of trying to understand the literal meaning of the texts, people link the songs with a symbol or proverb used to identify the individual. *Nantoh* (a small poisonous reptile) and *bawuna* (a bush cow) are the animals used to symbolize Ya Naa Yakuba I and Ya Naa Abdulai I, respectively, and the praise songs in honor of these kings accordingly bear the titles "Nantoh" and "Bawuna" (Mahama 1973). Members of the audience become familiar with the praise names for important officials because fiddlers regularly include them in songs. In the song text for "Nantoh" performed by Sulemana Iddrisu at the 1973 celebration of Tsimsi Tsugu in Yendi (see Song Text 4.1),[54] he improvises toward the middle of the song by calling out the names of Ya Naa Yakuba's sons who became Ya Naas (e.g., Abudu, Andani, Mahami), listing the names of the towns where they served as king, and referring to the praise name or proverb used to signify them. For example, in line 11, Iddrisu calls out Naa Abudu's praise name, Nagbiegu, which signifies that the king's might is comparable to a bush cow. Naanigoo (see line 12), the praise name for Naa Andani, alludes to the proverb, "Do not trust your enemy or he will turn into a thorn and prick you" (DjeDje 1978b:1475).

Song Text 4.1. Sulemana Iddrisu. "Nantoh." Performed at the Ya Naa's Palace during Tsimsi Tsugu. January 15, 1973.Yendi, Ghana.
TRANSLATED INTO ENGLISH BY FUSEINI ABDULLAHI (1974), ALHASSAN SULEMANA (2003), AND M. D. SULLEY (2003).

Chorus:
Purified one, God loves you.

Vocal Lead:
King, you are the chosen one. [Mankana, the sitting king, you are the chosen one.]
Great one, descendant of Bawuna [King Abudulai], you are the chosen one.
An individual should not worry about poverty. Oh king, you the son of a Kuntuli lady.
Oh, you the descendant of Mahama.
A life, no matter how short it is, cannot be given as a present to anybody.
An individual should not worry about poverty. One pair of trousers is enough.
An individual should not worry about poverty. One gown is enough.
An individual should not worry about poverty. One horse is enough.
Purified one, grandson of Gariba, may God prolong your life.
We have come to find out how you, oh king, and your people spent the night.
The great Abudu is the son of Yakuba, [his praise name is] bush cow [Nagbiegu].
The great Andani, Yakuba's son, the thorn of treachery [Naanigoo].
The great Kworli chief, Mahami, God's cloth takes precedence.

The great Bileima, Yakuba's son, the dog's bone. The hawk has picked the dog's bone and left it in front of the dog.

The great Mion chief, Mahami, Zenaba's [mother's name] son, water from well. People with patience will get water from a well with a rich water table.

A short life can't be transferred to a son, the son of Nantoh. [Life, no matter how short, can't be given as a present to another person.]

The great Sayibu, chief of Tugu, is the son of Nantoh, the fowl in the fetish grove.

A hawk has spotted a fetish fowl and slept in a shrine.

The great Savelugu chief, Bukali, the rainy season's pond. He who draws water from the pond in a rainy season will never go home dirty.

The great chief of Savelugu, Dahamani, Yakuba's son, the straw bangle. The straw bangle can never resemble the metallic bangle. [A bangle made of straw will never be as beautiful as that of metal.]

The great chief of Tampion, Sayibu, Yakuba's son, the slim-waist person's pearl beads. [The highly prized waist beads for a slim-waist person still belongs to her and no other has the right to the beads.]

The great Aduna, chief of Zangbalin. He is Nantoh's son.

Purified one, grandson of Gariba, God will give you good health.

Ruler of this generation, descendant of Gariba.

Purified one, grandson of Gariba, God will give you good health.

Oh, you, the descendant of Mahama.

This universe belongs to you, the descendant of Naa Gariba.

Purified one, grandson of Gariba, God will give you good health.

(DjeDje 1978b:770–771)

It is not only the Ya Naas who are given proverbial or praise names that suggest something special about their personality, character, or social circumstance, but most people in Dagbon. Mahama explains: "If a person is always in trouble with people and he is not a troublemaker, then people are looking for his downfall. So he has to carve a praise name that will tell them proverbially that they are not God, they cannot destroy him. If there is happiness within your folk, you will need a praise name that will put more happiness between you. If there is rivalry, you'll have a proverbial praise that will warn the other side" (1995).

After individuals choose or are identified with a praise name, they keep it for life (Mahama 1995). The manner in which performers and other individuals become acquainted with people's praise names demonstrates the importance of community in Dagbon. Sulley explains: "Performers [and members of the community] learn your praise name at various performances such as rituals, weddings, market places, festivals, funerals that you attend, if you continue calling it. Because you are a native of the place, you've got to attend a ritual or performance. So you can't say you will not attend" (1995).

Although two people can have the same praise name, the family genealogy and characteristics of an individual make the song distinct. Thus, praise names, which may be in the form of a proverb, become identifiers that musicians use to compose and perform songs. In explaining the composition process, Iddrisu states, "No song is composed without falling into a proverb form. Before we can compose songs for them, people must call their praise names or the proverbs. When we have a naming ceremony or a wedding ceremony, all that we do is play the praise names of the person or family concerned. Even if they don't put in any request, we know the elders [father or late father], and we know his praise name" (Iddrisu 1973). Sulemana indicates that some patrons either tell fiddlers the tune they want for their praise names or ask fiddlers to create praise names for them: "Sometimes somebody comes to you and says that 'I want this tune; play it for me.' If it is a new tune, then you begin practicing it. You can just play some improvisation at that point, and when you go back home, you practice that. Sometimes he comes and tells you 'Give me a name that suits me.' Then you will create something for him" (Sulemana 1995b).

Because gondze musicians constitute a social unit based on kinship, the song that one fiddler composes is learned and passed on to other members of the family. Thus, a set repertoire of songs is established both for royalty and commoners. Of course, when the songs in the repertoire are performed, they may be varied slightly because musicians have their individual performance style and are expected to improvise the text. Songs, however, tend not to be altered to the degree that they are unrecognizable from the original creation.

Gondze song texts may include words from one or more languages (Dagbani, Hausa, Gourmantché, Arabic, and some English),[55] which is not surprising considering the cultural history of Dagbon. However, Hausa and Gourmantché are more prominently used in songs that concern royalty. Commenting on the language of song texts, Salifu Lali states: "Civilization has modernized our way of performance. When our great-grandfathers introduced this instrument in Dagbon, they sang mostly in the language of the Grumas, Gourmantché. And since then, we have developed it so much to suit our own taste of singing; we have created two more languages to sing with it, mostly Hausa and Dagbani. It is we who are very old who can still perform and sing in the language of the Gourmantché. The present young man cannot recite a statement or a verse in the Gourmantché language" (Lali 1973). It is noteworthy that Lali refers to songs composed in Dagbani as "new" and the result of Westernization (or modernization), suggesting they are recently created: "We still keep to the old songs, but, besides the old songs, we also introduce new songs in our functions of everyday life. Because of Westernization, one might call a praise name in Dagbani, but this person would not know how to compose a song. So it is left to us to bridge the gap and complete it with our own sense of feeling or material which will be needed to polish the song. Equally, someone might just give a proverb or adage in Dagbani or Hausa, and it is left to us to compose a full sense out of this to play on the *gondze*" (Lali 1973).

When I asked Mahama what was most important, the text or the music, in composing new songs, his response indicated that the lyrics are essential. Not only is the text used to identify songs, but the Dagbani language, which is tonal, determines or plays a major role in defining the melody (Mahama 1995). Therefore when Dagbamba fiddlers, during the 1980s and 1990s, began to compose songs in Twi (the language of the Asante people) and English, this was a departure from tradition (Meiregah 1990). Songs in Dagbani and Hausa are based on proverbs and praise names in honor of royalty and commoners in Dagbon; those in English concern current issues of the day. Sulemana indicates that several languages are used in the songs included on the cassette recording that he made in 1992. One song, in English, dealt with apartheid in South Africa "just to tell the people what type of political system existed there and why there was a need for change" (Sulemana 1994). Although Mahama, who can be considered a traditionalist, had composed songs in Asante, probably because, like Dagbani, it is a tonal language, he was critical of young Dagbamba fiddlers who created songs in English because he felt the fiddle melody did not fit the text (Mahama 1995).

Because the use of Arabic in reciting the Qur'an continues to be commonplace among the Dagbamba, Arabic names are included in gondze songs. However, references to Allah occur only sparingly. More often gondze musicians use "Naawuni," the Dagbani term for God. In his performance of "Kuntag Zaa" (a praise song in honor of Bimbilla Naa Nantogma), Mahama states *Ndan Naawun zallo zalgu, Naawun zalgu,* which means "What the Lord God has written is written" or "What God has decreed is irrevocable" (DjeDje 1978b:737).

Because gondze musicians believe song texts play an important role in educating the public and promoting social responsibility, fiddlers comment on social issues even when the lyrics are concerned with historical events, individuals, or places. Not only do songs deal with behavior (e.g., gossip, greed, envy, worldliness) that the Dagbamba believe is unhealthy, but many also concern topics that aid in promoting social control and positive moral values. The lyrics to the recreation song "Sakpalenga," by Mahama, demonstrate the way in which a performer attempts to discourage gossiping:

> They can only gossip; they can't catch me.
> They can only talk out of sight; they can't catch me.
> They can only be angry; they can't catch me.
> I say, a swallow does not eat millet.
> They only talk in secret; they cannot catch me.
> They can only talk out of sight; they can't catch me.
> They can only gossip; they can't catch me.
> He is a trap, Mahama. (DjeDje 1978b:736)

The symbols and themes included in song texts vary among fiddlers in West Africa because the social history and values of each culture differ. Hausa fiddlers, for example, often mention the occupation and social standing of people they praise to emphasize their wealth or prestige, but such topics are rarely included in songs by Dagbamba fiddlers. Rather, gondze musicians warn people that material gains are insignificant when compared to the respect one obtains from others. In the recreation song "Nyun Taa Jilma," Mahama sings:

He who respects you is better than he who gives you gold.
He who respects you is better than he who gives you jewelry.
He who respects you is better than he who gives you gold.
What harm does respect cause?
It's better than he who gives you gold.
What harm does respect cause? (DjeDje 1978b:74)

References to animals are also common in Dagbamba song texts. Not only do fiddlers compare people to animals, but a tale or story about animals may be used as an analogy to describe the behavior of an individual. Animals are also used to comment on the qualities of rulers. For example, anyone who sings "Taaka Sannu" (used when the Ya Naa walks in a procession at formal events) normally alludes to animals in referencing the Dagbamba king (see below for lyrics to "Taaka Sannu" by Sulemana Iddrisu in January 1973 during Tsimsi Tsugu, and by Salifu Lali in May 1974 during the installation of Ya Naa Yakubu Andani; also see DjeDje 1978b:703, 788 for the complete texts). A few examples of lyrics that include animals include follow:

a. You, the elephant among bachelors,[56] walk slowly.
b. The dog does not go near the playground of lions.
c. Humble king, walk slowly, slowly. You, like the forehead of a bush cow, slowly, slowly.

In the recreation song "Yeda Binbeim Zugu" by Salisu Mahama, the behavior of two animals that are obvious enemies is described. The question posed in the song text is, How did the two animals come in contact? In essence, this tale advises individuals to beware of people in whom they have faith, trust, or confidence, for friends sometimes betray each other.

Hyena has caught monkey; how then has he caught the monkey?
Hyena does not roam by day; hyena has caught monkey. How then rattler?
Hyena has caught monkey; how did he catch him?
Hyena has caught monkey; how did they meet?
Hyena does not roam by day.
I say, hyena has caught monkey; hyena has caught monkey.
Hyena has caught monkey; how did he catch him?
Hyena does not roam by day; hyena has caught monkey. (DjeDje 1978b:739)

The allusion to animals in gondze texts may be an extension of the usage of animal taboos that are sacred in certain areas of Dagbon. Oppong explains, "While legal control of the land is vested in the chiefs, ritual control is in the Land Priests. The land is divided into a series of ritual areas or 'parishes.' Each 'parish' may be distinguished by reference to the animal taboo within its bounds, which is neither slain nor eaten in the area. Such an animal is in a sense the symbol of the mystical aspect of the earth. The sacred animal in the Yendi area is the lion, which is also the symbol of kingship. In some 'parishes' more than one animal is taboo" (Oppong 1973:17).

Form and Stylistic Features of Songs

Similar to Fulbe performances, gondze songs are generally played in a series without stopping. Within a fifteen- to twenty-minute period, as many as thirteen songs may be performed because the length of songs is short. The longest song performed might be four minutes while the shortest could be less than one minute. When I asked Mahama about the large number of songs he includes in performances, especially when performing for royalty, he stated: "When you are performing with no accompaniment or dancing with anyone on stage, it dawns on you at a particular time you need to change this tune or this text because the king is the principal listener here. He will be fed up with one tune. So he will like to listen to as many different variations as possible. So that's why it dawns on you to keep changing the melody so he will be full of joy" (Mahama 1995).

When a large number of songs (e.g., more than twenty) are performed at an event, the lead fiddler may play what Mahama calls *zugubu* (a tuning-up melody or introduction) after every four or five songs. Explaining the significance of the zugubu, Mahama states: "When I'm about to change the song, I have to change the musical bow. This is also to alert the rattler that I'm about to change the title. He will then get himself prepared before I give him the right tune" (Mahama 1995).[57] At formal events such as festivals or funerals for kings and other important officials, historical songs are generally performed in the order in which kings reigned. Thus, musicians must know and correlate the sequence of songs with events in history. "Nantoh" is generally followed by "Bawuna" because Ya Naa Yakuba Andani I's reign was succeeded by Ya Naa Abdulai I's. At other occasions (weddings, outdoorings, funerals), the leader of the group is not obliged to perform songs in a specific order. Rather, his choice may be based on who is in the audience, those who are dancing, or other factors.

Most gondze songs generally have a single theme (main melody, melodic cycle, ostinato) upon which the vocal leader, vocal chorus, and fiddlers create variations. Call and response, which takes place between the vocal leader and the zaabia, or vocal chorus, is important. The chorus does not repeat the exact statement performed by the vocal leader. Rather, a fragment of the melodic cycle is used as the choral response. In the event that a chorus is not used, the ostinato played by the fiddler serves as the response. Thus, the gondze's theme and variation structure is different from most *goge* songs but similar to some *nyanyeru* performances.

Generally gondze songs are organized into three brief sections: opening, middle, and closing.[58] In the opening, the leader introduces the melodic cycle (ostinato) on the fiddle. After repeating the ostinato slowly one or more times with some ornamentation, the lead fiddler begins playing the cycle *a tempo*, and it is at this point that the rattle accompaniment begins. In the middle section, the theme is established and developed through continuous repetition and some variation by the fiddlers, rattlers, and zaabia. The closing normally consists of the fiddler and rattler performing their statements one or two times without any singing.

While music performed on the gondze may extend to more than three octaves, most melodies are performed within a one-octave range. Like fiddle music in other parts of West Africa, most gondze music is based on an anhemitonic pentatonic scale. The rhythm used by the percussion in gondze songs is much simpler than that employed in Fulbe and Hausa fiddling. Rhythmic patterns performed by Dagbamba rattlers are organized in groups of three pulses, and the strong pulse is always on the first beat that is produced when the rattle is struck in the palm of the hand. The tempo of the song determines the pattern rattlers use (rhythm A and rhythm B in Figures 4.2 and 4.3); see foregoing. When the fiddle part is in duple and the rattlers play in triple, cross rhythms result. The use of additive rhythms in melodies occurs occasionally but is not prominent.

In some ways Dagbamba fiddle music is simpler than Hausa and Fulbe fiddling. For example, the linear development of gondze melodies is not extensive. In other ways Dagbamba fiddling is more complex, especially in the layering and interplay of the various melodic (vocal and fiddle) parts. Thus, the two features that most dramatically affect the performance style of gondze music are (1) the greater emphasis placed on the text and (2) the large number of fiddles included in the ensemble.

When greater emphasis is placed on the text, several things happen. Because the audience expects the leader of the group, who is both the lead singer and lead fiddler, to be witty and have a good voice, he devotes more attention to developing the song texts than improvising on the fiddle. His fiddle playing tends to be simple without a lot of ornamentation not only because he needs time to think of new lyrics, but he does not want to do anything that distracts or competes with his singing. Since the lead fiddler does not feel any pressure to demonstrate his virtuoso skills on the instrument, which is one of the primary reasons interludes are included in *goge* and *nyanyeru* performances, the length of the Dagbamba songs is shorter when compared to Fulbe and Hausa songs.

The size of the group affects both melodic organization and improvisation. With a large number of fiddlers, competing sounds are more likely, which can result in cacophony if the melodic parts are not organized systematically. To avoid competition and control improvisation, only one theme, which is derived from the praise name, is normally included in songs, and all fiddlers in the ensemble perform this theme with some variation. The theme serves as the melodic cycle and as a point of reference, which is important in large ensembles. Not only do the vocal leader and vocal chorus base their singing on the cyclic pattern played by fiddlers, but the rattlers also use it as a referent.

To examine how these characteristics are used by different performers, I have transcribed[59] and analyzed the music of three fiddlers who are leaders within the gondze family: Sulemana Iddrisu, Yamba Naa Salifu Issah's nephew who served as the lead gondze during performances at Tsimsi Tsugu in 1973; Salifu

Photo 4.1. Sulemana Iddrisu dancing at a wedding. Photograph by Jacqueline Cogdell DjeDje. January 1973.

Lali, the head gondze at Bimbilla and one of the persons who led gondze performances at the installation of Yakubu Andani in 1974; and Salisu Mahama, an instructor of gondze at the University of Ghana at Legon and another gondze who led songs at the 1974 installation rites for Ya Naa Yakubu Andani.

Music and Identity: Profiles of Three Dagbamba Fiddlers

Sulemana Iddrisu (1918–1991)

Born in Yendi, Sulemana Iddrisu's profession was performing gondze and farming. Iddrisu began his fiddle training when he was between five and eight years old; his father, who served as Yamba Naa between 1930 and 1954, taught him how play the fiddle (Sulemana 1995a). Because Iddrisu and his brothers were born into the gondze family, all performed the instrument. His elder brother, Abdulai Iddrisu, served as Yamba Naa from 1967–1971, and his uncle, Salifu Issah, was enskinned in 1971. Continuing in the family tradition, Sulemana Iddrisu's eleven children had been taught how to play the fiddle and rattle. Since his wives were not born into the gondze family, none participated in the musicking (Iddrisu 1973). Although he was not the Yamba Naa, Iddrisu led the gondze musicians in singing and playing the instrument at most formal

Example 4.1. Sulemana Iddrisu. "Nantoh." Measures 1–6.
Continued on the next page

occasions at the Ya Naa's palace. As a result, he probably knew the gondze reper-toire better than most fiddlers living outside Yendi.

During my research in Yendi, I observed Iddrisu performing in several con-texts: at a festival (Tsimsi), in the privacy of his home, and at a wedding. For this analysis, I focus on "Nantoh" (3:10), the first song performed by gondze musicians on the eve of Tsimsi Tsugu. "Nantoh" is also one of the most popular

Example 4.1. *Continued*

among Dagbamba fiddlers, probably because it praises Ya Naa Yakuba who en-skinned Abudulai Baako as Yamba Naa, the first fiddler in Dagbon to hold such a title (Mahama 1990a; Sulley 1971).[60]

The gondze melodies for "Nantoh" (Example 4.1) are based on twelve beats and performed within a one-octave range, and the call and response occurs between the vocal leader and vocal chorus.[61] Rhythm B is employed throughout, creating cross rhythms between the gondze and gagle (see the duple melody performed by the fiddle and triple rhythms in the percussion of Example 4.1).

The opening for "Nantoh" is distinct, probably because of performance context. Whereas most fiddlers in Dagbon and other parts of West Africa perform the most complex version of the melody in the opening, Iddrisu does just the opposite. Like the leader of a West African drum ensemble who taps out the bell pattern in a very simple manner (so that everyone hears and understands the tempo and the rhythmic timeline) before the rest of the group enters, Iddrisu does the same with the fiddle melody in the opening (see measure 1). Only after the melodic cycle is stated very simply two or three times does he introduce a slightly more complex variation of the melody (compare the gondze melody in measures 1–4 with 5–6) that serves as the cycle through the rest of the piece. Occasional variations occur during the middle section, but they are not extensive. Similar to Fulbe and Hausa fiddling, variation takes place in specified points. Variations in the fiddle melody most often occur between beats 3 and 6 of the cycle; notice that the first evidence of variation in "Nantoh" occurs on the second half of beat 6 in measure 3 of the gondze statement. In measures 5 and 6 (beats 3 to 6), the gondze statement is even more varied. "Nantoh" ends with the vocal chorus, fiddlers, and rattlers playing their parts. Then Iddrisu abruptly intervenes by performing the fiddle melodic cycle for "Bawuna," the next song, in a slow tempo (see DjeDje 1978b for the complete transcription).

Iddrisu's singing is the most melodically and rhythmically complex part of his performance. Toward the end of the first fiddle statement of "Nantoh," he begins by singing an elaborate version of the vocal chorus, probably to prepare those who will be singing this part later (see vocal leader part in measures 1–2). However, because he does this so early, the introduction is very short. During the rest of the song, Iddrisu does not sing the chorus but develops new material. Occasionally, he follows the general contour of the melodic cycle (compare the fiddle and vocal leader parts for measure 4, beats 5–7). Other times he creates a totally different melody because of the text he uses in singing the praises (compare the vocal leader and gondze parts in measures 3 and 4, beats 1–4, to see how Iddrisu's singing differs from the melodic cycle).

The part performed by the zaabia in "Nantoh" is somewhat different from the gondze cycle. In some instances the zaabia repeat the same phrase without changes. Other times the vocal chorus varies its repetitive phrase. No overlapping (homophony) takes place between the vocal leader and vocal chorus, but incidental harmony does occur on beats 8 and 9 within the vocal chorus of each cycle. Because of the interplay of the different melodic parts, polyphony is strongly apparent throughout the performance.

An analysis of Iddrisu's playing indicates that the size and organization of the fiddle ensemble, as well performance context, can affect performance style. Iddrisu places more emphasis on singing and developing the text at the festival but focuses more on fiddling at his home (see analysis of "Dunia Taali" in DjeDje 1978b). Without the need to impress the audience by improvising on the

Photo 4.2. Salifu Lali holding the *gondze*. Photograph by Jacqueline Cogdell DjeDje. January 1973.

lyrics, fiddle variations in his home performance are reserved, especially when his playing is compared with other Dagbamba fiddlers included in this study.

Salifu Lali (early 1930s–2001)

Salifu Lali was born in Gbulon, a town in western Dagbon. As head gondze, he lived in Bimbilla, which is about forty miles south of Yendi in eastern Dagbon. Lali began his gondze training when he was between four and five years old when an elder brother taught him. Before settling in Bimbilla, Lali and his family lived in southern Ghana in Accra. His work at the Accra Race Club, "taking care of the horses," did not allow him time to play gondze on a regular basis. Rather, he performed when people from all walks of life invited him on holidays or at weddings and outdoorings. Only when his elder brother requested that he return to the North to help him in Bimbilla did Lali choose fiddling as his primary profession. In addition to his ten children, his four younger brothers assisted him in performing his duties as gondze (Lali 1973). Lali was highly regarded by gondze musicians in Dagbon and his immediate family. He had the honor of serving as the head gondze during the installation celebration of the enskinment of Ya Naa Yakubu Andani in May 1974, and his kin often sent their children to him to learn about fiddling.

Lali's early experiences as a fiddler both in northern *and* southern Ghana gave him a perspective somewhat different from that of Sulemana Iddrisu, who spent much of his life in the north. While growing up and learning how to play the fiddle in Gbulon, Lali had the occasion to perform at all types of events associated with the divisional and village rulers based in western Dagbon. In Accra where he performed at events for both Dagbamba and non-Dagbamba, he probably modified his playing to appeal to a more diverse audience. While he knew the repertory of songs associated with the Ya Naa, he did not perform them as regularly as Iddrisu. In other words, Lali's experiences brought him in contact with a broader audience.

I observed fiddling by Salifu Lali in two different contexts: at his home during an interview in January 1973 and during his performance at the installation rites for Ya Naa Yakubu Andani.[62] At the interview, he performed three songs: "Bantchande" (1:11), a praise song in honor of a Gurma king; "Nantoh" (1:17); and "Karinbandana" (:52), a praise song for Yamba Naa Ntoli. Because it is longer, more developed, and can be used to compare fiddling by Sulemana Iddrisu, my analysis here is based on "Nantoh" (see Example 4.2). Lali sang the vocal lead and was the only fiddler; his ten-year-old daughter, Mariama, performed the rattle and sang the vocal chorus.

Although the three songs were played together in a series, Lali did not perform anything distinctive, such as a tuning-up melody, to connect them. After he played the last note in "Bantchande," he immediately performed the melodic cycle for "Nantoh." There are several differences in the performance of "Nantoh" by Iddrisu and Lali. First, not only is Lali's introduction longer (two statements instead of one), but it includes more ornamentation. Yet the ornaments that Lali employs are basically the same as those used by Iddrisu. Second, although the theme that Iddrisu and Lali employ is recognizable as "Nantoh," they are not exactly the same. While the music played between beats 5 and 11 is similar, the beginning of the song (music played between beats 1 and 4) by each performer differs (compare measure 1 of Example 4.1 with measure 3 of Example 4.2). This demonstrates that although the repertory for gondze songs is set, performers create variants of basic melodies.

Iddrisu and Lali also create intensity differently. Iddrisu's performance of "Nantoh" is faster (116 minutes per minute), and only quarter and eighth notes are prominently used. Lali creates the same energy by using more eighth and some sixteenth notes, but the tempo is slower (96 minutes per second). Thus, it is interesting how performers can produce the desired effect by modifying different aspects of the music.

Although the vocal lead is the most melodically and rhythmically complex part of Lali's performance of "Nantoh," he does not develop the text as extensively as Iddrisu. Instead of recounting several of the past Ya Naas, Lali focuses only on Ya Naa Yakuba by using proverbs and other praises that refer to the king's power and importance in Dagbon (see Song Text 4.2). However, as with Iddrisu's version, cross rhythms are used because the fiddler's part is performed in duple while the rattler performs in triple. The vocal chorus in Lali's perfor-

Example 4.2. Salifu Lali. "Nantoh." Measures 1–6.
Continued on the next page

Example 4.2. *Continued*

mance, which does not enter until measure 4, is not as melodically or rhythmically developed as Iddrisu's because only one person is performing.

Song Text 4.2. Salifu Lali. "Nantoh." Performed January 22, 1973. Bimbilla, Ghana.

TRANSCRIBED AND TRANSLATED BY M. IDDI. JULY 1974.
LEGON, GHANA.

Measure Number	Vocal Lead
2–3	A heavy object cannot defeat its carriers [No matter the weight of an object, its carriers will always carry it].
3–4	A heavy object cannot defeat its carriers. A lion's elder's son is a lion.
4–5	The owner of the world, Andani's son, we have come to see whether you are well.
5–6	All of the subjects of this land, commoners and princes alike, recognize you as their overlord, and we have come to see how well you are.

In summary, we find that Lali's performance style differs from Iddrisu's but not dramatically. Most likely the differences in style are due to (1) the size of the two groups, (2) the performances taking place in different settings, and (3) the fiddlers unique performance style. Although the melodic ornamentation used by Lali is similar to that employed by Iddrisu and other gondze musicians, Lali employs ornaments more prominently.

Salisu Mahama (1934–2001)

The life of Salisu Mahama, a musician well known throughout Dagbon for his wisdom and knowledge of the gondze tradition, differs from other Dagbamba fiddlers because it reflects a greater integration of traditional and nontraditional culture.

Mahama was born in Diare, a small village near Savelugu. In terms of his professional life, Mahama explains: "First and foremost is the gondze, second is farming, third is the weaving of hats, and fourth is another form of decoration that I make for chiefs in the North" (Mahama 1990b). Mahama has four children who all know how to play gondze and rattle.

Although Mahama's position at Legon gave him enormous visibility in Ghana, he was not without his critics. Sulley indicates that some gondze referred to Mahama as a "female son" because his inheritance came not from his father but his mother (Sulley 1995).[63] Since the Dagbamba are patrilineal, inheriting a profession through one's mother can be used to discredit legitimacy and credibility. Yet this factor did not affect Mahama's stature or popularity. Both

Photo 4.3. Salisu Mahama (seated and holding the *gondze*) with his group, including M. D. Sulley, who is seated on Mahama's right. Ahmadu Iddrisu (standing and holding the *gagle*). Photograph by Jacqueline Cogdell DjeDje. December 1994.

the young and the elderly in Dagbon often consulted him regarding details of gondze history. Many were also enthralled with Mahama's playing. Sulley explains: "Most younger performers come to him wanting to hear his voice, wanting to see his performances just to copy or imitate him. So he doesn't perform just everywhere. He has special occasions on which to perform" (Sulley 1995).

Salisu began his fiddle training when he was between the ages of six and seven. Yamba Naa Mahama Bla, his mother's younger brother who taught him how to play the instrument, had a major influence on him. Considering the times in which he lived, Mahama Bla was cosmopolitan in his behavior and thinking. Mahama states that not only was his uncle known throughout Dagbon, the uncle understood twelve to sixteen different languages and had taken several trips outside Ghana. When Salisu was in his late teens and early twenties, he lived for short periods (one to two years) in different regions of Ghana with other gondze family members, performing at major funerals and other events, which gave him greater experience, confidence, and notoriety as a fiddler.

Salisu's prominence as an outstanding gondze player is one of the reasons he was invited to work at the University of Ghana's Institute of African Studies (IAS). When he made the decision to accept the position, his music world changed and foreshadowed the role of gondze in Dagbon and modern Ghana.

After his retirement from IAS in 1983,[64] Mahama limited his fiddling to special performances. "When I stay in Accra, distinguished personalities invite me, a dignitary or visitor from outside Ghana. If a tourist comes to Ghana demanding to have good models of the instrument, I model the instruments and send them to him. Others write requesting instruments" (Mahama 1990). Overwhelmed with requests to perform toward the end of his life, Mahama restricted his engagements to only the most "important functions," festivals in major Dagbamba towns and funerals of rulers and other important people (Mahama 1995).

Because of his affiliation with the university, Salisu Mahama was one of the first fiddlers to receive attention from the media. In 1978, the Ghana Film Studio produced a cassette recording of his music that was sold in northern Ghana. He allowed the Ghana Broadcasting Company (GBC) to take five minutes from the recording to use "for Dagbani programs on the television and on the radio" (Mahama 1995). In addition, he made several trips to the United States and Europe.[65]

When I interviewed Mahama in 1995 and asked about changes in his life as a professional fiddler, he talked about transformations in his performance style:

> I do not play so vigorously like I used to do when I was in my middle thirties and forties. I sometimes get tired which can slow down the performance. I recall a visit to a village near Karaga, one of the divisional areas of Dagbon. There was a real performance. When I started playing the *gondze* around 9:00 PM, I never ceased till daybreak with some little resting intervals. Now I can't even do a quarter of a night because of old age. However, what I'm performing and the way I'm performing give me a lot of admirers and attention. I can say that my performance is equal to many other violinists or *gondze* players. I not only play at the university but I perform for the national level as well. I gain more experiences as I continue my daily performances because new ideas come.

As he grew older, he stated that God had become central to his life, causing changes in the lyrics of his songs.

> When you are old and elderly, you must think of God more often than anybody. When I was young, I hardly thought about God so much. So I just started singing praises to someone else instead of God. But today, I can't start a performance without singing praises to the Almighty God here.
>
> When I go to perform at the palace of the king. I will first of all remind the Ya Naa that God is the creator of the universe, and I have to sing His praises first. After having sung the praises to God, the Creator, then I will then remind the chief that now it's his turn. (Mahama 1995)

I have observed fiddle performances by Salisu Mahama at festivals, funerals, and in concerts at IAS and in the United States. In fact, I have audio and video recordings of more than seventy songs performed by him at music events and private sessions. Yet I find the music played during special recording sessions to be the most fascinating because he is more experimental in the type of songs he plays and the manner in which he performs them. During a recording session at

IAS on June 11, 1973, Mahama played the fiddle and sang the vocal lead, while Ahmadu Iddrisu, a cousin who was a member of his professional troupe, played the rattle and sang the vocal chorus.

During Mahama's 1973 performance, not only did he play praise music for the different Ya Naas and Yamba Naas, he also performed several proverbial, recreation, and possession songs. In total, there were twenty-eight songs, but here I analyze only two—"Yenchebli" (also spelled Yantsebli) (1:06) and "Dunia Taali" (1:50)—because they demonstrate how Mahama's performance style compares with that of other fiddlers in this study.

"Yenchebli" is significant because it praises the legendary figure believed to have introduced gondze into Gurma culture (Sulley 1971). Except for a brief mention of Grumaland in the last line to "Yenchebli" (see Song Text 4.3), Mahama's lyrics do not refer to the gondze history. Instead, he includes proverbs and other praises that allude to the power and greatness of chieftaincy in Dagbon.

Song Text 4.3. Salisu Mahama. "Yenchebli." Performed June 11, 1973. University of Ghana. Legon.
TRANSCRIBED AND TRANSLATED BY FUSEINI ABDULLAHI (JUNE 1974) AND M. D. SULLEY (AUGUST 2003). LEGON, GHANA.

Measure Number	Vocal
7–8	I have come to find out how you slept last night.
8–9	Son of Gariba, called Yenchebli.
10–11	Oh. Son of Gariba, called Yenchebli.
13–14	No king is comparable to Almighty God.
14–15	Below God, no other king but you.
16	Your enemy, Naa Muudu, has a face like that of a hyena.
18–19	I have come to find out how you slept last night.
20–21	I have come to find out how you slept last night.
23–24	There is no land as sweet and as homely for me, Yenchebli, as Grumaland.
25–26	There is no land as sweet and as homely for me, Yenchebli, as Grumaland.

Mahama's song texts for "Dunia Taali" are more developed (see Song Text 4.4). Since the theme of the song concerns people not knowing what causes problems in the world or what is considered a fault, Mahama improvises on the text by referring to different items people might have in their possession (e.g., a fine shirt, fine shorts, or a fine hat) to demonstrate that almost anything can be a fault. In some cases, Mahama uses two statements to make the same point: "A fine shirt is considered a fault. Fine shorts are considered a fault" (see measures 7–8 of Song Text 4.4). Other times, he uses two opposing statements to make his point: "Wealth is considered a fault. Poverty is considered a fault" (see measures 9–10 of Song Text). Because Mahama varies his text continuously, the singing in this part of the piece is involved with lots of melodic improvisation.

Song Text 4.4. Salisu Mahama. "Dunia Taali." Performed June 11, 1973. University of Ghana, Legon.

TRANSCRIBED AND TRANSLATED BY FUSEINI ABDULLAHI (JUNE 1974) AND M. D. SULLEY (AUGUST 2003). LEGON, GHANA.

Chorus:
No one can know one's faults in the world.

Measure Number	*Vocal Leader*
4	Wealth is the world. No man can tell what the world considers a fault.
5–6	Wealth is the world. Wealth is considered a fault.
7–8	A fine shirt is considered a fault. Fine shorts are considered a fault.
9–10	Wealth is considered a fault. Poverty is considered a fault.
11–12	A wealthy man is considered proud. A poor man is considered useless [a failure].
13–14	No man can tell what the world considers a fault. (twice)
15–16	A fine shirt is considered a fault. A pair of fine shorts is considered a fault.
17–18	Wealth is considered a fault. Poverty is considered a fault.
19–20	Wealth is considered a fault. Poverty is considered a fault.
21–22	A fine hat is the world. A pair of fine shorts is considered a fault.

Although Mahama's performance style is similar to that of other gondze musicians, he emphasizes different features, causing his fiddling to be varied and more improvisatory with extensive use of ornamentation. Mahama performs "Yenchebli" on the gondze without the accompaniment of rattle or vocal chorus, and the form is theme and variation (see Example 4.3). In the opening, he performs the twelve-beat melodic cycle in a highly improvisatory manner. Not only does he include grace notes and neighboring tones, but he also moves quickly from one octave to another to develop the melody. In measure 1, he uses a major tenth rather than a major third on beats 5–6 and 10. Instead of playing the melodic cycle once or twice in the opening before singing, he performs the cycle five times and rarely repeats it the same way (see measures 1–6). In the middle section, which starts at measure 7, Mahama confines his fiddle melody to one octave, but his use of large (thirds, fifths, and sixths) and small intervals (semitones and whole tones) is prominent in the rest of the song.

When singing the text for "Yenchebli," Mahama either stops playing the fiddle altogether or just repeats one note several times as if he were playing a drone (see fiddle part in measure 7, beats 8–11, and measure 8, beats 7–10). This

Example 4.3. Salisu Mahama. "Yenchebli." Measures 1–8.
Continued on the next page

indicates that developing the fiddle melody is just as important to him as singing, and he wants to produce something new in each part rather than sing and
play the fiddle in unison. Mahama ends the song by playing two statements of
the melodic cycle without any singing (see ending in DjeDje 1978b:1132).

Unlike other fiddlers who generally place significant pressure on the bow
when playing the gondze, Mahama uses a light bowing technique throughout

236 *Fiddling in West Africa*

Example 4.3. *Continued*

his performance of "Yenchebli" to produce a soft, scratchy sound on the fiddle, probably to suggest the way Yenchebli may have played for the Gurma ruler in an intimate private setting. While Mahama may use such light touch occasionally in other songs, it is rarely used throughout a piece.

In "Yenchebli," call and response takes place between the vocal and fiddle part (see measures 7 and 8). However, the fiddle dominates because of the amount of time and manner in which Mahama performs the fiddle melody. Instead of singing the melody and repeating it on the fiddle, the fiddle part stands alone and in some instances is more developed than the singing. Therefore, Mahama's fiddle playing in "Yenchebli" comes very close to the performance style of Hausa fiddlers.

Improvisation is also strongly apparent in Mahama's performance of "Dunia Taali" (see Example 4.4). Here, Mahama does not embellish the melody with grace notes and neighboring tones, but he also does not restrict his playing to an octave. In the opening, rather than play a major third (from G to B), he performs a major tenth (see beats 1 and 2 of measure 2). When Mahama sings the vocal lead, which, like other gondze performances, is the most melodically and rhythmically complex part of the song, he chooses one of several ways to perform the fiddle. He either stops fiddling (see measure 4) or creates a drone by

Example 4.4. Salisu Mahama. "Dunia Taali." Measures 1–6 and 13–16.
Continued on the next page

repeating one note several times (see measure 6), a technique he uses in other songs. Occasionally, he performs portions of the cycle lightly (see measure 14) or merely plays two notes to fill in an empty space (see measure 16) that results because of the structure of the lyrics (see Song Text 4.4).

What is most striking about Mahama's "Dunia Taali" is the interrelationship of parts. The time span for this piece is twenty-four beats because the rattler

Example 4.4. *Continued on the next page*

performs his three-pulse pattern eight different times during the melodic cycle. However, the fiddle melody for "Dunia Taali" is based on sixteen beats, which creates cross rhythms (two against three) between the fiddle and rattle parts (see beat 7 of measure 2 for the beginning of the cross rhythm between the percussion and fiddle part).

Call and response in Mahama's "Dunia Taali" takes place between the vocal leader and the vocal chorus. Normally, the vocal chorus performs a theme that is related or derived from the fiddle melodic cycle. What makes Mahama's

Example 4.4. *Continued*

performance of "Dunia Taali" distinctive is that Ahmadu Iddrisu (the rattler) uses the first five beats of the vocal chorus to sing a counter melody, which is different from the cycle (see measure 3 of Example 4.4). Or he sings a melody that produces harmony (homophonic parallelism) (Nketia 1974:161–163). For example, in measure 5 of Example 4.4, while Mahama performs the fiddle melody, Ahmadu Iddrisu sings either a minor third or perfect fourth higher.

The result is an interesting polyphonic sound that differs from the textures of performances by Sulemana Iddrisu and Salifu Lali.

Mahama's performance style is distinctive for its variety, ornamentation, and improvisation. Although he follows the rules, most often he deviates from them in interesting ways whether he is performing alone or with a group. Not only does he include more embellishments in his fiddling than other Dagbamba fiddlers, but he does not limit his music to a one-octave range. Yet Mahama's improvisations are not as extensive as the musicking by Hausa and Fulbe fiddlers primarily because of the emphasis that the Dagbamba place on developing the text rather than the fiddle melody.

Conclusion

West African fiddling is not a minor and unchanging tradition, but is dynamic and highly developed. In addition to the joy and pleasure to be found in simply listening to fiddle music, the sound of the instrument has a way of touching the spirit and soul of those who experience it. While some West African musicians became fiddlers because it was a spiritual calling, others indicate that fiddling is important because of its additional qualities. Many West Africans believe that fiddling also has the power to heal and empower; thus, using the fiddle to communicate with the ancestors and spirit world is not uncommon. As a link with the present and past, fiddling both reinforces and signifies cultural identity and social status for those who use it. To explain how fiddling gained importance and point out the distinctiveness of fiddle music in different societies, I focus here on several issues: intracultural influences, multiple identities, and musical style.

Intracultural Influences

Fiddling in West Africa is most often identified with people living in the Sudan, but the history of the tradition has not been documented. What is known about fiddling comes from scattered references to the instrument in audiovisual and print sources and local histories of societies. The earliest printed references to West African fiddling appear in two eighteenth century works: (1) the writings of Jean Baptiste Labat, a French monk who traveled widely on the continent, and (2) a poem written by Fulbe leader Shehu 'Uthman dan Fodio, who led the nineteenth-century jihad in Hausaland. Using these sources and Gerhard Kubik's methodology (1998) regarding the spread of music traits (through human migration, contacts between neighboring groups, long-distance travel, and the media), a history of fiddling in West Africa can be constructed, one that can be used as a basis for further scrutiny and analysis.

West African fiddling probably began between the eleventh and thirteenth centuries, because the earliest evidence of interactions between West and North Africans occurred during this time. The Fulbe, a nomadic people who originated in the Senegal valley and are kin to the Tukulor, were most likely responsible for the early dispersion of the fiddle when they began migrating across West Africa in the twelfth century. Since some scholars believe the Fulbe are responsible for the distribution of the plucked lute (Coolen 1983), crediting them with the dispersion of the bowed lute is not far-fetched.[1]

Contacts between neighboring groups helped reinforce and spread the fiddle tradition to others. Not only did Hausa speakers have contacts with people who traveled east and west, but also several cities in Hausaland were important commercial centers along northern and southern trans-Saharan trade routes. In addition to learning about the tradition from the Fulbe, who arrived in Hausaland in the fifteenth century, the Hausa may have been exposed to fiddling through the Kanuri (Kanembu), the Songhai, or the Tuareg, for all play the fiddle and had interactions with North Africans. However, the prominence of the Hausa term for the fiddle (goge and its variants) among people in the Central Sudan, the Volta Basin, and central and southern Nigeria indicate that the Hausa were responsible for the dispersion of the instrument in these areas.[2] Whether gender played a role in the use and adoption of the fiddle in different cultures is not known. Among the Tuareg, fiddling is identified primarily with women. Although males dominate as fiddlers in Hausa and Songhai societies, females in both cultures also perform the instrument.

Musicians throughout Sudanic West Africa have been involved in long-distance travel (moving to different locations for short time periods with the intention of returning to their homeland) since precolonial times (Kubik 1998: 297). Before fiddlers from Grumaland settled permanently in Dagbon, they traveled great distances performing for royalty in both locations. When new opportunities and modes of transportation developed during the colonial and postcolonial eras, fiddlers traveled even farther distances from their homes. Hausa fiddler Garba Liyo regularly performed in different locations in West Africa (Nigeria, Niger, Côte d'Ivoire). When Salisu Mahama accepted a position in the Institute of African Studies (IAS) at the University of Ghana, he not only continued his travels in different regions of Ghana, but he also visited the United States and countries in West Africa and Europe. Fulbe fiddlers have always traveled to various locations in the Western Sudan (The Gambia, Senegal, Guinea, Mali), but Juldeh Camara has gone further afield: he has toured Europe and North America and become a resident musician for performing arts centers in Great Britain. These contacts have led to a type of cosmopolitanism both within and outside Africa (Turino 2000). Because scholars place more focus on how Africans are affected by non-Africans, examining how travel and mobility *within* Africa affects creativity and identity has received little attention.[3]

Multiple Identities

The use of a multi-sited ethnography reveals that West African fiddling has multiple identities. While some commonalities exist (for example, almost everyone uses the fiddle for entertainment), many distinctions are also apparent. Thus, the role of the fiddle in West Africa, both interculturally and intraculturally, is multilayered. Not only do variations in location, history, and cultural systems account for differences in meaning, other factors (ethnicity, religion, social status) affect identity.

Fiddling among the Fulbe in Senegambia is not identified with a particular ceremony or social institution. Not only do most Fulbe performance occasions include fiddling, nyanyeru music can be heard in pan-ethnic settings. When

Senegambians participate collectively in ceremonial activities such as puberty rites, fiddle music serves as a symbol of Fulbe culture and provides entertainment to non-Fulbe (*Born Musicians* 1984). In the Senegambian media and tourist industry, the nyanyeru represents the Fulbe just as the kora and bala help to identify the Mande. The decline in popularity of Fulbe fiddling because of generational differences has not affected the instrument's role. As a symbol of identity that reflects and shapes ethnicity, fiddling not only allows the Fulbe to remember their heritage, but it makes them proud of their Fulbeness. Through fiddling, the Fulbe are able to affirm and assert a complex of identities with self, ethnicity, region, and nation; they are transformed from being Senegambians to being Fulbe in Senegambia.

The tensions that exist among practitioners of the two major religions (Bori and Islam) in Hausaland contribute to the complex multilayering of meanings identified with the goge in northern Nigeria. While Muslims regard fiddling as profane, believing it signifies the devil and everything evil, fiddling empowers marginalized Bori practitioners, who use fiddle music to call Bori spirits to help with their problems. As social outcasts, fiddlers do not have qualms about participating in so-called immoral activities at venues considered to be unacceptable by the moral authorities. Their low status and the fiddle's negative associations may be part of the reason they have been musically innovative and open to new ideas. Instead of members of the Hausa community turning against them, fiddlers have received support not only from the elite in both the traditional and modern governments, but also from those who invite them to perform at ceremonial occasions.

When Shari'a (Islamic law) was revived in northern Nigeria in the late twentieth century in resistance to Western influence, government leaders banned fiddling and Bori, causing the performance of goge music to go underground. Although the fiddle does not have the visibility it once had, fiddlers performing in the twenty-first century attribute the instrument's decline to generational changes, not Shari'a. Not only do the youth find other types of Hausa and Western music to their liking, the difficulty in learning to play the fiddle has caused it to be less popular. Because the Hausa are a people who welcome new ideas, some in Hausaland believe fiddling will never die because fiddlers always find new ways to re-invent themselves and the tradition (Hassan 2003).

The Dagbamba fiddle's association with royalty has deeply affected its identity. Unlike royal performers in some West African societies where serving as a court musician does not always translate into a high social standing, the situation among the Dagbamba differs because of their geographical location and history. Located in the Volta Basin, the Dagbamba have been isolated from many Sudanic populations. They did not develop a large empire or state comparable to societies in the Western and Central Sudan, and Islamic influence was slight, so the indigenous religion continued to be practiced by Dagbamba rulers and others in the society.

Because the gondze's history validates the social status of fiddlers, the oral tradition concerning fiddling has been preserved. While the early history of the fiddle is a topic of much debate among the Dagbamba, most musicians and nonmusicians agree that fiddling began because of a close bond that developed between one of the kings and a fiddler who was a foreigner and nobleman. To maintain the intimate relationship with the king, the people of Dagbon gave the fiddler a titled position comparable to the one in his homeland. When he intermarried with the Dagbamba, an exogamous social group based on kinship became identified with fiddling. People not born into the family are not allowed to perform the instrument. Therefore, because fiddling was introduced into Dagbon by the king, royalty became responsible for all needs (food, clothing, housing, etc.) of the fiddler and his family.

Unlike Hausa fiddlers who rely on innovation for their survival, continuity has been the factor that has contributed to the maintenance of fiddling in Dagbon. The cultural emphasis on preservation has not only influenced the repertoire and performance style of Dagbamba fiddlers, but the Dagbamba social organization and attitude toward fiddling have been affected also. Because of changes that took place in the political organization of Dagbamba society in the latter part of the twentieth century (disputes over the succession of kingship and fewer resources for kings to support fiddlers), however, some fiddlers believe that fiddling lost its importance because it no longer served its primary role—to perform for royalty.

Instead of declining, Dagbamba fiddling is, I believe, in a state of transition. The transformations the Dagbamba underwent in the late twentieth and early twenty-first centuries were similar to the changes the Fulbe and Hausa experienced earlier in the nineteenth and twentieth centuries.[4] Just as musicians in Senegambia were forced to establish a new patronage system because of the changes in kingship in the Western Sudan and Hausa fiddlers had to find other occasions at which to perform when Bori was attacked by Muslim followers, Dagbamba fiddlers will have to adjust to the political and social changes now taking place in Dagbon. Instead of relying solely on royalty for their livelihood, some Dagbamba fiddlers have already started performing for other patrons, creating new songs for nonroyal functions and pursuing other occupations (farming, trading, etc.) to supplement their incomes. Yet if the fiddling tradition is to continue to pass on to family, Dagbamba youth will need to have a more positive attitude about learning it. If this does not happen, nonkinsmen may take up fiddling and change it to suit their needs. When and if this happens, it will be interesting to see if the social status of Dagbamba fiddlers remains high.

Musical Style

One of the many goals of this study has been to examine the extent that musical style relates to identity. When variables such as ensemble organization, form, melody, and rhythm are analyzed, it becomes apparent that West African fiddling has its own enduring and generic characteristics yet the manner in which musical elements are fused gives each region, culture, and musician a unique quality. The fiddle traditions represented here fall into several geographical regions: dessert, grasslands, woodlands, and forest.

The organization of fiddle ensembles in West Africa varies. Groups may include fiddle and idiophone; fiddle and membranophone; fiddle, idiophone, and membranophone; or fiddle, idiophone, membranophone, and aerophone. On some occasions, another type of chordophone (the plucked lute) may be included. While a few societies such as the Dagbamba are known for performing with a number of fiddles in the ensemble, many groups use only one. Solo fiddling seems to be strongest in the Sahel or northern parts of West Africa. Many ensembles include percussion, indicating that the emphasis on rhythm that characterizes musicking in the forest region has influenced fiddling in the savannah. Regardless of the combination or number of instruments in an ensemble, vocal music is central to a performance. Not only is the fiddle used to accompany the voice, such as what occurs in Fulbe and Dagbamba fiddling, but the voice can be subservient to the fiddle, as in the performance practice employed by Hausa fiddlers. In either case, the text is important in determining melody.[5]

Although most fiddle songs are divided into three parts (opening, middle, and closing), what happens in the different sections varies. Dagbamba fiddling is the most straightforward. One fiddle melody is introduced in the opening of gondze songs and developed in the middle section by continuous repetition and minor variation; the song ends with performers simply restating their parts as they move to the next song. Only the lead vocalist in gondze performances improvises extensively by varying the song texts. Songs performed by Hausa and Fulbe fiddlers tend to be more developed and longer, partly because of the number of themes included in the songs, but the emphasis placed on fiddle improvisation is also a factor. While the Hausa may introduce as many as five or six themes in a song, the Fulbe use one or two. In addition to including improvisatory material in the opening and closing, Fulbe and Hausa fiddlers may introduce interludes in the middle section to develop themes or introduce new material.

Other features relevant to the form of African-derived music—call and response, repetition, and variation—are prominent in West African fiddling. Call and response, whether performed between the lead vocal and fiddle, fiddle and chorus, or a solo fiddler who divides his melodies into sections so that one part represents the call and the other part the response, reflects the communal aspects of West African music and culture. Instead of repetition and variation contradicting each other, they are complementary. The repetition of a melody or rhythm not only gives greater emphasis to the pattern, but repetition provides a basis for improvisation. Parts of the cycle may be selected for further development, or the cycle may serve as a referent while variation takes place. Therefore, the melodic and rhythmic cycles played by fiddlers and percussionists are critical to the success of a performance.

The melodic and rhythmic organization of fiddle music reveals much about the relationship of style to geography and ethnicity. Single-part textures (monophony), emphasis on melody, and melodic ornamentation are more extensive in the northern regions. Fiddlers in the desert (e.g., the Tuareg, Tukulor, and Wolof) include handclapping, but rarely are percussion instruments used. When multipart organization is found in the desert, normally it appears as heterophony or a drone. In the woodlands or areas closer to the forest region, multiparts (polyphony and homophonic parallelism) and greater emphasis on rhythm are more apparent because of the use of percussion and a vocal chorus in the fiddle ensemble.

When melody and rhythm are examined in relationship to ethnicity and musical style, findings reinforce what has already been discovered. The feature that most distinguishes Dagbamba fiddling from that of the Hausa and Fulbe is the lack of emphasis placed on developing fiddle melodies. Whereas goge and some nyanyeru melodic themes can be long with lots of embellishment, gondze melodies are simple, with the majority consisting of only two- or three-note ornaments (e.g., grace notes, neighboring, passing, and repeated tones), indicating that extensive ornamentation of the fiddle part is not as important as improvisation of the song text and vocal melody. Most gondze melodies are based on triplets within a rhythmic cycle of nine, twelve, or twenty-four beats, but Hausa and Fulbe fiddle melodies may be organized on either duple or triple rhythms. Although percussion is essential in all traditions, rhythmic accompaniment in gondze songs is not extensively developed and tends to be the same in each song, while the rhythmic timeline performed by the Fulbe and Hausa percussionists varies and can be quite developed. Dagbamba fiddlers rarely employ interludes, which precludes improvisation on the fiddle in the way that it occurs in Hausa and some Fulbe performances.

Because several melodic parts (vocal leader, lead fiddler, vocal chorus, and fiddle chorus) perform independently in gondze performances, more interplay occurs between melodic phrases, resulting in a thicker or denser polyphonic texture. Whereas Fulbe and Hausa melodies are more complex horizontally (linearly) because of the use of extended melodic phrases as well as complex ornaments and embellishments, Dagbamba music is more developed vertically or in the interrelationship of melodic parts. If the percussion in Hausa and Fulbe music were excluded, the texture of goge and nyanyeru music would be close to monophony or heterophony, a characteristic feature of Arab-derived music in North Africa. Excluding the percussion in Dagbamba gondze music would probably result in polyphony, one of the defining features of music in West Africa.

This study demonstrates that differentiation exists in the performance style of traditional musicians, which is significant because scholarship rarely focuses on the individual musical style of traditional performers. By analyzing musical style, it becomes apparent that fiddlers within societies create their own identities, confirming that traditional culture is not homogenous. Because of the different Fulbe dialect groups that reside in West Africa, several Fulbe fiddle traditions (ensemble organizations and performance styles) exist. Not only are the skills of the Fulbe fiddlers in Senegambia distinct, but each fiddler has a different specialization. When compared to Tamba Kandeh and Samba Bah, Juldeh Camara is not only the most accomplished and most technically competent fiddler, he is also the most innovative. The manner in which he improvises the text and fiddle melodies and fuses fiddling with dancing and singing makes his performances exciting. Bah was more well known for fire-eating than fiddling, a fact that probably accounted for him serving as an accompanying fiddler instead of the lead fiddler in his ensemble. By profession, Kandeh is a farmer who plays the fiddle occasionally to entertain kin at special ceremonies and events. Because his energies are not focused on fiddling to the same degree as Camara, who depends on fiddling for a livelihood, Kandeh's playing style is not as developed.

All Hausa fiddlers included in this study were highly competent. What set them apart was their specialization, which affected the type of music they played and manner in which they performed the fiddle. While some specialized in Bori, others focused on nightclub entertainment or music to promote nationalism. Virtuoso playing was a feature emphasized by some, but others were innovative by creating different song types or integrating new instruments and dancing into the performance. The role of the fiddler in the ensemble affected what each fiddler produced. Since Hausa fiddlers do not personally dance and rarely sing, they are able to focus on fiddling which accounts for the highly technical and sophisticated manner they perform the instrument. Of all of the fiddlers in the study, Hausa fiddling is the most complex melodically, rhythmically, and in terms of form and ensemble organization.

In Dagbamba societies, the institution to which a fiddler is attached affects his musical identity. Salisu Mahama, who performed in both traditional and nontraditional settings, was more innovative and creative than fiddlers such as Sulemana Iddrisu or Salifu Lali who regularly performed at traditional royal occasions. Although all fiddlers in Dagbon were allowed to vary the music, Mahama was the only one whose performance style included improvisation and ornamentation comparable to musicking by Fulbe and Hausa fiddlers. Other fiddlers in Dagbon used stylistic features that demonstrated maintenance rather than innovation.

Stereotypes and Untruths

In spite of the amount of research conducted on musicking in Africa, many stereotypes and untruths exist that affect our understanding of and approach to the study of musical style. This study reveals several. One, the belief that West Africa only consists of drum orchestras, is an obvious untruth. While drumming is prominent in this area of the continent, other performance traditions are equally important. Therefore, both examining traditions in geographical regions not normally investigated and looking beyond the stereotypes are vital if we are truly committed to appreciating the complex realities of African music.

Two, referring to fiddling in West Africa as an Arab tradition is a stereotype. After hundreds of years of innovation, West Africans have created their own ways of performing the fiddle; the features derived from North Africa and Southwest Asia (that is, emphases on melody and ornamentation) have been altered to reflect the aesthetics of West Africans. While outsiders may view certain characteristics as foreign, the people of West Africa regard these elements as part of their heritage. To put this stereotype in perspective, the situation should be viewed another way. Although the bowed lute in Europe and Africa have the same origins, how often do scholars refer to the Western violin as a tradition influenced by Southwest Asian (Arab) culture?

Three, to regard traditional or indigenous cultures as homogenous is also a stereotype.[6] Although studies on nontraditional musics regularly note that the characteristics of individual performers and composers are unique, this type of critical analysis is often missing in research on traditional music. While commonalities exist in all types of music, how musicians employ elements to create their own identity is significant regardless of the type of music performed. Furthermore, to suggest that studying traditional cultures is old fashioned (suggests bias on the part of researchers) is not only shortsighted, but raises other issues. Why do some scholars have such skewed views about traditional culture? Have they accepted and internalized the stereotypes of Westerners who believe that indigenous culture is backward or "primitive"? Traditional African music needs to be examined as critically as nontraditional idioms. Furthermore, many questions urgently need to be addressed when examining traditional music. How are individuals in traditional culture responding to modernity, especially when pressures from both inside and outside their local surroundings simultaneously affect them? How is contemporary music influencing traditional culture? How is the traditional informing contemporary music? Why is Western influence privileged when examining hybridity and fusions in modern Africa? Why has little research been devoted to intracultural or Arab influences?[7] Addressing these and other questions will stimulate discussion and suggest methods and theories that can inform studies in African musicology and ethnomusicology (Nketia and DjeDje 1984; DjeDje and Carter 1989; DjeDje 1992a).

As this analysis demonstrates, fiddling is a diverse and dynamic tradition, constantly adapting to the needs, pressures, and expressions of the people involved with it. As a result, West African fiddling has multiple identities not only because of varying forces affecting it but because fiddlers are sensitive to issues and musical tastes of their communities. As people and society continue to change, fiddlers generally respond by transforming.

Although this study provides much information on fiddling in West Africa, there are areas where more research needs to be done. History, both cross-cultural and within societies, is a topic that needs further investigation. Not only do researchers need to look more closely at terms used for the fiddle in

West Africa, the language of song texts and the relationship of language to fiddle melodies and rhythms need further scrutiny. It would also be helpful if comparable studies on fiddling were pursued in other parts of the continent. Doing so would provide both a fuller understanding of fiddling's multiple identities within Africa and a continental African perspective on a fascinating performance tradition that is practiced globally.

Appendix: Distribution of the One-Stringed Fiddle (Listed by Country)

Country	People	Language SubFamily (Family)	Location on Map 1.3	Term for Fiddle
Benin	Nago, Yoruba	Kwa (Niger-Congo)	34	*godié, goge, goje, kukuma*
Burkina Faso	Bisa	Mande (Niger-Congo)	20	*doudouga*
Burkina Faso	Bwa	Voltaic (Niger-Congo)	22	*soko*
Burkina Faso	Gurma	Voltaic (Niger-Congo)	19	*cohorougou, goge(?), gonje*
Burkina Faso	Mossi	Voltaic (Niger-Congo)	21	*duduga, düdügi, duuduga, rebec*
Burkina Faso	Songhai	Songhai	23	*godie, godje*
Cameroon	Bilala (Bulala)	Central Sudanic (Chari-Nile)	46	*coucouma, kukuma*
Cameroon	Bournauan (Borno)	Central Sudanic (Chari-Nile)	42	*coucouma*
Cameroon	Foulbé	Atlantic	3	*guegueru*
Cameroon	Kirdi	Eastern Sudanic (Chari-Nile)	39	?
Chad	Beriberi (Kanembu, Kanuri?)	Saharan	49	*kukuma*
Chad	Bilala (Bulala)	Central Sudanic (Chari-Nile)	46	*coucouma, kukuma*
Chad	Bournauan (Borno)	Central Sudanic (Chari-Nile)	42	*coucouma*
Chad	Kanembu (Beriberi?)	Saharan	51	?
Chad	Kanuri (Beriberi?)	Saharan	50	*ku'u*
Chad	Teda	Saharan	53	*kiiki, kudi*
Chad	Tubu	Saharan	52	*kiiki, kudi*
Côte d'Ivoire	Agni	Kwa (Niger-Congo)	14	*godye*
Gambia, The	Fulbe (Fula)	Atlantic (Niger-Congo)	3	*nyanyeru, nyaanyooru, nyanyuru, nyayur*
Gambia, The	Mandinka	Mande (Niger-Congo)	9	*susaa*
Gambia, The	Wolof	Atlantic (Niger-Congo)	1	*riti*

Country	People	Language SubFamily (Family)	Location on Map 1.3	Term for Fiddle
Ghana	Dagbamba	Voltaic (Niger-Congo)	15	*gondze, gonje, goondze*
Ghana	Frafra	Voltaic (Niger-Congo)	17	*duringa, durungu*
Ghana	Kusasi	Voltaic (Niger-Congo)	18	*gonje*
Ghana	Mamprussi	Voltaic (Niger-Congo)	16	*gondze*
Guinea	Foulah, Fulani	Atlantic (Niger-Congo)	3	*lélé, nhènhèru*
Guinea	Malinké	Mande (Niger-Congo)	9	*soke, soko*
Guinea	Soso (Susu)	Mande (Niger-Congo)	8	*kundye*
Guinea	Wolof	Atlantic (Niger-Congo)	1	*riti*
Guinea-Bissau	Fula	Atlantic (Niger-Congo)	3	?
Liberia	Mano	Mano (Niger-Congo)	13	?
Mali	Foula (Peul)	Atlantic (Niger-Congo)	3	*kalandé*
Mali	Malinké	Mande (Niger-Congo)	9	*kalâdé, kalani*
Mali	Sarakolle (Sarokolle)	Mande (Niger-Congo)	7	*ngime*
Mali	Sonhrai (Sonrai)	Songhai	24	*diarka, njarka, ndjarka*
Mali	Tuareg (Touareg)	Berber	25	*amz'ad, amzad, imzad, an-zad, imzhad, inzad*
Mauritania	Peul	Atlantic (Niger-Congo)	3	*arab, arbab*
Mauritania	Tukulor (Toucouleur)	Atlantic (Niger-Congo)	4	*gnagnour, nyanyur, rebec*
Niger	Adarawa	Chad	29	*kwambilo*
Niger	Bilala (Bulala)	Central Sudanic (Chari-Nile)	46	*coucouma, kukuma*
Niger	Bournauan (Borno)	Central Sudanic (Chari-Nile)	42	*coucouma*
Niger	Dendi	Songhai	27	*goge*
Niger	Djerma (Zaberma)	Songhai	26	*godie, godjié, goje, kwambilo, vièle gogué*

Country	Ethnic group	Language family	No.	Instrument names
Niger	Ful	Atlantic (Niger-Congo)	3	*gogeru*
Niger	Hausa (Haoussa)	Chad	28	*godie, godjie, gogué, guge, vièle gogué*
Niger	Kanuri	Saharan	50	*ku'u*
Niger	Maouri	Chad	30	*gogué*
Niger	Peul	Atlantic (Niger-Congo)	3	?
Niger	Songhai	Songhai	23	*godie, godje, godji, goje*
Niger	Sonrai	Songhai	24	*godie, godjié*
Niger	Teda	Saharan	53	*kiiki, kudi*
Niger	Tuareg (Touareg)	Berber	25	*amz'ad, amzad, anzad, imzad, imzhad, inzad*
Niger	Tubu	Saharan	52	*kiiki, kudi*
Niger	Zaberma (Djerma)	Songhai	26	*godie, godjié, goje, kwambilo, vièle gogué*
Nigeria	Arewa (Aregwa)	Benue-Congo/Bantu (Niger-Congo)	31	?
Nigeria	Beriberi (Kanembu, Kanuri?)	Saharan	49	*kukuma*
Nigeria	Bilala (Bulala)	Central Sudanic (Chari-Nile)	46	*coucouma, kukuma*
Nigeria	Bolewa	Chad	48	?
Nigeria	Bournauan (Borno)	Central Sudanic (Chari-Nile)	42	*coucouma*
Nigeria	Bura (Burra)	Chad	47	*kwakuma*
Nigeria	Burum (Biram Berom, Birom)	Benue-Congo/Bantu (Niger-Congo)	32	*goge*
Nigeria	Fali of Mubi	Chad	46	?
Nigeria	Fulani (Ful, Fulbe, Peul)	Atlantic (Niger-Congo)	40	*gogeru*
Nigeria	Gungawa	Benue-Congo/Bantu (Niger-Congo)	33	?

Country	People	Language SubFamily (Family)	Location on Map 1.3	Term for Fiddle
Nigeria	Gwari (Gbari)	Kwa (Niger-Congo)	36	*goje, gujeje*
Nigeria	Hausa	Chad	28	*goge, guge, kukuma*
Nigeria	Jukun	Benue-Congo/Bantu (Niger-Congo)	38	*?*
Nigeria	Kambari	Benue-Congo/Bantu (Niger-Congo)	35	*goge*
Nigeria	Kamu	Chad	41	*goge*
Nigeria	Kanembu (Beriberi?)	Saharan	51	*?*
Nigeria	Kanuri (Beriberi?)	Saharan	50	*ku'u*
Nigeria	Peul (Ful, Fulani)	Atlantic (Niger-Congo)	3	*?*
Nigeria	Tangale	Chad	44	*kakuma, goge*
Nigeria	Tera	Chad	43	*kwakuma*
Nigeria	Tiv	Benue-Congo/Bantu (Niger-Congo)	37	*goga*
Nigeria	Waja	Adamawa (Niger-Congo)	45	*goge*
Nigeria	Yoruba	Kwa (Niger-Congo)	34	*godié, goge, goje, kukuma*
Senegal	Koniagi (Konyagi)	Atlantic (Niger-Congo)	5	*anyanyir*
Senegal	Peul	Atlantic (Niger-Congo)	3	*riti*
Senegal	Serer	Atlantic (Niger-Congo)	2	*riti*
Senegal	Tukulor (Toucouleur)	Atlantic (Niger-Congo)	4	*nanur, nyanyur*
Senegal	Wolof	Atlantic (Niger-Congo)	1	*riti*
Sierra Leone	Fula (Foulah)	Atlantic (Niger-Congo)	3	*kalande, ngenge, nyanyaru, nyanyur, nyayaru*
Sierra Leone	Limba	Atlantic (Niger-Congo)	10	*kuliktu*

Sierra Leone	Mandingo (Madingo)	Mande (Niger-Congo)	9	*jurukele, kalande, kalani, karaning, ngime, soke, soko, soku*
Sierra Leone	Sarakole	Mande (Niger-Congo)	7	*ngime*
Sierra Leone	Sherbro	Atlantic (Niger-Congo)	12	*bondobai*
Sierra Leone	Soso (Susu)	Mande (Niger-Congo)	10	*akonde, kundye*
Sierra Leone	Temne	Atlantic (Niger-Congo)	11	*angbulu, gbulu, rafon*

Notes

Introduction

1. The term *gondze* (singular and plural) refers to the Dagbamba one-stringed fiddle, which in performance is held horizontally with the resonator placed near the performer's waist (when standing) and in the lap (when sitting). The term is also used as a designation for Dagbamba fiddler(s) and for fiddling (the act of playing the instrument).

2. The king of the Dagbamba monarchy is the Ya Naa, who resides in Yendi. In precolonial times, several hierarchies of rulers and a complex network of dynastic polities lay under the monarch. The kingdom was divided into three provinces: Karaga, Mion, and Savelugu, each of which was ruled by a royal "duke," known respectively as the Karaga Naa, Mionlana, and Yo Naa. Under them were other smaller polities with rulers (Staniland 1975:16–17). The head fiddler in service to the Ya Naa is known as the Yamba Naa.

3. Songs averaged about one to two minutes in length. The longest was three minutes, forty seconds (3:40), while the shortest was about forty seconds (:40). Part 1 consisted of twelve songs (23:20); part 2, twelve songs (24:52); part 3, thirteen songs (23:00); part 4, four songs (10:25); part 5, seventeen songs (27:00); and part 6, eleven songs (16:38).

4. Many terms are used for the fiddle in West Africa (see appendix). Therefore, it is difficult and, I believe, inappropriate to choose one over the other. For this reason, I employ "fiddle," the generic term for a bowed string instrument having a neck (Marcuse 1975:180). "Fiddle" is also better known in English than "bowed lute," the more technical term. In using this terminology, I am not suggesting that the fiddle is of less value or has a lower status than the "violin," a term often identified with Western classical (or art) music; nor am I trying to create a dialectic or opposition between so-called folk and high culture. I am also cognizant of the danger in using "fiddle," which as a verb in English implies spending time in aimless or fruitless activity (*Webster's New Collegiate Dictionary* 1974:426). In spite of possible negative connotations, I find "fiddle" to be less problematic than "violin." It is important for the instrument not to be identified with Europe, for fiddling in West Africa predates contact with Western cultures.

5. Much research on Africa has been conducted solely to address questions or issues (i.e., "missing links") related to cultures in other parts of the world. Comparative musicologists of the early twentieth century conducted research on non-Western cultures such as those in Africa because of their interests in determining the antecedents of European art music traditions (Myers 1992). Also, many investigations on music in the African diaspora use Africa as a springboard for discussing developments elsewhere. This study is Africa-centered; my interest is in the development of West African fiddling from its

earliest beginnings to the present, not in how it serves as a precursor to developments outside Africa.

6.   The few print publications that focus solely on West African fiddling include Borel (1989, 1991), Cogdell (1973, 1974), DjeDje (1978b, 1980, 1982, 1984a, 1992b, 1999), Gourlay (1980, 1982b), Sulley (1971), Wendt (1994), and Yakubu (1981). Works by Ames and King (1971), Bebey (1969, 1975), Kawada (2001), Mack (2004), Nikiprowetzky (1963, 1964b, 1966a, 1966b), Nketia (1974), Schlottner (2004), and Wegner (1984) include references to fiddling. The number of fiddle recordings on West Africa is large when compared to print sources, but small relative to drumming. Of the three audio recordings that focus on fiddling, two are devoted to the Hausa (*Alhaji Gɔrbo Leɗo* 1976; *Niger* 1999), while the other concerns the Dagbamba (*Master Fiddlers* 2001). Juldeh Camara, a Fulbe fiddler from Senegambia, made a CD in which six of the eleven pieces are devoted to his fiddling while the other selections are performed by Mande musicians playing other instruments (*Ancient Heart* 1990). Fulbe musicians from Futa Jalon in Guinea include four selections with fiddling (*Guinée* 1992). Laura Boulton collected four fiddle songs when she participated in the 1934 Straus expedition: one was from Senegal (Fatick), two were from Mali (Timbuktu), and one was from Niger (Niamey) (*Music and Culture* 2002). François Borel has helped to produced two recordings that contain several selections of fiddle music by the Tuareg (*Niger: Musique des Touaregs*. Vol. 1. Azawagh, 2002; *Niger: Musique des Touaregs*. Vol. 2. In Gall, 2002).When Arthur S. and Lois Alberts visited West Africa during the mid-twentieth century, they collected Mossi fiddle music from Burkina Faso (*Field Recordings* 1954).

7.   I conducted interviews with fiddlers, other musicians, and nonmusicians; attended and participated in performance events; visited the homes of fiddlers to interact with them and members of their families in an informal setting; made audio and video recordings of music performances; took photographs; and participated in other activities in the different communities I visited.

8.   In this study, Sudanic West Africa includes desert, grassland, and woodland areas that extend from the Atlantic Ocean to the eastern shore of Lake Chad (see further explanation in chapter 1).

9.   I use only aspects of the multi-sited ethnography outlined by George Marcus (1995). Issues concerning capitalist political economy and postmodernism are not included here because I do not feel they relate to this study.

10.   When I conducted research between 1972 and 1974, the majority of my time was spent in Ghana with stays in Nigeria. Although my focus was on fiddling among the Dagbamba and the Hausa, I was interested in the fiddle wherever it existed because I wanted to know how the traditions were similar or different. As a result, I also visited other locations—Benin, southwest Nigeria, Niger, Burkina Faso, and Côte d'Ivoire—where I thought the fiddle might be used. When I returned to this topic in the 1980s and 1990s, I interviewed several Hausa from northern Nigeria who were either studying in or visiting the United States. Three were UCLA graduate students: Lawan Danladi Yalwa (linguistics), Maina Gimba (linguistics), and Aliyu Moddibbo Umar (education). In addition, I met with Mamman Shata, a well-known Hausa singer-musician, when

he made a presentation at UCLA. At this time, I also broadened my examination to include Senegambia to determine if fiddling there was similar to what I discovered in Ghana and Nigeria. During the 1990s and later in 2003, I conducted research in Senegambia and follow-up fieldwork in Ghana and Nigeria.

11.   Since the mid-twentieth century, many ethnomusicologists have looked upon comparison with disfavor (Merriam 1982c). With growing interest in diaspora, urban, and global studies, however, the comparative method is prominently used, although music researchers may not admit that this is what they are doing. Like some scholars, I believe comparative analysis should not be discarded because it has been misused or researchers reached faulty conclusions. Rather, the methodology needs to be refined to fit the needs of the research question; also see Nettl (1983) and Nketia (1972).

12.   Christopher Small, who coined the term, states that "musicking" refers to the act of taking part in a musical performance (Small 1987:50; 1998). I use it because it includes all aspects of the performing arts (playing musical instruments, singing, dancing, etc.), which demonstrates that African performance is an integration of many components.

13.   The use of additive rhythms in duple, triple, and hemiola patterns is the hallmark of rhythmic organization in African music (Nketia 1974:131). Performing additive and divisive rhythms against each other not only creates tension that is exciting, but the juxtaposition adds a character to the music that differs from playing only divisive rhythms. Although there is much debate in the literature about these music concepts (see Agawu 2003), I find those employed by Nketia to be useful.

14.   In this study, "traditional" refers to traditions guided by ethnicity, kinship, and a common indigenous language. "Contemporary," on the other hand, refers to practices that go beyond this to linkages established through membership in educational and industrial institutions; churches; new social, political, and economic associations such as trade and market unions; and recreational associations such as sports clubs (Nketia 1995:1). Most importantly, traditional African culture is not static; it is dynamic with influences from both the past and the present. In modern Africa, the traditional exists alongside the contemporary, and sometimes the two are integrated. Some researchers refer to the latter as neo-traditional.

1. Fiddling in West Africa

1.   Although I visited many countries throughout West Africa to locate the fiddle, the three culture groups that are the primary focus of this study (Fulbe, Hausa, and Dagbamba) are located in Sudanic West Africa. As noted in the introduction, Sudanic West Africa extends from the Atlantic Ocean to Lake Chad, roughly 10° to 20° north latitude and 17° west to 15° east longitude (Hiskett 1984), and encompasses the desert scrubs of the Sahel as well as the woodland and grassland of the savannah. In this study, the terms *Sudanic* and *Sudan* are used interchangeably, and the word *Sudanese* relates to the people who live in the region. These terms should not be confused with the country (Sudan) or the people (Sudanese) located in northeast Africa. While some may find the

term *Sudan* dated because it references precolonial and colonial times, I find it useful for describing a distinct African culture and civilization. My discussion of the ancient history of Sudanic culture is derived from the work of several scholars—e.g., Christopher Ehret (2001, 2002); Fred Wendorf and Romuald Schild (1984)—whose analyses of archaeological and linguistic data as well as oral tradition provide us with a more deeply textured understanding of these early periods in Africa.

2.   Niger Bend refers to that portion of the Niger River in Mali that turns and flows southeastward.

3.   Some scholars refer to these socio-occupational classes or groups as "castes." Unlike the caste system found among Indians in South Asia, however, stratification in West Africa is not based on religious prohibitions. Thus, the two social systems are not the same (Hale 1998).

4.   The Atlantic subfamily of the Niger-Congo language family constitutes the people—e.g., Fulbe, Tukulor, Wolof, Serer, Jola (also spelled Jolla), and Balante—who live in the lower and middle Senegal basin along and inland from the Atlantic Ocean. Mande refers to descendants of the Mali Empire, which flourished from 1240 to 1500.

5.   Atlantic speakers (Wolof and Fulbe) along the Senegal valley had one of the most complex class systems. In the seventeenth century, the Wolof distinguished five occupational endogamous social groups: fishermen (*cubaalo*), weavers (*rabb-ser*), woodworkers (*lawbe*), smiths (*tegg*), and minstrels (*gewel*) (Conrad and Frank 1995a; Curtin 1975:31–32).

6.   During the first millennium CE, Senegambians in the Western Sudan were clearly differentiated between those who lived north and south of the Gambia River. In the south, the humidity and swamps caused Senegambians to be more isolated, which negatively impacted communication and the establishment of large-scale political structures through the fifteenth and sixteenth centuries. Because wide-open spaces did not offer groups in the north the same protection found in the south, northern Senegambians created kingdoms early in history, and horses became a powerful means of transport (Barry 1997:17–28).

7.   The trans-Saharan trade truly began when gold, mined in the upper Senegal and Niger Rivers, started to be transported between the Western Sudan and the Roman Empire at Carthage toward the close of the third century CE.

8.   Nominal allegiance to Islam was given possibly in the tenth century CE by the kings of Gao and later in the eleventh century (1040–1041) by Tukulor royalty (Ehret 2001:272; Hale 1990:23). The introduction of Islam took place later in the eleventh century (1067–1071 or 1080–1097) among Kanembu royalty (Hrbek 1992:40, 223; Ehret 2001:271; Murdock 1959:137; Brandily n.d.). During the first stage of Islamization, the powerful states and strong cultural and social identity of Sudanic kings surprised Muslim traders, who immediately began writing major ethnographic descriptions about them. Because of these circumstances, North Africans did not seek to convert or force the Sudanese to abandon their religious, cultural, and social practices during this period. Rather, they were content to coexist as merchants (Hrbek 1992:53–54).

What occurred among the Tukulor, who are closely related to the Fulbe, is noteworthy. Sheldon Gellar explains:

Tekrur, a densely populated kingdom situated in the middle Senegal River Valley and founded more than a thousand years ago, was one of the oldest and most prominent of Senegal's precolonial African states. Thanks to its strategic location reaching to the edge of the desert, Tekrur prospered from the trans-Saharan trade between North and West Africa, which involved gold and slaves moving north and cowries, salt, and weapons coming south. During the eleventh century, Tekrur's Tukulor ruler, War Jabi, came under the influence of Muslim traders and missionaries from North Africa and converted to Islam. The great majority of the Tukulor people soon followed War Jabi's example, and the Tukulor became the first major Senegalese ethnic group to embrace Islam en masse. From Tekrur arose the Almoravid movement, which swept through Morocco and Spain during the last third of the eleventh century. Over the years, Tekrur became a training ground for Muslim clerics and missionaries operating throughout modern Senegal and West Africa.

During the thirteenth century, Tekrur became a vassal state of the powerful Mandinka Mali Empire to the east. (Gellar 1995:2-3)

9.   By the fifteenth century, many West African Muslims were associated with Sufis (Muslim mystics) who stressed the personal relationship between Allah and man (Diouf 1998:5).

10. For most music scholars, North Africa refers to the Maghrib, a region encompassing Morocco, Algeria, Tunisia, and Libya, as well as areas reaching southward into the Sahara to include Mauritania and northern sections of Mali and Niger. Berber and West African influence in the Maghrib is what distinguishes its music from musicking in Egypt and Arabic-speaking Muslims in Southwest Asia (Wendt 1998a:532–533).

11. The debate on the admissibility of music in Islam has elicited views that vary from complete nonacceptance to full admittance of all musical forms and dance. The work of Abu Hamid al-Ghazzali (1058–1111), a religious reformer and mystic who integrated Sufism and orthodoxy, became the model for many writers because he specified when music could and could not be used. According to al-Ghazzali, music may be used (1) to encourage pilgrimage for whom pilgrimage is permissible, (2) to incite to battle, (3) to inspire courage on the day of battle, (4) to invoke lamentation and sorrow, (5) to arouse joy, (6) to elicit love and long, or (7) to evoke love of God. Music is prohibited (1) when produced by women under certain conditions, (2) if the instruments used are expressively prohibited, (3) when the listener is ruled by lust, or (4) if one listens to music for its own sake (Shiloah 1995:43–44; also see discussion in Faruqi 1985).

12. While some North Africans were thoroughly absorbed by Arab cultures, others—e.g., the Tuareg Berbers of the Sahel, the Berbers living in the Algerian mountains (Kabylie and Aurès), as well as the Gnawa (also spelled Ginnawa and Gnaoua) and other peoples of Morocco—remained so little influenced by other cultures that their music continued to be unarguably Berber (Lortat-Jacob 1980:517).

13. *Voltaic* refers to a small area south of the Niger Bend near the Black and White Volta Rivers (see DjeDje 1998).

14. The association of fiddling with royalty in West Africa is limited to select groups. In some societies, the use of the fiddle as a court instrument was shunned by kingship (see chapters 2–4).

15. *Melisma,* or *melismatic,* refers to the singing of a succession of several different notes on one syllable. This is a feature of Arab or Arab-influenced music.

16. Later in this chapter where I describe three fiddle styles—Sahelian, savannah, and forest—I discuss Arab influences in West African fiddling. The Sahelian style represents the Arab style most closely, and the savannah style explains the fusion of Arab elements with characteristics identified with forest West Africa. Simply put, the emphasis on a single melody with significant ornamentation is a feature that signifies "Arabness." Percussion and multipart structure represent influence from the forest. Different musical identities are created when musicians find interesting ways of combining melody with percussion and multipart structures.

17. Fiddles in Africa, Asia, and Europe are constructed in a variety of shapes and sizes. However, there are two basic forms: long-necked (often with spikes) and short-necked. Short-necked fiddles are most common in Europe (Diagram Group 1976:202). Some West African fiddles have more than one string. This study, however, concerns only one-stringed fiddles. The Hornbostel-Sachs figures for the one-stringed fiddle are 321.311.71 (Hornbostel and Sachs 1961:23).

18. Recent research indicates that the etymology and origin of the term "rabab" to denote chordophones is not known with certainty. Yet the first report on the instrument appears in Arabic texts of the ninth and tenth centuries ("Rabab" 2004). Although early Arab writers (see Levtzion and Hopkins 1981) make several references to African string instruments, the fiddle is not mentioned. Several reasons can be given for the omission: (1) Arab travelers did not visit Sudanese societies that used the fiddle, (2) the fiddle was not used in contexts observed by Arabs, or (3) writers may have thought it unimportant, especially since fiddling was not identified with kingship or highly regarded.

19. Besides those found in North Africa, at least three fiddle prototypes exist in Africa. The one in Ethiopia resembles the spike fiddle (a lute with a spike fixed to the resonator). A second type has a wide distribution in Sudanic West Africa and is the subject of this study. The tube fiddle, a third type, is found in eastern and central Africa (Nketia 1974:102–103; Marcuse 1975:372–373; Schuyler 1979; Thieme 1969).

20. Although the Nago/Yoruba were in contact with the Fon, the latter did not adopt the instrument. Nor did the Asante incorporate the fiddle into their culture, even though they were in contact with Dagbamba and appropriated the Dagbamba hourglass tension drum (Bowdich 1873:280; Wilks 1961; Trimingham 1970).

21. The map in Murdock (1959), which corresponds with maps in Robinson (1985:50–51), is useful because it provides a more detailed listing of Fulbe settlements that continue to be relevant in present day. Not only do large numbers of Kita Fulbe live in Mali, but the Liptako Fulbe are widespread in the Liptako-Gurma region located near the border of Mali, Niger, and Burkina Faso. On most modern-day maps, these Fulbe groups are not listed but are subsumed into the larger category of Masina Fulbe ("The Fula Kita of Mali" 1997; "The Liptako Fula" n.d.).

22. Michael Coolen is convinced that the Fulbe's "diasporatic movements have undoubtedly been partly responsible for the diffusion of the plucked lute"

(1983:481). He is referring primarily to migrations within Senegambia, but I believe the Fulbe may have been involved with the dispersion of both the plucked and bowed lutes to other parts of Sudanic Africa as well (also see Charry 1996). As explained in greater detail in chapter 2, the Tukulor and Fulbe, who are closely related, may have been among the first groups to adopt the fiddle because they were among the first to make substantial contact with Arab cultures (those in North Africa, Sudanic Africa, and East Africa). The Tukulor mainly stayed put; the pastoral Fulbe, however, who migrated east, may well have reinforced dispersion by introducing the fiddle to groups who did not themselves come in contact with people in the Sahel and North Africa.

23. Although most researchers place the Fulbe into the two categories nomadic and sedentary, John P. Paden indicates that the Fulbe in northern Nigeria should be placed into three groups because of differences in lifestyles and cultural patterns. One group is the pastoral nomads, a second is the rural settled Fulbe who mix farming with animal husbandry, and a third is the urban Fulbe, particularly those who dominated the administrative structures in the nineteenth and twentieth centuries (Paden 1973:32); see chapters 2 and 3.

24. While no information exists on the fiddle, the presence of some drums (*tambari*) and wind instruments (*kakaki* and *algaita*) in the Kanem-Bornu and Songhai kingdoms is the result of interactions with North Africans (Harris 1932:106; King 1980a:309; Surugue 1980:523; Gourlay 1982a:53; Erlmann 1983b:25; Ki-Zerbo and Niane 1997:107–108). Borrowings between the Central Sudan and North Africa occurred both ways. The *shantu*, a percussion tube used by Hausa women, is played in North Africa as a result of females being taken north into slavery. The Kanuri *ganga* (double-headed drum) as well as the Hausa and Songhai instrument of the same name are borrowings from West Africa that found their way into North Africa (Hause 1948:23).

25. The Teda, Saharan speakers in Chad and Niger, are among the few who play the fiddle in a vertical position, a performance practice resembling that used in parts of North Africa and the Eastern Sudan.

26. For details on the construction of fiddles in West Africa, see Laing (1825:148), Balandier and Jolivet (1962), Bowdich (1873:280), Brandily (1970:58), Lhote (1955:329), Pivin (195?), Bovis and Gast (1959), Borel (1989), and Wendt (1998a:542).

27. In terms of which gender performs the fiddle in various cultures, what seems to be most important is the lifestyle associated with fiddling rather than the act of playing the instrument. If those who perform the instrument are expected to participate in activities that are gender specific or identified with the behavior of males in those societies (e.g., traveling long distances), perhaps the instrument is relegated to men as opposed to women (see chapters 2, 3, and 4).

28. Because many African languages are tonal, membranophones, aerophones, and even chordophones (i.e., the fiddle) can be used as speech surrogates. When the highs and lows of the language are simulated on instruments, they become talking instruments.

29. Gourlay's English translation omits details included in the legend that appears in Rouch (1960). In the translation presented here, I have added those details

(see italics) so the translation more accurately reflects the myth found in Rouch.

30.   Spirit possession, a major component of Songhai religion, occurs during cere-
        monies in which visions and sounds are fused to re-create Songhai experiences
        from a mythic past (Stoller 1989:104). Possession ceremonies probably date to
        the reign of Askia Mohammed Touré (ca. late fifteenth and early sixteenth cen-
        turies) because this was a period of great sociocultural and religious upheaval.
        Not only were Askia Mohammed's attempts to Islamize the Songhai under-
        mining the locally based lineage as the principal government body of Songhai
        society, his efforts were decreasing the importance of the indigenous religion
        (Stoller 1989:163).

31.   Tuareg men play the three-stringed plucked lute, flute, and some drums
        (Wendt 1998b:587–592).

32.   Of the studies concerned with style, most concern the Tuareg: Holiday (1956),
        Nikiprowetzky (1964b, 1966a), Kimberlin (1976), and Wendt (1994, 1998b).
        The works by DjeDje focus on the Hausa and Dagbamba; see DjeDje (1978b,
        1984a, 1984b). Although I have identified almost sixty recordings of fiddle
        music (see discography), my analysis is based on forty-three examples. Thirty-
        eight are commercial recordings (the majority are in the UCLA Ethnomusi-
        cology Archive), and five are field recordings: two were collected by other
        researchers—Russell Schuh (1991) and the Institute of African Studies, Uni-
        versity of Ghana—and three were collected by me. The analysis is limited in
        several ways. Sound material for all groups in West Africa is not represented.
        In some cases, only one sample is available for a particular group. Because the
        commercial recordings were recorded and/or published between the 1940s
        and 1990s, covering roughly a fifty-year period, the discussion relates only to
        the performance practices of fiddlers from the middle to the late twentieth
        century. I have not included the 1934 sample recorded by Laura Boulton in the
        analysis because little is known about the person performing the fiddle (see
        Gibson and Reed 2002).

33.   Considered to be the oldest, the Ahaggar (the northernmost region in the
        center of the Sahara Desert in Algeria) style has a formulaic structure con-
        sisting of one or more principal tones surrounded by a cluster of neighboring
        pitches (mordents, accacciaturas, turns, or other figures) and stock melodic
        formulas or motives linked together to form phrases of varying lengths. When
        played rapidly, the effect is a melismatic music of rich texture. Rhythm is sub-
        ordinate to melody, and pulse is often difficult to discern. The Aïr (the fertile
        valley area of the country Niger) style is also based on formulas, but the units
        are more smoothly joined, making it difficult to determine where one ends
        and another begins. Long phrases of original or developed material are less
        elaborate, and Aïr's rhythms, like those in the Ahaggar style, are subordinate to
        melodies. The dominant feature of the Azawagh or Azawar (the southernmost
        region) style is the emphasis on rhythm: strongly accented rhythms based on
        regularly recurring pulses performed in a lively tempo. Although based on for-
        mulaic material, Azawagh's melodies are less elaborate and always subordinate
        to the rhythm, and music is often accompanied by handclapping and occa-
        sional dancing (Wendt 1994:93–100).

34.   In a field recording (of a fiddle solo performed in praise of one of Bai's patrons) by the Senegalese Tukulor fiddler Majaw Bai, characteristics identified with the Sahelian performance style can be heard (florid melodies with lots of ornaments and no percussion accompaniment), but features associated with the savannah (see below) are also included.

35.   Examples identified as Sahelian include Djerma (*Africa Noire,* B5), Sonrai (*Niger: La Musique de Griots,* A1), Tuareg (*Sahara 1: Chants des Touareg Ajjer,* A4; *Au Coeur de Sahara avec les Touareg Ajjer,* B1c; and *Tuareg Music of the Southern Saharan,* A3, A4, A5), and Wolof (*La Musique des Griots: Senegal,* A6). Two examples are field recordings: Russell Schuh is responsible for the Wolof piece, and I collected the Tukulor example.

36.   When transposed so G is tonic, the five-tone scale used by the Tuareg is similar to scales used by the Dagbamba, Hausa, and other groups in Sudanic West Africa. While most scales are anhemitonic (without semitones) pentatonic, some are hemitonic (with semitones) pentatonic (Nikiprowetzky 1964b:81–83; DjeDje 1978b:458–462).

37.   For examples of this singing technique, see Wendt (1994:91–92), which includes a transcription of a piece on *Tuareg Music of the Southern Sahara,* A3. Also see *Tuareg Music of the Southern Saharan,* A4, A5; Djerma (*Africa Noire,* B5); and Sonrai (*Niger: La Musique de Griots,* A1).

38.   For music examples representing fiddling in forest regions, see *Pondo Kakou: Musique de Société Secrète. Côte d'Ivoire-Dahomey-Guinée,* B3; *Musique Dahoméennes,* A1, A2; and *Afrique, Vol. 4: Mauritanie, Guinée, Dahomey, Côte d'Ivoire,* A3. I have not included a musical example of the forest style because of lack of space.

39.   Akayaa Atule (a Frafra music and dance teacher based in San Diego, California, who was born in Bolgatanga, Ghana) transcribed the song texts to the Frafra fiddle song. She states that this song in praise of the ancestors would be performed at funerals, weddings, and other social occasions. In English the lyrics mean "Our ancestors / Our ancestors in Zaboretongo" (name of a village in northern Ghana) (Atule 2002).

2. An Affirmation of Identity

1.   Senegambia refers to the region that encompasses the countries Senegal and The Gambia. The country is called "The Gambia" to distinguish it from the river, Gambia. The chapter concerns the Fulbe who live in The Gambia, but information about those who reside in Senegal is also included. *Nyanyeru* is the term for the fiddle in Fulfulde or Pulaar, the language of the Fulbe. Many Senegambian Fulbe also use the Wolof term, *riti,* for the instrument. However, I refer to the Fulbe fiddle as nyanyeru, which has several spellings.

2.   On all field trips to The Gambia (1990, 1994, and 2003), Tamba Kandeh served as my host and put me in contact with other fiddlers in the area.

3.   Besides "Supere Demba," "Mamareh Ko Bengel Kaddy Jatou," and "Jawara," other songs that Tamba performed at the wedding included "Poromandalli," a critical song he composed; "Dangingka," a song he adapted from Serahuli lute

players; "Burugy warama" ("Burugy Is Killed"), a song that documents an incident (the death of a man named Burugy in a market) that took place in URD during the 1970s; and "Cabral," a praise song composed by Demba Gabbi (a Fulbe fiddler from Guinea Bissau) in honor of Luis de Almeida Cabral (an African freedom fighter and former president of Guinea Bissau).

4. The people call themselves Fulbe (singular, Pullo). However, the people with whom they interact have given them different names: Fula (a Mandinka term) used in The Gambia and Sierra Leone; Peul (a Wolof term) used by French speakers; Fulani (a Hausa term) used in Nigeria and other parts of West Africa; Fellaata used by the Kanuri and others in the Chad Basin; Fellah used by the Arabs of the Western Sudan; and Fulbe used in German literature (Stenning 1960:140; 1965:323). In the mid-twentieth century, when there were well over 6 million speakers of Fulfulde, they were roughly distributed as follows: Nigeria (3,630,000), Mali (850,000), Guinea (720,000), Cameroon (305,000), Niger (269,000), The Gambia (58,700), Benin (54,000), Côte d'Ivoire and Burkina Faso (52,000), Guinea Bissau (36,000), Senegal and Mauritania (12,000), Ghana (5,000), and Central African Republic (no estimate). In the early 1990s, about 15 million spoke Fulfulde (Azarya, Eguchi, and VerEecke 1993; Schultz 1980; Stenning 1960, 1965; Mabogunje 1976).

5. By the nineteenth century, the nine Fulbe dialect groups living in Senegambia fell into three linguistic groupings: (1) Fulbe Firdu, Jombonko, Habobe, Rorobe, Hamanabi (Hammanabi); (2) Torodo, Jawando, Labo; and (3) Fulbe Futa/Fulbe Futo. The Rorobe, who live in URD on the north bank, came from Bundu (Bondu) in the east. In the urban centers of Banjul, Basse, and the suburban area of north Kombo are many Fulbe from Futa Jalon in Guinea. The Fulbe of Fuladu East migrated from Masina (Mali) on the Niger River. Sometimes called Firdu Fulbe, they have been in The Gambia for a long time, but their dialect is distinct from other groups in Casamance and Guinea Bissau who also call themselves Firdu Fulbe (Quinn 1967:40–44, 1972:20–21; Gamble 1981:i; Innes 1976).

6. Because the Fulbe, as Muslim leaders, were political masters over a considerable portion of Sudanic Africa when the Europeans arrived, theories of Caucasoid origin were popular in the early twentieth century. Several scholars even believed that the Fulbe were a group of Judeo-Syrians who entered Africa about 200 CE and that Fulfulde was Hamitic. The fact that many Fulbe were light skinned and some were conquerors who owned cattle helped to promote this theory. However, linguistic evidence indicates that the Hamitic theory was based more on racist conjecture than fact (Greenberg 1970:24–30). The people of Takrur and their descendants did not use "Tukulor" but called themselves "Hal Pulaaren," speakers of Pulaar or Fulfulde. Tukulor is believed to be a corruption of "Takruri," a term used by Arab geographers and historians to describe, first, the people of Takrur and later, loosely and very inaccurately, all Sudanic Muslims (even those who lived as far east as Borno in present-day Nigeria). Prior to movements to different parts of West Africa, the Halpulaaren had interactions with the Serer, Wolof, and northern Berbers (Mabogunje 1976; Hiskett 1984).

7. In colonial writings about people in the Western Sudan, social scientists

defined social structure in absolute terms with relationships into which individuals were born. This view denied individuals the capacity to negotiate personal identity in their social world. The status of people attached to occupational groups was viewed as a given inheritance, a preconceived legacy determining the shape and course of people's lives. Although scholars acknowledge that social stratification exists, many now suggest that it is not fixed (Conrad and Frank 1995a).

8. The tolerance that characterizes interethnic relations in Senegambia is due to a formal relationship (called *dankuto*) formed between ethnic groups in the precolonial period (Sidibe 2003). The relationship was initially established between the Mande and the Jola with the understanding that both parties swore to support each other in times of trouble, mediate on behalf of each other without causing offenses, and intermarry. The alliance was binding to unborn generations, and anyone who broke it was subjected to a curse (Sonko-Godwin 1988:7).

9. While living in Senegambia, Fulbe pastoralists often complained of heavy taxes, extortion, and exploitation by the Mandinka. The incident that sparked Alfa Molo's revolt occurred in 1867 when the Mandinka king of Jimara took a sheep from Molo's herd and refused to return it. The dispute, similar to many before it, quickly generalized because of the resentment that the Fulbe had toward their Mandinka landlords. Although Jimara called on Mande clans in the area for help, the Fulbe Firdu, led by Molo and free Lorobe Fulbe, attacked Jimara's town and destroyed it. The revolt later spread to other districts (Quinn 1971:428–429). The leaders and location of some jihads in Senegambia include Nasir al-Din in Futa Toro (1672–1677), Malik Sy in Bondu or Bundu (1690–1702), Alfa Ba in Futa Jalon (1726–1764), Abd al-Qadir in Futa Toro (1776–1797), Al-hajj Shaykh Umar Tall in Futa Jalon (1850s–1891), Maba Diakhou in Gambia (1861–1867), Shaykh Amadu Ba in Jolof (1869–1875), and Alfa Molo/Musa Molo in Gambia (1867–1890s) (Quinn 1971; Last 1974; Barry 1997).

10. The Serahuli (also referred to as Sarakolle, Sarakholle, and Seraculeh) are related to the Soninke, the rulers of Wagadu (the Ghana Empire) (Quinn 1971; Murdock 1959).

11. Bakari Sidibe, a Gambian (of mixed Mande-Fulbe ancestry) who was the former director of The Gambia's Cultural Archives and the author of several works on Gambian history and culture, indicates that *bulundu,* a concept synonymous with *kabilo* (a Mande term), is a Mandinka contribution to the administrative system in Senegambia that almost all ethnic groups have adopted (Sidibe 2003). The names of Fulbe dialect groups associated with bulundu are significant because of their relationship to the surnames of fiddlers. One of the bulundu in the Fulbe Firdu and Jombo dialect groups shares the names Baldeh, Bandeh, and Bah. Other bulundu names were Kandi, Kah; Umballo; Ha, Jamanka; Jowo; Buaru; Sidibi; Sow; Sabali; Saidai; Dem; Garno (Quinn 1971:431).

12. Gum arabic, used to glue or thicken various products or preserve their form, comes from the gum tree (*Acacia senegal*) and grows wild in the steppe country

of the Western Sudan (Curtin 1969:18). Because no reliable figures exist, the number of enslaved Africans taken from Senegambia is a matter of debate (Curtin 1969; Quinn 1972:8; Gailey 1975:117–118; Barry 1997:39–40).

13. Works by Adelaida Reyes Schramm (1979), William Belzner (1981), and Martin Stokes (1994a) are just some of the publications in ethnomusicology concerned with ethnicity. Stokes explains that ethnicity "allows us to turn from questions directed towards defining the essential and 'authentic' traces of identity 'in' music . . . to the questions of how music is used by social actors in specific local situations to erect boundaries, to maintain distinctions between us and them, and how terms such as 'authenticity' are used to justify these boundaries" (1994b:6). Because the material in *Ethnicity* (1996), edited by John Hutchinson and Anthony D. Smith, relates closely to this discussion, I use this work as the basis for many of my comments.

14. The population statistics for Senegambia indicate that there *is not* a significant variation in the percentage of people identified with different ethnicities. When compared with the demographics in Hausaland and Dagbon, where the Hausa and Dagbamba are much larger in number than other ethnic groups (see chapters 3 and 4), the situation in Senegambia is distinct.

15. When the Mande established the Kaabu kingdom in Senegambia, people captured in war were sometimes sold to the Fulbe herdsmen and called Manding Fulas (or Manding Puls). In Fulbe communities, according to Sidibe, "you will find two groups of Fulas: pure Fulas and the impure Fulas. Maybe now this is not the case because of the change in time, but the Fulas are very protective of their race. They guard their purity more than necessary" (Sidibe 2003; also Quinn 1967, 1971).

16. The amount of research conducted on the Fulbe is small in comparison to groups who live around them. Some research has been done on the Fulbe of the Central Sudan, but focus is on Nigeria and Cameroon. A small number of publications exists for the Fulbe of Niger and Burkina Faso. The situation for Senegambian Fulbe is more dismal. Yet much has been published on the music of the Mande and Wolof. To find materials on Gambian Fulbe music, one must review general works on the Fulbe or music publications about other ethnic groups living in the region; see publications in Gray (1991) and works by Charry, Duran (1994, 1999), Knight (1980, 2001), and N'Diaye (1990).

17. Much of this may be the result of the emphasis on a nationalist ideology that was prominent when The Gambia became an independent country. Rather than emphasize differences, nations attempted to unify and build on the similarities that existed among ethnic groups in their countries (Nketia 1995).

18. Henri Gaden's (1931) discussion of Fulbe groups in Futa Toro (Senegal) and Futa Jalon (Guinea) is based on data collected between 1910 and 1912, and in 1916 (also see Arnott 1980:20, 24; 2001). Although most spellings of music terms used here are from Gaden (1931), I occasionally employ other spellings (see Coolen 1984:124; Erlmann 1985).

19. Accounts about Gambian Fulbe music were obtained from interviews I conducted with several Fulbe fiddlers living in The Gambia in 1990, 1994, and 2003: Samba Juma Bah (originally from Guinea), Juldeh Camara (from Casamance, Senegal), Mamadou Baldeh (a Fulbe Firdu from URD), Maulday Bal-

deh (a Fulbe Firdu from MacCarthy Island Division, known as MID), Ngeya Kandeh (a Rorobe originally from URD), and Tamba Kandeh (a Rorobe also from URD). In addition, I interviewed Seiniwa Baldeh, a fiddler originally from Guinea Bissau who also played the tama; Ngansumana Jobateh, a Mandinka kora player born in MID, and several nonmusicians from The Gambia. These individuals ranged in age from thirty to sixty years. Although most musicians were born and raised in the provinces where they received their musical training, many were aware of musical practices in other parts of Senegambia. Their knowledge of the music in the precolonial and colonial periods came from oral tradition that had been passed down by kinsmen.

20. Tamba Kandeh (1994) stated that while he uses the term *jalijo*, the Fulbe Futa (from Futa Jalon) use the term *nyamakala* for a musician. For other terms, see Charters (1975:5) and Jessup (1981:39). The variety of terms is consistent with cultural practices of Gambian Fulbe; several Fulbe dialect groups exist with their own terms and pronunciation, and the spellings for terms are not standardized.

21. Sidibe uses "slaves" to refer to descendants of people captured in war during precolonial times and given slave status.

22. Although Fulbe Firdu in Fuladu were politically the most important group in the Gambian region in the nineteenth century, nomadic ("purer") Fulbe looked down upon them because Fulbe Firdu were considered to be of slave origin (Quinn 1967:41–42; 1972:19).

23. For example, while several of the fiddlers interviewed for this study went by the surname Baldeh, others went by Bah, Camara, and Kandeh. Even in Dagbon, where fiddlers claim a family lineage, gondze musicians within the same family have different surnames because the use of surnames in their culture is not what distinguishes a person as a professional musician. (Among the Senegambian Mande, however, a person with last name Diabate, Kouyate, or Susso is considered to be a jali or related to jalis.)

24. Scholars (e.g., Innes 1974:7) and the musicians I interviewed state that Musa Molo's court attracted a large number of griot families that lived in towns (Sotuma and Boraba) near Kesserkunda. Concerning Fulbe warriors who lived before Musa Molo (e.g., Alfa Molo or Maba Diakhou Ba), not only did the musicians I interviewed not know names of performers or musical activity associated with these leaders, they were not even familiar with the leaders' names. A Mandinka kora musician thought that Maba was a Wolof, probably because Maba's family came from Futa Toro. The responses of the musicians can be interpreted in several ways. First, whereas the role of the Fulbe performer as a court musician dates back to only the nineteenth century when Fulbe warriors rose to power, the Mandinka jalolu, who trace their beginnings to Sundiata, had already established themselves as court musicians because Mandinka landlords politically dominated the Gambian region until the nineteenth century. Second, the primary reason oral traditions that associate Gambian musicians with Musa Molo now exist is because Molo continues to be regarded as one of the greatest leaders in Fulbe history. The Fulbe and the Mandinka revere Musa Molo in the same manner that the Mandinka revere Sundiata. Third, the different opinions demonstrate that ethnicity in Senegambia is not clear-cut.

25. Written documentation of the lute in West Africa dates to the fourteenth century when Ibn Battuta mentioned its use in the Mali Empire. Henry George Farmer (1928:27) believes that a folk version of the lute was already in existence when the Arabs arrived.

26. The thinnest piece of wood used for the bridge, about four inches in length, is placed toward the base of the fiddle. The other piece—which is thicker, about six inches in length, and made from the same type of wood used for the bow—lies near the point where the horsehair string is tied to the ball of cord that connects the string to the leather twine. All Fulbe fiddlers I interviewed indicated that they constructed their own instruments.

27. While Majaw Bai (a Tukulor fiddler from Senegal) used the term *nyanyeru,* other Senegalese fiddlers I interviewed and recorded—Ousainou Chaw (a Serer who lived in Dakar) and Juldeh Camara (a Fulbe born in Casamance, Senegal)—referred to the instrument as *riti* (Bai 1990; Chaw 1990).

28. When a close examination is made of the various ethnic groups that use lutes (bowed and plucked), many have either had direct or indirect contact with the Fulbe. In some instances, people who intermarry with the Fulbe have become the performers and propagators of Fulbe culture (Coolen 1982:74; Dalby 1980:573; Charry 2000a:19; Murdock 1959:72).

29. Except for statements made by Tamba Kandeh (1990), there is no other evidence that the Balante of The Gambia play the fiddle. If the Wolof and Serer were not introduced to the fiddle at the same time as the Fulbe (i.e., around the eleventh or twelfth century), their adoption of the instrument could have occurred as a result of contacts with the Fulbe later. Yet the possibility that the Wolof and other groups were introduced to the instrument earlier, as a result of contacts with the Tukulor, should not be ruled out. When I asked Russell Schuh about the ethnicity of the fiddlers he recorded in Dakar in early 1991, he indicated that they were Wolof speakers but did not know if they would have identified their ethnicity as Wolof if he had inquired.

30. Buba Kandeh, who was born in 1975, states that youth in The Gambia find music from the West appealing. Reggae is the most popular, followed by rap and the fusion of reggae and rap. In 2003, some of the most popular musicians in The Gambia that performed these forms included Da Fugitivz, Dance Hall Masters, Rebellion, and Pencha Be (B. Kandeh 2003).

31. Three or four fiddlers performing during a male circumcision ceremony can be viewed in the film *Born Musicians* (1984).

32. Maulday Baldeh, the fiddler who provided the most detailed account about musicians attached to Musa Molo, stated that he acquired his information from his father and grandfathers. At the time of my interview with him in December 1994, Maulday stated that he was in his middle thirties. Except for short visits to towns in Senegal to perform the fiddle, he had spent most of his life at his home in the provinces. Maulday moved to the Banjul area in early 1994 to visit his younger brother, Abudullahi Baldeh, who had migrated to Banjul in 1990 to learn to drive and had not returned home. So Maulday traveled to find him (Maulday Baldeh 1994).

33. Maulday Baldeh states that Musa Molo's second name was Balla (the nickname

for anyone named Musa), so the song is called "Balla." "Sorronna" refers to the bow and arrow that Musa used when he went to war. The literal meaning of "Sodahnam Padeh Jelleh" is "buy high-heeled shoes for me." Composed by Maulday's brother, Abudullahi, "Sodahnam Padeh Jelleh" is in honor of one of Musa Molo's grandchildren because she, at one time, gave him a bull. At the time the brother decided to praise her for giving him the bull, she was wearing high-heeled shoes (Maulday Baldeh 1994).

34. Maulday Baldeh's account is confirmed by Ngansumana Jobateh (1994), a Mandinka kora player born in 1938 in Boraba in Fuladu, which is also located in MID. Jobateh identifies himself as a jali (professional musician). He was ten years old when he began taking kora lessons from his father, and his children actively participate in the profession. According to Jobateh (1994), Musa Molo was the first and greatest warrior in the Gambian region. Because Molo liked music and supported his musicians well, all types of performers (praise singers and instrumentalists) sang and played for him. Most lived in villages near Kesserkunda, where Musa Molo had appointed different men to serve as district heads or rulers. While Mandinka musicians lived in Boraba where Dembo Danso was ruler, Fulbe musicians lived in Basse where Falai Kora Tamba Sangsang was the political leader. When musicians went to Kesserkunda to entertain Molo, he oftentimes rewarded them with a bull to slaughter. Jobateh indicated that he knew of several Mandinka musicians who played for Musa Molo: Karunkah Jobateh, Jaturr Jobateh, Bamba Suso, and Madi Suso. Jobateh also stated that Mandinka musicians had composed historical songs for great leaders who lived during Musa Molo's time (Knight 1983; Charry 2000a).

35. Members of the Rorobe Fulbe group that Tamba and Ngeya Kandeh belong to were originally cattle herders. As they became more settled, they also began to farm. More importantly, both Tamba and Ngeya did not become fiddlers until early adulthood.

36. Several musicians I interviewed explained that they played for politicians. Seiniwa Baldeh, originally from Guinea Bissau, first visited Senegambia with a cultural troupe but decided to stay because he found that he could earn more money in The Gambia. Eventually, he became attached to Lamin Tuthi Baldeh, a Fulbe ruler in MID, who, according to Seiniwa, selected him to be his griot. Whenever the chief traveled, Seiniwa went with the chief and performed at government programs and other events. Later Seiniwa moved to the Banjul area where he performed at hotels, ceremonial occasions, and special programs (S. Baldeh 1994).

37. On the first anniversary of The Gambia's independence in February 1966, the government held a national competition to select the best cultural troupes to represent the different regions of the country. Four groups from the Basse region competed. Because Ngeya's group won first place, Ngeya eventually became known as the champion fiddler, and his group was often invited to perform on Radio Gambia and at government programs.

38. This positive view of fiddling in Senegambia comes from the perspective of the fiddler. In 1990, when I spoke with Mohammed Sissoho, a nonmusician and devout Muslim who considered himself to be of high status because he

worked with the secret service at the airport in The Gambia, about fiddling, he did not berate fiddlers or the profession. Similar to most Muslims, Sissoho did not believe that the playing of musical instruments or dancing was acceptable within Islam. But, like other nonmusicians in Senegambia, Sissoho did not defiantly oppose fiddling, which differs from the attitude of Muslims in Hausaland (see chapter 3).

39. At the time of my interview with him in December 1994, Mamadou Baldeh was thirty-seven years old. Although he did not receive formal lessons from his father, he states that his father advised him on how to play the instrument.

40. Because of Tamba and Ngeya Kandeh's association with a politician, they probably aren't regarded as "fake" griots by most nonmusicians in Fulbe society. However, people born into the profession and who received the necessary training to make them "professionals" (e.g., Maulday Baldeh, Mamadou Baldeh, and Juldeh Camara) might think differently.

41. Ngeya Kandeh was able to provide the genealogy of his fiddle training. His teacher was Sambaru Jawo, who lived near a village called Jawo. Sambaru Jawo received his fiddle instruction from Jajeh Nyalen, who lived in Sinchu Sambajawo. Nyalen learned from Nayang Baldeh, who lived in Sare Timbo. Samba Janabo, who lived in Sinchu Sara, taught Nayang.

42. Tamba Kandeh states that when he began performing the fiddle in the early 1960s, fiddle ensembles rarely included drums (2003). Yet Maulday and Mamadou Baldeh (1994) state that the nyanyeru and tama combination is now the most common instrumental organization used in the provinces. On occasion, other instruments may be added.

43. This performance practice is similar to that of the Hausa. The Hausa fiddler *rarely* sings while performing the fiddle (see chapter 3).

44. Because Maulday and Mamadou Baldeh were born into the fiddling profession and lived in the provinces most of their lives, this performance probably reflects how they were taught and indicates a playing style used by Fulbe in the eastern part of The Gambia.

45. Tamba's wife, Kumba Kandeh, won an award in 1966 for the most beautiful Fulbe lady (T. Kandeh 1994).

46. It is noteworthy that Ngeya Kandeh, someone who did not inherit the fiddle profession from kin, was the person who made innovations. Perhaps the fact that he was not born into the profession allowed him to be more open to changes.

47. Although some songs that Tamba Kandeh played at his brother's wedding were the same ones he played for me in his courtyard, his behavior was different in each context. He did not dance in either situation, but at the wedding he stood and was more physically involved in the performance.

48. Music scholars have noted the impact of tourism on the transmission, preservation, and performance of African music (Kirkegaard 2001). From these comments, it is apparent that Fulbe musicians associate fire-eating and acrobatics with traditional practices, which are not necessarily identified with fiddling but can be included in fiddle performances. Fulbe in other parts of West Africa use similar practices. Salifu Lali, a Dagbamba fiddler, indicated he had observed

Malian Fulbe musicians performing acrobatics with fire in Ghana (Lali 1995). Nigerians also employ fire-eating and acrobatics. Whether they are Nigerian Fulbe is not known; see Bollag (2002).

49. Dagbamba fiddlers, who also perform short phrases before and between a series of songs, call this material *zugubu* (a tuning-up melody or introduction); see chapter 4.

50. The oral tradition that explains how Juldeh Camara's father became a fiddler is fascinating and similar to the history of the Dagbamba gondze (see chapter 4). According to legend, Camara's grandfather, a hunter, wanted his son, Serif, to continue in the family occupation. However, when Serif was fifteen years old, he disappeared into the forest. Although many people thought Serif was dead, killed by hyenas, the father continued to search for his son in the forest. While searching one year later, the father heard a sound coming from a tree. When he came closer, he saw Serif sitting in the tree playing a golden violin, hypnotized by *djinni* (spirits). After many hours, the father was able to drive the djinni away, but the violin also disappeared. Although Serif followed his father home, he returned to the forest each day to learn more from the djinni. "When the time came, and Serif had become a fully trained musician and *marabout* [Islamic teacher with spiritual powers], the *djinni* took his eyesight in return" (Heilmann 2003).

51. Camara is featured on two recordings—*Ancient Heart: Mandinka and Fulani Music of the Gambia* (1990) and *Tramp* (1994)—and is an accompanist on several, including Zubop, *Hiptodisiac,* United Kingdom 33 Records CD (1997) Norway; Dee Ellington, *Vibe Me,* RCA (1997) United Kingdom; Positive Black Soul, *New York-Paris-Dakar,* Cassette and CD vol. 1 (1997) New York, Paris, and Dakar, Senegal; Ifang Bondi, *Gis Gis,* MW Records CD (1998) Netherlands; Various Artists, *Millennium Drum Salute,* Yellowgate CD (1999) The Gambia; Various Artists, *Kairo Sounds of the Gambia,* Arch CD (1999) The Gambia; Batanai Marimba, *Moto Moto,* Koni CD (2000) United Kingdom; Batanai Marimba, *Mudzimu Mudzimu,* Koni CD (2002) United Kingdom; Daykil Chosan Group, *Madirisa,* ECCO (2003) The Gambia; and ZubopGambia, *ZubopGambia,* 33 Records CD (2004). The recordings on which he serves as an accompanist are not included in the discography because too many details (titles, labels, etc.) are missing.

52. Camara did not give a formal title for any of his songs. I refer to the song concerning youth as the "African youth song" (see Song Text 2.1). Hausa fiddler Mamman Landi also composed a song about the youth (see chapter 3). In both cases, the fiddlers call on the youth to become more involved in helping their respective countries socially.

53. The lengths given for Camara's songs are rough estimates. The length of Tamba Kandeh's songs on August 19, 1990, may have been short because we were preparing to go to a wedding later in the day. Instead of being concerned about satisfying a patron who had paid him money to perform, Kandeh, on August 19, was more interested in testing the sound of the fiddle and his voice on a tape recorder.

54. Salif Badjie identified himself as a Jola. At the time of my interview with him, Badjie was twenty-eight years old. He was born in 1962 in Bakau Kachikali,

a town located near Serrekunda, and had lived in a town called Siga Shore in Casamance, Senegal, as well as other locations in The Gambia. In addition to the tama, which he learned to play between 1982 and 1984, Badjie performed the Wolof *sabar* and other drums used by the Mandinka and Fulbe that are similar in construction. Badjie referred to the Mandinka version of the sabar as *tentawo* and called the Fulbe version the "Fulbe sabar." Badjie stated that he was eleven years old when his grandfather started teaching him how to play the sabar, his first instrument. Except for him and his grandfather, no one else in his family were musicians. When I asked why he decided to play the tama, Badjie stated: "I learned tama because they invite me for these wedding ceremonies, birthday ceremonies, parties. I learned this to teach people that's paying me. I wanted to make this tama a profession of my own. And I respect it" (Badjie 1990). Camara and Badjie were not part of a permanent group. Rather, Badjie was a freelance drummer who played with a variety of musicians (Badjie 1990).

55. To refer to men as warriors was a compliment, which indicates that the individuals were strong in their cause (struggle), similar to Fulbe leaders Alfa Molo and his son, Musa Molo. The measure numbers refer to the music transcription.

56. The Fulbe textual variation serves the same purpose as the shouting by the *marok'i* (praise shouter) in Hausa fiddling. In some Hausa fiddle performances, the marok'i shouts praises to patrons and members of the group as well as makes comments about other aspects of the culture (see chapter 3). The fact that Camara mentions the desire to travel to the United States so early in the song indicates that this was something very important to him.

57. Before his performance, Camara asked me to give him the names of my close family members. I gave him my daughter's name, Dominique Abiba DjeDje.

58. The melodic organization of this piece is similar to Dagbamba fiddle music. The Dagbamba use only one theme, which is performed repeatedly throughout the composition by the vocal chorus and fiddlers. However, the Hausa may use two or more themes in their fiddle songs (see chapters 3 and 4).

59. See Examples 2.2 and 2.3 for the rhythmic patterns for the tama player. Of course, some variations take place in the ostinato as Badjie plays the song. For example, a slight change to the rhythm occurs in measure 15 when the tama is not played on the first half of beat 2 and neither on beat 6.

60. In the opening of the African youth song (i.e., the first thirty seconds when no singing is performed), Camara varies the B part of the main melody (inserting neighboring tones, passing tones, harmonics, as well as playing it an octave higher) much more than he does in the other parts (A, A, or B′). I am not sure why he chooses the B part (beats 4, 5, and 6) of the ABAB′ form for further development and improvisation. But other Fulbe fiddlers do the same thing. Portions of the main melody are improvised more than other parts.

61. Home ownership and owning land were important to Kandeh, who had lived in several parts of Senegambia, for he believed property ownership gave a person status and peace of mind. Considering that his ancestors were nomadic and cattle herders, this change in attitude represents a major shift in values and priorities. When I visited Kandeh in the 1990s, he was leasing a compound in Lamin where he and his family resided. On my return to The Gambia in 2003,

he had built and moved into a new compound on land he had purchased in another part of Lamin.

62. In 1960, Mali gained independence from the French and became the Republic of Mali. The first president was Modibo Keita. When a group of Malian military leaders overthrew Keita in 1968, Moussa Traoré, one of the leaders, took control of Mali's government as head of a military committee. Traoré was elected president of Mali in 1979 when the first elections under the country's new constitution were held (Spitzer 1987a). Traoré was both a military man and an elected official, which may explain why Kandeh refers to him both as "colonel" and "president."

63. In 1990, I was told this was the typical instrumentation for ensembles that performed at luxury hotels, but some groups *did not* include a flute. When I recorded a similar group (called the Fula Acrobats Johkerreh Endham) in 2003, the ensemble included all instruments but no fiddle. Although they had tried, members of the group stated they had not been able to find a fiddle replacement after Bah died in 2000.

64. "Nafa" alludes to the Fulani musicians' appreciation of gifts they receive from patrons. On *Guinée* (1992), "Nafa" is defined as "utility." In Mande, *nafa* means profit or benefit and it may have Arabic origins (Charry 2005). "Nafa" is played at hotels that European tourists often visit, such as Fajara, located northwest of Serrekunda in a town called Fajara (Barry 1990).

65. Not only were people attracted to the sound, I imagine some were interested in the dramatic acrobatic movement and fire-eating, neither of which took place during Camara's performance on September 1, 1990. The colors (red, white, and blue) of the attire worn by most members of the ensemble were similar to those worn by Camara. Bah was the only person who did not wear these colors. Except for the djembe drummer, everyone wore Sudanic-style trousers with various types of tops. Three persons (the fiddler and two horde players) had on sleeveless Western-style white T-shirts, and one person (the lala player) wore a short-sleeved Western-style T-shirt. The other two performers wore blue shirts of different designs: the djembe drummer wore African-style clothing while the flute player had on a shirt that was Western in design. Members of the audience did not wear clothing with bright colors.

66. As a fire-eater, Bah ignited the end of a long stick with some material attached and placed the torch inside his mouth without harming himself. In my interview with him, unfortunately, I did not inquire about how he learned fire-eating nor how long he had been doing it as an entertainer.

67. Because the sound of the music is so dense, determining the parts played by each percussionist is difficult. Probably because the lala is higher in pitch, the sound of this instrument can be heard more clearly than others. Therefore, except for the lala's playing, the notation of the other percussion parts is not included in Examples 2.7, 2.8A–F, and 2.9.

68. During the performance of "Churoi Wuro," Tamba joined in and played something totally different than Bah did. When I inquired about what had happened, I was told that it was not uncommon for one fiddler to play a drone or even a counter melody when several fiddlers are included in an ensemble.

69.   When embellishing the melody, Sanneh focuses on pitches surrounding C and A (see beats 5–8 of measure 25) as well as F and G (see beats 5–7 of measure 28). In many ways, the collective improvisation is similar to the performance practice used during dancing and acrobatic movements. Each person is given an opportunity to take the spotlight in front of the group. While this happens, others stay in the background until that person finishes. Then the next person steps to the front and showcases his talents.

3. Calling the Bori Spirits

1.   This poem by Shehu 'Uthman dan Fodio, one of the major Islamic reformists of the nineteenth century, was originally written when he was a youth (Erlmann 1986:38; Hiskett 1969:706).

2.   During my first field trip to northern Nigeria in 1974, several Hausa fiddlers I interviewed indicated that the use of the goge in Bori performances in the Kano area was common (Mohammadan 1974; Bande 1974). However, Lawan Danladi Yalwa, a Hausa born in Kano City who is a professor of linguistics at Abdullahi Bayero University and a devoted follower of Islam, argues that the *garaya* (plucked lute) was used more often at Bori performances in Kano than the goge (Yalwa 2003a).

3.   Ibraheem A. Garba, a Muslim and Hausa speaker born in Jos (Plateau State), Nigeria, indicates that Western-style nightclubs did not become prominent in northern Nigeria until the 1960s and 1970s. However, settings where people congregated for pleasure (e.g., beer bars)—to drink, interact with women, and play cards—have always existed in Hausa culture because "men like to go to places where they can chase women" (I. Garba 2003). In Garba's opinion, goge musicians frequented these places because they knew men wanted to show off in front of women by spending money; especially when praise songs were performed in their honor. Because owners of such establishments found that the sound of the fiddle attracted customers, they regularly invited goge musicians to perform. Garba believes that when both Muslim and Christian leaders began to preach more vehemently against "loose living" during the 1980s and 1990s, many of the clubs closed. Rafin Sanyi, a club in Jos that was popular for fiddling during the 1970s, closed in the 1990s due to protests by religious groups (I. Garba 2003).

4.   In an article written in 1942, P. G. Harris, a British district officer based in the Sokoto Province during the early decades of the twentieth century, documents three precolonial festivals that continued to be held annually at Argungu: *Gyaran Gari* (Putting the Town in Order), *Gyaran Ruwa* (Putting the Waters in Order), and *Fashin Ruwa* (Scattering or Breaking of the Waters) (Harris 1942:23–25). In addition to celebrating hunting, Fashin Ruwa marked the opening of the fishing and season, just as the festival I attended in 1974. In Harris' description of Fashin Ruwa, fiddling and Bori play important roles in the festivities.

5.   Class among youth in late-twentieth-century Sokoto is an issue in an article by Malami Buba and Graham Furniss (1999). The authors explain that Sokoto's two areas—the inner walled (old town) and the surrounding outskirts (new

town)—not only corresponded with the socio-economic status of those who lived there, but they also reflected the co-existence of modernity and tradition. The *'yan bariki* (children-of-outside-town) were the middle class (Western-educated professionals) while the *'yan cikin gari* (children-of-inside-of-town) were largely nonliterate and relied heavily on the old caliphate system of patronage to survive (Buba and Furniss 1999:33–34). In 1974, when I made my observations and interviewed city residents, nightclubs in Kano City fall into three categories, which attracted people in the lower, middle, and upper classes, respectively. The frequency of fighting between individuals served as a basis for distinguishing the different types of clubs, but other factors (club hours and music types) were also taken into account. Regardless of the factors, a relationship existed between the type of music preferred and socio-economic status. Duro Oni, a colleague who accompanied me to the clubs and knew many of the guests, stated that most people in the audience were northern and southern Nigerians who worked as clerks, civil servants, teachers, and in other occupations.

6. When Oni and I arrived at the Railway Nite Club entrance, between 8:45 and 9 PM, a ticket seller was stationed at the door. Fortunately, one of the Liyo's protégés saw us and told the ticket seller we were guests of the goge musician. We were allowed to enter without paying. Liyo's protégé may have been at the door waiting for our arrival, so we could gain entrance without a problem, which might be the reason Liyo sometimes sits outside the club before his performance. After we selected a table and sat down, one of Liyo's *marok'a* (chief praise singer of the group) came over, sat down, and talked with us about Liyo's life as a musician. The *marok'i* indicated that the fiddler had traveled to the United States and would be visiting other places in Nigeria as well as Côte d'Ivoire. He explained that they rarely performed with Bori initiates because Liyo and members of the group were "professional." Therefore, they played primarily at hotels and clubs where Bori performances were not wanted.

7. *'Dan kar'bi* is a double-membrane hourglass pressure drum, similar to but smaller than the kalangu. In performance, one person performs the two drums simultaneously. While sitting, the drummer holds the kalangu under his arm and squeezes the strings to get different pitches, while the 'dan karbi is strapped to his thigh. In this way, the drummer is able to alternately hit the membrane of both instruments with a single stick. The kuntuku is a single-membrane, snared bowl-shaped drum played with two sticks. *Masu amshi* (or *'yan amshi*) refer to the chorus. When singing a song, a *mawak'i* (solo singer) is answered by the *masu amshi*. The *marok'a* (plural; *marok'i,* masculine singular; *marok'iya,* feminine singular) are persons who praise or acclaim others, whether solicited or not, in the hope of obtaining a reward. The acclamation may be expressed in song (*waka*) or speech (*kirari*), with or without instrumental accompaniment. Several marok'a generally perform when there is a large audience (Ames and King 1971). In Figure 3.2, the second fiddler (Liyo's apprentice) is not depicted.

8. Mervyn Hiskett suggests that Bayajida (also spelled Bayajidda) may be a Hausa form of the classical Arab figure, Abu Zayd, the legendary leader of the Banu Hilal (Arab Bedouins who invaded North Africa during the eleventh century) (Hiskett 1984:69–73). While some versions of the tradition relate that Bayajida

and his followers were slaves of the sultan of Borno, other accounts indicate that Bayajida escaped from the treachery of the sultan of Borno who was plotting to kill him (Palmer 1928:95). Some scholars discredit this account because it reflects the situation in the sixteenth century, when the seven states that had survived the surrounding conflicts legitimized themselves by a legend claiming a prestigious eastern ancestry (Ki-Zerbo and Niane 1997; Ogot 1999; Abdulkadir 1975:42–43).

9. Before the sixteenth century, the inhabitants of present-day Hausaland were known by the names of kingdoms: Katsinawa, Kanawa, Gobirawa, and so on. For references to the early use of the term Hausa, see Ki-Zerbo and Niane (1997:105) and Hiskett (1984:72–73).

10. According to one version, the earliest inhabitants of Kano were referred to as Abagayawa (also known as Arna, Azna, Bunjawa, Maguzawa) (DjeDje 1978b). One of their ancestors, a blacksmith called Kano, is believed to have come from Gaya (east-southeast of Kano) in search of iron stone and settled near Dala (also spelled Dalla) Hill when the present site of the town was uninhabited (Gowers 1921:8). Some versions estimate that Bagauda [also spelled Bagoda], the first king and grandson of Bayajida, entered Kano in 999, and it was Bagauda's grandson, Gijimasu (1095–1134), who founded Kano at the foot of Dala Hill. Gijimasu began constructing the city walls, but his son, Tsaraki (1136–1194), completed them (Ki-Zerbo and Niane 1997:107).

11. Some scholars believe that the Hausa's first contact with the Kanuri and Kanembu of Kanem-Borno occurred in the thirteenth century, and Borno dominated the Hausa, politically and culturally, from the fifteenth to the eighteenth century (Hiskett 1984:60). Joseph Greenberg argues that Fulbe presence in Kano first took place during the reign of Yaji dan Tsamiya (1452–1463) when they migrated into Hausaland from Mali where they had adopted Islam from the Maghrib. The Malian Fulbe brought "books of divinity," and *sharifs* (Muslims of noble ancestry) also came (Greenberg 1960:479–480; Ki-Zerbo and Niane 1997:107–108).

12. When the Sahara and Azbin (Aïr) sent Arab and European goods (mirrors, paper, horses, camels, dates, henna, salt, swords, and other articles), Hausaland supplied slaves, clothes, fabrics, millet, hides, iron, gold dust, and kola nuts from Gwanja (Gonja). Borno offered the Hausa horses, natron, and salt in exchange for metal articles, gold dust, and kola nuts. To groups further south, the Hausa exported salt, swords, condiments, hides, clothes and fabrics, and slaves and horses, and received in return different European items, local iron, antimony, slaves and eunuchs, muskets from Nupe (for Kano), and kola nuts from Gwanja for domestic consumption (Ogot 1999:243).

13. Shari'a, or Islamic law, which regards only a restricted range of offenses as crimes, is limited to illicit sexual relations, theft, brigandage, drinking alcohol, and sometimes apostasy. Homicide and physical injury are not included (Lewis 1980:45). Although Shari'a was a political issue during the 1970s when a new constitution was drafted after Nigeria's civil war, it was never fully implemented (Maier 2000). However, when Ahmed Sani, the newly elected governor of Zamfara State, announced in 1999 that his state planned to adopt Islamic law, several northern states (Niger, Kano, Sokoto, and others) followed suit. In

2000, supporters of the law argued that the federal constitution, by guaranteeing freedom of religion, gave all Muslims the right to live under Shari'a and that it would only affect Muslims; the small minority (10 percent) of non-Muslims in the states would not be affected. In disputes involving Christian and Muslim communities, the non-Muslims could choose to settle the matter in a Shari'a or secular court (Maier 2000:14–15, 177).

14. According to Yalwa, *karuwa* (plural, *karuwai*) is an unmarried woman who sells her chastity to men (for money or material needs); she is a prostitute. Unmarried women who are honorable and respected are *zararawa* (singular, *bazawara*); they are either divorced or have lost their husbands and are looking for someone to marry (Yalwa 2003b). Buba and Furniss indicate that children of *'yan cikin gari* in Sokoto during the late twentieth century often rebelled against their Islamic upbringing by having a night out at the local *gidan karuwai* (house of prostitutes), which was "the main venue for visiting goge 'bowed instruments associated with *bori*' and *gambara* 'rap artist' groups" (Buba and Furniss 1999:34).

15. Although Qur'anic education dates to earlier times, it continues to be important in Sudanic Africa (Odoom 1968:70). In areas such as northern Nigeria, Qur'anic training is part of a child's daily activities. In some of the homes I visited in The Gambia in 2003, however, Qur'anic training occurs less frequently. In those cases, the mallams would visit compounds several times a week in the late afternoon or early evening and teach children.

16. After reading portions of my manuscript, Yalwa stated: "Many people do not agree with you that Bori (at least) *nowadays* is a 'religion.' In a nutshell Bori cannot be compared with any of the revealed religions. Idol worshipping or even belief in jinn's possession; it is just an entertainment. But that type that predates Islam or [was] practiced by Maguzawas is a religion as you correctly assume" (Yalwa 2003b). Likewise, Hassan states that in present-day Kano, "Bori is regarded more as superstition than as a religion" (Hassan 2003). Other Hausa refer to it as devil possession or temporary madness (Madauci 1968; Danfulani 1999:414–415). See Tremearne (1914) and Greenberg (1946) for other interpretations regarding Bori.

17. When I visited Kano City in 2003, several Hausa explained that Bori ceremonies continued to take place, but only the participants knew the place and time (Hassan 2003). When asked why Bori continues even though Shari'a prohibits such practices and many Hausa regard the religion to be superstition, Hassan stated: "Because it's one's habit. Once you inculcate a habit, it's very difficult for you to do away with it. Only until you fight your mind before you can do away with what you've inculcated. . . . So they are already used to this type of goge and garaya musicals. So it's already in their blood and everything. So it's only gradual that they will do away with it" (Hassan 2003).

18. John Gray's bibliography *African Music* contains citations on ethnographic, anthropological, and musicological studies from the 1890s to the early 1990s (Gray 1991:x). While forty-one sources are listed for the Hausa, there are fourteen for the Dagbamba, and none for the Fulbe of Senegambia. Yet the findings differ greatly when statistics for Nigeria are taken into account. Whereas 198 sources (roughly 75 percent) are listed for southern Nigeria, only 67 (25 per-

cent) appear for northern Nigeria. When I reviewed the literature published since the early 1990s, the percentage of material on northern and southern Nigeria had not changed.

19. Although several works—Ames (1970, 1973b), Besmer (1998), Borel (1991), Buba and Furniss (1999), Furniss (1996), (King 1980a, 2000), Kofoworola and Lateef (1987), Podstavsky (1992, 2004), and Rhodes (1977)—include a general discussion of Hausa music, the *Glossary of Hausa Music in Its Social Context* (1971) by David Ames and Anthony V. King is the most thorough and comprehensive with details on instruments, performers, patrons, occasions, and music performance. Research on Hausa music reflect features that characterize musicking in Hausaland. Most studies focus on singing and songs, followed by instruments, religion (Bori and Islam), performers, performance contexts, and musical style (see Gray 1991:114–117). Several recordings on Hausa music have been produced, but the two-volume set produced by David Ames (n.d.) remains one of the best in providing a cross-section of musical traditions. Numerous other recordings of Hausa music have been published in Nigeria, but few are available in the United States. My comments, therefore, are based on what has been accessible to me.

20. Except for chordophones (bowed and plucked lutes), Hausa instruments adopted from outsiders are associated with Hausa royalty and have high status. Court instruments such as the alghaita or algaita (oboe), kakaki (long trumpet), and tambari (drum) are believed to have been borrowed from either Borno or Songhai, while the kotso (drum) was originally Fulbe (Ames and King 1971:29; Arnott 2001; Erlmann 1983b:25). Instruments described in Harris (1942) are not included in Ames and King (1971) and Ames (1973b).

21. This was particularly true of instruments used by Hausa fiddlers I interviewed in 1974: Haruna Bande (also known as Harun Bande), Mamman Landi, Garba Liyo, Ibrahim Mohammadan, Momman Nabarau, and Ahmadu Samunaka. Only three fiddlers (Liyo, Mohammadan, and Nabarau) had constructed their instruments. Bande purchased his fiddle and stated that instead of goge musicians constructing instruments, many bought them from instrument makers (DjeDje 1978b:120). Interestingly, all Fulbe and Dagbamba fiddlers I interviewed indicated that they constructed their instruments.

22. While Gourlay relies almost entirely on secondary sources, DjeDje, Yakubu, and Kawada use both primary and secondary data. Yakubu is one of the few Hausa researchers to have conducted formal investigations on the goge. Maikudi Karaye, the Director of the Centre for the Study of Nigerian Languages at Abdullahi Bayero University, believes that the negative views that Muslims have about music and dancing are the primary reasons for the lack of research on this topic by Hausa scholars (Karaye 2003).

23. It is noteworthy that Mohammadan remained a Bori musician throughout his performance career. He began his career as a garaya musician, and, though he switched from the garaya (the two-stringed plucked lute) to the goge (the one-stringed bowed lute), he continued to perform for Bori.

24. Liyo did not give a detailed physical description of the sunsuma, but used gestures to demonstrate how it was played. However, I have not been able to find an instrument used by the Hausa that corresponds with his description. Both

Ames and King and Besmer discuss the sham'bara, also known as *kasam'bar* (or *kasambara*). Made from a guinea corn stalk, it is held between the palms of the hands and rotated in a rubbing motion to produce sound (Ames and King 1971:7; Besmer 1983:54).

25. I have not found an instrument with the name *gyandamma,* but Harris discusses the rattle (*chekki*) used to accompany the fiddle: "The *chekki* is a water-bottle gourd (*gyandamma*) filled with dried seeds . . . and is shaken rhythmically, producing a tinny [*sic*] sound like that of a tambourine when shaken" (Harris 1932:123). Could the term *gyandamma* refer to the gourd material that fiddlers used to construct instruments in earlier times, or could this be another instrument that Liyo references as a predecessor to the goge?

26. When I interviewed him in 2003, Musa dan Gado Saminaka stated that his age was fifty-five (yet he appeared to be in his sixties or early seventies). Although he was born in Kano State, his permanent residence was Saminaka, a town in Plateau State about fifty miles northeast of Jos. He moved with his parents and siblings to Saminaka when he was fifteen years old. At age twelve, he started playing the garaya before changing to the goge four years later. In the late 1990s, he gave up fiddling as a profession because he stated that he had "repented" from his evil ways. Yet later in his interview, he indicated that Shari'a would not stop a person from playing the fiddle.

27. The Zaberma (also spelled Zerma, Djerma, Dyerma) people live west of the Hausa in Songhai along the Niger River where its great bend touches the edge of the Sahara Desert. Linguistically, the Zaberma are related to the Dendi and the Songhai, whose languages belong to the Songhai linguistic family. All three groups came from the western part of Hausaland when they ascended the Niger to their present location around 700 CE. People of Songhai have had contacts with several Berber groups and others in the Sudan. The Adarawa speak a language belonging to the Hausa branch of the Chadic subfamily (Murdock 1959:137–138). Babba Mai Goge (whose birth name is Muhammadu Lawal) was born in Gaya, a town in Kano State, and received his Qur'anic training in the town of Borno, which is where he saw the Adarawa people from Niger playing the kwambilo (Yakubu 1981).

28. Balan Na Bassa did not give me his exact date of birth, but I estimate from our conversation that he was born in the mid-1920s. His birthplace is Bassa, a town in central Nigeria (Plateau State). He started playing the fiddle when he was thirteen or fourteen years old and, with his brother, became well known in many parts of Nigeria. He states that Nigeria Radio Kaduna still uses his fiddle music recordings to start some of their programs. Although Bassa's grandfather (Bawa mai Goge), father (Abdul Karim mai Goge), and elder brother (Ahmadu Na Bassa mai Goge) all played the *goge,* Bassa gave up the goge profession in 1962 to become a building contractor and trader (Bassa 2003). Born in the 1920s in Gombe State, Umarun Mayani identified his ethnicity as Waja, an ethnic group closely related to the Tangale of central Nigeria. However, he was a Hausa speaker, like most ethnic groups living in central Nigeria. Mayani started playing the fiddle in 1959, when he was in his early twenties. In addition to fiddling, he was also a farmer. Although his permanent residence was Kuba, a small village about twenty-one miles from the city of Jos, Mayani

spent time in Jos where he earned much of his income playing the goge. The *kwambilo* bow that Balan Na Bassa and Umarun Mayani described resembles the bow used by Dagbamba fiddlers (see chapters 1 and 4).

29. The Beri-Beri (a Hausa term, also spelled Beriberi) were part of Kanem-Borno but were strongly influenced by the Hausa, whose language some of them adopted (Ki-Zerbo and Niane 1997:110; Murdock 1959:136). Except for Meek's comments, there is no other evidence that the Beriberi played the fiddle, but fiddling among the Kanembu (Kanuri) has been documented (*Music of Kanem* n.d.). Fiddling among the Kanembu-Kanuri (Beriberi) is significant because of their close association with the Hausa. Since borrowings can occur both ways when two cultures make contact, perhaps the kukuma is evidence of this exchange. In other words, while the Hausa adopted the trumpet (e.g., the *kakaki*) from the people of Borno, possibly Kanem-Borno adopted the fiddle from Hausaland.

30. Using only nomenclature can be misleading in reconstructing the history of an instrument (Schuyler 1979:110). During the 1970s and 1980s, scholars (myself included) writing about the history and distribution of the fiddle in Hausaland used works by Farmer and Hause as major sources without scrutinizing their methodology. It was not until I had completed my research trip in Senegambia, where I learned that the terms *nyanyeru* and *riti* both refer to "rubbing," that I investigated whether similar meanings existed in Hausaland for the term *goge*. Junzo Kawada agrees that the Hausa introduced the *goge* term in North Africa and adds that enslaved Hausa in the Maghrib later formed spirit possession groups known as *stambâlî* (Kawada 2001:5). Lois Anderson indicates that *stambâlî* means "reunion" or "gathering" and is used in reference to Islamic events held by the Gnawa in North Africa (Anderson 1971:162; Charry 2000b:554).

31. Kawada dismisses Borno as a source for the introduction of fiddling in Hausaland because his findings indicate that the Kanuri do not use either the hourglass pressure drum or the fiddle, two instruments he believes are most often identified with the Hausa (Kawada 2001:4). Yet my research reveals that while the fiddle may not be one of their most prominent instruments, the Kanembu and Kanuri do use it; see Brandily (n.d.), Bornand (1999:15), and the appendix.

32. People from Niger feature prominently in Hausa oral traditions about fiddling. Both Musa dan Godo Saminaka (2003) and Ahmadu Doka (quoted in Yakubu 1981) refer to the Zaberma (Djerma) people (who, in earlier times, were located in present-day southwest Niger) as being responsible for introducing fiddling into Hausaland. Mohammadan (1974) believes that people from Damagarau, Niger, were responsible for introducing the instrument to the Hausa. Finally, it should not be overlooked that goge musician Haruna Bande was born in Niger. The role of the fiddle in Songhai religion corresponds with Bori and fiddling in Hausaland (see Rouch 1960; Stoller 1989; Bornand 1999).

33. When I asked Musa dan Gado Saminaka why fiddlers in Hausaland were not court musicians, he initially stated that this was a decision made by the fiddlers but later retracted and indicated that it was the decision of royalty. Yet Saminaka believes that fiddlers were financially better off than court musicians. He explains: "The chief or the emir would not satisfy their needs, financially.

So none of the goge musicians has taken himself to become a royal part. They would rather go into the public and perform and get five *naira*, ten naira, and another amount. The tambari person is the drummer that the emir decides that he wants under him. So he's responsible for his feeding and so on. However, they that perform the goge music outside are richer than he who stays with the emir. In fact, most of them [fiddlers] have to give gifts to the musicians inside [the emir's palace]" (Saminaka 2003).

34. Several fiddlers—Mohammadan (1974), Gobe Mudu (see Yakubu 1981), and Saminaka (2003)—started as either garaya or kukuma players before changing to goge. Erlmann (1983b:201) reports that with the end of colonial rule in the Cameroon, the younger Fulbe began "to challenge the role of Hausa and Kanuri musicians" for they realized the financial benefits of music-making. Abdoulaye Oumar (1995) confirms that young Fulbe in Cameroon during the early postcolonial period challenged the restrictions placed on musicking in traditional culture. Whether the same type of changes occurred among Fulbe living in northern Nigeria during the postcolonial period is not known.

35. A Bulala male playing the kukuma can be viewed on JVC Video (1988). The Bulala, who are located in Chad, also had contacts with Borno in precolonial times (see chapter 1).

36. When indirect rule was established by British colonialists in the early twentieth century, emirs in Hausaland lost much of the administrative, economic, and legal power they had exercised in their precolonial city-states. Emirs do continue to be visible as traditional rulers, living in palaces with courtiers and presiding over traditional festivities, ceremonies, and rituals; yet it is Nigeria's federal government that confirms who should hold office and provides the ruler with a salary and other support (see chapter 4).

37. Hawan salla usually occurs at annual Muslim feasts—the Lesser Feast, which is known as Kàrámár Sállà ('Id al-fitr), and the Great Feast, known as Bàbbár Sállà ('Id al-kabir) (Besmer 1974; Lewis 1966:70–71; also see chapters 2 and 4). Goge and other low-ranking musicians are present not because of their religious or political significance to the occasion, but because of their desire to provide entertainment to attendees and patrons who may have an important function at the ceremony (Ames and King 1971).

38. In 2003, when I ate meals in the restaurant of the Royal Tropicana Hotel where I was staying in Kano City, workers often turned the radio on to provide listening music for guests. On several occasions, I heard fiddle music on Radio Kano. Hassan states that fiddle music is regularly used as background sound for films. In his opinion, fiddling "sweetens the sound" (2003).

39. Titles are commonly used for court musicians. Like their patrons, they are chosen on the basis of the positions of their relatives.

40. Musicians often consult a Bori spirit called Sarkin Maka'da or Sarkim Maka'da (chief of drummers) when they have professional difficulties (Mohammadan 1974; Bassa 2003; Mayani 2003). Bori spirits (divine horsemen) are residents of the invisible city of Jangare "who mark their victims with illness and misfortune and then provide the source for its remedy" (Besmer 1983:1).

41. The most celebrated goge musicians associated with political parties were

Audu Yaron Goge and Garba Liyo. Audu Yaron was at first a supporter of NEPU (The Northern Elements' Progressive Union) before changing his support to the NPC (Northern Peoples Congress), while Garba Liyo was always a staunch supporter of NPC (Ames and King 1971:144). Before his death in 1966, Ahmadu Bello, the premier of the Northern Region, was the head of the Northern Peoples Congress (NPC) political party. Saminaka explains that "wherever Ahmadu Bello moved with his campaign team, he would search for somebody who was popular in that region. Then they would choose this person to play music . . . along with the campaign. It's not like he [Bello] always went together with musicians on his campaign. For instance, if he's going to Bauchi, he would like for someone who plays the instrument in Bauchi to perform" (Saminaka 2003). Garba Liyo's son, Shehu, indicates that his father often performed for military leaders such as Ibrahim Babangida (Nigerian president from the mid-1980s to the early 1990s) when they served as head of state (Liyo 2003).

42.   Bassa is alluding to the fact that the goge is a "talking" instrument (speech surrogate). As Hausa is a tonal language, the high and low pitches of the language often correspond to the contour of the fiddle melody, allowing the instrument to "talk." The goge is used to talk in all types of music—both Bori and non-Bori songs.

43.   In distinguishing between the kukuma and goge, Bassa states: "If you look at it, the kukuma is just like the goge fiddle. The sound is not the same, although they are similar [in physical appearance]. It's the kukuma [player] who sings praise songs. These are the type of people who normally go to clubs. When they go there, you here them talk as they are praising" (Bassa 2003). I believe that because kukuma music is less complex melodically and rhythmically than goge music, this may also be a reason people prefer the former for dancing.

44.   UCLA linguistics professor Russell Schuh states that the text *Goge mai kasha was molo kaifi* "is completely mistranslated. It should be 'Fiddle which deadens the sharpness of molo,' clearly meaning that the *molo*-lute is no match for the fiddle" (Schuh 1990).

45.   When I asked Shehu Liyo if he thought Shari'a would have stopped his father from playing the fiddle, his response was similar to Saminaka's: "No. That [Shari'a] would never stop him. It can stop him here [in Katsina State], but it can't stop him from performing. He would go elsewhere to places where they don't have Shari'a" (2003). Yet Mamman Landi's son felt that his father would have stopped performing because of Shari'a. He states, "If they [fiddlers] don't have back-up encouragement or patrons to support them, he probably would not play" (2003).

46.   When Bassa gave up fiddling, his family was more concerned about the loss in income than his leaving the family profession. In Senegambia and Dagbon, however, the situations are different (see chapters 2 and 4).

47.   In addition to participating in political party functions, kukuma players perform for wealthy merchants (*attajirai*), officials (*sarakuna*), and prostitutes, and their patrons. Young unmarried men and women, as well as married women, also play kukuma for pleasure (Ames and King 1971:85).

48.   When individuals in Hausaland choose fiddling as a profession, they sometimes add the instrument's name to their given name to identify themselves as

professional goge musicians. For example, Haruna Bande's professional name is Haruna Yaron Goge. Although the phrase, "yaron goge," implies that Haruna is "the son of goge," it also signifies that Haruna is a "young" or "new" performer of the instrument. One of the fiddlers Yakubu interviewed for his study uses Babba Mai Goge as his professional name, but his birth name is Muhammadan Lawal (Yakubu 1981). In this case, "mai goge" means that Babba is a professional goge player, or is the owner or possessor of goge. A similar situation exists in Dagbon where the word "gondze" is included as part of fiddlers' names to signify that their profession is fiddling and that they belong to the gondze clan (see chapter 4). Among Senegambian Fulbe, the naming of professional musicians is different primarily because the history of the fiddle and peoples in the region also differ.

49.	During the 1960s, most Hausa membranophone and aerophone players were expected to learn and continue the tradition of their father, particularly instrumentalists who served in the emir's court (Ames 1973b).

50.	Harouna Oumarou Sanaye (also called Harouna Goge) was born in Kara-Kara in the Gaya region of southern Niger (also called Dendi Country) (Bornand 1999). He should not be confused with Haruna Bande, whom I interviewed in Kano in 1974.

51.	It does not matter if the student is trained by a kinsman or apprenticed to a non-kinsman; training is the same. Although the teacher assumes social and professional responsibility for the pupil, no written contract is made between the two. The pupil addresses his master as "father" and treats him with the same degree of respect due to any male relative of his father's generation. The master treats his pupil as his son (or son-in-law). However, irrespective of age, the student is assigned "younger brother" status if his teacher has natural sons who are also apprentices, a practice that results in friction when age and achievement do not correspond with social placement (Besmer 1983:42–43). As noted in the foregoing, Saminaka also performed the garaya before changing to goge. Instead of studying with an established goge musician after he made the switch, he learned how to fiddle on his own by observing others (Saminaka 2003).

52.	Salihu Y. Ingawa (1974) states that goge ensembles, before the 1960s, often included two or more fiddlers with only calabash beaters (k'warya) as accompaniment. While some musicians used the second fiddler as a permanent and regular member of the group, others performed with another fiddler on an ad hoc basis (Grass 1976; Saminaka 2003). At the 1974 Argungu Festival and on the 1999 Ocora recording by Harouna Goge of the Gaya region of Niger, several instrumental combinations can be heard: fiddle alone, fiddle with calabash beater, fiddle with plucked lute, flute, and calabash beater (Bornand 1999:18).

53.	Although the entry in Richard Lander's journal, written in the nineteenth century, does not indicate the ethnicity of the performers (see Lander 1967:160–161), most scholars assume they are Hausa (Gourlay 1982b:229).

54.	A Fulbe born in Bauchi State during the mid-1930s, Usman Garba stated that he was about sixty-eight years old. Before becoming a marok'i in the early 1960s, he used to be a k'warya player in Balan Na Bassa's group. Regarding his profession, Garba states: "Since my master [Balan Na Bassa] stopped playing the fiddle, I have continued praise singing with just my mouth without any instrument during naming ceremonies and things like that. And when certain activities aren't taking place, I buy things and sell. So I'm also a trader" (U. Garba 2003).

55.   Ames (1973b) suggests that many of these changes became popular because of the media. When Hausa fiddlers during the 1960s saw that professional dancers were used in the performance of Arab and Indian music (in the movies and other entertainment events in Kano), some began to integrate dance in their performances. Thus, many dances were inspired by foreign elements—e.g., rumba and cha cha cha from Cuba, highlife from West Africa, and movements seen in Indian films (Ames 1982:134). During a performance for the Hausa Week celebrations by Ahmadu Samunaka in March 1974 at Abdullahi Bayero College in Kano City, professional dance teams performed in a linear formation of six or eight dancers. The dancers (three or four females and three or four males) entered the stage in one line and then separated into two lines (males in one line and females in the other). When doing the choreographed steps, sometimes they faced each other and paired off before returning to the single line formation to leave the stage.

56.   Rawan kashewa or rawan banjo are the same dance but known by different names. Ames (1982:131) states that the karuwai (unmarried females) were regarded as the expert dancers of rawan banjo, and goge musicians played for them. The twist became popular globally during the 1960s when an African-American man, Chubby Checker, recorded a song entitled "The Twist" (Belz 1969:93).

57.   In parts of Hausaland, goge music serves as source material for other musicians such as hourglass drummers (Ames 1982:118).

58.   Deleb is a type of root or food eaten (muruci) by people in Hausaland (DjeDje 1978b:589).

59.   On Liyo's recording (Grass 1976), the title of this song (track 3) is mislabeled as "Sarkin Mallamai Garba Kai" (praise song to a chief mallam [teacher]). Russell Schuh (1987) indicates that the correct title is "Alhaji Balan Gwaggo, Sarkin Shanu" (praise song to the chief of cattle).

60.   A similar practice occurs among the Dagbamba; proverbs and references to animals are common in gondze song texts.

61.   Homophonic parallelism refers to the performance of harmony either in thirds, sixths, fourths, or fifths (Nketia 1974:161–163).

62.   Except for the music by Garba Liyo, which is taken from a Folkways recording (Alhɔji Gɔrba Leɗo 1976), I recorded all of the goge music used for analysis in this study. Because there was no quiet, secluded place to make audio recordings at CNCS, Jim Vilée (a researcher and staff member at CNCS) and his wife, Sue, allowed me to use the courtyard in their home. We began each recording session around 10AM; only the performers, Duro Oni, and myself were present at the recording sessions.

63.   Bande did not know his age when I interviewed him in 1974, but he looked like he was in his thirties. On my return trip to northern Nigeria in 2003, I learned that he had died in the late 1990s (Landi 2003).

64. Technical problems (the electricity needed for the tape recorder kept going off) prevented the group from completing the recording session in one day.

65. When Bande performs these themes, the length may vary or he may play them differently. For example, when he performs theme C the first time, it is ninety-six beats in length, and the choral response that follows is also ninety-six beats. However, when Bande performs theme C about midway into the song, he only plays the first twenty-four beats of the theme. The chorus responds by singing the next twenty-four beats of theme C. The remaining forty-eight beats are not performed.

66. Examples of additive rhythms in Bande's fiddling can be seen in Example 3.1: theme A (the last two beats of measure 8 extending over to beat 1 of measure 9 on pitch G); theme B (beat 8 extending to beat 9 in measure 14 on pitch G); theme C (beats 11 and 12 in measure 30 extending over to beat 1 of measure 31 on pitch A); and theme D (beat 12 of measure 66 extending over to beat 1 of measure 67 on pitch G).

67. The Second World Black and African Festival of Arts and Culture, scheduled to take place in 1975, was postponed to 1977 and became known as FESTAC. Held January 15–February 12, 1977, FESTAC was the largest festival of its kind. Not only did it include participants from Africa, but groups from the African Diasporas (the Americas and Australia) also attended (Nketia 1995).

68. Because Landi's percussionist (name unknown) did not bring an instrument, he played his rhythms on a table top placed near the fiddler.

69. Most goge themes are based on the five pitches (primary tones) of the pentatonic scale, while secondary tones (pitches included in the performance that are not the primary tones) are used for ornamentation (DjeDje 1978b:431). Landi's use of secondary tones in "Wakakai" surpasses all songs included in the study (DjeDje 1978b:509).

70. The fiddler's call in "Ki'dan Kanawa" is much shorter than the chorus response. Landi only performs a short version of the melody for themes B and C, while the chorus sings the entire statement (see DjeDje 1978b, 1984a:98).

71. Grass does not explain the circumstances for making the recording nor does he give the names of the performers accompanying Liyo. Although the photograph on the back cover of the record jacket shows seven singers and seven instrumentalists—two goge (one performed by Liyo and another by his apprentice), two k'warya (calabashes), one kuntuku (bowl-shaped drum or what Grass refers to as "a small, ordinary drum"), and two sets of kalangu and 'dan kar'bi (hourglass-shaped pressure drums)—I use the instrumentation that Grass describes in the liner notes for this analysis.

72. When Russell Schuh and Lawan Danladi Yalwa, at my request, transcribed the lyrics to songs on the Folkways recording, they discovered that the titles for tracks 3 and 4 on side two had been reversed and the translations for some songs were not accurate. For example, according to Schuh, the correct title for "Ali Mai Sai da Mai Shell BP" is "Ali Mai Sai da Mai a Shal Bipi" (Schuh 1987).

73. Music produced and published by Motown Records during the 1960s and 1970s provides an excellent example of how an African-American record company made its product appealing to a diverse audience. Not only did Motown

artists tone down elements associated with African-American performance culture, but they integrated features identified with European Americans to make the music attractive to white youth (see Browne 1998; Gordy 1994; Person-Lynn 1998). Ensembles of hourglass- and bowl-shaped drums are popular among performers in northern and southern Nigeria; see Abdulkadir (1975) and Euba (1990).

4. In Service to the King

1. The terms Dagbon and Dagbamba are indigenous to the people of the region (Tamakloe 1931:2). "Dagomba" is the Anglicized version of "Dagbamba" and was first used by Europeans during the colonial period. Both terms are used interchangeably in this study.

2. In Dagbani, the term *tsugu* means "festival." Five annual festivals take place in Dagbon. The Great Feast, Lesser Feast, and Prophet's Birthday are known as Tsimsi, Ramadan (or Konyuri), and Damba, respectively. The other two festivals—the Guinea Fowl Festival (Kpini) and the Fire Festival (Buxim or Bugim)—are based on Islamic rituals but have been linked to traditional practices (Chernoff 1999:269–270).

3. Lunsi history indicates that the hourglass pressure drum originated during the reign of Naa Nyagsi (ca. 1353) with Prince Bizum, who gave up his royal heritage to devote his life to playing the instrument (Locke and Lunna 1990; Creighton 1999).

4. Sulemana Iddrisu, the nephew of Yamba Naa Salifu Issah (the chief of gondze in Dagbon), would be regarded as Issah's brother in some African societies.

5. When community members kill a ram at the festival, on one level the sacrifice symbolizes the sacrifice that Ibrahim made to God, but on another level it represents a sacrifice to the ancestral kings and rulers of Dagbon. Individuals also perform ancestral veneration rites during celebrations (Sulemana 1994).

6. The meaning of the title "queen mother" varies in African societies. It can be given to the mother, sister, aunt, niece, or cousin of the reigning monarch. In some cases, a woman with special military prowess is given the title to recognize her contributions. Generally, the title grants special privileges that also vary. Queen mothers may have their own residence, land holdings, attendants, and other entitlements. When I visited Yendi in 1973, the Ya Naa's eldest sister was the queen mother. Unfortunately, I have no other information about her or the position she held in Dagbon.

7. As a result of the first rearrangement, not only were the British given eastern Dagbon (and other parts of ex-German Togo) under the League of Nations mandate, but they were also allowed to administer the northern areas as integral parts of the Northern Territories Protectorate. Under the second rearrangement, Yendi initially was administered as a separate district (the Eastern Dagbamba District), but starting in 1932, a single Dagbamba District was established with headquarters at Yendi (Staniland 1975:12).

8. Adopted from the Asante, the timpani is a goblet-shaped drum associated with warriors and royalty.

9. Savelugu and Karaga are located in western Dagbon. At one time, the western province was known as Toma and ruled by a "Yo Naa" from Savelugu. Located in eastern Dagbon just west of Yendi, Mion (also known as Sambu, the capital of Mion, and Pigu) was ruled from Yendi (see Map 4.1). Savelugu, the largest and richest of the three provinces, was sometimes referred to as "Yendi of the West." Karaga was the next largest, and Mion was the smallest. To become a candidate for the Ya Naa, a person had to have served as either a Yo Naa (ruler of Savelugu), Karaga Naa (ruler of Karaga), or Mionlana (ruler of Mion) (Staniland 1975:20, 25, 192).

10. Before the government announced the decision, Colonel Acheampong met with Mohamadu Abudulai IV and other Yendi officials in Accra to inform them of the contents of the white paper, "and the deposed king was persuaded to remain in Accra until the installation of his successor was completed" (Staniland 1975:175). Mohamadu Abudulai did not return to northern Ghana until November 1974. He died in 1989. Sulemana states that "when Naa Mohamadu Abudulai came back to Yendi, the government called him the former Ya Naa but all other people [in Yendi] paid him the allegiance and assignments of a Ya Naa. There were two Ya Naas. Actually, he [Mohamadu Abudulai] was more powerful. He had a lot of support in Yendi" (Sulemana 1994); see Staniland (1975) for details about the history and other issues surrounding the Yendi Skin Crisis.

11. In addition to Hale (1990, 1998), other researchers who have written on this subject include Camara (1976), Cissé (1970), Johnson and Sosòkò (1992), Tamari (1991, 1995), and Wright (1989).

12. The use of surnames among the Dagbamba differs from practices in the West and among Mande musicians. Dagbamba male children may include a portion of the father's name in their given name, but not necessarily as the final element of a name. In this discussion, for example, Sulemana Iddrisu (the lead fiddler at the Tsimsi Tsugu festivities described at the beginning of this chapter) is the father of Alhassan Iddi Sulemana, a person whom I consulted about the history of gondze in Dagbon. As you will note, they are father and son, but they do not bear the same "surname."

13. IAS researchers include Dakubu and Reed, Iddi, Oppong, and Sulley. Similar to the scholarship in Nigeria and Senegambia, the number of publications on people in northern Ghana (and more specifically the Dagbamba) is small when compared to publications on groups that live in southern Ghana (e.g., the Ewe and the Asante); see Gray (1991) and recent works by Abdullai, Boamah, Chernoff, Creighton, DjeDje, Kolaan, Locke, Lunna, Neely and Seidu, and Stoller.

14. Works by Oppong (1970), DjeDje, Black, Iddi, and Chernoff (2001) focus on fiddling, while other researchers mention fiddling only briefly in their publications.

15. "Praise" songs and "praise name" songs are similar, but the former is the more general category, implying any song in a musician's repertoire that he or she uses to praise a client. A praise name song, by contrast, is a specific song identified with an individual, corresponding directly with the person's praise name. Praise name songs are one type of praise song.

16. In addition to musicians, there are *banyegu* (reciters) whose beginnings date to the time of Ya Naa Gbewa (Mahama 1972–1974; DjeDje 1978b:201). Similar to Hausa marok'a, Dagbamba banyegu shout praises to nobles and others at important events.

17. The Frafra live in Bolgatanga, the largest city in the Upper East Region (see Map 4.2). The Frafra fiddle is most often performed at pito bars for drinking and is not associated with chieftaincy (Lali 1995).

18. Abubakari Salifu Meiregah was born in 1960 in Bimbilla and started playing the fiddle between the ages of four and eight. He attended Western schools for ten years in Bimbilla before settling in Accra in 1980 to live with his elder brother. Meiregah started working at IAS during the 1980s. When I interviewed him in 1990, he was a member of the Ghana Dance Ensemble at the University of Ghana, a professional group that regularly traveled to other African nations and Europe for performances. In 2003, he was a lead dancer with the National Dance Ensemble at the National Theatre of Ghana in Accra, a position he had held for several years.

19. In addition to information collected from Salisu Mahama, I also interviewed other gondze musicians during the 1970s: (1) Yamba Naa Salifu Issah of Yendi was sixty-seven years old and started playing the gondze when he was fifteen; (2) Sulemana Iddrisu of Yendi was forty-five and began playing the gondze when he was between the age of five and eight; (3) Salifu Lali of Bimbilla was in his early forties and began his gondze training between the age of four or five; (4) Abu Gondze of Nyohini-Tamale was forty-five and began his gondze training when he was eight; (5) Alhassan Gondze of Savelugu, at eighty years old and the eldest fiddler interviewed in 1973, began his gondze training at age six; and (6) Iddrisu Gondze of Tampion was fifty-six years old and started playing gondze at age six.

20. Instead of relating the gondze's introduction to kings (Ya Naas) in Yendi, Alhassan Gondze refers to chiefships in Savelugu to document his version of gondze history. He believes the fiddle was introduced into Dagbon by their "great-grandfather" during the reign of Savelugu Naa Mahami. When Naa Mahami lost his life in a war against the Zabarimas in the late nineteenth century, their "grandfather" settled in Yendi (Alhassan 1973).

21. Mahama indicates that some details in Sulley's account are not correct. For example, the original version of this sentence reads: "Yantsebli's father as a child always chose to sit and converse amongst his colleagues." The story concerns Yantsebli, not "Yantsebli's father" as indicated in this account. I have made the correction. So the sentence now reads, "Yantsebli as a child. . . ."

22. Another error is the term for the rattle. In Sulley's account, the rattle is referred to as *zaabia*. Actually, the gourd rattle in Dagbani is known as *gagle*, while the musicians (both male and female) who perform the rattle are referred to as zaabia.

23. Using the fiddle for healing relates to the instrument's function in Hausa society wherein goge music is used to communicate with spirits to help people with their problems. This is evidence that fiddling in Dagbon may be related or influenced by the tradition in Hausaland.

24. Mondays and Fridays are special days of the week marked by taboos and alms-giving. In earlier times, titled men and village rulers paid their respects and brought tribute of goods or money to political leaders on these days. In modern times, they simply come and greet the king, who distributes kola nuts, and discuss news and views about village affairs and cases with him (Oppong 1973:27–28).

25. When the entourage from Fada N'Gurma arrived in Dagbon and learned that the fiddler (Abudulai) would be installed as a nobleman (Yamba Naa), this probably assuaged their concerns. Not only was the gondze going to have a position of importance, but also the fiddler would be receiving the entitlement that he deserved.

26. It was during Naa Yakuba's rule that political disputes started in Dagbon, and some oral histories report that he went mad during his reign. Mallam Alhasan was a nineteenth-century Muslim scholar who served as a scribe for at least two European colonialists: Adam Mischlich, a German administrator in the Togo Protectorate, and Count von Zech, another German colonial officer (Pilaszewicz 2000:7, 24, 226–227).

27. In Mallam Alhasan's manuscript, the fiddle is referred to as *gooro* (Pilaszewicz 2000:211).

28. While some may question why I limited my research to two versions of the gondze history, it is miraculous that I was able to obtain any data on this topic because most Dagbamba fiddlers had only committed to memory the oral tradition about Naa Sigli's travels to Grumaland. During one of my fiddle lessons with Salisu Mahama in the early 1970s, I asked him to perform the praise songs in honor of the different Yamba Naas so I could record them; see song texts and music transcriptions of Yamba Naa genealogy in DjeDje 1978b. When I returned to Ghana in 1990, Mahama agreed to work with me in developing a written narrative that explained the history of gondze from the beginnings to the present. From our interviews, a document was created (see Mahama 1990a). When I met Alhassan Iddrisu Sulemana in Ghana in 1994, we discussed Mahama's version of the gondze history. Believing that Mahama's narrative might be different from what he had been taught (because they supported different families in the Yendi dispute), Sulemana decided to compile an account to represent his family's interpretation of the history (see Sulemana 1995a). Thus, the disputes that have plagued the succession of Dagbamba kings can also be found in the gondze history.

29. In many parts of Hausaland, the leader of Bori is a woman named Magajia who is assisted by another woman called Magayaki (see Harris 1930:329 and chapter 3).

30. In 1973, both Salifu Lali and Salisu Mahama performed a praise song in honor Bantchande, yet neither provided details about the Gurma leader except to say that he was a king. For the song text and music transcription of "Bantchande" as performed by Lali, see DjeDje 1978b:699 and DjeDje 1978b:1113, respectively. What I have learned about Bantchande is minimal. When the Gurma were in the grips of civil war in the 1890s, with the central throne at Fada N'Gurma claimed by rival princes, the main contestants were Bantchande and

31. Lali's description is related to the fire-eating I observed among fiddlers in Senegambia (see chapter 2).

32. In many areas of traditional West Africa, an outdooring may also be called a naming ceremony, referring to the event during which a newborn child is formally named and introduced to his or her community. Generally, the ceremony takes place seven days after the birth of a child and is held in the open air, which explains the reason for referring to it as "outdooring."

33. In Mahama's narrative about the history of the gondze, he includes a section, entitled "How the Yamba Naa Is Enskinned, Rituals Involved," that gives a description of the clothing the Yamba Naa wears when he is enskinned (see Mahama 1990a).

34. The fact that much of Chernoff's information about fiddling comes from musicians based in Tamale, the most cosmopolitan city in Dagbon, is significant. When I conducted research in Tamale in the 1970s, fiddlers I met there were less interested in traditional practices (e.g., performing for royalty) than those residing in Yendi and other small villages. Since some people living in urban areas tend to initiate change more readily than their counterparts in rural areas (DjeDje and Meadows 1998:1), it is perhaps not surprising that the interpretation of gondze history by Tamale drummers differs from that of musicians in other parts of Dagbon (Sulemana 2003).

35. When Ghana's government officials, in April 1974, made a decision about the Yendi Skin Crisis and asked Mohamadu Abdulai IV to travel to Accra, Issah sent his nephew, Sulemana Iddrisu to be with the deposed king. Iddrisu remained with Mohamadu Abdulai until he and his entourage returned to Yendi in November 1974. After Mohamadu Abdulai's death in 1989, one of his sons replaced him as the opposing candidate to Andani, and Issah chose to serve the son rather than associate with Ya Naa Yakubu Andani. Sulemana argues that if Yamba Naa Issah and his family had been allowed to decide on their own about serving the new Ya Naa, the situation would not have been different. Instead, Ghana's central government "wanted to use force on them," says Sulemana. "When my father (Sulemana Iddrisu) came from Accra with Naa Mohamadu Abdulai IV, the soldiers (military) came to our house with an armored car mounted with a missile launcher, which is used in warfare to fire missiles at the enemy. They came to our house to arrest my father to send him under force of arms to the palace of the Ya Naa to perform his fiddle in honor of the new Ya Naa Yakubu. That was improper. This was the beginning of all the problems" (Sulemana 1994).

36. Although accessible reports do not describe in detail the burial for the former king and the installation of the new regent in April 2006, I can only assume that, because these were royal events, drumming and fiddling were included. Similarly, I would assume that with government recognition of the royal family, musicking has now returned to Dagbon.

37. When I attended the Damba festival in Kumbungu in August 1995, I observed that a specific part of the public festivities was reserved for Muslim chanting. At the appointed time, the imam and other religious leaders went into the

center of the circle and chanted for twenty or thirty minutes. After the Muslim leaders finished, the fiddlers and drummers entered the circle and continued their performance of praise songs as they had done earlier in the day.

38. During the 1970s, fiddlers in Tamale performed at pito bars and marketplaces more often than fiddlers in other towns in Dagbon. In Yendi, gondze musicians rarely, if ever, performed in such contexts.

39. Organized during the early 1990s, the troupe is led by Sulemana because of his age (he is the eldest by a few months) and his avid interest in fiddling. In addition to government officials in Ghana, individuals from Europe and North America (Canada and the United States), who taught at the secondary school in Yendi or were working in the community, also encouraged him to start his troupe. Officials may have commissioned Sulemana and his group, instead of asking the Ya Naa's court musicians, because the former are young and can appeal to the youth, but also because of Sulemana's popularity as a result of his commercial recording (see below).

40. When I asked him if the same instrument had been passed down from one Yamba Naa to the next, he stated: "If he [the new Yamba Naa] cannot get the metal, he would take the [old] Yamba Naa's metal neck and use it to construct his fiddle" (Sulemana 1994). Although Sulemana could not document when this tradition began, he cited the names of Yamba Naas—Iddrisu Sansani (1930–1953), Mahama Jia (1954–1967), Abudulai Iddrisu (1968–1971), and Salifu Issah (since 1971)—who had used fiddles with a metal neck. He was aware of this because children like himself often carried the Yamba Naa's instrument when the family traveled to and from performance events (Sulemana 1994).

41. After Ya Naa Yakubu Andani was enskinned, first Ziblim Napari (originally from Sambu, a small town located seven miles west of Yendi) and later Iddrisu Osumanu (Sulemana Iddrisu's relative who was based in Accra) moved to Yendi and took up residence in the Yamba Naa's house while performing for the new Ya Naa. At the same time they were serving as chief fiddlers at the palace, they recognized Issah as the Yamba Naa and paid him royalties that were supposed to be given to him by tradition (Mahama 1990a; Sulemana 1995a).

42. Osumanu had only occasional help when gondze from other areas of Ghana who supported Naa Yakubu Andani visited Yendi. Mahama believed that Issah should have put aside personal loyalties and served Yakubu Andani because this was what he did when Mohamadu Abudulai sat on the skins. In 1995, Mahama explained an incident that occurred in 1973: "This is when we were in Yendi, and there was this festival, the Tsimsi Tsugu festival. We entered the Ya Naa's inner court. He was dancing to the music of gondze and our praises. At one time, he [Naa Mohamadu Abudulai IV] asked Sulemana [Iddrisu, the person who was singing the vocal lead and playing the lead fiddle part at Tsimsi in 1973] to hand over his instrument to me to play for him. I had no other way but to bow down and play. Originally, I would not have done it at that time because that pride was also in me. With me being able to pay homage to the [former] Ya Naa without any confusion, why don't the other people [Issah and his family] want to pay homage to Yakubu Andani?" (Mahama 1995).

43. Several instances of the Ya Naa arranging a marriage between his daughter and

a fiddler can be found in the gondze history (see Mahama 1990a; Sulemana 1995a). These acts are significant, for they demonstrate the regard that the king has for fiddlers and the fiddlers' high social status. In Fulbe and Hausa societies, a political leader would never allow a member of his family to have intimate relations with fiddlers because the music profession and musicians have such a low social status (see chapters 2 and 3).

44. The Ya Naa has many wives; each of the socio-occupational groups in Dagbon (e.g., drummers, fiddlers, butchers, blacksmiths, barbers) is considered to be a "wife" of the king. Because the gondze musician is the *most beloved* wife, the fiddler is allowed to interact intimately with royalty (Sulemana 1995b).

45. As a result of the Yendi Skin Crisis, the title of Yamba Naa and his residence have become sensitive topics. The gondze historical narratives by Mahama and Sulemana indicate that the Yamba Naa has not always been based in Yendi but has lived in various towns in Dagbon. Since the 1930s, however, the Yamba Naa has resided in Yendi.

46. Sulemana explains that it is not compulsory for a woman's son to become a performer. From his experience, "the involvement of the sons of the daughters of fiddlers is due more to economic reasons" (Sulemana 1995b).

47. Sulemana now regrets having studied the sciences in school and indicates that he wishes he had studied music. He indicates that his contact with Westerners caused him to reassess the importance of fiddling. "When someone comes from North America or Europe and is interested in your own music, then it makes you start to go back to your roots; go back and hold firm to what you have rather than trying to imitate the West" (Sulemana 1994).

48. Preserving historical songs has become a mission for Sulemana. When I first met him in 1994, he indicated that he had begun collecting gondze praise songs. His intent was to establish an archive so that the gondze song texts would be preserved for future generations.

49. Seidu Gondze served Kumbungu Naa Issah when Ya Naa Abudulai II (1918–1938) was on the skins in Yendi and the kingdom was politically divided into western and eastern Dagbamba (Mahama 1995).

50. "Body swerves" refer to the turns that male performers, in particular, make when dancing to gondze music. Normally, men wear large smocks so that when they turn, their garments flair out.

51. In 1973, Iddrisu Gondze, the head gondze musician in Tampion, had only one daughter to accompany him on the rattle. When she was not available, he performed alone because his wife was not allowed to perform; she was not born into the gondze family. His brothers had either died or left the village to pursue careers in larger towns (Iddrisu Gondze 1973).

52. In some performances that I observed, rattlers abruptly stopped or struck the rattle in the palm of their hands to correspond with the movement of the dancers. When a rattler did this, he stood close to the dancer so the two could better coordinate their movements.

53. When Sulemana alludes to the people who made copies and sold the recording, he is referring to those involved in the pirate cassette industry found not only in Africa but other parts of the world.

54. Due to corrections made by Sulemana and Sulley, the texts found here may be slightly different from those that appear in DjeDje (1978b).

55. When UCLA linguistics professor Russell Schuh examined the gondze songs that I collected (approximately seventy-four were collected between 1972 and 1974, and fifteen were collected in 1990), he discovered that more than half were in Hausa or mixed with Hausa and other languages. Unfortunately, he was not able to determine whether the other African languages were Dagbani or Gourmantché.

56. Sulemana suggests that a more accurate translation for this phrase is: " 'You are a male elephant without a wife. You surpass on any provocation.' A male elephant without a wife is very aggressive and easily provoked into a fight. When he sees any couple, two elephants moving, it attacks the other male to take up the wife" (Sulemana 1995b).

57. Although Mahama did not state this, the zugubu (tuning-up melody) is also used to allow members of the ensemble to rest and give the lead singer, who is also the lead fiddler, time to think of other songs that he might want to perform. When Mahama and his cultural troupe performed for me in a recording session on December 15, 1994, they played twenty different songs with four tuning-up melodies interspersed, making the total number of pieces twenty-four. During the recording, Mahama walked around freely in the performance circle as he played the zugubu. In Fulbe fiddle ensembles, the performance of short melodies or phrases between or before songs is called *tenandagal* (testing songs) (T. Kandeh 1994).

58. Because the gondze songs are so short, I do not give the time for the different sections.

59. Due to lack of space, only excerpts of transcriptions are included here. Symbols used to indicate rhythm show not only the recurring three-note pattern but indicate the kinetic motion used to produce the desired rhythm. In the percussion part, the solid quarter note or the half note indicates that the rattle is struck in the palm of the hand, while the note with an X refers to beat(s) shaken in the air.

60. When I conducted interviews with gondze musicians in 1973 and asked each to play a fiddle example for me so I could analyze their performance technique, many performed "Nantoh." Even Meiregah notes that when learning to play gondze as a youngster, his family always began with "Nantoh" when they went to perform at the king's palace early in the morning (Meiregah 1990).

61. Each measure for "Nantoh" comprises twelve beats, which represents one melodic cycle (see Example 4.1).

62. Yakubu Andani's installation to the position of Ya Naa was a three-day celebration that took place on Thursday, Friday, and Saturday (May 30 and 31 and June 1, 1974). In addition to performances by the gondze, there was music by lunsi, yua, kikaa, timpani, and Gonja performers. Both Salifu Lali and Salisu Mahama took turns in leading the gondze musicians (see DjeDje 1978b).

63. The lineage of Mahama's father is linked to Naa Zagali (Zagli), a Dagbamba king who reigned during the seventeenth century, while Mahama's mother was the eldest daughter of Yamba Naa Sulemana Bla, the eldest surviving son of

Yamba Naa Sulemana Abudulai Baako (Mahama 1990b). Mahama states that his mother "would have been in a position to be head of the gondze clan in the whole of Dagbon if she was a male. She could sing and she could play the rattle. But part of her inheritance is what I am now enjoying or had made me what I am today" (Mahama 1990).

64.   From 1960 to 1969, Mahama worked as a visiting instructor at IAS because he needed to remain in Dagbon to care for an aging uncle. After the death of his uncle in 1969, Mahama settled in Accra and became a permanent staff person at IAS through 1983. When J. H. Kwabena Nketia, who served as director of IAS from the mid-1960s to the late 1970s, established the International Centre for African Music and Dance (ICAMD) in the early 1990s at the University of Ghana, Mahama returned to Legon and became an instructor at ICAMD (Nketia 1989), a position he held until his death in 2001.

65.   Mahama and his group visited the United States in 1975 and 1976 to partici-pate in the American Folklife Festival in Washington, D.C., and toured various parts of the United States (Black 1976:121; Sulley 2003). Other travels included visits to Europe and neighboring countries in West Africa. In 1977, Mahama was a member of the musical entourage that represented Ghana at FESTAC in Nigeria. He was the first gondze to have his music released on a Western record label; see *Africa: Ancient Ceremonies* (1979).

Conclusion

1.   The use of bowed instruments in Southwest Asia has been traced to the tenth century. By the eleventh century, Southwest Asians (including Arab Bedouins), Moors, and Berbers in North Africa had probably adopted the instrument and were in a position to introduce it to West Africans. Among the societies in West Africa that had early contact with North Africans were the Tukulor in the Western Sudan and the Kanembu in the Central Sudan. The Tukulor are believed to have adopted Islam in 1040–41 CE, while the Kanem converted be-tween 1080 and 1097 (see chapter 1).

2.   Because of the construction of the West African fiddle and the technique of playing it, most scholars believe that fiddling in the Sudan was influenced by traditions in northwest Africa (the Maghrib) instead of the northeast (Egypt). If true, this rules out the Kanuri (Kanembu), who were more influenced by the latter. Until further investigations are conducted on musicking among the Kanuri and other groups, many of the issues regarding the history of fiddling in West Africa cannot be resolved.

3.   Works by Lucy Duran (1987), Ladzekpo and Eder (1992), and Schmidt (1998) are among the few that include discussion of migration *within* Africa and its influence on creativity.

4.   The Dagbamba have been the last of the three groups to be affected by social changes. In other words, isolation has had an interesting impact on Dagbamba culture. Whereas the Fulbe and Hausa adopted Islam some time between the eleventh and fifteenth centuries, Islam did not reach Dagbon until the eigh-teenth. Other changes in the political and social system due to Westernization affected Senegambians in the early part of the colonial era but did not have an

impact on Dagbon until the postcolonial period. A similar situation is occurring with fiddling. Whereas Fulbe and Hausa fiddlers had to adjust to changes in the fiddle culture earlier in the twentieth century, the Dagbamba did not experience upheaval until the latter part of the twentieth century.

5. Percussion *is not* common in fiddle ensembles in East and North Africa (Nketia 1974). Just as researchers who realize the importance of language in drumming regularly study drum language, perhaps studies need to be done on fiddling to discover the affect of language on fiddle melodies and rhythms.

6. The use of binary terms such as "traditional" and "contemporary" (or nontraditional) has come under scrutiny (Appiah 1992). However, Nketia finds the terms useful (Nketia 1995:1). In my opinion, these concepts are helpful for discussing the range of contexts for musicking in Africa (also see Introduction).

7. Kelly M. Askew's work on Swahili culture in East Africa is one of the few exceptions (see Askew 2002).

References

Abdulkadir, Dandatti. 1975. "The Role of an Oral Singer in Hausa/Fulani Society: A Case Study of Mamman Shata." Ph.D. diss., Indiana University.

Abdullai, Haroon. 2003. "Music at the Court of Yaa Naa of Dagbon." Master's thesis, University of Ghana.

Abu Gondze. 1973. Personal interview with the author, January 27.

Adamu, Mahdi. 1986. "The Role of the Fulani and Tuareg Pastoralists in the Central Sudan, 1405–1903." In *Pastoralists of the West African Savanna: Selected Studies Presented and Discussed at the Fifteenth International African Seminar held at Ahmadu Bello University, Nigeria, July 1979.* Ed. by Mahdi Adamu and A. H. M. Kirk-Greene. Manchester, U.K.: Manchester University Press with the International African Institute, 55–61.

Africa: Ancient Ceremonies, Dance Music and Songs. 1979. Nonesuch H 72082. Recording and notes by Stephen Jay.

Agawu, Kofi. 2003. *Representing African Music: Postcolonial Notes, Queries, Positions.* New York: Routledge.

Ajayi, J. F. Ade. 1987. "Nigeria." In *The World Book Encyclopedia.* Vol. 14. Chicago: World Book, 414–423.

———. 1998. *Africa in the Nineteenth Century until the 1880s. General History of Africa.* Vol. 6. Abridged ed. Berkeley: University of California Press.

Alhᵭji Gᵭrba Leᵭo [Garba Liyo] and His Goge Music. 1976. Folkways FW 8860. Notes by Randall Grass.

Alhassan Gondze. 1973. Personal interview with the author, January 29.

"Ali Farka on Ali Farka." 1994. In *World Music: The Rough Guide.* Ed. by Simon Broughton, Mark Ellingham, David Muddyman, and Richard Trillo. London: The Rough Guides, 261.

Ames, David W. 1970. "Urban Hausa Music." *African Urban Notes* 5, no. 4 (Winter): 19–24.

———. 1973a. "Igbo and Hausa Musicians: A Comparative Examination." *Ethnomusicology* 17, no. 2 (May): 250–278.

———. 1973b [1989]. "A Sociocultural View of Hausa Musical Activity." In *The Traditional Artist in African Societies.* Ed. by Warren L. d'Azevedo. Bloomington: Indiana University Press, 128–161.

———. 1982. "Contexts of Dance in Zazzau and the Impact of Islamic Reform." In *African Religious Groups and Beliefs: Papers in Honor of William R. Bascom.* Ed. by Simon Ottenberg. Bloomington: Indiana University, Folklore Institute, 110–147.

———. n.d. *The Music of Nigeria: Hausa Music. Record II.* Bärenreiter BM 30 L 2307. Notes by David W. Ames.

Ames, David W., and Anthony V. King. 1971. *Glossary of Hausa Music and Its Social Context.* Evanston, Ill.: Northwestern University Press.

Ancient Heart: Mandinka and Fulani Music of The Gambia. 1990. Axiom-Island 314-510 148-2. Notes by Robert H. Browning.

"Andanis to Enskin Regent on Friday." 2006. Dagbon.Net http://www.dagbon.net/news.php?bo=showNewsCat&cat=21 (accessed February 8, 2007).

Anderson, Lois. 1971. "The Interrelation of African and Arab Musics: Some Preliminary Considerations." In *Essays in Music and History in Africa.* Ed. by Klaus P. Wachsmann. Evanston, Ill.: Northwestern University Press, 143–169.

Appiah, Kwame Anthony. 1992. *In My Father's House: Africa in the Philosophy of Culture.* New York: Oxford University Press.

"Argungu Annual Fishing and Cultural Festival Booklet." 1974. Kaduna, Nigeria: Commission for Information, Cultural and Social Development.

Armstrong, Donna. 1993. Letter written to the author, February 18.

Arnott, D. W. 1980. "Fulani Music." In *The New Grove Dictionary of Music and Musicians.* Vol. 7. Ed. by Stanley Sadie. London: Macmillan, 23–25.

———. 2001. "FulBe Music." In *The New Grove Dictionary of Music and Musicians.* Vol. 9. 2nd ed. Ed. by Stanley and John Tyrrell. London: Macmillan, 337–340.

Aruatu Gondze. 1995. Personal conversation with the author, August.

Askew, Kelly M. 2002. *Performing the Nation: Swahili Music and Cultural Politics in Tanzania.* Chicago: University of Chicago Press.

Astley, Thomas, ed. 1968 [1745–1747]. *A New General Collection of Voyages and Travels Consisting of the Most Esteemed Relations Which Have Been Hitherto Published in Any Language. Comprehending Everything Remarkable in Its Kind in Europe, Asia, Africa, and America.* 4 vols. London: Frank Cass and Company Ltd., Travels and Narratives No. 47.

Atule, Akayaa. 2002. Personal communication with the author, May 25.

Avorgbedor, Daniel. 1998. "Rural-Urban Interchange: The Anlo-Ewe." In *Africa: The Garland Encyclopedia of World Music.* Vol. 1. Ed. by Ruth Stone. New York: Garland, 389–399.

Azarya, Victor, Paul Kazuhisa Eguchi, and Catherine VerEecke. 1993. "Introduction." In *Unity and Diversity of a People: The Search for Fulbe Identity.* Ed. by Paul Kazuhisa Eguchi and Victor Azarya. Osaka, Japan: National Museum of Ethnology, 1–9.

Bâ, Amadou Hampate. 1966. "The Fulbe or Fulani of Mali and Their Culture." *Abbia: Cameroon Cultural Review* 14–15 (July–December): 55–87.

Badjie, Salif. 1990. Personal interview with the author, September 1.

Bah, Samba Juma. 1990. Personal interview with the author, August 23.

Bai, Majaw. 1990. Personal interview with the author, August 29.

Balandier, Georges, and André Jolivet. 1962. Liner notes. *La Musique des Griots: Sénégal.* Ocora OCR 15.

Baldeh, Mamadou. 1994. Personal interview with the author, December 8.

Baldeh, Maulday. 1994. Personal interview with the author, December 9.

Baldeh, Seiniwa. 1994. Personal interview with the author, December 9.

Bande, Haruna. 1974. Personal interview with the author, February 10–12.

Barry, Boubacar. 1997. *Senegambia and the Atlantic Slave Trade.* Cambridge: Cambridge University Press.

Barry, Ebrima. 1990. Personal interview with the author, August 23.

Bassa, Balan Na. 2003. Personal interview with the author, July 23.

Baumann, Hermann, and Diedrich Westermann. 1967 [1948]. *Les Peuples et les Civilisations de l'Afrique. Suivi de les Languages et l'Éducation.* Paris: Payot.

Bebey, Francis. 1969. *Musique de l'Afrique.* Paris: Horizons de France.

———. 1975. *African Music: A People's Art.* Trans. from French to English by Josephine Bennett. Westport, Conn.: Lawrence Hill and Co.

Belz, Carl. 1969. *The Story of Rock*. New York: Harper Colophon.

Belzner, William. 1981. "Music, Modernization and Westernization among the Macuma Shuar." In *Cultural Transformations and Ethnicity in Modern Ecuador*. Ed. by Norman E. Whitten. Urbana: University of Illinois Press, 731–748.

Berliner, Paul F. 1978 [1981]. *The Soul of Mbira: Music and Traditions of the Shona People of Zimbabwe*. Berkeley: University of California Press.

Besmer, Fremont E. 1972/1973. "Boori: Structure and Process in Performance." Unpublished manuscript. Kano: Centre for Nigerian Cultural Studies, Ahmadu Bello University.

———. 1973. "Avoidance and Joking Relationships Between Hausa Supernatural Spirits." *Studies in Nigerian Culture* 1, no. 1:26–51.

———. 1974. *Kidan Daran Salla: Music for the Muslim Festivals of Id al-Fitr and Id al-Kabir in Kano, Nigeria*. Bloomington: Indiana University, African Studies Program.

———. 1983. *Horses, Musicians, and Gods: The Hausa Cult of Possession-Trance*. Zaria, Nigeria: Ahmadu Bello University Press.

———. 1998. "Hausa Performance." In *Africa: The Garland Encyclopedia of World Music*. Vol. 1. Ed. by Ruth Stone. New York: Garland, 515–529.

Black, Cobey. 1976. "Salisu the Praise Singer." In *Black People and Their Culture*. Washington, D.C.: Smithsonian Institution Press, 120–122.

Blacking, John. 1977. "Some Problems of Theory and Method in the Study of Musical Change." *Yearbook of International Folk Music Council* 9:1–26.

Blench, Roger. 1984. "The Morphology and Distribution of Sub-Saharan Musical Instruments of North African, Middle Eastern, and Asian Origin." *Musica Asiatica* 4:155–191.

Blum, Stephen. 1994. "Conclusion." In *Music-Cultures in Contact: Convergences and Collisions*. Ed. by Margaret J. Kartomi and Stephen Blum. Australia: Gordon and Breach, 250–277

Boamah, Emmanuel. 1993. "Salma-Praise Songs of Dagbon: A Traditional Musical Style of the Dagbamba of Northern Ghana." Master's thesis, University of Ghana.

Bollag, Burton. 2002. "Notes from Academe: Dramatic Intervention." *The Chronicle of Higher Education* 48, no. 41:A48, June 21.

Borel, François. 1989. "Une vièle éphémère: L'*anzad* touareg du Niger." *Cahiers de Musiques Traditionnelles* 2:101–123.

———. 1991. "Les musiques du quotidien: Rôles de la musique chez les Haoussa du Niger." *Mondes en Musique*. Ed. by Laurent Aubert. Genève: Musée d'ethnographie, 39–48.

Bornand, Sandra. 1999. Liner notes. *Niger. Musique Dendi. Harouna Goge*. Ocora Radio France C 560135.

Born Musicians: Traditional Music from the Gambia. 1984. London: Repercussions. The Television Series. Third Eye Production Ltd. For BBC Channel 4 in Association with RM Arts. Commentary and Interviews by Sidia Jatta. Directed by Geoffrey Haydon.

Bovis, Marcel, and Marceau Gast. 1959. *Collections Ethnographiques. Planches, Album No. I. Touareg Ahaggar*. Paris: Arts et Métiers Graphiques.

Bowdich, T. Edward. 1873 [1819]. *Mission from Cape Coast Castle to Ashantee, With a Descriptive Account of That Kingdom*. New Edition. London: Griffith & Farran.

Brandily, Monique. 1970. Liner notes. *The Teda of Tibesti Instrumental Music*. Bulgische Radio en Televisie 6803 002.

———. 1980. Liner notes. *Tchad. Musique du Tibesti*. Le Chant du Monde LDX 74722.

———. n.d. Liner notes. *Music of Kanem*. Bärenreiter BM 30 L 2309.

Brenner, Louis. 1984. *West African Sufi: The Religious Heritage and Spiritual Search of Cerno Bokar Saalif Taali*. Berkeley: University of California Press.

Browne, Kimasi L. 1998. "Brenda Holloway: Los Angeles's Contribution to Motown." In *California Soul: Music of African Americans in the West*. Ed. by Jacqueline Cogdell DjeDje and Eddie S. Meadows. Berkeley: University of California Press, 321–351.

Buba, Malami, and Graham Furniss. 1999. "Youth Culture, Bandiri, and the Continuing Legitimacy Debate in Sokoto Town." *Journal of African Cultural Studies* 12, no. 1: 27–46.

Camara, Juldeh. 1990. Personal interview with the author, September 1.

———. 1991. Personal interview conducted by Mamma Kandeh, April 29.

Camara, Juldeh, and Duncan Noble. 2003. Email correspondence to the author, August 23.

Camara, Sory. 1976. *Gens de la parole: Essai sur la condition et le rôle des griots dans la société malinké*. Paris: Mouton.

Card, Caroline. 1982. "Social Classification of Tuareg Music." *Resound: A Quarterly of the Archives of Traditional Music* 2, no. 4 (October): 3.

Charry, Eric. 1996. "Plucked Lutes in West Africa: An Historical Overview." *The Galpin Society* 49 (March): 3–37.

———. 2000a. *Mande Music: Traditional and Modern Music of the Maninka and Mandinka of Western Africa*. Chicago: University of Chicago Press.

———. 2000b. "Music and Islam in Sub-Saharan Africa." In *The History of Islam in Africa*. Ed. by Nehemia Levtzion and Randall Pouwels. Athens: Ohio University Press, 545–573.

———. 2005. Personal communication, August.

Charters, Samuel. 1975. Liner notes. *The Griots: Ministers of the Spoken Word*. Folkways FE 4178.

Chaw, Ousainou. 1990. Personal interview with the author, August 30.

Chernoff, John Miller. 1985. "The Drums of Dagbon." In *Repercussions: A Celebration of African-American Music*. Ed. by Geoffrey Haydon and Dennis Marks. London: Century Publishing, 101–127.

———. 1997. "Music and Historical Consciousness among the Dagbamba of Ghana." In *Enchanting Powers: Music in the World's Religions*. Ed. by Lawrence E. Sullivan. Cambridge: Harvard University Center for the Study of Religion, 91–120.

———. 1999. "Spiritual Foundations of Dagbamba Religion and Culture." In *African Spirituality: Forms, Meanings, and Expressions*. Ed. by Jacob K. Olupona. New York: Herder and Herder; Crossroad Publisher Co., 257–274.

———. 2001. Liner notes. *Master Fiddlers of Dagbon*. Rounder Records 82161–5086–2.

Church, R. J. Harrison. 1994. "The Gambia: Physical and Social Geography." In *Africa South of the Sahara, 1994*. 23rd ed. London: Europa Publications, 392.

Cissé, Diango. 1970. *Structures des Malinké de Kita*. Bamaka: Editions Populaires.

Clapperton, Hugh. 1829. *Journal of a Second Expedition into the Interior of Africa, from the Bight of Benen to Soccatoo*. London: John Murray.

Clark, Andrew F. 1992. "The Challenges of Cross-Cultural Oral History: Collecting and Presenting Pulaar Traditions on Slavery from Bundu, Senegambia (West Africa)." *The Oral History Review* 20, nos. 1&2 (Spring-Fall): 1–21.

Cogdell, Jacqueline Delores. 1973. *A Research Study: Historical, Functional, and Musical Analysis of the Goondze Instrument in Dagomba Culture*. Legon, Ghana: Institute of African Studies, University of Ghana.

———. 1974a. Field journal notes from research in Hausaland.

————. 1974b. *Goge in Hausaland*. Legon, Ghana: Institute of African Studies, University of Ghana.

Cole, Johnnetta B. 1988. "Ritual and Belief Systems: Introduction." In *Anthropology for the Nineties: Introductory Readings*. Ed. by Johnnetta B. Cole. New York: Free Press, 381–388.

Cone, James H. 1972. *The Spirituals and the Blues: An Interpretation*. New York: Seabury.

Conrad, David C., and Barbara E. Frank. 1995a. "*Nyamakalaya*: Contradiction and Ambiguity in Mande Society." Introduction to *Status and Identity in West Africa: Nyamakalaw of Mande*. Ed. by David C. Conrad and Barbara E. Frank. Bloomington: Indiana University Press, 1–23.

Conrad, David C., and Barbara E. Frank, eds. 1995b. *Status and Identity in West Africa: Nyamakalaw of Mande*. Bloomington: Indiana University Press.

Coolen, Michael T. 1982. "The Fodet: A Senegambia Origin for the Blues." *The Black Perspective in Music* 10, no. 1 (Spring): 69–84.

————. 1983. "The Wolof Xalam Tradition of the Senegambia." *Ethnomusicology* 27, no. 3 (September): 477–498.

————. 1984. "Senegambia Archetypes for the American Folk Banjo." *Western Folklore* 43, no. 2 (April): 117–132.

————. 1991. "Senegambia Influences on Afro-American Musical Culture." *Black Music Research Journal* 11, no. 1 (Spring): 1–18.

Creighton, Leigh. 1999. "The Luna Drum as Social Mediator among the Dagbamba of Ghana." In *Turn Up the Volume! A Celebration of African Music*. Ed. by Jacqueline Cogdell DjeDje. Los Angeles: UCLA Fowler Museum of Cultural History, 114–123.

Curtin, Philip D. 1969. *The Atlantic Slave Trade: A Census*. Madison: University of Wisconsin Press.

————. 1971. "Jihad in West Africa: Early Phases and Inter-Relations in Mauritania and Senegal." *Journal of African History* 12, no. 1:11–24.

————. 1975. *Economic Change in Precolonial Africa: Senegambia in the Era of the Slave Trade*. Madison: University of Wisconsin Press.

Dakubu, M. E. Kropp, and Cathleen Reed. 1977. "Language and Music in the Luna Drumming of Dagbon: A Preliminary Study." Unpublished manuscript. Legon: Language Centre, University of Ghana, Linguistic Circle of Accra, April 5.

Dalby, Winifred. 1980. "Mali: Music and Society/Manding Music." In *The New Grove Dictionary of Music and Musicians*. Vol. 11. Ed. by Stanley Sadie. London: Macmillan, 573–575.

Danfulani, Umar Habila Dadem. 1999. "Factors Contributing to the Survival of the *Bori* Cult in Northern Nigeria." *NUMEN: International Review for the History of Religions* 46, no. 4:412–447.

Diagram Group. 1976. *Musical Instruments of the World: An Illustrated Encyclopedia*. New York: Paddington Press Ltd.

Diouf, Sylviane A. 1998. *Servants of Allah: African Muslims Enslaved in the Americas*. New York: New York University Press.

DjeDje, Jacqueline Cogdell. 1978a. Liner notes. *Music of the Dagomba from Ghana*. Recorded and produced by Verna Gillis with David Moises Perez Martinez. Ethnic Folkways Records 4324.

————. 1978b. "The One String Fiddle in West Africa: A Comparison of Hausa and Dagomba Traditions." Ph.D. diss., University of California, Los Angeles.

———. 1980. *Distribution of the One String Fiddle in West Africa*. Los Angeles: UCLA Program in Ethnomusicology, Department of Music.

———. 1982. "The Concept of Patronage: An Examination of Hausa and Dagomba One-String Fiddle Traditions." *Journal of African Studies* 9, no. 3 (Fall): 116–127.

———. 1984a. "The Interplay of Melodic Phrases: An Analysis of Hausa and Dagomba One String Fiddle Music." In *Selected Reports in Ethnomusicology*. Ed. by J. H. Kwabena Nketia and Jacqueline Cogdell DjeDje. Los Angeles: UCLA Program in Ethnomusicology, Department of Music, 5:81–118.

———. 1984b. "Song Type and Performance Practice in Hausa and Dagomba Possession (Bori) Music." *The Black Perspective in Music* 12, no. 2 (Fall): 166–182.

———. 1985. "Women and Music in Sudanic Africa." In *More than Drumming: Essays on African and Afro-Latin American Music and Musicians*. Ed. by Irene V. Jackson. Westport, Conn.: Greenwood, 67–89.

———. 1990. Field journal notes from research in Senegambia, Summer.

———, ed. 1992a. *African Musicology: Current Trends*. Vol. 2. of *A Festschrift Presented to J. H. Kwabena Nketia*. Los Angeles: UCLA International Studies and Overseas Program (ISOP)/The James S. Coleman African Studies Center/Crossroads Press/African Studies Association.

———. 1992b. "Music and History: An Analysis of Hausa and Dagbamba Fiddle Traditions." In *African Musicology: Current Trends*. Vol. 2 of *A Festschrift Presented to J.H. Kwabena Nketia*. Ed. by Jacqueline Cogdell DjeDje. Los Angeles: UCLA International Studies and Overseas Program (ISOP)/The James S. Coleman African Studies Center/Crossroads Press/African Studies Association Press, 151–179.

———. 1998. "West Africa: An Introduction." In *Africa: The Garland Encyclopedia of World Music*. Vol. 1. Ed. by Ruth M. Stone. New York: Garland, 442–470.

———. 1999. "The Fulbe Fiddle in The Gambia: A Symbol of Ethnic Identity." In *Turn Up the Volume! A Celebration of African Music*. Ed. by Jacqueline Cogdell DjeDje. Los Angeles: UCLA Fowler Museum of Cultural History, 98–113.

———. 2001. "A Diaspora within Africa: The Fiddle Tradition in West Africa." Paper presented at the meeting of the African Studies Association, Houston, Texas, November 18.

———. 2005. "African Musicology: Current State of Research and Future Directions." In *Multiple Interpretations of Dynamics of Creativity and Knowledge in African Music Traditions: A Festschrift in Honor of Akin Euba on the Occasion of His 70th Birthday*. Ed. by Bode Omojola and George Dor. Richmond, Calif.: Music Research Institute Press, 267–299.

DjeDje, Jacqueline Cogdell, and William G. Carter, eds. 1989. *African Musicology: Current Trends*. Vol. 1. of *A Festschrift Presented to J. H. Kwabena Nketia*. Los Angeles: UCLA African Studies Center/African Arts Magazine and Crossroads Press/African Studies Association.

DjeDje, Jacqueline Cogdell, and Eddie S. Meadows. 1998. "Introduction." In *California Soul: Music of African Americans in the West*. Berkeley: University of California Press, 1–19.

Duran, Lucy. 1987. "On Music in Contemporary West Africa: Jaliya and the Role of the Jali in Present Day Manding Society." *African Affairs: Journal of the Royal African Society* 86, no. 343 (April): 233–236.

———. 1994. "Music Created by God: The Manding Jalis of Mali, Guinea and Senegambia." In *World Music: The Rough Guide*. Ed. by Simon Broughton, Mark Ellingham, David Muddyman, and Richard Trillo. London: Rough Guides, 243–259.

———. 1999. "Mande Sounds: West Africa's Musical Powerhouse." In *World Music*. Vol. 1

of *Africa, Europe and the Middle East*. Ed. by Simon Broughton, Mark Ellingham, and Richard Trillo. London: Rough Guides, 539–562.

Duvelle, Charles. 1961. Liner notes. *Musique Bisa de Haute-Volta*. Ocora OCR 58.

———. 1966. Liner notes. *Musiques Dahoméennes*. Ocora OCR 17.

Ehret, Christopher. 2001. "Sudanic Civilization." In *Agricultural and Pastoral Societies in Ancient and Classical History*. Ed. by Michael Adas. Philadelphia: Temple University Press, 224–274.

———. 2002. *The Civilizations of Africa: A History to 1800*. Charlottesville: University Press of Virginia.

Elmer, Laurel. 1983. *The Gambia: A Cultural Profile*. Banjul, The Gambia: The American Embassy.

Emms, Craig, and Linda Barnett. 2001. *The Gambia: The Bradt Travel Guide*. Chalfont St. Peter, England: Bradt Travel Guides Ltd.

Erlmann, Veit. 1982a. "Music and Body Control in the Hausa Bori Spirit Possession Cult." In *Papers Presented at the Second Symposium on Ethnomusicology*. Grahamstown: International Library of African Music, 23–27.

———. 1982b. "Trance and Music in the Hausa *Bòori* Spirit Possession Cult in Niger." *Ethnomusicology* 26, no. 1 (January): 49–58.

———. 1983a. "Marginal Men, Strangers and Wayfarers: Professional Musicians and Change Among the Fulani of Diamare (North Cameroon)." *Ethnomusicology* 27, no. 2 (May): 187–225.

———. 1983b. "Notes on Musical Instruments Among the Fulani of Diamare (North Cameroon)." *African Music* 6, no. 3:16–41.

———. 1985. "Model, Variation and Performance: Ful'be Praise-Song in Northern Cameroon." *Yearbook for Traditional Music* 17:88–112.

———. 1986. *Music and the Islamic Reform in the Early Sokoto Empire: Sources, Ideology, Effects*. Stuttgart: Kommissionsverlag F. Steiner Wiesbaden.

Euba, Akin. 1971. "Islamic Musical Culture among the Yoruba: A Preliminary Survey." In *Essays in Music and History in Africa*. Ed. by Klaus P. Wachsmann. Evanston, Ill.: Northwestern University Press, 171–181.

———. 1990. *Yoruba Drumming: The Dùndún Tradition*. Bayreuth: Bayreuth University; Lagos: Elekoto Music Centre, University of Lagos.

Farmer, Henry George. 1928. "A North African Folk Instrument." *The Journal of the Royal Asiatic Society of Great Britain and Ireland*, 25–34.

———. 1929a. [1967]. *A History of Arabian Music to the XIIIth Century*. London: Luzac and Co.

———. 1929b. "Meccan Musical Instruments." *The Journal of the Royal Asiatic Society of Great Britain and Ireland*, 489–505.

———. 1939. "Early References to Music in the Western Sudan." *The Journal of the Royal Asiatic Society of Great Britain and Ireland* (October): 569–579.

———. 1960. "The Music of Islam." In *New Oxford History of Music*. Vol. 1. Ed. by Egon Wellesz. London: Oxford University Press, 421–477, 500–503.

Faruqi, Lois Ibsen al-. 1985. "Music, Musicians and Muslim Law." *Asian Music* 17, no. 1:3–36.

Ferguson, Phyllis. 1973. "Islamisation in Dagbon: A Study of the Alfanema of Yendi." Ph.D. thesis, Cambridge University.

The Field Recordings of African Coast Rhythms: Tribal and Folk Music of West Africa. 1954. Riverside RLP 4001. Notes by Arthur S. Alberts, Melville J. Herskovits, and Richard A. Waterman.

"The Fula Kita of Mali." 1997. http://www.global12project.com/2004/profiles/p_code3/ 1154.html (accessed February 12, 2007).

Furniss, Graham. 1996. *Poetry, Prose and Popular Culture in Hausa*. Washington, D.C.: Smithsonian Institution Press.

Fynn, J. I. 1971. "Ghana—Asante (Ashanti)." In *West African Resistance: The Military Response to Colonial Occupation*. Ed. by Michael Crowder. New York: Africana Publishing Corp., 19–52.

Gaden, Henri. 1931. *Proverbes et Maximes Peuls et Toucouleurs: Traduits, Expliqués et Annotés*. Paris: Institute d'Ethnologie.

Gailey, Harry A. 1975. *Historical Dictionary of The Gambia*. African Historical Dictionaries, no. 4. Metuchen, N.J.: Scarecrow.

Gamble, David P. 1967. *The Wolof of Senegambia, Together with Notes on the Lebu and the Serer*. 2nd ed. London: International African Institute.

———. 1981. *Gambian Fulbe Stories Told by Mary Umah Baldeh*. San Francisco: D. P. Gamble, Gambian Studies, No. 13.

Gamble, David P., Linda K. Salmon, with Alhaji Hassan Njie. 1985. *Peoples of the Gambia I. The Wolof*. San Francisco: San Francisco State University, Anthropology Dept.

Garba, Ibraheem A. 2003. Personal conversation with the author, July 19.

Garba, Usman. 2003. Personal interview with the author, July 23.

Gaye, Dieynaba. 2004. Personal conversation with the author, November 29.

Gellar, Sheldon. 1995 [1982]. *Senegal: An African Nation Between Islam and the West*. 2nd ed. Boulder, Colo.: Westview Press.

Gibson, Gloria J., and Daniel B. Reed, eds., 2002. *Music and Culture of West Africa: The Straus Expedition*. CD-ROM. Bloomington: Indiana University Press.

Gordy, Berry, Jr. 1994. *To Be Loved: The Music, The Magic, The Memories of Motown, An Autobiography*. New York: Warner Books.

Gourlay, Kenneth A. [1980?]. "The Bowed Lute of Northern Nigeria." Unpublished manuscript.

———. 1982a. "Long Trumpets of Northern Nigeria—In History and Today." *African Music* 6, no. 2:48–72.

———. 1982b. "Who Invented the 'Goge'?" *Studies in Nigerian Culture* 2, no. 1:224–268. Originally entitled "The Bowed Lute of Northern Nigeria."

Gowers, W. J. 1921. "Gazetteer of Kano Province." *Gazetteers of the Northern Provinces of Nigeria*. Vol. 1, *The Hausa Emirates (Bauchi, Sokoto, Zaria, Kano)*. London: Frank Cass and Co.

Grass, Randall. 1976. Liner notes. *Alhɔji Gɔrbo Lɛɗo [Garba Liyo] and His Goge Music*. Folkways Records FW 8860.

Gray, J. M. 1940. *A History of the Gambia*. London: Cambridge University Press.

Gray, John. 1991. *African Music: A Bibliographical Guide to the Traditional, Popular, Art, and Liturgical Musics of Sub-Saharan Africa*. New York: Greenwood.

Greenberg, Joseph H. 1946. *The Influence of Islam on a Sudanese Religion*. New York: J. J. Augustin.

———. 1960 [1941]. "Some Aspects of Negro-Mohammedan Culture-Contact Among the Hausa." In *Cultures and Societies of Africa*. Ed. by Simon and Phoebe Ottenberg. New York: Random House, 477–488.

———. 1970. *The Languages of Africa*. Bloomington: Indiana University Press.

Guinée: Les Nyamakala du Fouta Djallon [Guinea: The Nyamakalas from Futa Jalon]. 1992. Musique du Monde. SDRM 92530-2. Notes by Roger Botte.

Hale, Thomas A. 1990. *Scribe, Griot, and Novelist: Narrative Interpreters of the Songhay Empire.* Gainesville: University of Florida Press/Center of African Studies.

———. 1998. *Griots and Griottes: Masters of Words and Music.* Bloomington: Indiana University Press.

Harris, P. G. 1930. "Notes on Yauri (Sokoto Province), Nigeria." *The Journal of the Royal Anthropological Institute of Great Britain and Ireland* 60:283–334.

———. 1932. "Notes on Drums and Musical Instruments Seen in Sokoto Province, Nigeria." *The Journal of the Royal Anthropological Institute of Great Britain and Ireland* 62:105–125.

———. 1942. "The Kebbi Fishermen (Sokoto Province, Nigeria)." *The Journal of the Royal Anthropological Institute of Great Britain and Ireland* 72:23–31.

Hassan, Mohammad Kassim. 2003. Personal interview with the author, July 10.

Hause, Helen Engel. 1948. "Terms for Musical Instruments in the Sudanic Languages: A Lexicographical Inquiry." *Journal of the American Oriental Society.* Suppl. No. 7. 68, no. 1 (January–March): 1–71.

Heilmann, Guro Gardsjord. 2003. "Juldeh Camara: Biographical Notes." Unpublished.

Hiskett, Mervyn. 1969. "Hausa Islamic Verse: Its Sources and Development Prior to 1920." Ph.D. diss., University of London.

———. 1984. *The Development of Islam in West Africa.* London: Longman Group.

Hoffman, Barbara. 1990. "The Power of Speech: Language and Social Status Among Mande Griots and Nobles." Ph.D. diss., Indiana University.

———. 1995. "Power, Structure, and Mande *Jeliw.*" In *Status and Identity in West Africa: Nyamaka-law of Mande.* Ed. by David C. Conrad and Barbara E. Frank. Bloomington: Indiana University Press, 36–45.

Holiday, Geoffrey. 1956. "The Tuareg of the Ahaggar." *African Music* 1, no. 3:48–53.

Holiday, Geoffrey, and Finola Holiday. 1960. Liner notes. *Tuareg Music of the Southern Sahara.* Folkways FE 4470.

Hornbostel, Erich M. von, and Curt Sachs. 1961 [1914]. "Classification of Musical Instruments." Translated by Anthony Baines and Klaus P. Wachsmann. *Galpin Society Journal* 14 (March): 3–29.

Hrbek, I., ed. 1992. *Africa from the Seventh to the Eleventh Century. General History of Africa.* Vol. 3. Abridged ed. Berkeley: University of California Press.

Hughes, Arnold. 1994. "The Gambia: Recent History." In *Africa South of the Sahara, 1994.* 23rd ed. London: Europa, 392–394.

Hutchinson, John, and Anthony D. Smith. 1996. "Introduction." In *Ethnicity.* Oxford: Oxford University Press, 3–16.

Iddi, M. Dasana. 1973. "The Case of Salisu Mahama: A Fiddler Who Also Belongs to the Drummer Group." Field Notes. Dagomba, 1969–1972. Legon: Institute of African Studies, University of Ghana, 115–116.

Iddrisu Gondze. 1973. Personal interview with the author, January 30.

Iddrisu, Sulemana. 1973. Personal interview with the author, January 21.

Ingawa, Salihu Y. 1974. Personal communication with the author, February.

Innes, Gordon. 1974. *Sunjata: Three Mandinka Versions.* London: School of Oriental and African Studies University of London.

———. 1976. *Kaabu and Fuladu: Historical Narratives of the Gambian Mandinka.* London: School of Oriental and African Studies University of London.

Institute of African Studies. n.d. Field recording of fiddle music by the Frafra in northern Ghana. University of Ghana. Legon–Accra, Ghana, West Africa.

Isa, Yusuf. 2003. Personal conversation with the author, July 19.

Issah, Salifu. 1973. Personal interview with the author, January 20.

Jallow, Jansewo. 2003. Personal conversation with the author, August 23.

Jessup, Lynne. 1981. "Musical Instruments of The Gambia." *Gambia Museum Bulletin* (February): 39–42.

"J. H. Kwabena Nketia: A Biobibliographical Portrait." 1989. In *African Musicology: Current Trends.* Vol. 1 of *A Festschrift Presented to J.H. Kwabena Nketia.* Ed. by Jacqueline Cogdell DjeDje and William G. Carter. Los Angeles: UCLA African Studies Center/African Arts Magazine and Crossroads Press/African Studies Association, 3–29.

Jobateh, Ngansumana. 1994. Personal interview with the author, December 10.

Johnson, John, and Fa-Digi Sisòkò. 1992 [1986]. *The Epic of Son-Jara: A West African Tradition.* 2nd ed. Bloomington: Indiana University Press.

Johnson, Kathleen. 1983. Liner notes. *Rhythms of the Grasslands: Music of Upper Volta.* Vol. 2. Nonesuch-H 72090.

Johnston, H. A. S. 1967. *The Fulani Empire of Sokoto.* London: Oxford University Press.

The JVC Video Anthology of World Music and Dance: Middle East and Africa III. Vol. 18, *Chad/Cameroon.* 1988. Tokyo: JVC Victor Company of Japan, Ltd.

Kandeh, Buba. 2003. Personal conversation with the author, August 27.

Kandeh, Mamma. 1990. Personal interviews with the author, August–September.

Kandeh, Ngeya. 1990. Personal interview with the author, August 19.

———. 1994. Personal interview with the author, December 10.

Kandeh, Tamba. 1990. Personal interviews with the author, August 19–25.

———. 1994. Personal interviews with the author, December 8–11.

———. 2003. Personal interviews with the author, August.

Karaye, Maikudi. 2003. Personal conversation with the author, July 10.

Kawada, Junzo. 2001. "Continuité et discontinuité dans les cultures sonores ouest-africaines: rapports internes et interculturels." In *Cultures Sonores d'Afrique II: Aspects Dynamiques.* Ed. by Junzo Kawada and Kenichi Tsukada. Japan: Hiroshima City University, 3–20.

Kimberlin, Cynthia Tse. 1976. "Masinqo and the Nature of Qenet." Ph.D. diss., University of California, Los Angeles.

———. 1989. "Ornaments and Their Classification as a Determinant of Technical Ability and Musical Style." In *African Musicology: Current Trends.* Vol. 1 of *A Festschrift Presented to J.H. Kwabena Nketia.* Ed. by Jacqueline Cogdell DjeDje and William G. Carter. Los Angeles: UCLA African Studies Center/African Arts Magazine and Crossroads Press/African Studies Association, 265–306.

King, Anthony V. 1980a. "Hausa Music." In *The New Grove Dictionary of Music and Musicians.* Vol. 8. Ed. by Stanley Sadie. London: Macmillan, 309–312.

———. 1980b. "Nigeria." In *The New Grove Dictionary of Music and Musicians.* Vol. 13. Ed. by Stanley Sadie. London: Macmillan, 235–243.

———. 2000. "Hausa Music." *Grove Music Online.* www.grovemusic.com (accessed July 8, 2002). Ed. by Laura Macy. Also in *The Revised New Grove Dictionary of Music and Musicians.* Ed. by Stanley Sadie. London: Macmillan.

Kirkegaard, Annemette. 2001. "Tourism Industry and Local Music Culture in Contemporary Zanzibar." In *Same and Other: Negotiating African Identity in Cultural Production.* Ed. by Maria Eriksson Baaz and Mai Palmberg. Stockholm: Nordiska Afrikainsitutet, 59–76

Ki-Zerbo, Joseph, and Djibril Tamsir Niane, eds. 1997. *Africa from the Twelfth to the*

Sixteenth Century. General History of Africa. Vol. 4. Abridged ed. Berkeley: University of California Press.

Klein, Martin A. 1969. "The Moslem Revolution in Nineteenth Century Senegambia." In *Western African History*. Boston University Papers on Africa 4, ed. by Daniel F. McCall, Norman R. Bennett, and Jeffrey Butler. New York: Frederick A. Praeger, 69–101.

———. 1972. "Social and Economic Factors in the Muslim Revolution in Senegambia." *Journal of African History* 13, no. 3:419–441.

Knight, Roderic C. 1972. Record Review. *Le Mali du Fleuve: les Peuls*. Bärenreiter BM 30L2502. *Ethnomusicology* 16, no. 2 (May): 301–302.

———. 1980. "Gambia." In *The New Grove Dictionary of Music and Musicians*. Vol. 7. Ed. by Stanley Sadie. London: Macmillan, 139–142.

———. 1983. "Manding/Fula Relations as Reflected in the Manding Song Repertoire." *African Music* 6, no. 2:37–47.

———. 2001. "The Gambia." In *The New Grove Dictionary of Music and Musicians*. Vol. 9. 2nd ed. Ed. by Stanley and John Tyrrell. London: Macmillan, 491–495.

Koetting, James T. 1975. "The Effects of Urbanization: The Music of the Kasena People of Ghana." *World of Music* 17, no. 4:23–31.

———. 1979/1980. "The Organization and Functioning of Migrant Kasena Flute and Drum Ensembles in Nima/Accra." *African Urban Studies* 6, no. 1 (Winter): 17–30.

Kofoworola, Ziky, and Yusef Lateef. 1987. *Hausa Performing Arts and Music*. Lagos: Department of Culture, Federal Ministry of Information and Culture.

Kolaan, B. A. 1991. "Dagomba Women in Music: Their Work and Play Songs in Gulkpegu-Tamale." Diploma in African Music. University of Ghana.

Kubik, Gerhard. 1998. "Intra-African Streams of Influence." In *Garland Encyclopedia of World Music*. Vol. 1. Ed. by Ruth Stone. New York: Garland, 293–326.

Kuckertz, Josef. 1980. "Origin and Development of the Rabab." *Sangeet Natak* (New Delhi) 15 (January–March): 16–30.

Ladzekpo, Kobla, and Alan Eder. 1992. "*Agahu:* Music Across Many Nations." In *African Musicology: Current Trends*. Vol. 2. of *A Festschrift Presented to J.H. Kwabena Nketia*. Ed. by Jacqueline Cogdell DjeDje. Los Angeles: UCLA International Studies and Overseas Program (ISOP)/The James S. Coleman African Studies Center/African Studies Association Press, 181–190.

Laing, Alexander Gordon. 1825. *Travels in the Timannee, Kooranko, and Soolima Countries in Western Africa*. London: John Murray.

Lali, Salifu. 1973. Personal interview with the author, January 22.

———. 1995. Personal interview with the author, July 26.

Lamm, Judith Ann. 1968. "Musical Instruments of Sierra Leone." Master's thesis, University of Wisconsin, Madison.

Lander, Richard. 1967 [1830]. *Records of Captain Clapperton's Last Expedition to Africa*. Vol. 1. London: Frank Cass & Co.

Landi, Auwalu. 2003. Personal conversation with the author, July 12.

Landi, Mamman. 1974. Personal interview with the author, February 22.

Last, Murray. 1974. "Reform in West Africa: the Jihad movements of the Nineteenth Century." In *History of West Africa*. Vol. 2. Ed. by J. F. A. Ajayi and Michael Crowder. London: Longman Group, 1–29.

Levtzion, Nehemia, and J. F. P. Hopkins, eds. 1981. *Corpus of Early Arabic Sources for West African History*. Trans. J. F. P. Hopkins. Cambridge and New York: Cambridge University Press.

Lewis, I. M., ed. 1966. *Islam in Tropical Africa: Studies Presented and Discussed at the*

Fifth International African Seminar, Ahmadu Bello University, Zaria, January 1964. London: International African Institute and Oxford University Press.

———. 1980. *Islam in Tropical Africa.* 2nd ed. Bloomington and London: International African Institute in association with Indiana University Press.

Leymarie-Ortiz, Isabelle. 1979. "The Griots of Senegal and Change." *Africa* (Rome) 34 (September): 183–197.

Lhote, Henri. 1955. *Les Touaregs du Hoggar (Ahaggar).* 2nd ed. Paris: Payot.

"The Liptako Fula." n.d. Jamtan Fulani. http://www.jamtan.com/jamtan/fulani.cfm?chap=4&linksPage=365 (accessed February 12, 2007).

"List of Nigerian States by Population." Wikipedia. http://en.wikipedia.org/wiki/List_of_Nigerian_states_by_population (accessed December 29, 2006).

Liyo, Garba (G∂rbo Le∂o). 1974. Personal interview with the author, February 19.

Liyo, Shehu Garba. 2003. Personal interview with the author, July 13.

Locke, David, with Abubakari Lunna. 1990. *Drum Damba: Talking Drum Lessons.* Crown Point, Ind.: White Cliffs Media Co.

Lortat-Jacob, Bernard. 1980. "Berber Music." In *The New Grove Dictionary of Music and Musicians.* Vol. 2. Ed. by Stanley Sadie. London: Macmillan, 517–519.

Lunna, Abubakari. 1996. *Drum Damba Music of the Damba Festival of the Dagbamba People.* A recording. Crown Point, Ind.: White Cliffs Media Co.

Mabogunje, Akin L. 1976 [1971]. "The Land and Peoples of West Africa." In *History of West Africa.* Vol. 1. 2nd ed. Ed. by J. F. A. Ajayi and Michael Crowder. London: Longman Group, 1–32.

Mack, Beverly B. 2004. *Muslim Women Sing: Hausa Popular Song.* Bloomington: Indiana University Press.

Madauci, Y. I. 1968. *Hausa Customs.* Zaria: Northern Nigerian Publishing Co.

Mahama, Salisu. 1972–1974. Personal interviews with the author, University of Ghana, Legon, Ghana.

———. 1973. Personal interview with the author, January.

———. 1990a. "A History of *Gondze* in Dagbon. As Told by Salisu Mahama, Tamale, Ghana." Trans. from Dagbani to English by M. D. Sulley. Unpublished manuscript has been deposited in the UCLA Ethnomusicology Archive.

———. 1990b. Personal interview with the author, August.

———. 1994. Personal interview with the author, December 14.

———. 1995. Personal interview with the author, July–August.

Maier, Karl. 2000. *This House Has Fallen: Nigeria in Crisis.* London: Penguin Books.

Marcus, George E. 1995. "Ethnography in/of the World System: The Emergence of Multi-Sited Ethnography." *Annual Review of Anthropology* 24:95–117.

Marcuse, Sibyl. 1975 [1964]. *Musical Instruments: Comprehensive Dictionary.* New York: W. W. Norton.

Master Fiddlers of Dagbon. 2001. Rounder Records CD 82161-5086-2. Notes by John M. Chernoff.

Mayani, Umarun. 2003. Personal interview with the author, July 23.

Mbiti, John S. 1989. *African Religions and Philosophy.* 2nd rev., enl. ed. Oxford: Heinemann International Literature and Textbooks.

McCall, Daniel F. 1969. *Africa in Time-Perspective: A Discussion of Historical Reconstruction from Unwritten Sources.* New York: Oxford University Press.

Meek, Charles Kingsley. 1921. *The Northern Tribes of Nigeria: An Ethnographical Account of the Northern Provinces of Nigeria Together with a Report on 1921 Decennial Census.* Vols. 1 and 2. London: Oxford University Press.

Meiregah, Abubakari Salifu. 1990. Personal interview with the author, August 9.

Merriam, Alan P. 1982a [1973]. "The Bala Musician." In *African Music in Perspective.* New York: Garland, 321–356.

———. 1982b [1980]. "The Basongye Musicians and Institutionalized Social Deviance." In *African Music in Perspective.* New York: Garland, 357–388.

———. 1982c. "On Objections to Comparison in Ethnomusicology." In *Cross-Cultural Perspectives on Music.* Ed. by Robert Falck and Timothy Rice. Toronto: University of Toronto Press, 174–190.

Miller, Joseph C., ed. 1980. *The African Past Speaks: Essays on Oral Tradition and History.* London: Wm. Dawson and Sons.

Mohammadan, Ibrahim. 1974. Personal interview with the author, February 5.

Monts, Lester P. 1982. "Music Clusteral Relationships in a Liberian-Sierra Leonean Region: A Preliminary Analysis." *Journal of African Studies* 9, no. 3 (Fall): 101–115.

———. 1984. "Conflict, Accommodation, and Transformation: The Effect of Islam on Music of the Vai Secret Societies." *Cahiers d'Etudes Africaines* 24, no. 3:321–342.

"More Progress in Dagbon." 2006. Dagbon.Net http://www.dagbon.net/news.php?bo= showNewsCat&cat=21 (accessed February 8, 2007).

Murdock, George P. 1959. *Africa: Its Peoples and Their Culture History.* New York: McGraw Hill.

Music and Culture of West Africa: The Straus Expedition. 2002. A CD-ROM compiled and ed. by Gloria J. Gibson and Daniel B. Reed. Bloomington: Indiana University Press.

Music of Kanem. n.d. Bärenreiter BM 30 L 2309. Notes by Monique Brandily.

Myers, Helen. 1992: "Ethnomusicology." In *Ethnomusicology: An Introduction.* Ed. by Helen Myers. New York: W. W. Norton, 3–19.

Nabarau, Momman. 1974. Personal interview with the author, February 7.

Naqar, 'Umar al-. 1969. "Takrur: The History of a Name." *Journal of African History* 10, no. 3:365–374.

The National Atlas of the Federal Republic of Nigeria. 1978. Lagos: Federal surveys.

N'Diaye, Diana Baird. 1990. "Tradition and Cultural Identity in Senegal." In *Festival of American Folklife (1990), June 27–July 1/July 4–8.* Ed. by Peter Seitel. Washington, D.C.: Smithsonian Institution, 38–47.

Neely, Paul, and Abdullai Seidu. 1995. "Pressing Patrons with Proverbs: Talking Drums at the Tamale Market." *Institute of African Studies Research Review.* Suppl. 9:98–108.

Nettl, Bruno. 1983. *The Study of Ethnomusicology: Twenty-nine Issues and Concepts.* Urbana: University of Illinois Press.

———. 1997. "Music of the Middle East." In *Excursions in World Music.* 2nd ed. Ed. by Bruno Nettl. Upper Saddle River, N.J.: Prentice Hall, 42–68.

Niger. Musique Dendi. Harouna Goge. 1999. Ocora Radio France C 560135. Notes by Sandra Bornand.

Niger: Musique des Touaregs. Vol. 1, *Azawagh.* 2002. Disques Gallo VDE CD-1105. Notes by François Borel.

Niger: Musique des Touaregs. Vol. 2, *In Gall.* 2002. Disques Gallo VDE CD-1106. Notes by François Borel.

"Nigeria's Kano State Celebrates Sharia." 2000. BBC News. http://news.bbc.co.uk/2/hi/ africa/798630.stm (accessed March 3, 2007).

Nikiprowetzky, Tolia. 1963. "The Griots of Senegal and Their Instruments." *Journal of the International Folk Music Council* 15:79–82.

———. 1964a. Liner notes. *Niger: La Musique de Griots.* Ocora OCR 20.

———. 1964b. "L'Ornamentation dans la Musique des Touareg de l'Air." *Journal of the International Folk Music Council* 16:81–83.

———. 1966a. "Les Instruments de Musique au Niger." In *Trois Aspects de la Musique Africaine: Mauritanie, Senegal, Niger.* Paris: Office de Cooperative Radiophonique.

———. 1966b. *Trois Aspects de la Musique Africaine: Mauritanie, Sénégal, Niger.* Paris: Office de Coopération Radiophonique, Ocora.

———. 1967. Liner notes. *Nomades du Niger: Musique des Touareg Musique des Bororo.* Ocora OCR 29.

———. 1980. "Senegal." In *The New Grove Dictionary of Music and Musicians.* Vol. 17. Ed. by Stanley Sadie. London: Macmillan, 127–129.

Njie, Saihou. 1970a. "A Look at Gambian Praise Songs and Singers, Part One." *The Gambia News Bulletin* 87 (August 6): 3.

———. 1970b. "Praise Song for the Great Man of the Village, Part Two." *The Gambia News Bulletin* 88 (August 8): 2.

———. 1970c. "Wedding Praise Song, Part Three." *The Gambia News Bulletin* 89 (August 11): 3.

Nketia, J. H. Kwabena. 1963. *Drumming in Akan Communities of Ghana.* London: Thomas Nelson, for University of Ghana.

———. 1968. *Our Drums and Drummers.* Accra: Ghana Publishing House.

———. 1972. "The Present State and Potential of Music Research in Africa." In *Perspectives in Musicology. The Inaugural Lectures of the Ph.D. Program in Music at the City University of New York.* Ed. by Barry S. Brook, Edward O. D. Downes, and Sherman van Solkema. New York: W. W. Norton, 270–289.

———. 1974. *The Music of Africa.* New York: W. W. Norton.

———. 1978. "Tradition and Innovation in African Music." *Jamaica Journal* 11, no. 3/4:3–9.

———. 1987. "Music and Religion in Sub-Saharan Africa." In *The Encyclopedia of Religion.* Ed. by Mircea Eliade. Macmillan, 172–176.

———. [1995?]. "National Development and the Performing Arts of Africa." Unpublished paper.

———. 1998. "The Scholarly Study of African Music: A Historical Review." In *Africa: The Garland Encyclopedia of World Music.* Vol. 1. Ed. by Ruth M. Stone. New York: Garland, 13–73.

Nketia, J. H. Kwabena, and Jacqueline Cogdell DjeDje. 1984. *Studies in African Music.* Special issue, *Selected Reports in Ethnomusicology* 5. Los Angeles: UCLA Program in Ethnomusicology, Department of Music.

Nzewi, Meki. 1974. "Melo-Rhythmic Essence and Hot Rhythm in Nigerian Folk Music." *The Black Perspective in Music* 2, no. 1 (Spring): 23–28.

———. 1997. *African Music: Theoretical Content and Creative Continuum. The Culture-Exponent's Definitions.* Oldershausen, Germany: Institut für Didaktik Populärer Musik.

Obichere, Boniface I. 1971. *West African States and European Expansion: The Dahomey-Niger Hinterland, 1885–1898.* New Haven and London: Yale University Press.

Odoom, K. O. 1968. "Islamic Education in Yendi." Field Notes of Yendi Project Report. No. 8. Legon: Institute of African Studies and Program of African Studies, Northwestern University.

Ogawa, Ryo. 1993. "Ethnic Identity and Social Interaction: A Reflection of Fulbe Identity." In *Unity and Diversity of a People: The Search for Fulbe Identity.* Ed. by Paul Kazuhisa Eguchi and Victor Azarya. Osaka, Japan: National Museum of Ethnology, 119–137.

Ogot, Bethwell A., ed. 1999. *Africa from the Sixteenth to the Eighteenth Century.* Vol. 5 of *General History of Africa.* Abridged ed. Berkeley: University of California Press.

Oliver, Roland, and J. D. Fage. 1970. *A Short History of Africa.* 3rd ed. Middlesex, England: Penguin Books.

Oppong, Christine. 1966a. "The Dagomba Response to the Introduction of State Schools." *Ghana Journal of Sociology* 2, no. 1:17–25.

———. 1966b. "A Note on Royal Genealogy." *Research Review* (Legon) 3, no. 1:71–74.

———. 1967. "The Context of Socialization in Dagbon." *Research Review* (Legon) 4, no. 1:7–18.

———. 1968. "A Note on a Dagomba Chief's Drummer." *Research Review* (Legon) 4, no. 2:63–65.

———. 1969. "A Preliminary Account of the Role and Recruitment of Drummers in Dagbon." *Research Review* (Legon) 6, no. 1:38–51.

———. 1970. "A Note on Dagomba Fiddlers." *Research Review* (Legon) 6, no. 2:27–33.

———. 1973. *Growing Up in Dagbon.* Accra-Tema: Ghana Publishing Corp.

Osumanu, A. M. n.d. *Dagomba History.* Yendi: n.p.

Oumar, Abdoulaye. 1995. Telephone interview with the author, June 10.

Paden, John N. 1973. *Religion and Political Culture in Kano.* Berkeley: University of California Press.

Palmer, H. R. 1928. "Kano Chronicle." *Sudanese Memoirs Being Mainly Translations of a Number of Arabic Manuscripts Related to the Central and Western Sudan* 3:92–132.

Pâques, Viviana. 1964. *L'Arbre Cosmique dans la Pensée Populaire et dans la Vie Quotidienne de Nord-ouest Africain.* Paris: Institut d'Ethnologie, Musée de l'Homme.

Person-Lynn, Kwaku. 1998. "Insider Perspectives on the American Afrikan Popular Music Industry and Black Radio. Part I: The Popular Music Industry: An Interview with Al Bell." In *California Soul: Music of African Americans in the West.* Ed. by Jacqueline Cogdell DjeDje and Eddie S. Meadows. Berkeley: University of California Press, 179–197.

Pevar, Susan Gunn, and Marc D. Pevar. 1978. Liner notes. *Music from Gambia.* Vol. 1. Folkways FE 4521.

Phyfferoen, Dominik. 2006. "Traditional Music and Dance in Ghana: A Comparative Study of the Traditional Music and Dance of the Dagomba of Northern Ghana." Unpublished manuscript.

Pilaszewicz, Stanislaw. 2000. *Hausa Prose Writings in Ajami by Alhaji Umaru from A. Mischlich / H. Sölken's Collection.* Berlin: Dietrich Reimer Verlag.

Pivin, José. [195?]. Liner notes. *Sahara: 1. Chants des Touareg Ajjer.* Le Chant de Monde LDY-4160.

———. 1961. Liner notes. *Au Coeur de Sahara avec les Touareg Ajjer.* Le Chant du Monde LDM 8239 or LDM 4254.

Podstavsky, Sviatoslav. 1992. "Hausa *Roko* and *Maroka:* Social Dimension of Professional Entertainment in Argungu, Northern Nigeria." Ph.D. diss., Columbia University.

———. 2004. "Hausa Entertainers and Their Social Status: A Reconsideration of Sociohistorical Evidence." *Ethnomusicology* 48, no. 3 (Fall): 348–377.

"President Declares State of Emergency." 2002. *The Ghanaian Times.* March 28, 1, 3.

Quinn, Charlotte Alison. 1967. "Traditionalism, Islam and European Expansion: The Gambia 1850–1890." Ph.D. diss., University of California, Los Angeles.

———. 1968. "Maba Diakhou Ba: Scholar-Warrior of the Senegambia." *Tarikh: Six Aspects of African History* 2, no. 3:1–12.

———. 1971. "A Nineteenth Century Fulbe State." *Journal of African History* 12, no. 3: 427–440.

———. 1972. *Mandingo Kingdoms of the Senegambia: Traditionalism, Islam, and European Expansion.* Evanston, Ill.: Northwestern University Press.

———. 1979. "Maba Diakhou and the Gambia Jihad, 1850–1890." In *Studies in West African Islamic History.* Vol. 1 of *The Cultivators of Islam.* Ed. by John Ralph Willis. London: Frank Cass and Co., 233–258.

"Rabab." 2004. *Grove Music Online.* www.grovemusic.com (accessed September 6, 2004).

Racy, A. Jihad. 1983. "Music." In *The Genius of Arab Civilization: Source of Renaissance.* 2nd ed. Ed. by J. R. Hayes. Cambridge: MIT Press, 121–145.

———. 1996. "Heroes, Lovers, and Poet-Singers: The Bedouin Ethos in the Music of the Arab Near-East." *Journal of American Folklore* 109, no. 434:404–424.

———. 1999. "The Lyre of the Arab Gulf: Historical Roots, Geographical Links, and the Local Context." In *Turn Up the Volume! A Celebration of African Music.* Ed. by Jacqueline Cogdell DjeDje. Los Angeles: UCLA Fowler Museum of Cultural History, 134–139.

———. 2006. Personal communication with the author, June.

Reynolds, Dwight F. 1993. *Sirat Bani Hilal: A Guide to the Epic and Its Performance.* Detroit: ACCESS Cultural Arts Program.

Rhodes, Willard. 1977. "Musical Creativity of Hausa Children." *Yearbook of the International Folk Music Council* 9:38–49.

———. 1983. "Foreword." In *Horses, Musicians, and Gods: The Hausa Cult of Possession-Trance* by Fremont E. Besmer. Zaria, Nigeria: Ahmadu Bello University Press, viii–x.

Riesman, Paul. 1977 [1974]. *Freedom in Fulani Social Life: An Introspective Ethnography.* Trans. Martha Fuller. Chicago: University of Chicago Press. Originally published as *Société et liberté chez les Peul Djelgôbé de Haute-Volta.*

Robinson, David. 1973. "Abdul Qadir and Shaykh Umar: A Continuing Tradition of Islamic Leadership in Futa Toro." *The International Journal of African Historical Studies* 6, no. 2:286–303.

———. 1985. *The Holy War of Umar Tal: The Western Sudan in the Mid-Nineteenth Century.* Oxford: Clarendon.

Rosellini, Jim. 1980. "Upper Volta." In *The New Grove Dictionary of Music and Musicians.* Vol. 19. Ed. by Stanley Sadie. London: Macmillan, 456–460.

Rouch, Jean. 1960. *La Religion et la Magie Songhay.* Paris: Presses Universitaires de France.

Rouget, Gilbert. 1980. "Guinea." In *The New Grove Dictionary of Music and Musicians.* Vol. 7. Ed. by Stanley Sadie. London: Macmillan, 819–822.

———. 1985. *Music and Trance: A Theory of the Relations between Music and Possession.* Chicago: University of Chicago Press.

Saminaka, Musa dan Gado. 2003. Personal interview with the author, July 19.

Samunaka, Ahmadu. 1974. Personal interview with the author, March.

Schaeffner, André. 1955–1956. Liner notes. *The Columbia World Library of Folk and Primitive Music.* Vol. 2, *African Music from the French Colonies.* Columbia KL 205 or ML 4942 and SL 205.

Schlottner, Michael. 2004. "Amplifiers for 'No Names.' Local Concepts of Contemporary Music in Ghana and the Periphery of Global Pop." *Ntama: Journal of African Music and Popular Culture:* http://ntama.uni-mainz.de/content/view/49/37/ (accessed February 8, 2007).

Schmidt, Cynthia. 1989. "Womanhood, Work and Song Among the Kpelle of Liberia." In *African Musicology: Current Trends.* Vol. 1 of *A Festschrift Presented to J.H. Kwabena*

Nketia. Ed. by Jacqueline Cogdell DjeDje and William G. Carter. Los Angeles: UCLA African Studies Center/African Arts Magazine and Crossroads Press/African Studies Association, 237–263.

———. 1998. "Kru Mariners and Migrants of the West African Coast." In *Africa: The Garland Encyclopedia of World Music.* Vol. 1. Ed. by Ruth M. Stone. New York: Garland, 370–382.

Schramm, Adelaida Reyes. 1979. "Ethnic Music, the Urban Area, and Ethnomusicology." *Sociologus* 29, no. 2:1–21.

Schuh, Russell. 1987. Letter written to the author, January 29.

———. 1990. Letter written to the author, August.

———. 1991. Field recording of fiddle music by a Wolof from Senegal.

Schultz, Emily A. 1980. "Introduction." In *Image and Reality in African Interethnic Relations: The Fulbe and Their Neighbors.* Studies in Third World Societies, no. 11, ed. by Emily A. Schultz. Williamsburg, Virginia, v–xiv.

Schuyler, Philip Daniel. 1979. "A Repertory of Ideas: The Music of the *Rwais,* Berber Professional Musicians from Southwestern Morocco." Ph.D. diss., University of Washington.

Seavoy, Mary. 1982. "The Sisaala Xylophone Tradition." Ph.D. diss., University of California, Los Angeles.

———. 1994. Personal communication with the author, November.

Seydou, Christiane. 1972. *Silamaka and Poullori: récit epique peul raconté par Boubacar Tinguidji.* Paris: Armand Colin.

Seyire, Augustine. 1968. "Dagomba Traditional Religion." Field Notes of Yendi Project Report, No. 9. Legon: Institute of African Studies and Program of African Studies, Northwestern University.

Shiloah, Amnon. 1995. *Music in the World of Islam: A Socio-Cultural Study.* Detroit: Wayne State University Press.

Sidibe, Bakari K. 1990. Personal interview with the author, August 24.

———. 2003. Personal interview with the author, August 20.

Sidibe, Bakari K., and Winifred F. Galloway. 1975. *Senegambian Traditional Families: An Occasional Paper.* Banjul: Gambia Cultural Archives.

Sillah, Kawsu. 1973. "Origins of Fulas and Other Facts Relating to Them." Oral Tradition Collected by Bakari Sidibe in Latrikunda, The Gambia, February 27.

Sissoho, Mohammed. 1990. Personal interview with the author, August.

Small, Christopher. 1987. *Music of the Common Tongue: Survival and Celebration in Afro-American Music.* London: John Calder.

———. 1998. *Musicking: The Meanings of Performing and Listening.* Hanover, N.H.: Wesleyan University Press.

Smith, Abdullahi. 1976 [1971]. "The Early States of the Central Sudan." In *History of West Africa.* Vol. 1. 2nd ed. Ed. by J. F. A. Ajayi and Michael Crowder. London: Longman Group, 152–195.

Smith, Michael G. 1965. "The Hausa of Northern Nigeria." In *Peoples of Africa.* Ed. by James L. Gibbs, Jr. New York: Holt, Rinehart and Winston, 119–155.

———. 1973 [1957]. "The Social Functions and Meaning of Hausa Praise-Singing." In *Peoples and Cultures of Africa: An Anthropological Reader.* Ed. by Elliott P. Skinner. Garden City, N.Y.: The Doubleday/Natural History Press, 554–579. First published in *Africa* 27, no. 1 (January 1957): 26–45.

Smith, Patrick. 1994. "Economy." In *Africa South of the Sahara 1994.* 23rd ed. London: Europa Publications, 660–675.

Sonko-Godwin, Patience. 1988 [1985]. *Ethnic Groups of the Senegambia. A Brief History.* Banjul, The Gambia: Sunrise Publishers.

Sow, Abdoul Aziz. 1993. "Fulani Poetic Genres." *Research in African Literatures* 24, no. 2 (Summer): 61–77.

Spitzer, Leo. 1987a. "Mali." In *The World Book Encyclopedia.* Vol. 13. Chicago: World Book, 105–109.

———. 1987b. "Songhai Empire." In *The World Book Encyclopedia.* Vol. 18. Chicago: World Book, 592.

Staniland, Martin. 1975. *The Lions of Dagbon: Political Change in Northern Ghana.* Cambridge: Cambridge University Press.

Stenning, Derrick J. 1960. "Transhumance, Migratory Drift, Migration: Patterns of Pastoral Fulani Nomadism." In *Cultures and Societies of Africa.* Ed. by Simon and Phoebe Ottenberg. New York: Random House, 139–159.

———. 1965. "The Pastoral Fulani of Northern Nigeria." In *Peoples of Africa.* Ed. by James L. Gibbs, Jr. New York: Holt, Rinehart and Winston, 363–401.

Stokes, Martin, ed. 1994a. *Ethnicity, Identity and Music: The Musical Construction of Place.* Oxford: Berg.

———. 1994b. "Introduction: Ethnicity, Identity and Music." In *Ethnicity, Identity and Music: The Musical Construction of Place.* Oxford: Berg, 1–27.

Stoller, Jay. 1997. "Takai and Tora Musics of the Dagbamba: A Sociocultural Study." Diploma in African Music. University of Ghana.

Stoller, Paul. 1989. *The Taste of Ethnographic Things: The Senses in Anthropology.* Philadelphia: University of Pennsylvania Press.

Sulemana, Alhassan Iddi. 1994. Personal interview with the author, December 13.

———. 1995a. "A Brief History of Dagomba Fiddlers." Unpublished manuscript has been deposited in the UCLA Ethnomusicology Archive.

———. 1995b. Personal interview with the author, July 26.

———. 2003. Personal interview with the author, August 4.

Sulley, M. D. 1971. "How Goondze Started and Was Introduced in Dagbon." In *Notes and Observations Collected in Yendi. Three Collections of Reports on Culture.* Legon: Institute of African Studies, University of Ghana.

———. 1973. Personal communication with the author, January.

———. 1995. Personal communication with the author, August.

———. 2003. Personal interview with the author, August 2.

Suret-Canale, J., and Boubacar Barry. 1976 [1971]. "The Western Atlantic Coast to 1800." In *History of West Africa.* Vol. 1. 2nd ed. Ed. by J. F. A. Ajayi and Michael Crowder. London: Longman Group, 456–511.

Surugue, Bernard. 1972. "Contribution à l'Étude de la Musique Sacrée Zarma Songhay (Republique de Niger)." *Étude Nigeriennes* 30:1–63.

———. 1980. "Songhay Music." In *The New Grove Dictionary of Music and Musicians.* Vol. 18. Ed. by Stanley Sadie. London: Macmillan, 523–524.

Swanson, Richard Alan. 1985. *Gourmantché Ethnoanthropology: A Theory of Human Being.* Lanham, Md.: University Press of America.

Swift, Lloyd B., Kalifu Tambadu, and Paul G. Imhoff. 1965. *Fula, Basic Course.* Washington, D.C.: Foreign Service Institute.

Tamakloe, Emmanuel Forster. 1931. *A Brief History of the Dagbamba People.* Accra: Government Printing Office.

Tamari, Tal. 1991. "The Development of Caste Systems in West Africa." *Journal of African History* 32:221–50.

———. 1995. "Linguistic Evidence for the Existence of West African 'Castes.'" In *Status and Identity in West Africa: Nyamaka-law of Mande*. Ed. by David C. Conrad and Barbara E. Frank. Bloomington: Indiana University Press, 61–85.

Thieme, Darius L. 1969. "A Description Catalogue of Yoruba Musical Instruments." Ph.D. diss., The Catholic University of America.

Tomoaki, Fujii, ed. 1988. *The JVC Video Anthology of World Music and Dance. Middle East and Africa III*. Vol. 18, *Chad/Cameroon*. Tokyo, Japan: JVC Victor Company of Japan.

Tracey, Hugh. 1948. *Chopi Musicians: Their Music, Poetry, and Instruments*. London: Oxford University Press.

Tremearne, A. J. N. 1914. *The Ban of Bori: Demons and Demon-Dancing in West and North Africa*. London: Heath, Cranton, & Ouseley.

Trimingham, John Spencer. 1970 [1962]. *A History of Islam in West Africa*. Paperback ed. London: University of Glasgow, Oxford University Press.

Turino, Thomas. 2000. *Nationals, Cosmopolitans, and Popular Music in Zimbabwe*. Chicago: University of Chicago Press.

Van Oven, Cootje. 1980. "Sierra Leone." In *The New Grove Dictionary of Music and Musicians*. Vol. 17. Ed. by Stanley Sadie. London: Macmillan, 302–304.

———. 1981. *An Introduction to the Music of Sierra Leone*. Wassenaar, Netherlands: Cootje van Oven.

VerEecke. 1993. "Sub-National Fulbe Identity in Nigeria? Responses to Political Change in Post-Independence Times." In *Unity and Diversity of a People: The Search for Fulbe Identity* ed. Paul Kazuhisa Eguchi and Victor Azarya. Osaka, Japan: National Museum of Ethnology, 163–179.

Wachsmann, Klaus P., ed. 1971. *Essays on Music and History in Africa*. Evanston, Ill.: Northwestern University Press.

Wallerstein, Immanuel. 1988. "Ghana." In *World Book Encyclopedia*. Vol. 8. Chicago: World Book, 178–180.

Webster, J. B., A. A. Boahen, with H. O. Idowu. 1967. *History of West Africa: The Revolutionary Years—1815 to Independence*. New York: Praeger.

Webster's New Collegiate Dictionary. 1974. Springfield, Mass.: G. & C. Merriam Co.

Wegner, Ulrich. 1984. *Afrikanische Saiteninstrumente*. Berlin: Museum für Völkerkunde.

Wendorf, Fred, and Romuald Schild. 1984. *Cattle-keepers of the Eastern Sahara: The Neolithic of Bir Kiseiba*. Dallas, Texas: Department of Anthropology and Institute for the Study of Earth and Man, Southern Methodist University.

Wendt, Caroline Card. 1994. "Regional Style in Tuareg *Anzad* Music." In *To the Four Corners. A Festschrift in Honor of Rose Brandel*. Ed. by Ellen C. Leichtman. Detroit: Harmonie Park Press, 81–106.

———. 1998a. "North Africa: An Introduction." In *Africa: The Garland Encyclopedia of World Music*. Vol. 1. Ed. by Ruth Stone. New York: Garland, 532–548.

———. 1998b. "Tuareg Music." In *Africa: The Garland Encyclopedia of World Music*. Vol. 1. Ed. by Ruth Stone. New York: Garland, 574–595.

Wilks, Ivor. 1961. *The Northern Factor in Ashanti History*. Legon: Institute of African Studies, University of Ghana.

Wilson, Sule Greg. 1992. *The Drummer's Path: Music, the Spirit with Ritual and Traditional Drumming*. Rochester, Vt.: Destiny Books.

Wright, Bonnie. 1989. "The Power of Articulation." In *Creativity of Power: Cosmology and Action in African Societies*. Ed. by William Arens and Ivan Karp. Washington, D.C.: Smithsonian Institution Press, 39–57.

Yakubu, Sanusi Mohammed. 1981. "Kidan Goge a Kasar Hausa [Goge Music in Hausa-land]." Paper presented in partial fulfillment of the Bachelor's Degree. Department of Nigerian Languages, Abdullahi Bayero University, Kano. Trans. from Hausa to English by Naseer Saeed.

Yalwa, Lawan Danladi. 1989. Personal interview with the author, August 15.

———. 2003a. Personal conversation with the author, July 15.

———. 2003b. Personal notes written to the author, July 15.

"Yaa Na Goes Home Finally." 2006. Dagbon.Net http://www.dagbon.net/news.php?bo=showNewsCat&cat=21 (accessed February 8, 2007).

"Ya-Na Killed." 2002. *The Ghanaian Times*, March 28:1, 3.

"Yendi Crisis Committee of Enquiry Inaugurated." 2002. *The Ghanaian Times*, May 7:1, 3.

Zubairu, Mohammed. 2003. Personal conversation with the author, July 9.

Zubko, Galina V. 1993. "Ethnic and Cultural Characteristics of the Fulbe." In *Unity and Diversity of a People: The Search for Fulbe Identity*. Ed. by Paul Kazuhisa Eguchi and Victor Azarya. Osaka, Japan: National Museum of Ethnology, 201–214.

Discography and Videography: Selected Recordings of One-Stringed Fiddle Music from West Africa

Central Sudan

Bilala (Bulala) and Bournaun (Borno)

1966   *Music of Chad.* Folkways FE 4337. Fiddle performed by Amadou Coucouma. Notes by Charles Hofmann, Elizabeth Dyer, and W. Gurnee Dyer.

1988   *The JVC Video Anthology of World Music and Dance. Middle East and Africa III. Vol. 18. Chad/Cameroon.* Fiddle performed by Dungus Mohammed from Chad. Tokyo: JVC Victor Company of Japan, Ltd. Edited by Fujii Tomoaki.

Burum (Biram)

1975   *Musiques de Plateau.* Ocora OCR 82. Notes by Benoit Quersin. Recorded in Dengi, Nigeria, in 1972.

Djerma

1955–56   *The Columbia World Library of Folk and Primitive Music, Vol. II: African Music from the French Colonies.* Columbia KL 205 or ML 4942 and SL 205. Notes by André Schaeffner. Recorded in Niger in 1950 by Jean Rouch.

1964   *Niger: La Musique de Griots.* Ocora OCR 20. Fiddle performed by Abdou Badié. Notes by Tolia Nikiprowetzky. Recorded in Dosso, Niger, in 1963.

1965   *Afrique Noire. Panorama de la Musique Instrumentale.* Boîte à Musique LD 409A. Notes by Charles Duvelle. Recorded in Tillabery, Niger, in 1961.

Fulbe

1956   *Musique du Nord-Cameroun: Peuples Kirdi et Foulbé.* Boîte à Musique-LD 331. Notes by Jacques Biltgen. Recorded in Kaélé, Cameroon, in 1956.

Hausa

n.d.   *The Music of Nigeria: Hausa Music. Record II.* Bärenreiter BM 30 L 2307. Notes by David Wason Ames. Recorded in the Emirate of Zaria (Northern Nigeria) between 1963 and 1964.

n.d.   *Momo Duka and His Goge Group.* Rainbow RSO 92 ZR 183-184 45 rpm. Momo Duka.

1958?   *Musique Touareg et Haoussa de la Région d'Agadez.* Boîte à Musique LD 353. Notes by Jacques Biltgen.

1962   *Rythmes et Chants du Niger.* Ocora SOR 4. Fiddle performed by Oumarou Kaka. Notes by Charles Duvelle. Recorded in Massalata, Niger.

1964   *Niger: La Musique de Griots.* Ocora OCR 20. Fiddle performed by Saloufou. Notes by Tolia Nikiprowetzky. Recorded in Zinder, Niger, in 1963.

1976   *Alhǝji Gǝrba Leɗo [Garba Liyo] and His Goge Music.* Folkways FW 8860. Fiddle performed by Gǝrba Leɗo. Notes by Ronald F. Grass. Recorded April 11, 1976, at Radio-Television Kaduna Studios in Nigeria.

1984   *Studies in African Music,* ed. J. H. Kwabena Nketia and Jacqueline Cogdell DjeDje. Special issue, *Selected Reports in Ethnomusicology* 5. A cassette recording that accompanies this book includes fiddle music by Salisu Mahama and Haruna Bande. An article titled "The Interplay of Melodic Phrases: An Analysis of Dagomba and Hausa One String Fiddle Music," by Jacqueline Cogdell DjeDje, includes discussion of the music on the tape. Recorded in Legon, Ghana, and Kano, Nigeria, in 1974.

1999   *Niger. Musique Dendi. Harouna Goge.* Ocora Radio France C 560135. Fiddle performed by Harouna Oumarou Sanaye. Notes by Sandra Bornand. Recorded in Niamey, Niger, in 1996.

2001   *Africa and the Blues: Connections and Reconnections.* Neatwork AB 101. Fiddle performed by Adamou Meigogue Garoua. Notes by Gerhard Kubik. Recorded in Yoko, Cameroon, in 1964.

Kanembu (Kanuri)

n.d.   *Music of Kanem.* Bärenreiter BM 30 L 2309. Notes by Monique Brandily. Recorded in Chad in 1963.

Maouri

1964   *Niger: La Musique de Griots.* Ocora OCR 20. Fiddle performed by Yahaya. Notes by Tolia Nikiprowetzky. Recorded in Dogondoutchi, Niger, in 1963.

Sonrai

1964   *Niger: La Musique de Griots.* Ocora OCR 20. Fiddle performed by Yankori. Notes by Tolia Nikiprowetzky. Recorded in Ayerou, Niger, in 1963.

1992   Ali Farka Touré. *The Source.* World Circuit/Hannibal HNCD 1375. Fiddle performed by Ali Farka Touré. Notes by Affel Bacoum, trans. by Emma Barn. Recorded in London and Brixton, Great Britain, in 1991.

Tangale

1971   *Music from the Villages of Northeastern Nigeria.* Asch Mankind Series AMH 4532. Notes by Paul Newman, Eric Davidson, and Lyn Davidson. Recorded in 1969.

Teda

1970   *The Teda of Tibesti Instrumental Music.* Bulgische Radio en Televisie 6803
        022. Notes by Monique Brandily. Recorded in Tibesti and Fezzan, Chad, in
        1969.

1980   *Tchad. Musique du Tibesti.* Le Chant du Monde LDX 74722. Notes by Monique
        Brandily. Recorded in Tibesti, Chad, between 1969 and 1979.

Tiv

1966   *Music of the Jos Plateau and Other Regions of Nigeria.* Folkways FE 4321.
        Notes by Victor Grauer and Stanley Diamond.

Tuareg

195?   *Sahara 1: Chants des Touareg Ajjer.* Le Chant du Monde LDY 4160. Notes by
        José Pivin.

1958?   *Musique Touareg et Haoussa de la Région d'Agadez.* Boîte à Musique LD 353.
        Notes by Jacques Biltgen.

1960   *Tuareg Music of the Southern Sahara.* Folkways FE 4470. Notes by Finola
        Holiday and Geoffrey Holiday.

1961   *Au Coeur de Sahara avec les Touareg Ajjer.* Le Chant du Monde LDM 8239 or
        LDM 4254. Notes by José Pivin.

1967   *Nomades du Niger: Musique des Touareg et des Bororo.* Ocora OCR 29. Fiddle
        performed by Sinkirehane. Notes by Tolia Nikiprowetzky. Recorded at Talak,
        Niger, in 1963.

1994   *Hoggar: Musique des Touareg.* Le Chant du Monde LDX 274974. Notes by
        Jean-Louis Lamande and Nadia Mecheri Saada.

2002   *Niger: Musique des Touaregs. Vol. 1. Azawagh.* Disques Gallo VDE CD-1105.
        Notes by François Borel.

2002   *Niger: Musique des Touaregs. Vol. 2. In Gall.* Disques Gallo VDE CD-1106.
        Notes by François Borel.

Unknown

2002   *Music and Culture of West Africa: The Straus Expedition.* A CD-ROM com-
        piled and edited by Gloria J. Gibson and Daniel B. Reed. Bloomington: In-
        diana University Press. Recorded by Laura Boulton in Niger in 1934.

Eastern Forest Region (of West Africa)

Yoruba/Nago

195?   *Afrique, Vol. 4: Mauritanie, Guinée, Dahomey, Côte d'Ivorie.* Vogue EXTP
        1032. Fiddle performed by Adjado. Notes by Gilbert Rouget.

1959   *Pondo Kakou: Musique de Sociéte Secrète: Côte d'Ivoire-Dahomey-Guinée.* Con-
        trepoint MC 20141. Fiddle performed by Adjado. Notes by Gilbert Rouget.

1964?   *Iyawo ati Oko and Omo Iwoyi.* 45 rpm. Philips West African (Lagos) 393070
        PFB 070. Performed by Oseni Ejire and His Group.

1966   *Musiques Dahoméennes.* Ocora OCR 17. Notes by Charles Duvelle. Ensemble directed by Akansaa Sikirou. Recorded in 1963.

Voltaic

Bisa

1961   *Musique Bisa de Haute-Volta.* Ocora OCR 58. Notes by Charles Duvelle. Recorded in Yarkatenga in 1961.

Bwa

1983   *Rhythms of the Grasslands: Music of Upper Volta, Volume II.* Nonesuch H 72090. Fiddle (*soko*) performed by Moussa Dembele. Notes by Kathleen Johnson. Recorded in Bobo-Dioulasso between 1973 and 1975.

Dagbamba (Dagomba)

n.d.   *Ghana: Ancient Ceremonies, Dance Music and Songs.* Nonesuch 79711. Fiddle performed by Salisu Mahama.

1961   *New Sounds from a New Nation: The Republic of Ghana.* Tempo 7007. Performed by the Saaka Gonje Ensemble of Tamale.

1978   *Music of the Dagomba from Ghana.* Folkways FE 4324. Performed by the Youth Gonje Group led by fiddler Alhasan Ibrahim. Notes by Jacqueline Cogdell DjeDje and Verna Gillis. Recorded in Tamale, Ghana, in 1976 by Verna Gillis with Davis Moises Perez Martinez.

1979   *Africa: Ancient Ceremonies, Dance Music and Songs.* Nonesuch H 72082. Fiddle performed by Salisu Mahama. Recorded and notes by Stephen Jay.

1984   *Studies in African Music,* ed. J. H. Kwabena Nketia and Jacqueline Cogdell DjeDje. Special issue, *Selected Reports in Ethnomusicology* 5. A cassette recording that accompanies this book includes fiddle music by Salisu Mahama and Haruna Bande. An article titled "The Interplay of Melodic Phrases: An Analysis of Dagomba and Hausa One String Fiddle Music," by Jacqueline Cogdell DjeDje, includes discussion of the music on the tape. Recorded in Legon, Ghana, and Kano, Nigeria, in 1974.

2000   *Ghana. Rhythms of the People: Traditional Music and Dance of the Ewe, Dagbamba, Fante, and Ga People.* Multicultural Media MCM 3018.

2001   *Master Fiddlers of Dagbon.* Rounder CD 82161-5086-2. Fiddles performed by Mahama Braimah (group leader), Alhassan Braimah, Masahudu Mahama, and Inusah Seidu with Abdulsamed Mahama and Yamba Mahama on rattle. Notes by John Chernoff. Recorded in Tamale, Ghana, in 1991.

2002   *Nonesuch Explorer Series. African Music Sampler.* Nonesuch. Fiddle performed by Salisu Mahama.

Kusasi

1978   *Ghana: Music of the Northern Tribes.* Lyrichord LLST 7321. Fiddle performed by Mr. Akurugu. Notes by Verna Gillis and Larry Godsey. Recorded in Bolgatanta in 1976.

Mossi

1954   *The Field Recordings of African Coast Rhythms: Tribal and Folk Music of West Africa. Recorded in French Guinea, Gold Coast, Ivory Coast, Upper Volta, and Liberia.* Riverside RLP 4001. Notes by Arthur S. Alberts. Recorded in Ouagadougou, Burkina Faso, in 1949.

1975   *Les Trésors du Mogho: Le Larle-Naaba et sa troupe folklorique.* Club Voltaiqute du Disque CVD 003. Notes by Titinga Pacéré. Recorded by Saïdou Compaoré.

1977   *Les Trésors du Mogho: Le Larle-Naaba et sa troupe folklorique.* Vol. 2. Club Voltaiqute du Disque CVD 004. Notes by Titinga Pacéré. Recorded by Saïdou Compaoré.

Western Sudan

Fulbe/Fula/Peul

1961   *Sons Nouveaux d'une Nation: Presentation Haute-Fidelité; Les Rhythmes de l'Ouest Africain.* Tempo 7008. Performed by Sory Bambara. Recorded in the Fouta Djallon region of Guinea.

1971   *Le Mali du Fleuve: Les Peuls.* Baerenreiter Musicaphon-BM 30 L 2502.

1975   *The Griots: Ministers of the Spoken Word.* Folkways FE 4178. Fiddle performed by Satala Kurubally. Notes by Samuel Charters. Recorded in The Gambia, in 1974.

1984   *Born Musicians: Traditional Music from the Gambia.* London: Repercussions. The Television Series. Third Eye Production Limited. For BBC Channel 4 in Association with RM Arts. Commentary and Interviews by Sidia Jatta. Directed by Geoffrey Haydon. Recorded in The Gambia.

1990   *Ancient Heart: Mandinka and Fulani Music of The Gambia.* Axiom-Island 314-510 148–2. Fiddles performed by Juldeh Camara and Korreh Jalow. Notes by Robert H. Browning. Recorded in Brikama, The Gambia, in 1990. Produced by Bill Laswell and Foday Musa Suso.

1992   *Guinée: Les Nyamakala de Fouta Djallon.* Musique du Monde. SDRM 92530–2. Fiddles performed by Yéro Diouma Bah (track 2), Djouma Woûga Bah (track 4), Samba Diouldé Barry dit Moustâsi (track 8), and Kawou Samîna Lafou Diallo (track 12). Notes by Roger Botte. Recorded in Conakry and throughout Futa Djallon in November 1991.

1994   *Tramp.* Knut Reiersrud. Norwegian CD. Featuring Juldeh Camara with other Gambian musicians and the Blind Boys of Alabama.

Mande

1978   *Music from Gambia, Vol. 1.* Folkways FE 4521. Fiddle performed by Ibrahima Nyas. Notes by Susan Gunn Pevar and Marc D. Pevar. Recorded in Brikama, The Gambia, between 1971 and 1972.

1993   *Wassoulou Foli.* STCD 1047. Salimanta Sidibe (Mali). Song comes from *The Essential Guide to Africa.* 3 CD set. ESGCD203. Compilation 2005. Union Square Music Ltd. www.unionsquare.music.co.uk.

Maure

n.d. *Rèpublique Islamique de Mauritanie.* Uni-Dixc EX 33239. Notes by Monique Amiel.

n.d. *Chants et Musique: Chants et Musique Maures.* Institut Francais d'Afrique Noire IFAN 3–4. Notes by P. Potentier.

Serer and Wolof

1962 *La Musique des Griots: Sénégal.* Ocora OCR 15. Fiddle performed by Balla Diouf. Notes by Georges Balandier and André Jolivet. Recorded in Bambey, Senegal.

2002 *Music and Culture of West Africa: The Straus Expedition.* A CD-ROM compiled and edited by Gloria J. Gibson and Daniel B. Reed. Bloomington: Indiana University Press. Recorded by Laura Boulton in Fatick, Senegal, in 1934.

Index

Italicized page numbers indicate illustrations.

Abu Gondze (Ghana), 200, 205, 290n19
Abudulai (Gurma), 291n25
Accra. *See under* Ghana
acrobats, 62, 76, 95, 96, 272n48, 275nn65,66
Adamawa, *27*, 49, 117. *Also see* Cameroon
Adamu, Mahdi, 114, 133
African American. *See under* United States
"African Youth Song," 82–88, 273n52
Aïr (Azbin), *15*, 16, 37, 114, 264n33, 278n12
"Albanda," 4
Algeria. *See* North Africa
"Alhaji Balan Gwaggo, Sarkin Shanu," 151, 286n59
Alhassan Gondze (Ghana), 200, 290nn19,20
"Ali Mai Sai da Mai a Shal Bipi," 164–165, *166, 167,* 168, 287n72
Allah, 35, 71, 83, 122, 149, 150, 160–161, 219, 260n9
"Allah Gaba," 174
Ames, David, 125, 135, 137, 139, 141, 142, 148, 149, 258n6, 277n7, 280nn19,20,24, 286nn55,56,57
Americas. *See* United States; Western culture
anzad (anzhad). *See under* string instruments
Arab: and African fiddling, 9, 23, 27, 36, 66, 247, 262nn16,22, 296n1; Bedouins, 33, 296n1; fiddle and fiddling, 22–23, 33, 37, 85–86, 123, 262n18; history, 114, 116, 260nn7,8; influence, 7, 10, 14–17, 18–19, 21, 22–23, 26–27, 33, 36, 42, 66, 105, 117, 120–121, 123, 131, 132, 134, 149, 181, 195, 262nn15,16,22, 266n6, 278n12, 286n55; instruments, 19, 22, 23, 33, 37, 105; language (*see under* languages); music, 18–19, 21, 22–23, 37, 105, 183, 249, 261n11, 262n15; southwest Asia (*see under* Asia)
Argungu. *See under* Nigeria
Arnott, David, 59, 61–62, 64, 268n18
Aruatu Ghana (Ghana), 205
Asante (Ashanti) people, 17, 172, 176–178, 262n20
Asia, 56; south (India and Indian), 105, 138, 183, 260n3, 286n55; southwest, 14, 17, 18,

48, 134, 183, 249, 261n10, 296n1. *See also* Arab
Atlantic speakers. *See under* languages
Audu Yaron Goge (Nigeria), 283n41
Australia, 81, 287n67

Baako, Sulemana Abdulai (Ghana), 296
Babayo, Shehu (Nigeria), 154
Babba Mai Goge (Muhammadu Lawal) (Nigeria), 281n27, 284n48
Babu Gondze (Ghana), 3, 4, 5
Badjie, Salif, 82, 84, 273n54, 274n59
Bagirmi people, 12, 14
Bah, Samba Juma, 66, 70, 87–88, 93, *94,* 95–102, 248, 268n19, 275nn63,65,66
Bai, Majaw (Senegal), 66, 67, 265n34, 270n27
bala (balafon). *See under* xylophone
Balante people, 54, 66, 260n4, 270n29
Baldeh, Abudullahi (Gambia), 270nn32,33
Baldeh, Mamadou, 70, 71, 72, 73, 74, 268n19, 272nn39,40,42,44
Baldeh, Maulday, 69, 70, 71–72, 73, 74, 268n19, 270nn32,33, 271n34, 272nn40,42,44
Baldeh, Metta (Gambia), 74
Baldeh, Nayang (Gambia), 272n41
Baldeh, Seiniwa (Gambia/Guinea Bissau), 268n19, 271n36
"Balla," 69, 270n33
Bande, Haruna, 106, 108, 128, 136, 138, 149, 150, 152, 153, *154,* 155, 157–158, 160, 165, 276n1, 280n21, 285n50, 286n63, 287nn65,66
banjo. *See under* string instruments
Banjul. *See* Gambia
"Bantchande," 228, 291n30
Barahaza, 136, 138, 149, 150, 152, 153, 154–155, *156, 157, 158*
Bariba people, 19
Barro, Hawa (Gambia), 74
Barry, Ebrima (Gambia/Guinea), 95, 97, 99, 275n64
Barry, Ousman (Gambia/Guinea), 95
Bassa, Balan Na, 130, 133, 137–138, 142, 143,

144–145, 158, 281n28, 284nn42,43,46, 285n54

Bassa mai Goge, Ahmadu Na (Nigeria), 281n28

Bawa mai Goge (Nigeria), 281n28

bawdi. *See under* drums and drumming

"Bawuna," 4, 6, 216, 221

Bedouins. *See under* Arab

Benin (former Dahomey), 17, 23, 39, 104, 163

Berbers, 14, 19, 26, 27, 48, 53, 66, 114, 130–131, 261nn10,12, 281n27, 296n1. *See also* North Africa

Beri-Beri people, 131, 282n29

Berom. *See* Biram

Besmer, Fremont, 103, 120–121, 132, 136, 143, 144, 145, 283n37, 283n40, 285n51

Biram (Birom), 40, 114, 124

Bisa people, 40

Bori, 8, 103–104, 106, 108, *109,* 113, 120–124, 128, 130, 131, 134, 135, 136, 138, 143, 147, 148, 150, 153, 154, 184, 192, 244, 276nn1,4, 279nn14,16,17, 280n23, 282n32, 283n40, 284n42, 290n23, 291n29. *See also* religion

Borno (Bornu), 26, 116, 131, 132, 133, 134, 278n12, 280n20, 282n31, 283n34. *See also* Kanem

bowed lute. *See* fiddle and fiddling

British. *See under* Europe

Bulala people, 283n34

Bundu, 49, *52,* 266n5. *See also* Fulbe

Burkina Faso, 5, 23, 59, 193, 195, 262n21

"Burugy warama," 265n3

Burum. *See* Biram

Bwa people, 40

"Cabral," 265n3

calabash, 22, 28, 31, 39, 40, 62, 64, 66, 73, 82, 95, 96, 107, 108, 111, 129, 131, 132, 136, 144, 145, 146, 155, 156, 157, 158, 164, 165, 167–168, 193; horde, 64, 73, 82, 95; igba, 39; k'warya, 107, 108, 110, 126, 136, 144, 145, 146, 155, 156, 165, *166, 167,* 285n54, 287n71. *See also* rattle and rattlers

Camara, Juldeh, 68–69, 70–71, 76, 77, 78, *79,* 80–88, 91, 92, 93, 95, 97, 98, 99, 102, 150, 243, 248, 258n6, 268n19, 270n27, 272n40, 273nn50,51,52,53,54, 275n65

Cameroon, 23, 26, 58, 105; Fulbe in, 60, 64, 283n34. *See also* Adamawa

Casamance. *See* Senegal

Central Sudan. *See under* Sudanic West Africa

Chad (country), 19, 23, 26, 37, 105, 131, 163, 263n25, 283n34

"Le chameau qui boite," *38*–39

Chari-Nile. *See under* languages

Charry, Eric, 18, 20, 21, 42, 66, 133, 275n64, 282n30

Chaw, Ousainou (Senegal), 66, 67, 270n27

"Chemedo," 81

Chernoff, John, 173, 185, 188, 195, 196, 288n2, 289nn13,14

children, 2, 3, 5, 6, 43, 90, 119, 171, 180, 205

chorus. *See* singing and singers

Christianity, 17, 120, 124, 181

"Churoi Wuro," 95, 275n68

class. *See* social status, social structure, and social system

clothing (attire): in Dagbon, 1, 3, 5–6, 181; in The Gambia, 43, 46, 75, 82, 275n65; Muslim style, 1, 44, 105, 106, 108, 181; in Nigeria, 105, 107, 108, 110–111, 137

colonial period (colonization), 20, 48, 50–51, 58; in Gambia, 53, 74, 90–91, 296n4; in Ghana, 177, 288nn1,7, 291nn26,27, 296n4; and Islam, 58, 291n26; in Nigeria, 116, 120, 133–134, 283n36

Conrad, David C., 184, 260n5

contemporary (nontraditional) culture, 10, 68–69, 97, 134, 231, 259n14, 297n6. *See also* modernity; postcolonial period

Coolen, Michael, 64, 66, 268n18, 270n28

Côte d'Ivoire (Ivory Coast), 23, 163, 193, 243

Dagbamba (Dagomba) and Dagbon: Bimbilla, 223, 227, 231, 290nn18,19; clothing (attire), 1, 3, 5–6, 172, 181; Diare, 176, 231; economy, 170, 180, 201; ethnicity (*see* ethnicity); festivals, 169, 172–175, 184, 185, 198, 200, 212, 213, 216, 217, 221, 222, 224, 226, 233, 288nn2,5, 292n37, 293n42; fiddle and fiddling (*see* gondze); Fulbe, 192, 193; Gbulon, 227, 228; Gonja (*see* Gonja); Gurma (*see* Gurma people); Hausa, 176, 181, 193–195; history, 169, 175–180, 197–198, 201, 204, 207, 243, 244, 288n1, 296n4; identity (*see* identity); instruments, 125, 172, 184, 185–187, 195, 295n62; interactions with Asante, 176–178, 288n8; Karaga, (town and province), 176, 181, 191, 200, 257n2, 289n9; kingdom (Dagbon), 1, 3, 14, 169, 175–*178,* 180, 228, 257n2, 288n7, 292n36, 294n49; Kumbungu, 209, 292n37, 294n49; language (*see under* languages); living quarters (pattern), 2, 3, 170; Mamprussi (*see* Mamprussi people); Mande, 176, 181; map, *178;* migrations, 176; Mion,

181, 257n2, 289n9; music and musicians, 124, 172–173, 184–187, 195, 198, 279n18, 288n8, 289nn13,14, 290n16; peoples of, 1, 8, 9, 19, 21, 103, 177, 289n12; political system (kingdom), 1, 2, 3, 14, 180, 181–182, 244, 257n2, 288n7, 292n36, 294n49; religion, 171, 175–176, 181, 186, 219; rulers (kings and chiefs), 2, 3, 4, 169, 170, 171–175, 176–77, 181–182, 186, 189–190, 191, 194, 195, 196, 197–198, 199, 200, 201, 204, 206, 207, 209, 212, 213–214, 215, 216–217, 219, 220, 221, 223, 227, 228, 231, 233, 234, 243, 244–245, 257n2, 288nn3,5,6,8, 289nn9,10, 290nn16,20, 291nn25,26,26,30, 292nn34,35,36, 293n39,41,42,43, 294nn44,49, 295nn62,63; Salaga, 177; Savelugu (*see* Savelugu); social system (structure), 170, 171, 180–181, 199, 288n8, 289n12, 294nn44,46; Tamale (*see* Tamale); Tampion, 193, 290n19, 294n51; Tsimsi Tsugu, 169, 172–175, 222, 224, 288n2, 289n12, 293n42; urbanism, 171, 181, 292n34; West Africans, 176, 244; Yendi (*see* Yendi). *See also* Islam

Dagomba people. *See* Dagbamba and Dagbon

Dahomey. *See* Benin

Dakar. *See under* Senegal

dancing: in Dagbamba culture, 6, 172, 173, 174, 175, 203, 209–211, 212–213, 221, 293n42; in Fulbe culture, 46, 47, 62, 71–72, 74, 82, 209, 272n47; in Hausa culture, 107, 108, *110,* 111, 112, 113, 121, 131, 136, 138, 139, 141, 144, 147–148, 209, 248, 284n43, 286nn55,56

Danfulani, Umar Habila Dadem, 103, 121, 122–123, 124, 129, 279n16

"Danginka," 265n3

'dan kar'bi. *See under* drums and drumming

Darfur, 14, 16

diaspora, 296n3; African, 257n5, 259n11, 286nn55,56, 287n67; Fulbe, 26, 29, 30, 47–50, 56, 58, 59, 60, 62, 66, 114, 192–193, 242–243, 262nn21,22, 263n23, 266nn4,5,6, 268n16, 272n48, 278n11; Mande, 26, 28, 49, 54, 114, 116, 133, 176

diffusion. *See* distribution

distribution, 23–28, 42, 95, 107, 283nn34,35

DjeDje, Jacqueline Cogdell, 8, 9, 20, 21, 34, 35, 38, 42, 59, 64, 82, 108, 125, 127, 128, 151, 152, 157, 158, 161, 163, 165, 180, 184, 185, 188, 195, 216, 217, 219, 220, 226, 258n6, 264n32, 265n36, 286n58, 287nn69,70, 289nn13,14, 292n34, 295nn54,62

djembe. *See under* drums and drumming

Djenne, 16, 177

Djerma (Zabermawa) people, 34, 38, 40, 107, 130, 131, 281n27, 282n32

Doka, Ahmadu (Nigeria), 282n32

drama and theater, 76, 96, 134, 147, 148, 275n65

drone. *See under* melody

drums and drumming, 19, 21, 22, 28, 39, 42, 62, 64–65, 69, 73, 80, 95, 107, 111, 113, 117, 121, 123, 125–126, 141, 144, 145, 146, 165, 172, 173, 174, 175, 185, 188, 195, 198, 202, 203, 248, 262n20, 263n24, 273n54, 277n7, 280n20, 282n31, 286n58, 287n71,73, 288nn3,8, 292nn34,36, 294n44, 295n62; bawdi, 65, 69, 73, 82; 'dan kar'bi, 111, 144, 146, 287n71; djembe, 64–65, 73, 95, 275n65; kalangu, 107, 108, 111, 112, 139, 144, 146, 165, *166, 167,* 287n71; kuntuku, 111, 144, 165, *166, 167,* 287n71; lunsi, 172–173, 174, 195–196, 198, 203, 213, 288n3, 295n62; sakara, 39; tama (tema), 21–22, 63, 64, 69, 73, 74, 82, 84, 272n42, 273n54

duduga. *See under* string instruments

"Dunia Taali," 234, 235, 237–241, *238–240*

Duran, Lucy, 20, 21, 268n16

Dyula people. *See* Mande

Eastern Sudan, 14, 26. *See also* Sudanic West Africa

Egypt. *See under* North Africa

Ehret, Christopher, 12, 14, 19, 182, 259n1, 260n8

English (people). *See under* Europe: Great Britain

epics. *See under* songs

Ethiopia, 14, 130

ethnicity, 8, 67, 243, 268n13; in Dagbamba culture, 191–192; in Fulbe culture, 8, 43, 47–48, 54, 56, 58–59, 60–61, 63, 67, 68, 266nn4,5,6,7, 268n14, 269n24, 270nn28,29, 271n35; in Hausa culture, 112, 281n28, 282n29

ethnography: multi-sited, 8, 9, 243, 258n9

Europe (Europeans), 17–18, 20, 23, 44–45, 50–51, 53, 58, 68, 75–76, 80, 81, 83, 105, 124, 159, 183, 233, 243, 257n5, 275n64, 278n12, 290n18, 293n39, 294n47, 296n65; France, 17, 43, 53, 177; Germany, 177, 288n7, 291n26; Great Britain and United Kingdom, 17, 53, 56, 80, 81, 97, 133, 177–178, 180, 243, 288n1; The Netherlands, 80; Norway, 80, 81; Portugal, 53. *See also* Western culture

FESTAC (Second World Black and African Festival of Arts and Culture), 104, 159, 287n67, 296n65

festivals, 21, 33, 36, 296n65. *See also under* Dagbamba and Dagbon; Fulbe; Hausa

Fezzan. *See under* North Africa

fiddle and fiddling: attitude toward, 80–81, 90, 95, 103, 283n34, 293n43, 294n44; classification, 22–23; clothing (attire), 1, 3, 74, 75, 82, 95, 108; composition, 76–77, 81, 83, 91; construction, 22–23, 31, 44, 193, 196–197, 262n17, 263n26, 270n25; context and cultural significance, 21, 31, 33–36, 45–47, 64, 70–71, 103–113, 123, 141–142, 169, 196, 198–199, 219; distribution patterns, 23–28, 42, 95, 107, 283nn34,35; ensemble organization, 37–42, 82, 91, 95–96, 98–99, 107, 111, 211, 246; forest performance style, 39–41, 262n16, 265n38; generational differences, 68, 139, 197, 205, 208; history, 22–23, 34, 42, 66, 131–132, 242, 262n18, 268n19, 283n34, 296nn1,2; learning and playing technique, 32–33, 71, 72–73, 78, 80, 81, 87–88, 90, 94–95, 128, 142, 143–144, 153, 158, 163, 204–209, 218, 223, 227, 228, 232, 272nn39,41,42, 281n28, 283n34, 285n51, 290n19; modernization, 110, 196, 197, 198–199, 201, 213–214; playing technique, 32–33; performance contexts, 33–36, 290n17; performance style and analysis, 9–10, 37–42, 77–102, 107, 111, 113, 151–153, 211–214, 245–248, 262n16, 263n25, 264nn32,33; 265nn34,35,37,38; physical features and construction, 28–32, 65, 110, 131, 138, 193; recruitment (*see under* musicians); religion, 34, 35, 36, 83, 103, 108–109; rulers (kingship), 34, 36, 61, 63, 76, 197–198, 261n14; Sahel (Sahelian) performance style, 37–38, 262n16, 265nn34,35; savannah performance style, 40–42, 262n16; social status, 71, 72, 73, 140–142; songs, 35, 45, 61, 69, 71, 76–78, 82–84, 95, 96, 106, 111, 113, 143–144, 148–151, 201; song texts, 36–37, 76, 82–84, 91–92, 96–98, 106, 143, 149–151, 193, 194, 195, 203–204, 216–217, 219; sources on, 7, 258n6, 268nn18,19, 273n51, 280nn19,20, 289n14; terms for, 28, 61, 64, 65, 257nn1,4, 270n27, 282n30; tuning, 31. *See also* goge; gondze; nyanyeru; musicians

flute. *See under* wind instruments

forest region. *See under* West Africa

Frafra people, 40, 188, 191, 265n39, 290n17

France. *See under* Europe

Frank, Barbara E., 184, 260n5

Fula Acrobats Johkerreh Endham (Gambia/Guinea), 275n63

Fula people. *See* Fulbe

Fuladu, 50–51, *52*, 60, 62, 69, 78, 88, 90, 266n5, 267n9, 269n22. *See also* Fulbe

Fulani Musicians (Gambia/Guinea), 97–102, 275n65

Fulani people. *See* Fulbe

Fulbe, 8, 9, 14, 19, 21, 26–27, 29, 31, 43–102, 103, 191, 242, 243–244, 260nn4,5,6, 268n16; Adamawa (*see* Adamawa); and Berbers (*see* Berbers); Bundu (*see* Bundu); clothing (attire), 43, 44, 46, 74, 75, 95; and Dagbamba, 192, 193; economy, 48, 49, 50, 51; ethnicity (*see* ethnicity); festivals, 68; fiddle and fiddling (*see* nyanyeru); Fuladu (*see* Fuladu); and Hausa, 49, 59, 60, 64, 103, 105, 114, 116, 117, 124, 131, 132, 133, 140, 278n11; Futa Jalon (*see* Futa Jalon); Futa Toro (*see* Futa Toro); history, 48–51, 60, 69, 133, 266nn4,5,6, 267nn8,9,11, 271n35, 296n4; identity (*see* identity); instruments, 1, 21, 42, 61–62, 63–65, 66, 67–68, 107, 125, 131, 262n22, 270n28, 273n54, 283n34; jihad, 49, 50, 57, 58, 59, 103, 133; language, 47–48, 56, 59, 67, 76, 117, 133, 260nn4,5, 266nn4,5; living quarters, 44, 273n61; and Mande, 49–50, 54, 56, 58–59, 62, 64, 69, 269n24; Masina (*see* Masina); migrations (*see under* diaspora); music and musicians, 42, 45, 59–102, 124, 268nn16,17,18,19, 269nn20,24, 271nn34,36,37,38, 273n54, 279n18; nomadism, 26, 48–49, 57, 58, 62, 88, 90, 105, 133, 242, 262n22, 263n23, 269n22, 274n74; political system, 49, 50, 57–58; pulaaku (pulaagu), 56–57, 67; religion, 48, 49, 51, 60, 62, 83, 133; rulers, 50–51, 58, 59, 63, 69, 70, 193, 267n9, 269n24, 270nn32,33, 271n34, 277n54; rural, 133; sedentary, 26, 48–50, 58, 133; and Serer, 266n6; social system (structure), 51, 58, 266n7, 268n15, 269nn21,22; Sokoto (*see* Sokoto); and Tuareg, 49; and Tukulor (*see* Tukulor people); urbanism, 26, 51, 133, 133, 266n5; wedding, 45–47, 272n47; and Wolof, 60, 64, 66–67, 266n6. *See also* Islam; languages; Tukulor people

Fulfulde. *See under* languages

Futa Jalon, 14, *27*, 48, 49, 50, *52*, 53, 54, 58–59, 60, 62, 63, 66, 94, 258n6, 267n9, 268n18. *See also* Fulbe

Futa Toro, 14, *27*, 48, 54, 58, 59, 60, 61, 62, 267n9, 268n18. *See also* Fulbe

Gabbi, Demba (Guinea Bissau), 265n3

Gaden, Henri, 57–58, 59, 61, 62, 268n18

"Gagara Sarki," 154

gagle. *See under* rattle and rattlers: in Dagbamba culture

Gambia, The (country), 23, 30, 37, 43, 47, 51–54, 58, 75, 78, 95, 243, 265nn1,2; Banjul, 43, 44, 45, *55,* 59, 68, 70, 80, 81, 90, 91, 270n32, 271n36; Basse, 44, 69, 70, 78, 271n34; government, politics and political system, 53, 69, 70, 74, 75–76, 90, 91, 96, 98, 271nn36,37; history, 53–54; Kesserkunda, 69, 269n24; Lamin, 44, 83, 90, 91, 97, 274n74; map, *55;* music and musicians in, 59–102, 270n30, 271nn34,36,37,38; peoples (ethnic groups), 54, 266n4, 270n29; population, 50, 53–54; regions (provinces), 45, 46, 47, 51, *55,* 67–68, 69, 70, 71, 72, 76, 81, 90, 265n3, 266n5, 268n19; Serrekunda, 46, 67–68, 98, 273n54; urbanism in, 67–68, 266n5

Gambia river, 48, 50, 53

Gao (Kawkaw), 14, 16, 260n8

garaya. *See under* string instruments

Garba, Usman (Nigeria), 146, 285n54

Gellar, Sheldon, 260n8

gender, 6, 8, 22, 32, 80, 96, 243, 263n27; men's role, 32, 35, 37, 45–47, 51, 71, 73, 74, 105, 108, 122, 125, 131, 135, 136, 142, 144, 147, 148, 173, 194, 196, 199, 205, 206, 211, 243, 270n31, 279n14, 284n47, 286n56, 290n22, 294nn46,50; women's role, 8, 32, 34, 35–36, 37, 43, 45–47, 51, 73, 74, 81, 82, 105, 108, 122, 125, 131, 135, 136, 142, 144, 147, 148, 171, 173, 194, 196, 197, 199, 205, 206, 211, 212–213, 243, 263n24, 272n45, 279n14, 284n47, 286nn55,56, 288n6, 290n22, 294nn44,46, 295n63

geography, 7, 8, 9, 40, 124, 258n8, 259n1

Ghana (country), 8, 258n10; Accra, 1, 43, 170, 194, 201, 227, 228, 233, 290n18, 296n64; Bolgatanga, 265n39, 290n17; central Ghana, 172; government, politics, and political system, 170, 181–182, 198, 199, 200, 289n10, 292n35, 293n39; history, 177–178, 180, 201, 288n7, 292n35; Kumasi, 201; map, *179;* music and musicians in, 105, 184, 192, 213, 289nn13,14; northern Ghana, 1–3, 18, 19, 21, 23, 44, 104, 169, 170, 171, 177–178, *179,* 192, 193, 195, 227, 228, 231, 233, 265n39, 288n7, 289nn10,13, 292nn35,36; peoples of, 172, 194, 219; population, 181; religion in, 181; Savelugu (*see* Savelugu); southern Ghana, 170, 180, 227, 228, 289n13; Tamale (*see* Tamale); University of, 1, 3, 104, 169, 184, 223, 232, 233, 234, 243, 290n18, 296n64; Upper East, 290n17; urbanism in, 1, 67–68, 201; Yendi (*see* Yendi)

Ghana (empire). *See* Wagadu

goge (and variant spellings), 9, 28, 103–168, 258n10; attitude toward, 103, 106, 123, 128, 139–140, 204, 244; clothing (attire), 108, *110,* 111; dancing, 108, *110,* 111, 113, 141, 145, 147–148; distribution, 26–27, 103, 107; ensemble organization, 107, 108, 111, 137, 138, 144–147, 154, 159, 211, 285nn52,53, 287n71; generational differences, 139–140, 144, 244; history, 26–27, 34, 103, 127–134, 144–145, 146, 147, 191, 193–194, 282nn30,31,32, 296n4; innovations, 137–138, 140, 147; musicians, 34, 106, 107, 113, 134, 137–138, 140–142, 153–168, 205, 284n48; patronage and gift giving, 136–142, 146–147, 150, 152, 155, 160, 161, 163–164, 284n45; performance contexts, 103–113, 122–123, 128, 131, 134–135, 137, 141–142, 143–144, 145, 147, 153, 159, 163, 192, 276n1,3,4, 279n14, 280n23, 282n33, 283nn37,38,41, 284n45, 286n55, 286n62, 290n23; performance style, 108, 111, 113, 137, 139, 140, 145–147, 151–153, 154–155, 157–168, 221, 222, 237, 241, 245–248, 274nn56,58, 277n7, 284n43, 286n55; physical description and construction, 127, 130, 132, 133, 137, 187, 194, 280n21; religion and Islam, 34, 35, 103; social structure, 135–136; songs and composition, 111, 113, 137, 138, 147, 148–151, 152, 153, 154–155, 157–158, 159–163, 164–168, 219, 286nn59,60,62; terminology, 28, 131, 282n30

Gold Coast. *See* Ghana

gondze (gondje, gonje), 28, 35, 40, 43, 258n10, 257n1, 289n14; attitude toward, 199, 201–202, 204, 245, 293n43, 294n44; clothing (attire), 1, 3; dancing, 174, 294nn49,50,52; ensemble organization, 146, 211–214, 226; generational differences, 197, 205, 208; history, 2, 5, 127, 169, 187, 188–198, 199, 200, 201, 224–225, 232, 234, 244–245, 289n12, 290n1921,22,23, 291nn25,27,28, 292nn33,34,35,36, 293nn40,41,42,43, 294n45, 296n4; innovations, 187–188, 197, 198–199, 201, 208, 213–214, 233, 245, 293n39; living quarters (patterns), 2, 199; musicians, 3, 9, 70, 169, 204–209, 212–213, 284n48; patronage and gift giving, 175, 200, 201–203, 209, 210, 211, 212–213, 245,

293n39; performance contexts, 108, 169, 173–174, 189, 190, 191, 198–199, 200, 201, 202, 203, 212, 217, 218, 226, 232, 245, 290n23, 292n32, 293n38,41,42, 295nn60,62; performance style, 3–6, 146, 153, 173–174, 208, 210, 213, 221–222, 224–227, 228, 231, 232, 233–241, 245–248, 295n57; physical description and construction, 127, 187, 193, 194, 196–197, 280n21, 293n40; religion and Islam, 191, 198, 205; social significance, 202–203, 204, 219, 290n23; social structure and status, 9, 169, 183–184, 188, 199–204, 211, 245, 293nn43,46, 295n63; songs and composition, 173–174, 191, 200, 201, 203, 206, 212, 214–221, 286n60, 294n48, 295nn55,56,57,58; Yamba Naa (chief of gondze), 5, 175, 190, 191, 194–195, 197, 199–200, 201, 211, 222, 223, 228, 232, 234, 288n4, 291n25, 293nn40,41,42, 294nn44,45, 295n63; zaabia, 3, 6, 205, 211–212, 221, 226, 290n22; zugubu, 4, 6, 221, 228, 273n49, 295n57

Gonja (Gwanja) people, 173, 176, 278n12, 295n62

gourd. *See* calabash

Gourlay, Kenneth, 23, 31, 34, 35, 128, 132, 258n6, 263nn24,29, 280n22, 285n53

Gourmantché. *See* languages

Grass, Randall, 111, 113, 163, 285n53, 286n59, 287n71

griot. *See* musicians

Grumaland (Gruma). *See* Gurma people

Guinea (Guinea Conakry), 17, 23, 48, 54, 58, 66, 73, 94, 95, 98, 99, 243, 258n6, 266n5

Guinea-Bissau, 23, 58, 90, 265n3, 266n5

guitar. *See under* string instruments

Gurma people, 5, 14, 16. 28, 35, 176, 189–190, 191, 192, 193, 195, 196, 228, 234, 237, 243, 262n21, 291n30

Gurmi. *See under* string instruments

Gwanja people. *See* Gonja

halam (xalam). *See under* string instruments

Hale, Thomas A., 169, 183, 188–189, 260nn3,8, 289n11

harp. *See under* string instruments

Harris, P. G., 121, 127, 136, 145, 276n4, 280n20, 281n25, 291n29

Hausa (Hausaland), 8, 9, 14, 19, 26–27, 28, 29, 34, 35, 40, 43, 191, 192, 193, 194–195; attitude toward fiddling, 103, 123, 129, 140–142, 276n3; Bauchi, 285n54; Biram (Berum, Birom, Burom) (*see* Biram); and Borno (Bornu) (*see* Borno); clothing (attire), 106, 108; and Dagbamba, 176, 181, 193–195;

Daura, 114; economy, 116, 118; ethnicity (*see* ethnicity); festivals, 104, 106–108, 121, 134, 153, 159, 276n4, 285n52; fiddle and fiddling (*see* goge); and Fulbe, 49, 64, 103, 116–117, 124, 131, 132, 133, 140; Gobir, 114, 116; and Gurma, 194, 195; Gwari, 114, 131; history, 26–27, 114–120, 124, 277n8, 278nn9,10,11,12, 296n4; identity (*see* identity); instruments, 28, 105, 107, 108, 110, 111, 112, 123, 125–126, 131, 144, 280n24, 281n25, 282n31, 290n23; jihad, 103, 116–117, 242; Jukun, 114, 116, 124; and Kanem (*see* Kanem); Kano (*see* Kano); Katsina, 114, 116; Kebbi, 114, 143; Kwararafa, 116; language (*see under* languages); living pattern, 118; and Mande, 114, 116; map, *115*; migrations, 27, 35, 103, 133, 242–243; music and musicians, 20, 118, 124–126, 133, 135–136, 144, 184, 279n18, 280nn19,20,21,22, 285n49, 290n16; and North Africans, 130, 132, 133; Nupe, 114, 124, 278n12; peoples of, 124; political system, 118–119, 140; Rano, 114; religion (*see* Bori; Islam; religion); rulers, 103, 105, 114, 116, 117, 118–119, 124, 128, 132, 134–135, 137, 140, 141, 142, 149, 159, 194–195, 280n20, 282n32, 283n36, 285n49; rural, 104, 114, 117, 135; social system (structure), 51, 58, 117–118, 119, 133–134, 135–136, 150, 276n4; Sokoto (*see* Sokoto); and Songhai, 133, 281n27; trade, 116, 130, 133, 278n12; and Tuareg, 114, 133; urbanism, 103, 104, 114, 117, 118, 121, 135; and West Africans, 103, 125, 132, 133, 176, 195, 278n12; Yawuri, 114; Yoruba (*see* Yoruba people); Zamfara, 114, 116, 130, 176, 278n13; Zaria (*see* Zaria)

hip hop (rap). *See under* popular music and musicians

history: of Dagbamba fiddling, 2, 5, 127, 169, 187, 188–198, 199, 200, 201, 224–225, 232, 234, 244–245, 289n12, 290n19,21,22,23, 291nn25,27,28, 292nn33,34,35,36, 293nn40,41,42,43, 294n45, 296n4; of Dagbamba people (*see under* Dagbamba and Dagbon); of Fulbe fiddling, 63, 65–68, 69, 71, 73–75, 133, 192–193, 270nn28,29, 296n4; of Fulbe people (*see under* Fulbe); of Hausa fiddling, 26–27, 34, 103, 127–134, 144–145, 146, 147, 191, 193–194, 282nn30,31,32, 296n4; of Hausa speakers (*see under* Hausa); of West African fiddling, 9, 22–23, 26–28, 34, 63, 65–68, 72

hoddu. *See under* string instruments

horde. *See under* calabash

horn. *See under* wind instruments
Hutchinson, John, 54, 56, 268n13

Iddrisu, Abudulai (Ghana), 293n40
Iddrisu, Ahmadu (Ghana), *232*, 234, 240
Iddrisu Gondze (Ghana), 200, 290n19, 294n51
Iddrisu, Sulemana, 173, 175, 211, 212, 216,
    218, 220, 222, *223*, 223–227, 228, 231,
    241, 248, 288n4, 289n12, 290n19, 292n35,
    293nn41,42
identity, 9, 39, 242, 245, 249; in Dagbamba cul-
    ture, 6, 184, 202–204, 223, 289n12, 294n44;
    in Fulbe culture, 43, 56–59, 65, 67, 72–73,
    82–83, 97, 102, 117, 244; in Hausa culture,
    103, 117, 124, 140, 153, 164–165; in Tuareg
    culture, 36; multiple identities, 7–8, 67,
    242, 243–245, 249, 250; and musical style,
    245–248
Igbo people, 107, 124
imzad (anzad). *See under* string instruments
India (Indian). *See under* Asia
Ingawa, Salihu (Danjume), 103, 106, 108, 138,
    144, 150, 152, 285n52
instruments, 7. *See also* calabash; drums and
    drumming; rattle and rattlers; string instru-
    ments; wind instruments; xylophone
Islam (Islamic and Muslim): attitude to-
    ward musicking, 44, 71, 103, 123, 261n11,
    280n22; call to prayer (chanting), 18, 36, 39,
    123, 174, 198; celebrations (holidays and
    festivals), 68, 116, 135, 169, 172–175, 198,
    283n37, 288n2; clothing (attire) (*see under*
    clothing); culture, 28, 103, 106, 109, 117,
    120–124, 140; in Dagbamba culture, 169,
    171, 172, 174, 176, 180–181, 191, 198, 205,
    288n2, 291n25, 292n37; education, 18, 119,
    128, 142, 279n15; and fiddling, 23, 26, 28,
    35, 66, 103, 109, 123, 128, 133, 135, 139, 140,
    142, 150, 191, 271n38; in Fulbe culture, 48,
    49, 50–51, 57–58, 62, 181, 260n8, 271n38,
    276n3, 278n11; in Gao, 260n8; in Hausa
    culture, 8, 103, 104, 114, 116, 117, 119,
    120–124, 128, 132, 133, 140, 142, 181, 244,
    278nn11,13, 283n37; history, 14–17, 260n8;
    jihad, 16–17, 26, 49, 50–51, 57, 103, 116,
    267n9; in Kanem, 260n8; in North Africa,
    282n30; Shari' a, 117, 124, 135, 139, 141, 244,
    278n13, 284n45; state system, 58; in Sudanic
    West Africa, 14–17, 18, 28, 66, 131,132, 181,
    260n8; Sufism, 19, 260n9; traders, 16, 114,
    260n8; urbanism and, 17, 26, 117
Issah, Salifu, 175, 197, 200, 205, 213, 214, 222,
    223, 288n4, 290n19, 293nn40,41,42
Ivory Coast. *See* Côte d'Ivoire

"Jabula," 138, 149, 152, 153, 154, 158
Jallow, Felli (Gambia/Guinea), 95
Jallow, Jansewo (Gambia/Guinea), 95
"Jam Tara," 193
Janabo, Samba (Gambia), 272n41
"Jawara Aa Hebe Kodo," 45, 91–93, 100, 265n3
Jawo, Daddaa (Gambia), 74
Jawo, Subbah (Gambia), 74
Jawo, Sambaru (Gambia), 272n41
jazz. *See under* popular music and musicians
jembe. *See* under drums and drumming
Jia, Mahama (Ghana), 293n40
jihad. *See under* Islam
jali (jalo, jeli), 20, 62, 63, 69. *See also* musicians
Jobateh, Jatuur (Gambia), 271n34
Jobateh, Karunkah (Gambia), 271n34
Jobateh, Ngansumana (Gambia), 268n19,
    271n34
Jola (Jolla) people, 54, 260n4, 266n7, 273n54

kalangu. *See under* drums and drumming
kamanje. *See under* string instruments
Kandeh, Kumba (Gambia), 74, 272n45
Kandeh, Mamma, 46, 68, 81, 83, 268n19
Kandeh, Ngeya, 46, 70, 71, 73, 74–75, 76–77, 80,
    90, 268n19, 271nn35,37, 272nn40,41,46
Kandeh, Tamba, 43–45, 63–64, 66, 68, 70, 71,
    72, 73, 74, 76–77, 78, 81, 82, 87, 88, *89*, 90–
    93, 95, 98, 99, 100, 102, 248, 265nn2,3,
    269nn20,23, 270n29, 271nn35,37,
    272nn40,41,42,47, 274n61, 295n57
Kanem, 21, 26, 27, 40, 243, 260n8, 282nn2931,
    296nn1,2. *See also* Kanem-Borno
Kanem-Borno, 14, 16, 26, 114, 263n24, 278n11.
    See also Borno
Kanembu people. *See* Kanem
Kano (city and state), 104, 105, 106, 107, 108,
    109, 110, 111, 114, 116, 117, 119–120, 128,
    129, 133, 134, 139, 144, 145, 150, 152, 158,
    159, 160, 163, 177, 276nn1,5, 278n10,11,
    279n17, 281n26, 286n55
Kanuri, 21, 27, 116, 243, 278n11, 282n31,
    296n2. *See also* Kanem and Kanem-Borno
Karaga. *See under* Dagbamba and Dagbon
Karim mai Goge, Abdul (Nigeria), 281n28
"Karinbandana," 5, 228
Kawada, Junzo, 128, 131–132, 133, 280n22,
    282nn30,31
Kawkaw. *See* Gao
"Ki'dan Banjo," 138, 149, 152, 153, 154–155
"Ki'dan Barahaza," 136, 138, 149, 150, 152, 153,
    154–155, *156*, *157*, *158*
"Ki'dan Kanawa," 150, 153, 159, 162, 287n70
"Ki'dan Sarki Kano," 159

"Ki'dan Sarkin Rafi," 138, 154, 159
"Ki'dan Wanzami," 138
King, Anthony, 20, 21, 26, 133, 135, 149, 258n6, 277n7, 280nn19,20
kings (kingship). *See* rulers
Ki-Zerbo, Joseph, 114, 116, 278nn9,10,11, 282n29
kora. *See under* string instruments
Koran. *See* Qur'an
Kubik, Gerhard, 9, 242, 243
kukuma. *See under* string instruments
Kumasi. *See under* Ghana
"Kuntag Zaa," 219
kuntigi. *See under* string instruments
kuntuku. *See under* drums and drumming
Kusasi people, 40, 191
kwambilo. *See under* string instruments
k'warya. *See under* calabash

Lake Chad, 9, 16, 26, 97, 176
lala. *See* rattle and rattlers: in Fulbe culture
Lali, Salifu, 185, 187, 188, 192–193, 194, 218, 220, 222, 223, *227*–231, 241, 248, 272n48, 290n19, 291n30, 292n31, 295n62
Landi, Mamman, 128, 142, 147, 149, 150, 151, 153, 154, 158, *159*, 160–163, 164, 165, 273n52, 280n21, 287nn68,69,70
languages: Afroasiatic, 26, 114; Arabic, 17, 19, 82, 83, 114, 116, 117, 181, 195, 218, 219, 261n10, 262n18, 275n64; Atlantic, 12, 19, 20, 21, 26, 47, 48, 66, 260nn4,5; Bariba, 19; Benue-Congo (Bantu), 26, 27; Berber, 11, 26; Chad, 11, 19, 26–27, 114, 281n27; Chari-Nile, 11, 12, 19, 26; Dagbani, 169, 176, 193–194, 212, 218, 219, 295n55; English, 82, 158, 218, 219; Fulfulde and Pulaar, 47, 48, 56, 57, 67, 76, 82, 117, 133, 193, 260nn4,5, 265n1, 266nn4,6; Gourmantché (Gruma or Gurma), 193, 194, 195, 218, 295n55; Gur, 176, 195; Hausa, 28, 114, 116, 117, 124, 149, 191, 193, 194, 195, 203, 218, 219, 295n55; Kwa, 27; Mande, 12, 19, 21, 26; Mossi, 19, 176; Niger-Congo, 11, 12, 176, 260n4; Nilo-Saharan, 26; Saharan, 11, 19, 26, 263n25; Songhai, 11, 19, 26, 281n27; Sudanic West African, 11, 26, 82, 260nn 4,5, 263n28, 296n5; Twi, 219; Voltaic, 27
Lawal, Muhammadu (Baba Mai Goge) (Nigeria), 281n27
Leo, Garba. *See* Liyo, Garba
Liberia, 18
Libya. *See* North Africa
Liyo (Leo), Garba, 109–111, 113, 128–130,

137, 139, 142, 151, 153, 154, 163, *164*, 165–168, 243, 277n6, 280nn21,24, 283n41, 286nn59,62
love songs. *See under* songs
lunsi. *See under* drums and drumming
lute (bowed). *See* fiddle and fiddling
lute (plucked). *See under* string instruments

Maghrib. *See under* North Africa
"Maginin Zaman Banza," 150
Maguzawa people, 121, 129, 130, 279n16
Mahama, Salisu, 1–6, 7, 9, 169, 171, 185, 186, 187, 188, 189–190, 191, 193, 195, 196–197, 199, 200, 201, 202–203, 205, 205, 206, 207, 209–210, 214, 215, 216, 218–219, 221, 222, 223, 225, 231, *232*, 233–241, 243, 248, 290nn19,21, 291nn28,30, 292n33, 293nn41,42,43, 294n49, 295nn57,62,63, 296nn64,65
Mahama Bla Gondze (Ghana), 232
Mali (country), 16, 17, 23, 54, 58, 59, 83, 91, 95, 192, 193, 243, 258n6, 261n10, 262n21, 275n62; Timbuktu, 258n6
Mali Empire, 14, 48, 49, 60, 66, 76, 176, 260nn4,8, 270n24
"Mamareh Ko Bengel Kaddy Jatou," 45, 91, 265n3
Mamprussi people, 40, 176, 177, 191, 195
Mande (Manding), 16, 19, 26, 43, 48, 54, 61, 133, 215, 244, 260n4, 266n7, 268n15; European influence in, 53, 59; fiddling, 36, 40; Fulbe interactions with, 49–50, 54, 59, 60, 62, 69, 266n7, 268n15, 269n24; Hausa interactions with, 114, 116; instruments, 20, 21, 28, 31, 42; Mandinka, 36, 37, 53, 59, 60, 63, 67, 260n8, 269n24; migrations (*see under* diaspora); music and musicians, 20, 43, 59, 61, 63, 183, 258n6, 269n24; rulers, 53, 215
Mandinka people. *See* Mande
Manjago people, 54
Maouri people, 29, 34, 40
Marcus, George, 8, 9, 258n9
Mariama Gondze (Ghana), 228, 294n51
marok'i, 111, 113, 144, 146–147, 152, 155, 158, 165, 285n54. *See also* singing and singers
Masina, 14, *27*, 49, *52*, 58, 60, 62, 66, 76, 88, 262n21, 266n5. *See also* Fulbe
Mauritania, 16, 23, 48, 59, 261n10
Mayani, Umarun, 130, 144, 281n28
media, 67, 83, 90, 105, 109, 135, 137, 138, 139–140, 163–164, 168, 204, 213–214, 219, 217n37, 233, 242, 244, 271n37, 273n51,

281n28, 283n38, 285n53, 286nn55,56, 287n71,72,73, 293n39, 294n53

Meiregah, Abubakari Salifu, 188, 206–207, 219, 290n18, 295n60

melody, 10, 18, 19, 22, 34, 37–42, 245, 246, 247, 248, 250, 264n33, 265n34; in Dagbamba culture, 4, 6, 184, 203–204, 210, 211, 218–219, 221, 222, 225, 226, 228, 231, 235, 236, 237, 239–240, 241, 273n49, 274n58, 295nn57,61; drone, 22, 275n68; in Fulbe culture, 45, 47, 73, 74, 76–78, 82, 84–87, 91–93, 98–100, 102, 274n60, 275n68, 276n69; in Hausa culture, 105, 113, 121, 123, 143, 144, 145, 146, 148, 151–155, 157, 158, 160–162, 165, 167, 273n49, 274nn58,60, 275n68, 276n69, 284n43, 286n61, 287nn65,69,70; melodic instruments, 7, 18, 19, 22, 40, 66, 73, 95, 211, 218–219; scale, 38, 39, 40, 78, 153, 222, 265n36, 287n69

Middle East. *See* Arab

migration. *See under* diaspora; Fulbe; Hausa

modernity, 32, 67–68, 69, 70–71, 72, 73–75, 76, 83, 84, 90–91, 95, 96, 110, 111, 113, 119, 120, 138, 144, 147, 149, 150–151, 180, 183, 196, 197, 208–209, 213–214, 218, 219, 232, 249. *See also* urbanism; postcolonial period

Mohammadan, Ibrahim, 106, 108, 120, 128, 142, 143, 151, 276n1, 280nn21,23, 283n34

molo. *See under* string instruments

Monts, Lester, 8, 18, 21

Morocco. *See under* North Africa

Mossi people, 14, 16, 19, 40, 176, 191, 192

Mudu, Gobe (Nigeria), 283n34

Muhammad. *See* Prophet Muhammad

multiple identities. *See* identity

multi-sited ethnography. *See* ethnography

Musa Molo. *See under* Fulbe: rulers

musicians: clothing, 74, 75, 95, 137; patronage, 20, 61–62, 66, 68, 69, 70, 73, 80, 83, 90–91, 95, 96–97, 102, 125, 135–140–142, 145, 146–147, 161, 169, 215, 244, 271nn34,36, 274n57, 282n33, 283nn40,41; popular (commercial), 40, 68, 73, 81, 139, 164; professional, 20, 32, 43, 61–62, 66, 67, 80–81, 82, 90–91, 102, 110, 125, 140–142, 164, 169, 182–185, 205, 223, 231–233, 272nn40,44,46; recruitment, 69–70, 142–143, 153, 158–159, 163, 204, 223, 227, 281n26; social organization, 19–20, 61–62, 63, 68–71, 182–184, 211, 218; social status, 20–21, 32, 61–62, 63, 68, 72–73, 90–91, 123, 133–134, 139, 140–142, 169, 182–184, 205, 231, 232–233, 244, 269nn22,23

Muslim. *See* Islam

"Naanigoo," 4

Nabarau, Momman, 106, 128, 143, 280n21

"Nafa," 95, 96–102, 275n64

Nago people, 23, 39

Namumba people, 176

"Nantoh," 4, 174, 194, 216–217, 221, *224–225, 226–227, 228, 229–230,* 231, 295nn60,61

Napari, Ziblim (Ghana), 200, 293n41

Near East. *See* Arab

Niane, D. T., 114, 116

Niger (country), 16, 23, 31, 35, 104, 105, 107, 128, 163, 243, 258n6, 261n10, 262n21, 264n33, 282n32, 285n50; Adarawa people, 281n27; Damagarau, 128, 153, 282n32; Djerma (Zabermawa) people (*see* Djerma); Fulbe people, 193; Gaya (Dendi), 285n50; Hausa people, 136, 285n50; Niamey, 258n6; peoples of, 107, 130, 131, 136, 263n25

Niger bend, 12, 16, 17, 49, 260n2. *See also* Niger river

Niger river, 31, 51, 177, 260n7, 281n27

Nigeria, 8, 58, 243, 258n10; Argungu, 103, 106, 107–108, 285n52; Bida, 105, 107; central Nigeria, 130, 243, 281n28; Dala, 129; educational institutions and universities, 104, 105–106, 130, 276n2, 280n22, 286n55; FESTAC (*see* FESTAC); festivals, 104, 107–108, 159, 287n66, 296n65; Fulbe (Fulani) in, 59, 105; Funtua, 110, 163; government, politics and political system, 104, 105, 106, 107, 117, 134, 136–137, 141, 145, 147, 148, 159, 163, 278n13, 283n36, 283n41; Hadejia, 163; history, 119–120, 283n36; Ibadan, 104, 105; Jos, 130, 138, 144, 148, 276n2, 281nn26,28; Kaduna, 131, 144; Kano (city and state) (*see* Kano); Kebbi (*see under* Hausa); Lagos, 104, 119–120, 144; map, *115;* Minna, 107; music and musicians in, 106, 107, 279n18, 280nn19,20,21,22; Muslim states, 104; nightclubs, 104, 109–113, *110,* 128, 135, 138, 153, 163, 276nn3,5, 277n6, 279n14; northern Nigeria, 19, 23, 26, 64, 103–106, 107, 112, 124, 130, 131, 132, 134, 140, 143, 148, 165, 244, 258n10, 276n3, 278n13, 279n18, 283nn34,41; Northeastern State, 107; Northwestern State, 104, 106, 107, 143, 144–145; peoples of, 17, 39, 59, 64, 105, 107, 119–120; Plateau (Plateau-Benue) State, 107, 276n3, 281n26, 281n28; population, 119; religion (*see* religion); Rivers, 107; Saminaka, 281n26; Second World Black and African Festival of Arts and Culture (*see* FESTAC); social structure, 109, *112,* 163, 168; Sokoto (*see* Sokoto); southern Nigeria, 104, 105, 112, 165, 243, 277n6, 279n18; urbanism in, 105, 109, 136–137, 140, 144, 148, 276n3; Wudil, 128; Zaria (*see* Zaria)

"Ninsali Nim Bori Naawuni Nyebu," 194

Nketia, J. H. Kwabena, 9–10, 27, 42, 67, 214, 215, 240, 249, 258n6, 259nn11,13,14, 262n19, 268n17, 287n67

Nkrumah, Kwame, 178, 180, 185

nomads. *See under* Fulbe

North Africa, 7, 14, 18, 21, 22, 42, 130, 247, 249, 261n12; Algeria, 16, 107, 261n10, 264n33; Almoravid, 260n8; contacts (interactions) with, 23, 26, 66, 132, 176, 242, 243, 260nn7,8, 262n22, 263n24, 296nn1,2; Egypt, 14, 22–23, 261n10; Fezzan, 26; instruments in, 21, 22, 23, 132, 263n24; Libya, 14, 26, 261n10; Maghrib, 17, 132, 261n10, 278n11, 282n30, 296n2; Morocco, 14, 16, 22, 260n8, 261n10; peoples of, 261n12, 282n30, 296nn1,2; Tripoli, 16; Tunisia, 16, 261n10

Nupe, 17, 49, 278n12

Nyalen, Jajeh (Gambia), 272n41

nyanyeru, 28, 31, 40, 43–102, 243–244, 265n1; attitude toward, 71; clothing (attire), 74, 75, 95; dancing, 71–72, 82; distribution, 26, 66–67; ensemble organization, 73–76, 82, 91, 95–96, 98–99, 144, 146, 211, 272n42, 275n63; generational differences, 68; history, 63, 65–68, 69, 71, 73–75, 133, 192–193, 270nn28,29, 296n4; innovations, 74–76, 77; musicians, 68–73, 78–102, 205; performance contexts, 68–69, 80, 192–193, 270n31, 271nn34,36,3; performance style, 74–102, 146, 153, 221, 222, 241, 245–248, 272nn42,43,47,48, 274nn56,58,59,60, 275n67,68, 276n69; physical description and construction, 65, 187, 193, 270n26, 280n21; songs and composition, 76–77, 81, 84, 91, 150; tenandagal, 77, 295n57; terminology, 28, 282n30. *See also* fiddle and fiddling

"Nyun Taa Jilma," 219–220

oboe. *See under* wind instruments

Oni, Duro, 110–111, 276n5, 277n6, 286n62

Oppong, Christine, 180, 181, 184, 204, 205, 208, 220, 289nn13,14, 291n25

oral tradition. *See* history

Osumanu, Iddrisu (Ghana), 200, 214, 293nn41,42

Paden, John N., 117, 133, 263n23

patronage. *See under* musicians

percussion instruments, 37, 165, 167–168. *See*

also calabash; drums and drumming; and rattle and rattlers

percussion vessel. *See* calabash

Peul people. *See* Fulbe

popular music and musicians, 68, 81, 112; cha cha cha, 286n55; highlife, 286n55; hip hop (rap), 68, 73, 139, 270n30, 279n14; jazz, 68, 139; reggae, 68, 139, 270n30; rumba, 286n55

"Poromandalli," 265n3

Portuguese. *See under* Europe

postcolonial period, 18, 20, 21, 32, 36, 56, 59, 63, 67, 68, 70–71, 74–75, 76, 90–91, 104, 117, 118–119, 120, 138–139, 149, 243, 283n34

praise songs. *See* songs

precolonial period, 21, 34, 42, 51, 54, 63, 64, 69, 243; in Dagbamba culture, 175–177, 181, 186; in Fulbe culture, 266nn5,6, 267nn8,9; in Hausa culture, 103, 104, 116, 120, 131, 133–134, 140

Prophet Muhammad, 22, 35, 83, 106

pulaaku (pulaagu). *See under* Fulbe

pulaagu (pulaagu). *See under* Fulbe

Pulaar. *See* Fulbe: language

Pullo. *See* Fulbe

Quinn, Charlotte, 47–48, 50, 51, 53, 60, 266n5, 267nn9,10,11,12, 266n6, 268n15, 269n22

Qur'an (Koran), 18–19, 36, 59, 83, 116–117, 119, 122, 128, 142, 219, 279n15, 281n27

rabab. *See under* string instruments

Racy, A. J., 8, 18, 22–23, 27, 37

Ramadan. *See under* Islam

Rano, Bala (Nigeria), 154

rap (hip hop). *See under* popular music and musicians

rattle and rattlers, 21, 40, 41; in Dagbamba culture, 3–6, 173, 175, 186, 196, 205, 209, 210, 211–212, 213, 220, 221, 222, 223, 228, 231, 232, 234, 235, 239, 240, 290n22, 294nn51,52, 295nn59,63; in Fulbe culture, 21, 62, 64, 73, 80, 95, 99, 275nn65,67; in Hausa culture, 107, 126, 129, 145, 281n25

reed pipe. *See under* wind instruments

reggae. *See under* popular music and musicians

religion, 8, 19, 120, 243; in Dagbamba culture, 181, 184–185, 244, 288nn2,3; in Fulbe culture, 48, 49–50, 51, 60, 62, 83; in Hausa culture, 8, 103, 106, 108–109, 114, 116–117, 120–124, 129, 132, 136, 141, 142, 244, 276n3, 278n13, 279nn15, 16, 17; in Songhai, 34–35, 264n30, 282n32. *See also* Bori; Islam; Sudanic West Africa

rhythm, 6, 10, 18, 22, 37, 39, 40, 42, 47, 73, 74,

75, 78, 84, 87, 91, 92, 98–99, 121, 146, 147, 155, 157, 162, 163, 165–168, 172, 184, 211, 222, 225–226, 228, 237, 238–239, 246, 247, 259n13, 274n59, 287n66, 295n59
riti. *See under* string instruments
royalty. *See* rulers
rulers, 11, 12, 16, 17, 18, 20, 21, 63, 260n8, 282n33. *See also under* Dagbamba and Dagbon; Fulbe; Hausa; Islam; Mande; Takrur

Sahara, 14, 19, 53, 66, 106, 261n10, 264n33; trade in, 17, 23, 177, 243, 260n7, 278n12
Sahel (Sahelian). *See under* fiddle and fiddling
sakara, 39–40. *Also see* drums and drumming
"Sakpalenga," 6, 219
Salisu, Iddrisu (Ghana), 2, 3, 4
"Sambo Yariga," 193
Saminaka, Musa dan Gado, *30*, 130, 133, 139–140, 141, 142, 281n26, 282nn32,33, 283nn34,41, 285nn51,52
Samunaka, Ahmadu, 128, 147, 280n21, 286n55
Sanaye, Harouna Oumarou (Niger), 143, 285nn50,52
Sankara, Ali (Nigeria), 154
Sanneh, Gallah (Gambia/Guinea), 95, 96, 99, 100, 276n69
Sansani, Iddrisu (Ghana), 293n40
Sarakolle people. *See* Serahuli people
"Sarkin Mallamai Garba Kai," 286n59
savannah, 7, 17, 21, 22. *See also* Sudanic West Africa
savannah performance style. *See under* fiddle and fiddling
Savelugu (town and province), 1, 2–6, 181, 231, 257n2, 289n9, 290nn19,20
Schuh, Russell, 151, 265n35, 270n29, 284n44, 287n72, 295n55
Seidu Gondze (Ghana), 209, 294n49
Senegal, 9, 17, 23, 26, 44, 48, 53, 54, *55*, 59, 73, 95, 243, 258n6, 260n8, 265n1; Casamance, 76, 78, 80, 90, 266n5, 270n27; capital city of, Dakar, 66, 67, 270n27
Senegal river, 48, 260n7
Senegal valley, *27*, 97. *See* Senegal
Senegambia, 8, 21, 54, 56, 243–244, 260n6, 265nn1,2, 296n4; map, *52;* music of, 59–65, 243–244, 258n6, 271n38; peoples of, 28, 29, 43, 48, 49, 54, 58–59, 66, 67, 95, 103, 260nn4,6, 266n5, 267nn8,9,11, 268nn14,15. *See also* Fulbe
Serahuli people, 50, 54, 61, 62, 67, 265n3, 267n10. *See also* Soninke people; Wagadu
Serer people, 26, 38, 40, 48, 49, 54, 66, 67, 260n4, 270nn27,29

Serrekunda. *See* Gambia, The
Shari' a. *See under* Islam
Shata, Mamman (Nigeria), 258n10
shawm. *See under* wind instruments
Sherbro people, 29
Shiloah, Amnon, 18–19, 183, 261n11
Sidibe, Bakari, 51, 58–59, 60, 62, 267nn8,11, 268n15, 269n21
Sierra Leone, 17, 18, 23, 29, 30, 32, 66
simbi. *See under* string instruments
singing and singers, 4–6, 22, 33, 37, 39, 45, 47, 61, 62, 69, 74, 75, 76, 77, 78, 82, 84, 85, 87, 92, 95, 99, 102, 105, 111, 117, 144, 145–147, 150, 152, 155, 157, 165, 172, 173, 193, 194, 200, 205–206, 211, 221, 222, 225, 226, 228, 234, 235, 239, 240, 246, 247, 248, 272n43, 277n7, 285n54, 287nn65,69,70, 290n16
Sissoho, Mohammed, 43–44, 271n38
sistrum. *See* rattle and rattlers
slavery, 12, 17, 62; Asante, 176; Dagbamba, 176, 183; Fulbe, 50, 51, 62, 269n22, 269n21; transatlantic, 53, 267n12
Smith, Anthony D., 54, 56, 268n13
social status, social structure (stratification or class), and social system, 12, 14, 19, 243, 260nn3,5; in Dagbamba culture, 8, 182–184, 199; in Fulbe culture, 71, 72, 73, 266n7; in Hausa culture, 103, *112–113*, 117–118, 276n5, 283nn39,41, 284n48
"Sodahnam Padeh Jelleh," 69, 270n33
Sokoto (city and state), *27*, 34, 60, 104, 106, 116, 144–145, 276n5
Sokuato, Garba (Nigeria), 154
"Song in Praise of the Ancestors," 40–41
"Song to Encourage African Youth," 82–88, 273n52
Songhai, 12, 14, 19, 21, 26, 27, 34, 49, 66, 116, 133, 134, 243, 263n24, 264n30, 280n20, 281n27, 282n32
songs, 10, 246, 247, 258n6; Arab, 19; Dagbamba, 4–6, 184–185, 192, 193–194, 195, 203–204, 205, 206, 207, 208, 209, 211, 212, 214–221, 233, 234, 235, 245, 257n3, 294n48, 295nn55,56; epic, 33, 61, 66; Fulbe, 45, 61–62, 69, 76–78, 81, 82, 91, 193, 247, 272n47, 273n53; Gurma, 193, 195; Hausa, 106, 111, 113, 121, 138–139, 145, 148–151, 159–160, 164–168, 248, 284nn42,43, 286nn59,62; historical, 21, 67, 69, 207, 215, 221, 294n48; love, 33, 35, 36–37; political, 36, 125, 134, 136, 139, 148, 149; possession, 34–35, 36 (*see also* Bori); praise, 4–6, 21, 45, 62, 69, 82, 91, 192, 194, 207. 208, 209, 215, 216, 217–218, 233, 284n43, 289n15; texts (Lyr-

ics), 5, 33, 36–37, 76, 82–84, 85, 87, 91–92, 96–98, 99, 102, 143, 147, 148–151, 160–161, 165, 193, 194, 195, 196, 202, 203–204, 205, 207, 208–209, 211, 212, 214–220, 234–235, 246, 247, 248, 250, 265n39, 284n44, 286n60, 295nn54,55,56; Tuareg, 35
Soninke people, 43. *See also* Serahuli people
Sonni, Ali, 49
Sonrai people, 38
"Sorronna," 69, 270n33
Soso people. *See* Susu people
South Africa, 219
Southwest Asia. *See under* Asia
speech surrogation, 145, 152, 284n42
spirits and spirit possession, 31, 33, 34, 35–36, 120–124, 125, 129, 136, 137, 143, 148, 150, 158, 273n50, 282n30, 290n23. *See also* religion
Staniland, Martin, 176, 177, 180, 181, 182, 192, 257n2, 289n10
status. *See* social status, social structure, and social system
string instruments, 7, 37, 62, 105, 123, 131; anzad, anzhad, or imzad, 28, 33, 36, 38; bolong, 21; banjo, 138; duduga, 28 (*see also* fiddle and fiddling); garaya, 126, 129, 130, 132, 136, 139–140, 143, 276n1, 279n17, 280n23, 281n26; goge (*see* goge); gondze (gondje, gonje) (*see* gondze); guitar, 138; gurmi, 139; halam or xalam, 64, 67; harp, 21, 28, 42, 62, 64; hoddu, 61, 62, 63, 64; imzad or anzad, 28. 38, 39; kamanje, 132; kora, 21, 28, 62, 67, 73, 244 (*see also* harp); kukuma, 28, 126, 127, 131, 134, 139, 142, 282n29, 283n34, 284nn43,47; kuntigi, 139; kwambilo, 130, 281n27; lute, 19, 21, 42, 61, 62, 64, 66, 67, 107, 185, 262n22, 265n3, 270nn25,28; molo, 64, 131, 141, 284n44; nyanyeru (*see* nyanyeru); rabab, 22, 33, 132, 262n18; riti, 28, 65, 67, 265n1, 270n27, 282n30; simbi, 21; susaa, 36, 65; violin, 7, 33, 257n4; xalam or halam, 64, 67
Sudan. *See* Sudanic West Africa; Eastern Sudan
Sudanic West Africa, 9, 22, 34, 37, 242, 243, 258n8, 259n1; Central Sudan, 14, 19–22, 26–27, 28, 31, 34, 37–38, 40, 59, 65, 103, 116, 124, 132, 133, 134, 195, 243, 244; clothing, 44, 46, 75, 95; clusters in, 19, 28, 34, 40, 59, 64; economy, 12, 14; geography (physical environment), 7, 124, 258n8, 259n1; history of, 11–18, 26, 42, 48, 66, 130–131, 134, 192, 219; instruments, 21–22, 23, 37, 39, 40, 41, 42; Islam in, 14–17, 18, 28, 44, 260n8; languages of, 11 (*see also* languages); map,

13; music of, 18–22, 37–42, 59–65, 124–127, 184–187; musicians (*see* musicians); religion in, 11–12, 14–17, 34, 35, 114, 180–181, 260nn8,9; peoples in, 23, 26, 56; political system of, 11–12; rulers in, 16, 17, 34, 49, 61, 63, 189–190, 192, 197, 215, 260n8; Sahel (*see under* West Africa); savannah (*see under* West Africa); social system (stratification) and status (*see* social status, social structure, and social system); Voltaic, 19–22, 27, 28, 34, 35, 40, 64, 65, 133, 176, 181, 192, 243, 244, 261n13; Western Sudan, 14, 19–22, 28, 34, 35, 38, 40, 43, 53, 64, 66, 215, 243, 244, 260nn6,7
Sufism. *See under* Islam
Sulemana, Alhassan Iddi, 8, 185, 191, 193, 194–195, 197, 198, 199, 200, 202, 203–204, 205–206, 207, 208, 209, 210, 213, 214, 216, 218, 219, 288n5, 289nn10,12, 291n28, 292nn34,35, 293nn39,40,41,43, 294nn44,46,47,53, 295n56
Sulemana Bla (Ghana), 295n63
Sulley, M. D., 1, 3, 4, 169, 170, 173, 189–190, 210, 216, 217, 225, *232*, 234, 258n6, 290nn21,22
"Supere Demba," 45, 70, 91, 265n3
susaa. *See under* string instruments
Suso, Bamba (Gambia), 271n34
Suso, Madi (Gambia), 271n34
Susu people, 14

"Taaka Sannu," 174, 175, 220
Takrur (Tekrur), 14, 48, 260n8, 266n6; ruler (War Jabi), 260n8
tama (tema). *See under* drums and drumming
Tamale, 1, 2, 169–170, 176, 195, 201, 205, 290n19, 292n34, 293n38
Tangale people, 40, 281n28
"Tapa Tura," 76–77
Teda people, 37, 40, 263n25
Tembo, Maro (Guinea), 94
Temne people, 32, 66
theme (melody). *See* melody
Timbuktu, 16. *Also see* Mali
Tiv people, 124
Togo, 177, *178*, 193
tourism, 68–69, 75–76, 80, 91, 97, 104, 106, 159, 244, 272n48, 275nn63,64
traditional culture, 10, 68, 84, 96, 113, 117–118, 124, 134, 135, 171, 180, 181, 197, 199, 207, 219, 231, 249, 259n14, 272n48, 288n2, 297n6
Tripoli. *See* North Africa
Tsimsi Tsugu. *See under* Dagbamba and Dagbon

Tuareg people, 27, 28, 30, 31, 32, 35–36, 37, 38, 39, 42, 66, 114, 134, 243, 258n6, 264nn31,32,33, 265n356

Tukulor people, 26, 28, 38, 48, 60, 61, 66, 67, 242, 260nn4,8, 262n22, 265n35, 266n6, 270nn27,29, 296n1. *See also* Takrur and Fulbe

United States, 56, 67, 68, 80, 83, 97, 105, 107, 233, 243, 258n10, 296n65; and African American, 112, 138, 139, 147, 149, 152, 158, 286n55, 287n73. *See also* popular music and musicians

University of California, Los Angeles (UCLA), 107, 258n10, 284n44, 295n55

University of Ghana, Legon. *See under* Ghana

urbanism, 51, 59, 67, 68, 69, 201, 259n11, 266n5, 292n34. *See also under* Gambia; Ghana; Nigeria; Dagbamba; Fulbe; Hausa; Islam

'Uthman dan Fodio, Shebu, 103, 116, 121, 131, 133, 142, 242, 276n1

violin. *See under* string instruments

vocal, vocal chorus, and vocal music. *See* singing and singers

Voltaic. *See under* Sudanic West Africa

Wadai, 14, 176

Wagadu, 14, 16, 22, 48, 178, 180

"Wakakai," 149, 153, 159, *160–163,* 287n69

Wangara people. *See* Mande

"Wanzami," 154

War Jabi. *See* Takrur

weddings: in Dagbamba culture, 198, 212, 217, 218, 221, 224; in Fulbe culture, 45–47; in Hausa culture, 118, 121, 127, 134, 135, 153, 159

Wendt, Caroline Card, 18, 28, 32, 33, 36, 258n6, 261n10, 264nn32,33, 265n37

West Africa: culture of, 33, 72, 130; forest, 7, 23, 27, 39–41, 42, 133; history of, 48, 66, 103, 130; influence of, 103, 261n10; map in eleventh century, *15;* meaning and significance of, 11; music of, 59–65, 72, 76–77, 96, 110, 133, 247, 263n24; people of, 18; Sahel, 37, 37–38, 48; savannah, 7, 33, 40–42, 48

West Atlantic. *See* languages

West Asia. *See* Arab

Western culture: influence of, 6, 17–18, 20, 23, 30, 31, 37, 40, 44–45, 50–51, 53, 58–59, 63,

67–68, 73, 75–76, 105, 110, 112, 119, 132, 138, 148, 149, 158, 168, 180, 187, 197, 208, 244, 275n65, 288n1, 293n39, 294n47, 296n4

Western Sudan. *See under* Sudan; Sudanic West Africa

wind instruments: flute, 21, 42, 62, 63–64, 73, 95, 96, 99–100, 102, 107, 172, 174, 175, 186; horn, 107, 186, 263n24; kakaki, 280n20, 282n29; oboe, 28; reed pipe, 21, 186, 263n24, 280n20; shawm, 19; trumpet, 28, 282n29; types of, 21, 28, 42, 105, 126, 145, 174–175, 186, 263n24, 295n62

Windy, Seidou (Gambia), 72

Wolof, 26, 28, 31, 38, 40, 44, 48, 49, 54, 64, 65, 67, 260nn4,5, 270n29; interactions with Fulbe, 50, 59, 60, 63, 64, 65, 66–67; music and musicians, 59, 61, 63, 67, 69, 73, 265n1, 268nn16,17, 273n54

women. *See under* gender

"Wotare," 95, 96

xalam (halam). *See under* string instruments

xylophone, 7, 21, 28, 42, 95; bala (balafon), 21, 95, 244

Ya Naa (king of Dagbon). *See under* Dagbamba: rulers

Yakubu, Sanusi Mohammed, 128, 130, 131, 132–133, 258n6, 280n22, 281n27, 284n48

Yalwa, Lawan Danladi, 129, 133, 151, 258n10, 276n1, 279nn14,16, 287n72

Yamba Naa (chief of gondze). *See under* gondze; rulers

"Yeda Binbeim Zugu," 220

"Yeda Nai Ya," 5

"Yenchebli," 4–5, 234, 235–237, *236–237*

Yendi, 170–175, 176, 177, 182, 197, 198, 199, 200, 201, 208, 216, 220, 223, 224, 227, 228, 257n2, 288nn6,7, 289nn9,10, 290nn19,20, 291n28, 292n34, 293nn38,39,41,42, 294nn45,49, 295n62. *See also* Dagbamba

Yo Naa. *See under* Dagbamba: rulers

Yoruba people, 17, 23, 39, 114, 124, 262n20

youth, 47, 68, 81, 82, 139, 148, 150, 159, 208, 214, 244, 270n30, 273n52, 276nn1,5, 283n34, 293n39. *See also* children

zaabia. *See under* gondze

Zabermawa people. *See* Djerma people

Zaria, 104–105, 114, 116, 128, 134, 142, 193

zugubu. *See under* gondze

JACQUELINE COGDELL DJEDJE is Professor and Chair of Ethnomusicology and former Director of the Ethnomusicology Archive at the University of California, Los Angeles (UCLA). She received her Ph.D. from UCLA with a specialization in African music. Her publications include three monographs, numerous articles, and several edited books on African and African-American music, including *Turn Up the Volume: A Celebration of African Music* and *African Musicology: Current Trends*, volumes 1 and 2.